# THE COMPLETE MEDITERRANEAN DIET

## cookbook 2021

500 QUICK AND EASY RECIPES TO EMBRACE LIFELONG
HEALTH BY BRINGING THE MEDITERRANEAN KITCHEN IN
YOUR VERY OWN HOME

## Gwenda Smith

# TABLE OF CONTENTS

Introduction                                                                          8

Chapter 1.
10 TIPS FOR SUCCESS                                                                   13

Chapter 2.
APPETIZER AND SNACK RECIPES                                                          16

1. Roasted Beet Salad with Ricotta Cheese                                            17
2. Baked Fish with Tomatoes and Mushrooms                                            17
3. Goat Cheese and Walnut Salad                                                      18
4. Grilled Spiced Turkey Burger                                                      18
5. Tomato Tea Party Sandwiches                                                       19
6. Veggie Shish Kebabs                                                               19
7. Crispy Falafel                                                                    20
8. onion Fried Eggs                                                                  20
9. Black Bean Cake with Salsa                                                        21
10. Pickled Apple                                                                    21
11. Baked Clams Oreganata                                                            22
12. Tuna Tartare                                                                     22
13. Cod Cakes                                                                        23
14. Grilled Vegetable Kebabs                                                         23
15. Vegetable Fritters                                                               24

Chapter 3.
APPETIZER AND SNACK RECIPES PART 2                                                   26

16. Marinated Feta and Artichokes                                                    27
17. Tuna Croquettes                                                                  27
18. Smoked Salmon Crudités                                                           28
19. Citrus-Marinated Olives                                                          28
20. Olive Tapenade with Anchovies                                                    29
21. Greek Deviled Eggs                                                               29
22. Manchego Crackers                                                                30
23. Burrata Caprese Stack                                                            30
24. Zucchini-Ricotta Fritters with
Lemon-Garlic Aioli                                                                   31
25. Salmon-Stuffed Cucumbers                                                         31
26. Goat Cheese–Mackerel Pâté                                                        32
27. Taste of the Mediterranean Fat Bombs                                             32
28. Cream of Cauliflower Gazpacho                                                    33
29. Avocado Gazpacho                                                                 33
30. Tuscan Kale Salad with Anchovies                                                 34

Chapter 4.
APPETIZER AND SNACK RECIPES PART 3                                                   36

31. Classic Hummus                                                                   37
32. Roasted Garlic Hummus                                                            37
33. Red Pepper Hummus                                                                38
34. White Bean Hummus                                                                38
35. Kidney Bean Dip with Cilantro,
Cumin, and Lime                                                                      39
36. White Bean Dip with Garlic and Herbs                                             39
37. Black Bean Dip                                                                   40
38. Salsa Verde                                                                      40
39. Greek Eggplant Dip                                                               41
40. Baba Ghanoush                                                                    41
41. Chickpea, Parsley, and Dill Dip                                                  42

42. Instant Pot® Salsa                                                               42
43. Sfougato                                                                         43
44. Skordalia                                                                        43
45. Pinto Bean Dip with Avocado Pico                                                 44

Chapter 5.
APPETIZER AND SNACK RECIPES PART 4                                                   46

46. Power Pods & Hearty Hazelnuts with
Mustard-y Mix                                                                        47
47. Peppery Potatoes                                                                 47
48. Turkey Spheroids with Tzatziki Sauce                                            48
49. Cheesy Caprese Salad Skewers                                                     48
50. Leafy Lacinato Tuscan Treat                                                      49
51. Greek Guacamole Hybrid Hummus                                                    49
52. Portable Packed Picnic Pieces                                                    50
53. Perfect Pizza & Pastry                                                           50
54. Margherita Mediterranean Model                                                   51
55. Fowl & Feta Fettuccini                                                           51
56. Very Vegan Patras Pasta                                                          52
57. Scrumptious Shrimp Pappardelle Pasta                                            52
58. Mixed Mushroom Palermitani Pasta                                                 53
59. Mediterranean Macaroni with
Seasoned Spinach                                                                     53
60. Frittata Filled with Zesty
Zucchini & Tomato Toppings                                                           54

Chapter 6.
BREAKFAST RECIPES                                                                    56

61. Avocado Egg Scramble                                                             57
62. Breakfast Tostadas                                                               57
63. Parmesan Omelet                                                                  58
64. Menemen                                                                          58
65. Watermelon Pizza                                                                 59
66. Ham Muffins                                                                      59
67. Morning Pizza with Sprouts                                                       60
68. Banana Quinoa                                                                    60
69. Avocado Milk Shake                                                               61
70. Egg Casserole with Paprika                                                       61
71. Cauliflower Fritters                                                             62
72. Creamy Oatmeal with Figs                                                         62
73. Baked Oatmeal with Cinnamon                                                      63
74. Almond Chia Porridge                                                             63
75. Cocoa Oatmeal                                                                    64

Chapter 7.
BREAKFAST RECIPES PART 2                                                             66

76. Berry Breakfast Smoothie                                                         67
77. Mediterranean Omelet                                                             67
78. Hearty Berry Breakfast Oats                                                      68
79. Garden Scramble                                                                  68
80. Summer Day Fruit Salad                                                           69
81. Egg, Pancetta, and Spinach Benedict                                             69
82. Peach Sunrise Smoothie                                                           70
83. Oat and Fruit Parfait                                                            70
84. Savory Avocado Spread                                                            71
85. Cheesy Stuffed Tomatoes                                                          71

86. Fresh Tomato Pasta Bowl — 72
87. Garlicky Broiled Sardines — 72
88. Heart-Healthful Trail Mix — 73
89. Citrus-Kissed Melon — 73
90. Café Cooler — 74

91. Spring Caponata with Olives and Pomegranate — 77
92. Smoked Salmon Appetizer with Fresh Cucumber — 77
93. Cypriot Tomato Salad — 78
94. Tangerine and Olive Salad — 78
95. Farfalle with Avocado — 79
96. Salad of Squid, Apples, and Green Peas — 79
97. Three Bean Salad with French Sauce — 80
98. Sandwich with Tongue, Arugula and Champignons — 80
99. Pineapple Raspberry Smoothie — 81
100. Morning Cake with Oatmeal, Bananas, and Blueberries — 81
101. Pita Chicken Salad — 82
102. Salad with Spinach, Tomatoes, and Poached Egg — 82
103. Potato Scallops with Truffle Oil — 83
104. Mediterranean Pasta with Basil — 83
105. Pita with Greens, Fried Onions, and Bacon — 84

106. Banana Oats — 87
107. Breakfast Sandwich — 87
108. Breakfast Couscous — 88
109. Avocado and Apple Smoothie — 88
110. Mini Frittatas — 89
111. Sun-Dried Tomatoes Oatmeal — 89
112. Breakfast Egg on Avocado — 90
113. Brekky Egg- Potato Hash — 90
114. Basil and Tomato Soup — 91
115. Butternut Squash Hummus — 91
116. Savory Muffins — 92
117. Farro Salad — 92
118. Cranberry and Dates Squares — 93
119. Lentils and Cheddar Frittata — 93
120. Tuna Sandwich — 94

121. Chicken Shawarma — 97
122. Honey Balsamic Chicken — 97
123. Garlic and Lemon Chicken Dish — 98
124. High-Quality Belizean Chicken Stew — 98
125. Crispy Mediterranean Chicken Thighs — 99
126. Greek Penne and Chicken — 99
127. Yogurt-Marinated Chicken Kebabs — 100
128. Braised Chicken with Roasted Bell Peppers — 100
129. Chicken Stew with Artichokes, Capers, and Olives — 101
130. Zaatar Chicken Tenders — 101
131. Lemon Chicken with Artichokes and Crispy Kale — 102
132. Sumac Chicken with Cauliflower and Carrots — 102
133. Harissa Yogurt Chicken Thighs — 103
134. Braised Chicken with Wild Mushrooms — 103
135. Braised Duck with Fennel Root — 104

136. Turkey Burgers with Mango Salsa — 107
137. Herb-Roasted Turkey Breast — 107
138. Chicken Sausage and Peppers — 108
139. Chicken Piccata — 108
140. One-Pan Tuscan Chicken — 109
141. Chicken Kapama — 109
142. Spinach and Feta-Stuffed Chicken Breasts — 110
143. Rosemary Baked Chicken Drumsticks — 110
144. Chicken with Onions, Potatoes, Figs, and Carrots — 111
145. Chicken Gyros with Tzatziki — 111
146. Eggplant Casserole — 112
147. Dijon and Herb Pork Tenderloin — 112
148. Steak with Red Wine-Mushroom Sauce — 113
149. Greek Meatballs — 113
150. Lamb with String Beans — 114

151. Greek Lamb Chop — 117
152. Skillet Braised Cod with Asparagus and Potatoes — 117
153. Savory Vegetable Pancakes — 118
154. Mediterranean Tuna Noodle Casserole — 118
155. Acquapazza Snapper — 119
156. Eggplant Brown Rice Bowl — 119
157. Extra-Crispy Veggie-Packed Pizza — 120
158. Greek Turkey Burgers — 120
159. Beef and Lamb Kofta Lettuce Wraps — 121
160. Chicken Souvlaki — 121
161. Spicy Chicken Shawarma — 122
162. Lemon Chicken Pita Burgers with Spiced Yogurt Sauce — 122
163. Lamb Chop with Pistachio Gremolata — 123
164. Pita Salad with Cucumber, Fennel and Chicken — 123
165. Halibut with Lemon-Fennel Salad — 124

166. Tuscan Beef Stew — 127
167. Mediterranean Beef Stew — 127
168. Cabbage Roll Casserole with Veal — 128
169. Slow Cooked Daube Provencal — 128
170. Osso Bucco — 129
171. Slow Cooker Beef Bourguignon — 139
172. Balsamic Beef — 130
173. Veal Pot Roast — 130
174. Mediterranean Rice and Sausage — 131
175. Spanish Meatballs — 131
176. Lamb Shanks with Red Wine — 132
177. Leg of Lamb with Rosemary and Garlic — 132
178. Lemon Honey Lamb Shoulder — 133
179. Italian Shredded Pork Stew — 133
180. Parmesan Honey Pork Loin Roast — 134

181. Passion Fruit and Spicy Couscous — 137
182. Spring Sandwich — 137
183. Springtime Quinoa Salad — 138
184. Seafood Souvlaki Bowl — 138
185. Spaghetti Nicoise — 139
186. Tomato Poached Fish with Herbs and Chickpeas — 139
187. Garlic Prawn and Pea Risotto — 140
188. Honey and Vanilla Custard Cups with Crunchy Filo Pastry — 140

189. Mediterranean Tostadas — 141
190. Vegetable Ratatouille — 141
191. Citrus Cups — 142
192. Mixed Berry Pancakes and Ricotta — 142
193. Mediterranean Frittata — 143
194. Caponata — 143
195. Fresh Deli Pasta — 144

196. Balsamic Asparagus — 147
197. Lime Cucumber Mix — 147
198. Walnuts Cucumber Mix — 148
199. Cheesy Beet Salad — 148
200. Rosemary Beets — 149
201. Squash and Tomatoes Mix — 149
202. Balsamic Eggplant Mix — 150
203. Sage Barley Mix — 150
204. hickpeas and Beets Mix — 151
205. Creamy Sweet Potatoes Mix — 151
206. Cabbage and Mushrooms Mix — 152
207. Lemon Mushroom Rice — 152
208. Paprika and Chives Potatoes — 153
209. Bulgur, Kale and Cheese Mix — 153
210. Spicy Green Beans Mix — 154

211. Pistachio Arugula Salad — 157
212. Potato Salad — 157
213. Raisin Rice Pilaf — 158
214. Lebanese Delight — 158
215. Mediterranean Sweet Potato — 159
216. Flavorful Braised Kale — 159
217. Bean Salad — 160
218. Basil Tomato Skewers — 160
219. Olives with Feta — 161
220. Black Bean Medley — 161
221. Mediterranean Quiche — 162
222. Grilled Fish with Lemons — 162
223. Pesto Walnut Noodles — 163
224. Tomato Tabbouleh — 163
225. Lemon Faro Bowl — 164

226. Baked Bean Fish Meal — 167
227. Mushroom Cod Stew — 167
228. Spiced Swordfish — 168
229. Anchovy Pasta Mania — 168
230. Shrimp Garlic Pasta — 169
231. Vinegar Honeyed Salmon — 169
232. Orange Fish Meal — 170
233. Shrimp Zoodles — 170
234. Asparagus Trout Meal — 171
235. Kale Olive Tuna — 171
236. Tangy Rosemary Shrimps — 172
237. Asparagus Salmon — 172
238. Tuna Nutty Salad — 173
239. Creamy Shrimp Soup — 173
240. Spiced Salmon with Vegetable Quinoa — 174

241. Baked Cod with Vegetables — 177
242. Slow Cooker Salmon in Foil — 177
243. Dill Chutney Salmon — 178
244. Garlic-Butter Parmesan Salmon and Asparagus — 178

245. Lemon Rosemary Roasted Branzino — 179
246. Grilled Lemon Pesto Salmon — 179
247. Steamed Trout with Lemon Herb Crust — 180
248. Roasted Trout Stuffed with Veggies — 181
249. Lemony Trout with Caramelized Shallots — 181
250. Easy Tomato Tuna Melts — 182
251. Mackerel and Green Bean Salad — 182
252. Hazelnut Crusted Sea Bass — 183
253. Shrimp and Pea Paella — 183
254. Garlic Shrimp with Arugula Pesto — 184
255. Baked Oysters with Vegetables — 184

256. Grilled Whole Sea Bass — 187
257. Pan-Cooked Fish with Tomatoes — 187
258. Fish Steamed in Parchment with Veggies — 188
259. Swordfish Souvlaki — 188
260. Stuffed Monkfish — 189
261. Shrimp Santorini — 189
262. Greek-Style Shrimp Cocktail — 190
263. Fried Calamari — 190
264. Stuffed Squid — 191
265. Octopus with Figs and Peaches — 191
266. Octopus with Potatoes — 192
267. Feta Crab Cakes — 192
268. Steamed Mussels with White Wine and Fennel — 193
269. Seafood Rice — 193
270. Mixed Seafood with Wine and Capers — 194

271. Greek Stuffed Collard Greens — 197
272. Walnut Pesto Zoodles — 197
273. Cauliflower Steaks with Eggplant Relish — 198
274. Mediterranean Lentil Sloppy Joes — 198
275. Gorgonzola Sweet Potato Burgers — 199
276. Zucchini-Eggplant Gratin — 199
277. Grilled Stuffed Portobello Mushrooms — 200
278. Stuffed Tomatoes with Tabbouleh — 200
279. Polenta with Mushroom Bolognese — 201
280. North African Peanut Stew over Cauliflower Rice — 201
281. Italian Baked Beans — 202
282. Cannellini Bean Lettuce Wraps — 202
283. Israeli Eggplant, Chickpea, and Mint Sauté — 203
284. Mediterranean Lentils and Rice — 203
285. Brown Rice Pilaf with Golden Raisins — 204

286. Vegetarian Quinoa Pilaf — 207
287. Roasted and Curried Cauliflower — 207
288. Easy and Healthy Baked Vegetables — 208
289. Green Beans and Tomatoes — 208
290. Crunchy Kale Chips — 209
291. Zucchini Lasagna — 209
292. Garlic Parmesan Artichokes — 210
293. Roasted Brussels Sprouts And Pecans — 210
294. Parmesan Veggies Mix — 211
295. Almond Kale — 211
296. Tomato Basil Cauliflower Rice — 212
297. Allspice Okra — 212
298. Garlicky Rosemary Potatoes — 213
299. Creamy Carrot Chowder — 213
300. Cauliflower Hash Brown — 214

| | |
|---|---|
| 301. Mediterranean Veggie Bowl | 217 |
| 302. Grilled Veggie and Hummus Wrap | 217 |
| 303. Spanish Green Beans | 218 |
| 304. Rustic Cauliflower and Carrot Hash | 218 |
| 305. Roasted Cauliflower and Tomatoes | 219 |
| 306. Roasted Acorn Squash | 219 |
| 307. Sauteed Garlic Spinach | 220 |
| 308. Garlicky Sauteed Zucchini with Mint | 220 |
| 309. Stewed Okra | 221 |
| 310. Sweet Veggie-Stuffed Peppers | 221 |
| 311. Moussaka | 222 |
| 312. Vegetable-Stuffed Grape Leaves | 222 |
| 313.Grilled Eggplant Rolls | 223 |
| 314. Crispy Zucchini Fritters | 223 |
| 315. Cheesy Spinach Pies | 224 |

CHAPTER 23.
SOUP AND STEW RECIPES    226

| | |
|---|---|
| 316. Minestrone Soup | 227 |
| 317. Chicken Wild Rice Soup | 227 |
| 318. Classic Chicken Soup | 228 |
| 319. Cucumber Soup | 228 |
| 320. Squash and Turmeric Soup | 229 |
| 321. Leek, Potato, and Carrot Soup | 229 |
| 322. Bell Pepper Soup | 230 |
| 323. Yucatan Soup | 230 |
| 324. Zesty Taco Soup | 231 |
| 325. Southwestern Posole | 231 |
| 326. Spring Vegetable Soup | 232 |
| 327. Seafood Corn Chowder | 232 |
| 328. Beef Sage Soup | 233 |
| 329. Cabbage Borscht | 233 |
| 331. Ground Beef Soup | 234 |

CHAPTER 24.
SOUP AND STEW RECIPES PART 2    236

| | |
|---|---|
| 331. Mexican Tortilla Soup | 237 |
| 332. Chicken Noodle Soup | 237 |
| 333. Cheesy Broccoli Soup | 238 |
| 334. Rich Potato soup | 238 |
| 335. Mediterranean Lentil Soup | 239 |
| 336. Sausage Kale Soup with Mushrooms | 239 |
| 337. Classic Minestrone | 240 |
| 338. Turkey Meatball and Ditalini Soup | 240 |
| 339. Mint Avocado Chilled Soup | 241 |
| 340. Split Pea Soup | 241 |
| 341. Butternut Squash Soup | 242 |
| 342. Beef Stroganoff Soup | 242 |
| 343. Creamy Low Carb Butternut Squash Soup | 243 |
| 344. Baked Shrimp Stew | 243 |
| 345. Cinnamon Squash Soup | 244 |

CHAPTER 25.
SOUP AND STEW RECIPES PART 3    246

| | |
|---|---|
| 346. Bulgarian Lentil Soup | 247 |
| 347. White Bean Soup | 247 |
| 348. Cauliflower Soup | 248 |
| 349. Moroccan Pumpkin Soup | 248 |
| 350. Potato Soup | 249 |
| 351. Leek, Rice and Potato Soup | 249 |
| 352. Carrot and Chickpea Soup | 250 |
| 353. Broccoli, Zucchini and Blue Cheese Soup | 250 |
| 354. Beetroot and Carrot Soup | 251 |
| 355. Roasted Red Pepper Soup | 251 |
| 356. Lentil, Barley and Mushroom Soup | 252 |
| 357. Spinach Soup | 252 |
| 358. Spinach and Feta Cheese Soup | 253 |
| 359. Nettle Soup | 253 |
| 360. Thick Herb Soup | 254 |

CHAPTER 26.
VEGETARIAN RECIPES    256

| | |
|---|---|
| 361. Rice with Vermicelli | 257 |
| 362. Fava Beans and Rice | 257 |
| 363. Buttered Fava Beans | 258 |
| 364. Freekeh | 258 |
| 365. Fried Rice Balls with Tomato Sauce | 259 |
| 366. Spanish-Style Rice | 269 |
| 367. Zucchini with Rice and Tzatziki | 260 |
| 368. Cannellini Beans with Rosemary and Garlic Aioli | 260 |
| 369. Jeweled Rice | 261 |
| 370. Asparagus Risotto | 261 |
| 371. Vegetable Paella | 262 |
| 372. Eggplant and Rice Casserole | 262 |
| 373. Many Vegetable Couscous | 263 |
| 375. Bulgur with Tomatoes and Chickpeas | 263 |
| 374. Kushari | 264 |

CHAPTER 27.
VEGETARIAN RECIPES PART 2    266

| | |
|---|---|
| 376. Cauliflower Steaks with Olive Citrus Sauce | 267 |
| 377. Pistachio Mint Pesto Pasta | 267 |
| 378. Burst Cherry Tomato Sauce with Angel Hair Pasta | 268 |
| 379. Baked Tofu with Sun-Dried Tomatoes and Artichokes | 268 |
| 380. Baked Mediterranean Tempeh with Tomatoes and Garlic | 269 |
| 381. Roasted Portobello Mushrooms with Kale and Red Onion | 269 |
| 382. Balsamic Marinated Tofu with Basil and Oregano | 270 |
| 383. Ricotta, Basil, and Pistachio-Stuffed Zucchini | 270 |
| 384. Farro with Roasted Tomatoes and Mushrooms | 271 |
| 385. Baked Orzo | 271 |
| 386. Barley Risotto with Tomatoes | 272 |
| 387. Chickpeas and Kale with Spicy Pomodoro Sauce | 272 |
| 388. Roasted Feta with Kale and Lemon Yogurt | 273 |
| 389. Roasted Eggplant and Chickpeas with Tomato Sauce | 273 |
| 390. Baked Falafel Sliders | 274 |

CHAPTER 28.
VEGETARIAN RECIPES PART 3    276

| | |
|---|---|
| 391. Portobello Caprese | 277 |
| 392. Mushroom and Cheese Stuffed Tomatoes | 277 |
| 393. Tabbouleh | 278 |
| 394. Spicy Broccoli Rabe and Artichoke Hearts | 278 |
| 395. Shakshuka | 279 |
| 396. Spanakopita | 279 |
| 397. Tagine | 280 |
| 398. Citrus Pistachios and Asparagus | 280 |
| 399. Tomato and Parsley Stuffed Eggplant | 281 |
| 400. Ratatouille | 281 |
| 401. Gemista | 282 |
| 402. Stuffed Cabbage Rolls | 282 |
| 403. Brussels Sprouts with Balsamic Glaze | 283 |
| 404. Spinach Salad with Citrus Vinaigrette | 283 |
| 405. Kale Salad with Pistachio and Parmesan | 284 |

CHAPTER 29.
SALAD RECIPES    286

406. Peppers and Lentils Salad — 287
407. Cashews and Red Cabbage Salad — 287
408. Apples and Pomegranate Salad — 288
409. Cranberry Bulgur Mix — 288
410. Chickpeas, Corn and Black Beans Salad — 289
411. Olives and Lentils Salad — 289
412. Lime Spinach and Chickpeas Salad — 290
413. Minty Olives and Tomatoes Salad — 290
414. Beans and Cucumber Salad — 291
415. Tomato and Avocado Salad — 291
416. Arugula Salad — 292
417. Chickpea Salad — 292
418. Chopped Israeli Mediterranean Pasta Salad — 293
419. Feta Tomato Salad — 293
420. Greek Pasta Salad — 294

Chapter 30.
SALAD RECIPES PART 2 — 296

421. Pork and Greens Salad — 297
422. Mediterranean Duck Breast Salad — 297
423. Mediterranean Chicken Bites — 298
424. Mediterranean Chicken and Tomato Dish — 298
425. Creamy Chicken Salad — 299
426. Chicken and Cabbage Mix — 299
427. Chicken and Quinoa Salad — 300
428. Simple Pork Stir Fry — 300
429. Beef Tartar — 301
430. Melon Salad — 301
431. Celery Citrus Salad — 302
432. Broccoli Crunch Salad — 302
433. Summer Tomato Salad — 303
434. Cheese Beet Salad — 303
435. Cauliflower and Cherry Tomato Salad — 304

Chapter 31.
SALAD RECIPES PART 3 — 306

436. Watermelon Salad — 307
437. Orange Celery Salad — 307
438. Roasted Broccoli Salad — 308
439. Tomato Salad — 308
440. Feta Beet Salad — 309
441. Cauliflower & Tomato Salad — 309
442. Tahini Spinach — 310
443. Pilaf with Cream Cheese — 310
444. Easy Spaghetti Squash — 311
445. Roasted Eggplant Salad — 311
446. Penne with Tahini Sauce — 312
447. Roasted Veggies — 312
448. Zucchini Pasta — 313
449. Asparagus Pasta — 313
450. Feta & Spinach Pita Bake — 314

Chapter 32.
DESSERT RECIPES — 316

451. Vanilla Cream — 317
452. Blueberries Bowls — 317
453. Brownies — 318
454. Strawberries Coconut Cake — 318
455. Cocoa Almond Pudding — 319
456. Nutmeg Cream — 319
457. Vanilla Avocado Cream — 320
458. Raspberries Cream Cheese Bowls — 320
459. Mediterranean Watermelon Salad — 321
460. Coconut Apples — 321
461. Orange Compote — 322
462. Pears Stew — 322
463. Lemon Watermelon Mix — 323
464. Rhubarb Cream — 323

465. Mango Bowls — 324

Chapter 33.
DESSERT RECIPES PART 2 — 326

466. Chocolate Ganache — 327
467. Chocolate Covered Strawberries — 327
468. Strawberry Angel Food Dessert — 328
469. Fruit Pizza — 328
470. Bananas Foster — 329
471. Cranberry Orange Cookies — 329
472. Key Lime Pie — 330
473. Rhubarb Strawberry Crunch — 330
474. Chocolate Chip Banana Dessert — 331
475. Apple Pie Filling — 331
476. Ice Cream Sandwich Dessert — 332
477. Cranberry and Pistachio Biscotti — 332
478. Cream Puff Dessert — 333
479. Fresh Peach Dessert — 333
480. Blueberry Dessert — 334

Chapter 34.
DESSERT RECIPES PART 3 — 336

481. Good Sweet — 337
482. A Taste of Dessert — 337
483. Honey Carrots — 338
484. Fresh Cherry Treat — 338
485. Milky Peachy Dessert — 339
486. Citrus Sections — 339
487. After Meal Apples — 340
488. Warm Nut Bites — 340
489. Dipped Sprouts — 341
490. Pecans and Cheese — 341

Chapter 35.
DESSERT RECIPES PART 4 — 342

491. Hazelnut Cookies — 343
492. Fruit Dessert Nachos — 343
493. Honey Yogurt with Berries — 344
494. Caramelized Apples with Yogurt — 344
495. Ricotta Brulee — 345
496. Chocolate Quinoa Bars — 345
497. Almond Honey Ricotta Spread — 346
498. Apricot Energy Bites — 346
499. Pistachio Snack Bars — 347
500. Oat Berry Smoothie — 347

Chapter 36.
7-DAY MEAL PLAN — 348

CONCLUSION — 351

# INTRODUCTION

## About the Mediterranean Diet

The Mediterranean diet is full of never-ending varieties of healthy, fresh, and delicious foods. However, there is more of an emphasis on certain types of foods, nothing is excluded. People who try a Mediterranean diet can enjoy the dishes they love while also learning to appreciate how good the freshest, healthiest foods can be.

Transitioning into the Mediterranean diet is mainly about bracing yourself for a new way of eating, adapting your attitude toward food into one of joyful expectation and appreciation of good meals and good company. It's like a mindset as anything else, so you'll want to make your environment unite so you can quickly adapt to the lifestyle in the Mediterranean way.

## Benefits of the Mediterranean Diet

Boosts Your Brain Health: Preserve memory and prevent cognitive decline by following the Mediterranean diet that will limit processed foods, refined bread, and red meats. Have a glass of wine versus hard liquor.

Improves Poor Eyesight: Older individuals suffer from poor eyesight, but in many cases, the Mediterranean diet has provided notable improvement. An Australian Center for Eye Research discovered that the individuals who consumed a minimum of 100 ml (0.42 cup) of olive oil weekly were almost 50% less likely to develop macular degeneration versus those who ate less than one ml each week.

Helps to Reduce the Risk of Heart Disease: The New England Journal of Medicine provided evidence in 2013 from a randomized clinical trial. The trial was implemented in Spain, whereas individuals did not have cardiovascular disease at enrollment but were in the 'high risk' category. The incidence of major cardiovascular events was reduced by the Mediterranean diet that was supplemented with extra-virgin olive oil or nuts. In one study, men who consumed fish in this manner reduced the risk by 23% of death from heart disease.

The Risk of Alzheimer's disease is reduced: In 2018, the journal Neurology studied 70 brain scans of individuals who had no signs of dementia at the onset. They followed the eating patterns in a two-year study resulting in individuals who were on the Med diet had a lesser increase of the depots and reduced energy use - potentially signaling risk for Alzheimer's.

Helps Lessen the Risk of Some Types of Cancer: According to the results of a group study, the diet is associated with a lessened risk of stomach cancer (gastric adenocarcinoma).

Decreases Risks for Type 2 Diabetes: It can help stabilize blood sugar while protecting against type 2 diabetes with its low-carb elements. The Med diet maintains a richness in fiber, which will digest slowly while preventing variances in your blood sugar. It also can help you maintain a healthier weight, which is another trigger for diabetes.

Suggests Improvement for Those with Parkinson's disease: By consuming foods on the Mediterranean diet, you add high levels of antioxidants that can prevent your body from undergoing oxidative stress, which is a damaging process that will attack your cells. The menu plan can reduce your risk factors in half.

## Mediterranean Diet Pyramid

The Mediterranean Diet Pyramid is a nutritional guide developed by the World Health Organization, Harvard School of Public Health, and Oldways Preservation Trust in 1993. It is a visual tool that summarizes the Mediterranean diet, suggested eating patterns, and guides how frequently specific mechanisms should be eaten. It allows you to break healthy eating habits and not overfill yourself with too many calories.

Olive oil, fruits, vegetables, whole grains, legumes, beans, nuts & seeds, spices & herbs: These foods form the Mediterranean pyramid base. If you did observe, you would notice that these are mostly from plant sources. You should try and include a few variations of these items into each meal you eat. Olive oil should be the primary fat in cooking your dishes and endeavor to replace any other butter or cooking oil you may have been using to cook.

Fish & seafood: These are essential staples of the Mediterranean diet that should be consumed often as a protein source. You would want to include these in your diet at least two times a week. Try new varieties of fish, either frozen or fresh. Also, incorporate seafood like mussels, crab, and shrimp into your diet. Canned tuna is also great to include on sandwiches or toss in a salad with fresh vegetables.

Cheese, yogurt, eggs & poultry: These ingredients should be consumed in more moderate amounts. Depending on the food, they should be used sparingly throughout the week. Keep in mind that if you are using eggs in baking or cooking, they will also be counted in your weekly limit. You would want to stick to more healthy cheese like Parmesan, ricotta, or feta that you can add a topping or garnish on your dishes.

Red meat & sweets: These items are going to be consumed less frequently. If you are going to eat them, you need to consume only small quantities, most preferably lean meat versions with less fat when possible. Most studies recommend a maximum of 12 to 16 ounces per month. To add more variety to your diet, you can still have red meat occasionally, but you would want to reduce how often you have it. It is essential to limit its intake because of all the health concerns of sugar and red meat. The Mediterranean diet improves cardiovascular health and reduces blood pressure, while red meat tends to be dangerous to your cardiovascular system. The Greece population ate very little red meat and instead had fish or seafood as their main protein source.

Water: The Mediterranean diet encourages you to stay hydrated at all times. It means drinking more water than your daily intake. The Institute of Medicine recommends a total of 9 cups each day for women and 13 cups for men. For pregnant or breastfeeding women, the number should be increased.

Wine: Moderate consumption of wine with meals is encouraged on the Mediterranean diet. Studies shown that moderate consumption of alcohol can reduce the risk of heart disease. That can mean about 1 glass per day for women. Men tend to have higher body mass so that they can consume 1 to 2 drinks. Please keep in mind what your doctor would recommend regarding wine consumption based on your health and family history.

# CHAPTER 1
# 10 TIPS FOR SUCCESS

The healthy Mediterranean way of life is about eating balanced foods rich in vitamins, minerals, antioxidants, and healthy fatty acids. However, the Mediterranean diet is just one aspect of it. The Mediterranean way of life calls for regular physical exercise, plenty of rest, healthy social interaction, and fun. Balancing all these aspects was the secret of the excellent health of the Mediterranean folk back in the day. However, only the Mediterranean diet is the primary focus of this book, and we will spend most of our time talking about just that.

## 1.    Eat Healthy Fats

The Mediterranean diet is not low-fat diet at all, but the fat included in this diet is considered healthy for the body, and the heart in particular. Remember: not all fats are created equal. Certain kinds of fats are beneficial, while others do more harm than good. Monosaturated fats and polyunsaturated omega-3 fatty acids, for example, are considered healthy. Omega-6 polyunsaturated fatty acids and saturated fats are unhealthy, and these harmful fats are primarily present in most of the typical food worldwide. The United States, for example, absolutely loves saturated fats. According to a survey, saturated fats constitute 11% of an average American's total calories, which is a very high number compared to an average Mediterranean resident, who consumes less than 8% of his/her calories through saturated fat. If you wish to switch to the healthy Mediterranean way of life, the first thing to do is change the oils you consume. Eliminating fats like butter and lard in favor of more nourishing oils like olive oil would be the place to start.

## 2.    Consume Dairy in Moderation

We all love cheese. Dairy products are delicious, nutritious, and excellent sources of calcium and should be consumed in moderation if you're following the Mediterranean diet. It is usually a good idea to drink two to three servings of full-fat dairy products in a single day, where one serving can mean an 8-ounce glass of milk, or an ounce of cheese or 8 ounces of yogurt.

### 3.      Consume Tons of Plant-Based Foods

As we saw in the pyramid, fruits, vegetables, legumes, and whole grains form the basis of the Mediterranean diet. So, it is a good idea to eat five to ten servings of these in a single day, depending on your appetite. Eat as many as you want, but don't overeat. Plant-based foods are naturally low in calories and high in fiber and nutrients. Fresh, unprocessed plants are best, so always be on the lookout for the best sources of these around you!

### 4.      Spice Things Up with Fresh Spices and Herbs

Fresh herbs and spices make most of the recipes insanely delicious while also providing health benefits. If you already use these in your daily cooking, more power to you! If not, we got you covered!

### 5.      Consume Seafood Weekly and Meat Monthly

As we've talked about before, one benefit of living close to the sea is easy access to seafood. However, seafood holds a lower priority than plant-based foods in the Mediterranean diet and should be consumed in moderation. If you're a vegetarian, consider taking fish oil supplements to get those omega-3 fatty acids into your system.

Consume Meat Monthly: Red meat used to be a luxury for the Mediterranean people back in the day. Although not completely off-limits, you should try and reduce your red-meat intake as much as possible. If you love red meat, consider consuming it no more than two times per month. And even when you eat it, make sure the serving size of the meat in the dish is small (two to three-ounce serving). The main reason to limit meat intake is to limit the number of unhealthy fats going into your system. As we talked before, saturated fats and omega-6 fatty acids are not suitable for health, but unfortunately, red meat contains significant quantities. As a beef lover myself, I eat a two-ounce serving of it per month, and when I do eat it, I make sure there are lots of vegetables on the side to satiate my hunger.

Drink Wine! Love wine? Well, it is your lucky day. Drinking 1 glass of wine along with your meal at dinner is a common practice in the Mediterranean regions. Red wine is especially useful for the heart and it is a good idea to consume 1 glass of red wine twice in 1 week. Excess of everything is bad, and wine is no exception so keep it in check. Also, if you're already suffering from health conditions, it is a good idea to check with your doctor before introducing wine to your daily diet.

## 6.    Work Your Body

Now you don't have to hit the gym like a maniac to work your body. Walking to your destination instead of driving, taking the stairs instead of the lift, or kneading your dough can all get the job done. So, be creative and work your body when you can. Better yet, play a sport or just hit the gym like a maniac. You don't have to, as I said at the start, but it will help… a lot.

## 7.    Enjoy a Big Lunch

Lunch was usually the meal of the day when the Mediterranean residents sat with their families and took their time enjoying a big meal. This strengthens social bonds and relaxes the mind during the most stressful time of the day, when you're just halfway done with your work, probably.

## 8.    Have Fun with Friends and Family

Just by spending time and doing something fun with your loved ones is great for de-stressing. Today, we don't understand the importance of this, and people feel lonely, and in some cases, even depressed. Just doing this one thing has the power to solve a huge chunk of the problems our modern society faces.

## 9.    Be Passionate

The Mediterranean people are passionate folk. Living on or close to sun-kissed coasts, their passion for life is naturally high. Being passionate about something in life can take you a long way towards health and wellness.

## 10.    Planning Your Meals

If you're a beginner and have not yet made the switch to the Mediterranean diet, you will need to identify what changes you need to make to your current diet to make it match closely with the Mediterranean diet. In time, the Mediterranean diet will come to you naturally, but to start, you will need to plan. You will need to plan your portion sizes, and how often you eat certain foods. The changes are small but will benefit you in the long run.

# CHAPTER 2
# APPETIZER AND SNACK RECIPES

# 1. ROASTED BEET SALAD WITH RICOTTA CHEESE

**COOKING: 60'**    **PREPARATION: 10'**    **SERVES: 4**

## INGREDIENTS

- » Red beets (8.8 oz, large, wrapped in foil)
- » Yellow beets (8.8 oz, small, wrapped in foil)
- » Mesclun (4.3 oz)
- » Mustard Vinaigrette (4.4 oz)
- » Ricotta cheese (2.1 oz)
- » Walnuts (0.1 oz, chopped)

**NUTRITIONS:**
290 Calories, 6g Fat, 6g Protein

## DIRECTIONS

Bake at 400 F for 1 hour.

Cool the beets slightly. Trim the root and stem ends and pull off the peels.

Cut the red beets crosswise into thin slices.

Cut the yellow beets vertically into quarters.

Arrange the sliced red beets in circles on cold salad plates. Toss the mesclun with half the vinaigrette.

Drizzle the remaining vinaigrette over the sliced beets.

Situate small mound of greens in the center of each plate.

Arrange the quartered yellow beets around the greens.

Sprinkle the tops of the salads with the crumbled ricotta and walnuts (if using).

# 2. BAKED FISH WITH TOMATOES AND MUSHROOMS

**COOKING: 12'**    **PREPARATION: 25'**    **SERVES: 4'**

## INGREDIENTS

- » Fish (4, whole and small, 12 oz each)
- » Salt (to taste)
- » Pepper (to taste)
- » Dried thyme (pinch)
- » Parsley (4 sprigs)
- » Olive oil (as needed)
- » Onion (4 oz, small dice)
- » Shallots (1 oz, minced)
- » Mushrooms (8 oz, chopped)
- » Tomato concassed (6.4 oz)
- » Dry white wine (3.2 Fl oz)

## DIRECTIONS

1. Scale and clean the fish but leaves the heads on. Season the fish inside and out with salt and pepper and put a small pinch of thyme and a sprig of parsley in the cavity of each.
2. Use as many baking pans to hold the fish in a single layer. Oil the pans with a little olive oil.
3. Sauté the onions and shallots in a little olive oil about 1 minute. Add the mushrooms and sauté lightly.
4. Put the sautéed vegetables and the tomatoes in the bottoms of the baking pans.
5. Put the fish in the pans. Oil the tops lightly. Pour in the wine.
6. Bake at 400F for 15-20 minutes.
7. Remove the fish and keep them warm.
8. Remove the vegetables from the pans with a slotted spoon and check for seasonings. Serve a spoonful of the vegetables with the fish, placing it under or alongside each fish.
9. Strain, degrease, and reduce the cooking liquid slightly. Just before serving, moisten each portion with 1-2 tbsp of the liquid.

**NUTRITIONS:**
Calories: 434 kcal Fat: 35g Carbs: 27g Protein: 6.7g

# 3. GOAT CHEESE AND WALNUT SALAD

**COOKING: 15'**  **PREPARATION: 10'**  **SERVES: 3**

## INGREDIENTS

» Beet (2 oz)
» Arugula (3 oz)
» Bibb lettuce (2 oz)
» Romaine lettuce (9 oz)
» Breadcrumbs (1/4 cup, dry)
» Dried thyme (1/4 tbs)
» Dried basil (1/4 tbs)
» Black pepper (1/3 tsp)
» Fresh goat's milk cheese (6.35 oz, preferably in log shape)
» Walnut pieces (1.1 oz)
» Red wine vinaigrette (2 fl. Oz.)

## DIRECTIONS

1. Trim, wash, and dry all the salad greens.
2. Tear the greens into small pieces. Toss well.
3. Mix the herbs, pepper, and crumbs.
4. Slice the cheese into 1 oz pieces. In the seasoned crumbs mix, roll the pieces of cheese to coat them
5. Place the cheese on a sheet pan. Bake at the temperate of 425 F for 10 minutes.
6. Simultaneously, toast the walnuts in a dry sauté pan or the oven with the cheese.
7. Toss the greens with the vinaigrette and arrange on cold plates. Top each plate of greens with 2 pieces of cheese and sprinkle with walnuts.

## NUTRITIONS:
460 Calories, 40g Fat, 17g Protein

# 4. GRILLED SPICED TURKEY BURGER

**COOKING: 15'**  **PREPARATION: 20'**  **SERVES: 3**

## INGREDIENTS

» Onion (1.8 oz, chopped fine)
» Extra Virgin Olive Oil (1/3 tbsp)
» Turkey (14.4 oz, ground)
» Salt (1/3 tbsp)
» Curry powder (1/3 tbsp)
» Lemon zest (2/5 tsp, grated)
» Pepper (1/8 tsp)
» Cinnamon (1/8 tsp)
» Coriander (1/4 tsp, ground)
» Cumin (1/8 tsp, ground)
» Cardamom (1/8 tsp, ground)
» Water (1.2 Fl oz)
» Tomato Raisin Chutney (as desired)
» Cilantro leaves (as desired)

## DIRECTIONS

1. Cook the onions in the oil. Cool completely.
2. Combine the turkey, onions, spices, water, and salt in a bowl. Toss.
3. Divide the mixture into 5 oz portions (or as desired). Form each portion into a thick patty.
4. Broil but do not overcook it.
5. Plate the burgers. Put spoonful of chutney on top of each.

## NUTRITIONS:
250 Calories, 14g Fat, 27g Protein

# 5. TOMATO TEA PARTY SANDWICHES

**COOKING: 15'**  **PREPARATION: 0'**  **SERVES: 4**

## INGREDIENTS

» Red beets (8.8 oz, large, wrapped in foil)
» Yellow beets (8.8 oz, small, wrapped in foil)
» Mesclun (4.3 oz)
» Mustard Vinaigrette (4.4 oz)
» Ricotta cheese (2.1 oz)
» Walnuts (0.1 oz, chopped)

## DIRECTIONS

1. Toast bread to your preference.
2. Spread 2 tsp. olive oil on each slice of bread. Add the cheese.
3. Top with tomato, then sprinkle with basil and pepper.
4. Serve with lemon water and enjoy it!

**NUTRITIONS:**
290 Calories, 6g Fat, 6g Protein

# 6. VEGGIE SHISH KEBABS

**COOKING: 10'**  **PREPARATION: 0'**  **SERVES: 3**

## INGREDIENTS

» Cherry tomatoes (9)
» Mozzarella balls (9 low-fat)
» Basil leaves (9)
» Olive oil (1 tsp.)
» Zucchini (3, sliced)
» Dash of pepper

### For serving
» Whole Wheat Bread (6 slices)

## DIRECTIONS

1. Stab 1 cherry tomato, low-fat mozzarella ball, zucchini, and basil leaf onto each skewer.
2. Situate skewers on a plate and drizzle with olive oil. Finish with a sprinkle of pepper.
3. Set your bread to toast. Serve 2 bread slices with 3 kebobs.

**NUTRITIONS:**
349 Calories, 5.7g Fat, 15g Protein

# 7. CRISPY FALAFEL

**COOKING: 20'**     **PREPARATION: 8'**     **SERVES: 3**

## INGREDIENTS

- » Chickpeas (1 cup, drained and rinsed)
- » Parsley (½ cup, chopped with stems removed)
- » Cilantro (1/3 cup, chopped with stems removed)
- » Dill (¼ cup, chopped with stems removed)
- » Cloves garlic (4, minced)
- » Sesame seeds (1 tbsp., toasted)
- » Coriander (½ tbsp.)
- » Black pepper (½ tbsp.)
- » Cumin (½ tbsp.)
- » Baking powder (½ tsp.)
- » Cayenne (½ tsp.)

## DIRECTIONS

1. Thoroughly dry your chickpeas with a paper towel.
2. Place the parsley, cilantro, and dill in a food processor.
3. Mix chickpeas, garlic, coriander, black pepper, cumin, baking powder, and cayenne.
4. Transfer the mixture to an airtight container and chill for about an hour.
5. Take out from the refrigerator and mix the baking powder and sesame seeds.
6. Scoop the mixture into a pan with 3 inches of olive oil over medium heat to create patties. Keep in mind as you create the patties that you are aiming to make 12 with the mixture.
7. Let the falafel patties fry for 1-2 minutes on each side.
8. Once your falafel patties are nicely browned, transfer them to a plate lined with paper towels to finish crisping.
9. Dip, dunk, fill, and enjoy!

**NUTRITIONS:**
328 Calories, 10.8g Fat, 24g Protein

# 8. ONION FRIED EGGS

**COOKING: 15'**     **PREPARATION: 91'**     **SERVES: 4**

## INGREDIENTS

- » Eggs (11)
- » White mushroom (1 cup)
- » Feta cheese (4 oz, crumbled)
- » Sun-dried tomatoes (1/2 cup, chopped)
- » Onion (2 large, sliced)
- » Garlic clove (2, minced)
- » Olive oil (2.5 tbsp.)

## DIRECTIONS

1. Put a pan with the olive oil over medium-low heat.
2. Once hot, stir onions and mushrooms into the oil.
3. Allow the onion and mushroom mix to cook for about one hour. Stir them every 5-7 minutes to ensure they cook evenly.
4. After the onions have browned, add the sun-dried tomatoes and garlic, and let cook for 2 minutes.
5. Once the sun-dried tomatoes and garlic are fragrant, spread all the ingredients out into an even, thin layer across the pan.
6. Crack the eggs overtop the ingredients already in the pan.
7. Sprinkle your feta cheese and pepper over top of the eggs.
8. Cover the pan with its corresponding lid and let the eggs sit to cook for about 10-12 minutes. Gently shake the pan at 10 minutes to check on the consistency of the egg yolks. Continue to cook until they reach your desired level of doneness.
9. Remove pan from heat and divide the mixture between two plates.

**NUTRITIONS:**
360 Calories, 27g Fat, 20g Protein

# 9. BLACK BEAN CAKE WITH SALSA

**COOKING: 15'**  **PREPARATION: 18'**  **SERVES: 10**

## INGREDIENTS

» Olive oil (1 Fl oz)
» Onion (16 oz,)
» Garlic (2-4 cloves)
» Jalapenos
» Ground cumin (2 tsp)
» Black beans (32 oz.)
» Oregano (1 tsp)
» Salsa cruda (450 ml)

## DIRECTIONS

1. Heat the olive oil in a sauté pan over low heat.
2. Add the garlic and onions, cook until soft. Do not brown.
3. Add the ground cumin and jalapeño. Cook for a few more minutes.
4. Add the oregano and beans. Cook until they are heated through.
5. Place the mixture in a food processor and blend in a puree.
6. Season well.
7. Divide the mixture into 2 oz portions. Form into small, flat cakes.
8. Brown the cakes lightly on both sides in hot olive oil in a sauté pan.
9. Serve 2 cakes per portion with 1 ½ Fl oz salsa.

**NUTRITIONS:**
260 Calories, 12g Fat, 9g Protein

# 10. PICKLED APPLE

**COOKING: 10'**  **PREPARATION: 20'**  **SERVES: 6**

## INGREDIENTS

» Water (1/2 cup)
» Maple syrup (3 ½ oz)
» Cider vinegar (1/2 cup)
» Sachet:
» Peppercorns (3-4)
» Mustard seed (1/4 tsp)
» Coriander seed (1/4 tsp)
» Salt (1/4 tsp)
» Granny smith apple (2,)
» Italian parsley (1 tbsp,)

## DIRECTIONS

1. Combine the water, maple syrup, vinegar, sachet, and sat in a saucepan. Bring to a boil.
2. Pour the liquid and the sachet over the apples in a nonreactive container.
3. Let it be refrigerated for 3-4 hours or overnight.
4. Drain the apples before serving and toss with the parsley.

**NUTRITIONS:**
50 Calories, 0.1g Fat, 0.3g Protein

# 11. BAKED CLAMS OREGANATA

**COOKING: 30'**          **PREPARATION: 13'**          **SERVES: 10**

## INGREDIENTS

- » Cherrystone clams (30)
- » Olive oil (2 Fl oz)
- » Onions (1 oz, chopped fine)
- » Garlic (1 tsp, finely chopped)
- » Lemon juice (1 Fl oz)
- » Fresh breadcrumbs (10 oz)
- » Parsley (1 tbsp, chopped)
- » Oregano (3/4 tsp, dried)
- » White pepper (1/8 tsp)
- » Parmesan cheese (1/3 cup)
- » Paprika (as needed)
- » Lemon wedges (10)

## DIRECTIONS

1. Open the clams. Catch the juice in a bowl.
2. Remove the clams from the shell. Place them in a strainer over the bowl of juice. Let them drain 15 minutes in the refrigerator. Save the 30 best half-shells.
3. Chop the clams into small pieces.
4. Heat the oil in a sauté pan. Add the onion and garlic. Sauté about 1 minute, but do not brown.
5. Use half of the clam juice, then reduce it over high heat by three-fourths.
6. Remove from the heat and add the crumbs, parsley, lemon juice, white pepper, and oregano. Mix gently to avoid making the crumbs pasty.
7. If necessary, adjust the seasonings.
8. Once the mixture has cooled. Mix in the chopped clams.
9. Place the mixture in the 30 clamshells. Sprinkle with parmesan cheese and (very lightly) with paprika.
10. Place on a sheet pan and refrigerate until needed.
11. For each order, bake 3 clams in a hot oven (450 F) until they are hot and the top brown.
12. Garnish with a lemon wedge.

**NUTRITIONS:**
180 Calories, 8g Fat, 10g Protein

# 12. TUNA TARTARE

**COOKING: 0'**          **PREPARATION: 15'**          **SERVES: 8**

## INGREDIENTS

- » Sashimi quality tuna (26.5 g, well-trimmed)
- » Shallots (1 oz, minced)
- » Parsley (2 tbsp, chopped)
- » Fresh tarragon (2 tbsp, chopped)
- » Lime juice (2 tbsp)
- » Dijon-style mustard (1 Fl oz)
- » Olive oil (2 Fl oz)

## DIRECTIONS

1. Use a knife to mince the tuna.
2. Mixed the rest of the ingredients with the chopped tuna.
3. Use a ring mold to make a beautifully presented tuna tartare.
4. Season to taste with pepper and salt.

**NUTRITIONS:**
200 Calories, 12g Fat, 21g Protein

# 13. COD CAKES

**COOKING: 30'**  **PREPARATION: 25'**  **SERVES: 10**

## INGREDIENTS

- » Cod (12 oz, cooked)
- » Turnips puree (12 oz.)
- » Whole eggs (2 ½ oz, beaten)
- » Egg yolk (1 yolk, beaten)
- » Salt (to taste)
- » White pepper (to taste)
- » Ground ginger (pinch)

### Standard Breading Procedure:
- » Whole wheat flour
- » Egg wash
- » Breadcrumbs
- » Tomatoes sauce
- »

## DIRECTIONS

1. Shred the fish.
2. Combine with the turnips, egg, and egg yolk.
3. Season with salt, pepper, and ground ginger.
4. Divide the mixture into 2 ½ oz portions. Shape the mixture into a ball and then slightly flatten the mixture cakes.
5. Put the mixture through the Standard Breading Procedure.
6. Deep-fry at 350 F until golden brown.
7. Serve 2 cakes per portion. Accompany with tomato sauce.

**NUTRITIONS:**
280 Calories, 6g Fat, 23g Protein

# 14. GRILLED VEGETABLE KEBABS

**COOKING: 12'**  **PREPARATION: 13'**  **SERVES: 6**

## INGREDIENTS

- » Zucchini (6 oz, trimmed)
- » Yellow Summer Squash (6 oz, trimmed)
- » Bell pepper (6 oz, red or orange, cut into 1 ½ in. squares)
- » Onion (12 oz, red, large dice)
- » Mushroom caps (12, medium)
- » Olive oil (12 Fl oz)
- » Garlic (1/2 oz, crushed)
- » Rosemary (1 ½ tsp, dried)
- » Thyme (1/2 tsp, dried)
- » Salt (2 tsp)
- » Black pepper (1/2 tsp)

## DIRECTIONS

1. Cut the zucchini and yellow squash into 12 equal slices each.
2. Arrange the vegetables on 12 bamboo skewers. Give each skewer an equal arrangement of vegetable pieces.
3. Place the skewers in a single layer in a hotel pan.
4. Mix the oil, garlic, herbs, salt, and pepper to make a marinade.
5. Pour the marinade over the vegetables, turning them to coat completely.
6. Marinate 1 hour. Turn the skewers once or twice during margination to ensure the vegetables are coated.
7. Remove the skewers from the marinade and let the excess oil drip off.

**NUTRITIONS:**
50 Calories, 3g Fat, 1g Protein

# 15. VEGETABLE FRITTERS

**COOKING: 6'**         **PREPARATION: 15'**         **SERVES: 2**

## INGREDIENTS

- » Egg (3, beaten)
- » Milk (8 Fl oz)
- » Whole wheat flour (8 oz)
- » Baking powder (1 tbsp)
- » Salt (½ tsp)
- » Maple syrup (1/2 oz)
- »

## Vegetables:

- » Carrot (12 oz,)
- » Baby lima beans (12 oz)
- » Asparagus (12 oz)
- » Celery (12 oz)
- » Turnip (12 oz)
- » Eggplant (12 oz)
- » Cauliflower (12 oz)
- » Zucchini (12 oz)
- » Parsnips (12 oz)

## NUTRITIONS:

140 Calories, 6g Fat, 4g Protein

## DIRECTIONS

1. Combine the eggs and milk.
2. Mix the flour, baking powder, salt, and maple syrup. Add to the milk and eggs and mix until smooth.
3. Let the batter stand for several hours in a refrigerator.
4. Stir the cold, cooked vegetable into the batter.
5. Drop with a No. 24 scoop into deep fat at 350 F. Toss the content from the scoop carefully in the hot oil. Fry until golden brown.
6. Drain well and serve.

# CHAPTER 3
# APPETIZER AND SNACK RECIPES PART 2

# 16. MARINATED FETA AND ARTICHOKES

**COOKING: 0'**   **PREPARATION: 10' + 4 HOURS**   **SERVES: 4**

## INGREDIENTS

- » 4 ounces traditional Greek feta, cut into ½-inch cubes
- » 4 ounces drained artichoke hearts, quartered lengthwise
- » 1/3 cup extra-virgin olive oil
- » Zest and juice of 1 lemon
- » 2 tablespoons roughly chopped fresh rosemary
- » 2 tablespoons roughly chopped fresh parsley
- » ½ teaspoon black peppercorns

## DIRECTIONS

1. In a glass bowl, combine the feta and artichoke hearts. Add the olive oil, lemon zest and juice, rosemary, parsley, and peppercorns and toss gently to coat, being sure not to crumble the feta.
2. Cover and chill for 4 hours before serving.

**NUTRITIONS:**
235 Calories, 23g Fat, 4g Protein

# 17. TUNA CROQUETTES

**COOKING: 25'**   **PREPARATION: 40'**   **SERVES: 12**

## INGREDIENTS

- » 6 tablespoons extra-virgin olive oil, plus 1 to 2 cups
- » 5 tablespoons almond flour, plus 1 cup, divided
- » 1¼ cups heavy cream
- » 1 (4-ounce) can olive oil-packed yellowfin tuna
- » 1 tablespoon chopped red onion
- » 2 teaspoons minced capers
- » ½ teaspoon dried dill
- » ¼ teaspoon freshly ground black pepper
- » 2 large eggs
- » 1 cup panko breadcrumbs

## DIRECTIONS

1. In a huge skillet, heat 6 tablespoons olive oil over medium-low heat. Add 5 tablespoons almond flour and cook, stirring constantly, until a smooth paste forms and the flour browns slightly, 2 to 3 minutes.
2. Increase the heat to medium-high and gradually add the heavy cream, whisking constantly for 5 minutes.
3. Pull out from heat and stir in the tuna, red onion, capers, dill, and pepper.
4. Pour into 8-inch square baking dish that is well coated with olive oil and allow to cool to room temperature. Cover and chill for 4 hours.
5. To form the croquettes, set out three bowls. In one, beat together the eggs. In another, add the remaining almond flour. In the third, add the panko. Line a baking sheet with parchment paper.
6. Situate a tablespoon of cold prepared dough into the flour mixture and roll to coat. Shake off excess and, using your hands, roll into an oval.
7. Dip the croquette into the beaten egg, then lightly coat in panko. Set on lined baking sheet and repeat with the remaining dough.
8. In a small saucepan, cook 1 to 2 cups of olive oil over medium-high heat.
9. Once the oil is heated, fry the croquettes 3 or 4 at a time.

**NUTRITIONS:**
245 Calories, 22g Fat, 6g Protein

# 18. SMOKED SALMON CRUDITÉS

**COOKING: 0'**      **PREPARATION: 10'**      **SERVES: 4**

## INGREDIENTS

- » 6 ounces smoked wild salmon
- » 2 tablespoons Roasted Garlic Aioli
- » 1 tablespoon Dijon mustard
- » 1 tablespoon chopped scallions
- » 2 teaspoons chopped capers
- » ½ teaspoon dried dill
- » 4 endive spears or hearts of romaine
- » ½ English cucumber

## DIRECTIONS

1. Cut the smoked salmon. Add the aioli, Dijon, scallions, capers, and dill and mix well.
2. Top endive spears and cucumber rounds with a spoonful of smoked salmon mixture and enjoy chilled.

**NUTRITIONS:**
92 Calories, 5g Fat, 9g Protein

# 19. CITRUS-MARINATED OLIVES

**COOKING: 0'**      **PREPARATION: 10' + 4 HOURS**      **SERVES: 4**

## INGREDIENTS

- » 2 cups mixed green olives with pits
- » ¼ cup red wine vinegar
- » ¼ cup extra-virgin olive oil
- » 4 garlic cloves, finely minced
- » Zest and juice orange
- » 1 teaspoon red pepper flakes
- » 2 bay leaves
- » ½ teaspoon ground cumin
- » ½ teaspoon ground allspice

## DIRECTIONS

1. In a jar, mix olives, vinegar, oil, garlic, orange zest and juice, red pepper flakes, bay leaves, cumin, and allspice. Cover and chill for 4 hours, tossing again before serving.

**NUTRITIONS:**
360 Calories, 27g Fat, 20g Protein

# 20. OLIVE TAPENADE WITH ANCHOVIES

**COOKING: 0'**  **PREPARATION: 70'**  **SERVES: 4**

## INGREDIENTS

- » 2 cups pitted Kalamata olives
- » 2 anchovy fillets
- » 2 teaspoons capers
- » 1 garlic clove
- » 1 cooked egg yolk
- » 1 teaspoon Dijon mustard
- » ¼ cup extra-virgin olive oil

## DIRECTIONS

1. Wash olives in cold water and drain well.
2. In a food processor, mix drained olives, anchovies, capers, garlic, egg yolk, and Dijon.
3. With the food processor running, slowly stream in the olive oil.
4. Wrap and refrigerate at least 1 hour. Serve with Seedy Crackers.

**NUTRITIONS:**
179 Calories, 19g Fat, 2g Protein

# 21. GREEK DEVILED EGGS

**COOKING: 15'**  **PREPARATION: 45'**  **SERVES: 4**

## INGREDIENTS

- » 4 large hardboiled eggs
- » 2 tablespoons Roasted Garlic Aioli
- » ½ cup feta cheese
- » 8 pitted Kalamata olives
- » 2 tablespoons chopped sun-dried tomatoes
- » 1 tablespoon minced red onion
- » ½ teaspoon dried dill
- » ¼ teaspoon black pepper

## DIRECTIONS

1. Slice the hardboiled eggs in half lengthwise, remove the yolks, and place the yolks in a medium bowl. Reserve the egg white halves and set aside.
2. Smash the yolks well with a fork. Add the aioli, feta, olives, sun-dried tomatoes, onion, dill, and pepper and stir to combine until smooth and creamy.
3. Spoon the filling into each egg white half and chill for 30 minutes, or up to 24 hours, covered.

**NUTRITIONS:**
147 Calories, 11g Fat, 9g Protein

# 22. MANCHEGO CRACKERS

**COOKING: 15'**　　　**PREPARATION: 55'**　　　**SERVES: 4**

## INGREDIENTS

- » 4 tablespoons butter, at room temperature
- » 1 cup Manchego cheese
- » 1 cup almond flour
- » 1 teaspoon salt, divided
- » ¼ teaspoon black pepper
- » 1 large egg

## DIRECTIONS

1. Using an electric mixer, scourge butter and shredded cheese.
2. Mix almond flour with ½ teaspoon salt and pepper. Mix almond flour mixture to the cheese, mixing constantly to form a ball.
3. Situate onto plastic wrap and roll into a cylinder log about 1½ inches thick. Wrap tightly and refrigerate for at least 1 hour.
4. Preheat the oven to 350°F. Prep two baking sheets with parchment papers.
5. For egg wash, blend egg and remaining ½ teaspoon salt.
6. Slice the refrigerated dough into small rounds, about ¼ inch thick, and place on the lined baking sheets.
7. Egg wash the tops of the crackers and bake for 15 minutes. Pull out from the oven and situate in wire rack.
8. Serve.

**NUTRITIONS:**
243 Calories, 23g Fat, 8g Protein

# 23. BURRATA CAPRESE STACK

**COOKING: 0'**　　　**PREPARATION: 5'**　　　**SERVES: 0**

## INGREDIENTS

- » 1 large organic tomato
- » ½ teaspoon salt
- » ¼ teaspoon black pepper
- » 1 (4-ounce) ball burrata cheese
- » 8 fresh basil leaves
- » 2 tablespoons extra-virgin olive oil
- » 1 tablespoon red wine

## DIRECTIONS

1. Slice the tomato into 4 thick slices, removing any tough center core and sprinkle with salt and pepper. Place the tomatoes, seasoned-side up, on a plate.
2. On a separate rimmed plate, slice the burrata into 4 thick slices and place one slice on top of each tomato slice. Top each with one-quarter of the basil and pour any reserved burrata cream from the rimmed plate over top.
3. Drizzle with olive oil and vinegar and serve with a fork and knife.

**NUTRITIONS:**
153 Calories, 13g Fat, 7g Protein

# 24. ZUCCHINI-RICOTTA FRITTERS WITH LEMON-GARLIC AIOLI

**COOKING: 25'**     **PREPARATION: 30'**     **SERVES: 4**

## INGREDIENTS

- » 1 large zucchini
- » 1 teaspoon salt, divided
- » ½ cup whole-milk ricotta cheese
- » 2 scallions
- » 1 large egg
- » 2 garlic cloves
- » 2 tablespoons fresh mint (optional)
- » 2 teaspoons grated lemon zest
- » ¼ teaspoon freshly ground black pepper
- » ½ cup almond flour
- » 1 teaspoon baking powder
- » 8 tablespoons extra-virgin olive oil
- » 8 tablespoons Roasted Garlic Aioli

## DIRECTIONS

1. Place the shredded zucchini in a colander or on several layers of paper towels. Sprinkle with ½ teaspoon salt and let sit for 10 minutes. Using another layer of paper towel, press down on the zucchini to release any excess moisture and pat dry.

2. In a large bowl, combine the drained zucchini, ricotta, scallions, egg, garlic, mint (if using), lemon zest, remaining ½ teaspoon salt, and pepper and stir well.

3. Blend almond flour and baking powder. Mix in flour mixture into the zucchini mixture and let rest for 10 minutes.

4. In a large skillet, working in four batches, fry the fritters. For each batch of four, heat 2 tablespoons olive oil over medium-high heat. Add 1 heaping tablespoon of zucchini batter per fritter, pressing down with the back of a spoon to form 2- to 3-inch fritters. Cover and let fry 2 minutes before flipping. Fry another 2 to 3 minutes, covered.

5. Repeat for the remaining three batches, using 2 tablespoons of the olive oil for each batch.

6. Serve with aioli.

**NUTRITIONS:**
448 Calories. 42g Fat, 8g Protein

# 25. SALMON-STUFFED CUCUMBERS

**COOKING: 0'**     **PREPARATION: 10'**     **SERVES: 4**

## INGREDIENTS

- » 2 large cucumbers, peeled
- » 1 (4-ounce) can red salmon
- » 1 medium very ripe avocado
- » 1 tablespoon extra-virgin olive oil
- » Zest and juice of 1 lime
- » 3 tablespoons chopped fresh cilantro
- » ½ teaspoon salt
- » ¼ teaspoon black pepper

## DIRECTIONS

1. Slice the cucumber into 1-inch-thick segments and using a spoon, scrape seeds out of center of each segment and stand up on a plate.

2. In a medium bowl, mix salmon, avocado, olive oil, lime zest and juice, cilantro, salt, and pepper.

3. Spoon the salmon mixture into the center of each cucumber segment and serve chilled.

**NUTRITIONS:**
159 Calories, 11g Fat, 9g Protein

# 26. GOAT CHEESE-MACKEREL PÂTÉ

**COOKING: 0'**  **PREPARATION: 10'**  **SERVES: 4**

## INGREDIENTS

- » 4 ounces olive oil-packed wild-caught mackerel
- » 2 ounces goat cheese
- » Zest and juice of 1 lemon
- » 2 tablespoons chopped fresh parsley
- » 2 tablespoons chopped fresh arugula
- » 1 tablespoon extra-virgin olive oil
- » 2 teaspoons chopped capers
- » 2 teaspoons fresh horseradish (optional)

## DIRECTIONS

1. In a food processor, blender, or large bowl with immersion blender, combine the mackerel, goat cheese, lemon zest and juice, parsley, arugula, olive oil, capers, and horseradish (if using). Process or blend until smooth and creamy.
2. Serve with crackers, cucumber rounds, endive spears, or celery.

**NUTRITIONS:**
118 Calories, 8g Fat, 9g Protein

# 27. TASTE OF THE MEDITERRANEAN FAT BOMBS

**COOKING: 0'**  **PREPARATION: 15' + 4 HOURS**  **SERVES: 6**

## INGREDIENTS

- » 1 cup crumbled goat cheese
- » 4 tablespoons jarred pesto
- » 12 pitted Kalamata olives
- » ½ cup finely chopped walnuts
- » 1 tablespoon chopped fresh rosemary

## DIRECTIONS

1. Mix goat cheese, pesto, and olives. Cool for 4 hours to harden.
2. Create the mixture into 6 balls, about ¾-inch diameter. The mixture will be sticky.
3. In a small bowl, place the walnuts and rosemary and roll the goat cheese balls in the nut mixture to coat.

**NUTRITIONS:**
166 Calories, 15g Fat, 5g Protein

# 28. CREAM OF CAULIFLOWER GAZPACHO

**COOKING: 25'**  **PREPARATION: 15'**  **SERVES: 6**

## INGREDIENTS

- » 1 cup raw almonds
- » ½ teaspoon salt
- » ½ cup extra-virgin olive oil
- » 1 small white onion
- » 1 small head cauliflower
- » 2 garlic cloves
- » 2 cups chicken stock
- » 1 tablespoon red wine vinegar
- » ¼ teaspoon freshly ground black pepper

## NUTRITIONS:
505 Calories, 45g Fat, 10g Protein

## DIRECTIONS

1. Boil almonds to the water for 1 minute. Drain in a colander and run under cold water. Pat dry. Discard the skins.

2. In a food processor or blender, blend together the almonds and salt. With the processor running, drizzle in ½ cup extra-virgin olive oil, scraping down the sides as needed. Set the almond paste aside.

3. In a stockpot, cook remaining 1 tablespoon olive oil over medium-high heat. Sauté onion for 4 minutes. Add the cauliflower florets and sauté for another 3 to 4 minutes. Cook garlic for 1 minute more.

4. Add 2 cups stock and bring to a boil. Cover, reduce the heat to medium-low, and simmer the vegetables until tender, 8 to 10 minutes. Pull out from the heat and allow to cool slightly.

5. Blend vinegar and pepper with an immersion blender. With the blender running, add the almond paste and blend until smooth, adding extra stock if the soup is too thick.

6. Serve warm, or chill in refrigerator at least 4 to 6 hours to serve a cold gazpacho.

# 29. AVOCADO GAZPACHO

**COOKING: 0'**  **PREPARATION: 15'**  **SERVES: 4**

## INGREDIENTS

- » 2 cups chopped tomatoes
- » 2 large ripe avocados
- » 1 large cucumber
- » 1 medium bell pepper
- » 1 cup plain whole-milk Greek yogurt
- » ¼ cup extra-virgin olive oil
- » ¼ cup chopped fresh cilantro
- » ¼ cup chopped scallions
- » 2 tablespoons red wine vinegar
- » Juice of 2 limes or 1 lemon
- » ½ to 1 teaspoon salt
- » ¼ teaspoon black pepper

## DIRECTIONS

1. In a blender or in a large bowl, if using an immersion blender, combine the tomatoes, avocados, cucumber, bell pepper, yogurt, olive oil, cilantro, scallions, vinegar, and lime juice. Blend until smooth. If using a stand blender, you may need to blend in two or three batches.

2. Season with salt and pepper and blend to combine the flavors.

3. Chill for 2 hours before serving. Serve cold.

## NUTRITIONS:
147 Calories, 11g Fat, 9g Protein

# 30. TUSCAN KALE SALAD WITH ANCHOVIES

**COOKING: 0'**  **PREPARATION: 45'**  **SERVES: 4**

## INGREDIENTS

- » 1 large bunch Lacinato
- » ¼ cup toasted pine nuts
- » 1 cup Parmesan cheese
- » ¼ cup extra-virgin olive oil
- » 8 anchovy fillets
- » 2 to 3 tablespoons lemon juice
- » 2 teaspoons red pepper flakes (optional)

## DIRECTIONS

1. Remove the rough center stems from the kale leaves and roughly tear each leaf into about 4-by-1-inch strips. Situate torn kale in a large bowl and add the pine nuts and cheese.

2. Blend the olive oil, anchovies, lemon juice, and red pepper flakes (if using). Drizzle over the salad and toss to coat well. Let sit at room temperature 30 minutes before serving, tossing again just prior to serving.

**NUTRITIONS:**
337 Calories, 25g Fat, 16g Protein

# CHAPTER 4
# APPETIZER AND SNACK RECIPES PART 3

# 31. CLASSIC HUMMUS

**COOKING: 30'**       **PREPARATION: 8'**       **SERVES: 6**

## INGREDIENTS

» 1 cup dried chickpeas
» 4 cups water
» 1 tablespoon plus ¼ cup extra-virgin olive oil
» 1/3 cup tahini
» 1½ teaspoons ground cumin
» ¾ teaspoon salt
» ½ teaspoon ground black pepper
» ½ teaspoon ground coriander
» 1/3 cup lemon juice
» 1 teaspoon minced garlic

## DIRECTIONS

1. Position chickpeas, water, and 1 tablespoon oil in the Instant Pot®. Close, select steam release to Sealing, click Manual, and time to 30 minutes.

2. When the timer rings, quick-release the pressure and open lid. Press the Cancel button and open lid. Drain, reserving the cooking liquid.

3. Blend chickpeas, remaining ¼ cup oil, tahini, cumin, salt, pepper, coriander, lemon juice, and garlic in a food processor. Serve.

**NUTRITIONS:**
152 Calories, 12g Fat, 4g Protein

# 32. ROASTED GARLIC HUMMUS

**COOKING: 25'**       **PREPARATION: 40'**       **SERVES: 12**

## INGREDIENTS

» 1 cup dried chickpeas
» 4 cups water
» 1 tablespoon plus ¼ cup extra-virgin olive oil, divided
» 1/3 cup tahini
» 1 teaspoon ground cumin
» ½ teaspoon onion powder
» ¾ teaspoon salt
» ½ teaspoon ground black pepper
» 1/3 cup lemon juice
» 3 tablespoons mashed roasted garlic
» 2 tablespoons chopped fresh parsley

## DIRECTIONS

1. Situate chickpeas, water, and 1 tablespoon oil in the Instant Pot®. Cover, press steam release to Sealing, set Manual button, and time to 30 minutes.

2. When the timer beeps, quick-release the pressure. Select Cancel button and open. Strain, reserving the cooking liquid.

3. Place chickpeas, remaining ¼ cup oil, tahini, cumin, onion powder, salt, pepper, lemon juice, and roasted garlic in a food processor and process until creamy. Top with parsley. Serve at room temperature.

**NUTRITIONS:**
104 Calories, 6g Fat, 4g Protein

# 33. RED PEPPER HUMMUS

**COOKING: 34'**     **PREPARATION: 7'**     **SERVES: 4**

## INGREDIENTS

- » 1 cup dried chickpeas
- » 4 cups water
- » 1 tablespoon plus ¼ cup extra-virgin olive oil, divided
- » ½ cup chopped roasted red pepper, divided
- » 1/3 cup tahini
- » 1 teaspoon ground cumin
- » ¾ teaspoon salt
- » ½ teaspoon ground black pepper
- » ¼ teaspoon smoked paprika
- » 1/3 cup lemon juice
- » ½ teaspoon minced garlic

## DIRECTIONS

1. Put chickpeas, water, and 1 tablespoon oil in the Instant Pot®. Seal, put steam release to Sealing, select Manual and time to 30 minutes.

2. When the timer rings, quick-release the pressure. Click Cancel button and open it. Drain, set aside the cooking liquid.

3. Process chickpeas, 1/3 cup roasted red pepper, remaining ¼ cup oil, tahini, cumin, salt, black pepper, paprika, lemon juice, and garlic using food processor. Serve, garnished with reserved roasted red pepper on top.

**NUTRITIONS:**
96 Calories, 8g Fat, 2g Protein

# 34. WHITE BEAN HUMMUS

**COOKING: 40'**     **PREPARATION: 11'**     **SERVES: 12**

## INGREDIENTS

- » 2/3 cup dried white beans
- » 3 cloves garlic, peeled and crushed
- » ¼ cup olive oil
- » 1 tablespoon lemon juice
- » ½ teaspoon salt

## DIRECTIONS

1. Place beans and garlic in the Instant Pot® and stir well. Add enough cold water to cover ingredients. Cover, set steam release to Sealing, select Manual button, and time to 30 minutes.

2. Once the timer stops, release pressure for 20 minutes. Select Cancel and open lid. Use a fork to check that beans are tender. Drain off excess water and transfer beans to a food processor.

3. Add oil, lemon juice, and salt to the processor and pulse until mixture is smooth with some small chunks. Pour into container and refrigerate for at least 4 hours. Serve cold or at room temperature.

**NUTRITIONS:**
57 Calories, 5g Fat, 1g Protein

# 35. KIDNEY BEAN DIP WITH CILANTRO, CUMIN, AND LIME

**COOKING: 51'**  **PREPARATION: 13'**  **SERVES: 16**

## INGREDIENTS

- » 1 cup dried kidney beans
- » 4 cups water
- » 3 cloves garlic
- » ¼ cup cilantro
- » ¼ cup extra-virgin olive oil
- » 1 tablespoon lime juice
- » 2 teaspoons grated lime zest
- » 1 teaspoon ground cumin
- » ½ teaspoon salt

## DIRECTIONS

1. Place beans, water, garlic, and 2 tablespoons cilantro in the Instant Pot®. Close the lid, select steam release to Sealing, click Bean button, and cook for 30 minutes.

2. When the timer alarms, let pressure release naturally, about 20 minutes. Press the Cancel button, open lid, and check that beans are tender. Drain off extra water and transfer beans to a medium bowl. Gently mash beans with potato masher. Add oil, lime juice, lime zest, cumin, salt, and remaining 2 tablespoons cilantro and stir to combine. Serve warm or at room temperature.

**NUTRITIONS:**
65 Calories, 3g Fat, 2g Protein

# 36. WHITE BEAN DIP WITH GARLIC AND HERBS

**COOKING: 48'**  **PREPARATION: 10'**  **SERVES: 16**

## INGREDIENTS

- » 1 cup dried white beans
- » 3 cloves garlic
- » 8 cups water
- » ¼ cup extra-virgin olive oil
- » ¼ cup chopped fresh flat-leaf parsley
- » 1 tablespoon fresh oregano
- » 1 tablespoon d fresh tarragon
- » 1 teaspoon fresh thyme leaves
- » 1 teaspoon lemon zest
- » ¼ teaspoon salt
- » ¼ teaspoon black pepper

## DIRECTIONS

1. Place beans and garlic in the Instant Pot® and stir well. Add water, close lid, put steam release to Sealing, press the Manual, and adjust time to 30 minutes.

2. When the timer beeps, release naturally, about 20 minutes. Open and check if beans are soft. Press the Cancel button, drain off excess water, and transfer beans and garlic to a food processor with olive oil. Add parsley, oregano, tarragon, thyme, lemon zest, salt, and pepper, and pulse 3–5 times to mix. Chill for 4 hours or overnight. Serve cold or at room temperature.

**NUTRITIONS:**
47 Calories, 3g Fat, 1g Protein

# 37. BLACK BEAN DIP

**COOKING: 53'**　　　**PREPARATION: 14'**　　　**SERVES: 16**

## INGREDIENTS

- » 1 tablespoon olive oil
- » 2 slices bacon
- » 1 small onion,
- » 3 cloves garlic
- » 1 cup low-sodium chicken broth
- » 1 cup dried black beans
- » 1 (14.5-ounce) can diced tomatoes
- » 1 small jalapeño pepper
- » 1 teaspoon ground cumin
- » ½ teaspoon smoked paprika
- » 1 tablespoon lime juice
- » ½ teaspoon dried oregano
- » ¼ cup minced fresh cilantro
- » ¼ teaspoon sea salt

## DIRECTIONS

1. Press the Sauté button on the Instant Pot® and heat oil. Add bacon and onion. Cook for 5 minutes. Cook garlic for 30 seconds. Add broth and scrape any browned bits from bottom of pot. Add beans, tomatoes, jalapeño, cumin, paprika, lime juice, oregano, cilantro, and salt. Press the Cancel button.

2. Close lid, let steam release to Sealing, set Bean button, and default time of 30 minutes. When the timer rings, let pressure release naturally for 10 minutes. Press the Cancel button and open lid.

3. Use an immersion blender blend the ingredients. Serve warm.

## NUTRITIONS:
60 Calories, 2g Fat, 3g Protein

# 38. SALSA VERDE

**COOKING: 21'**　　　**PREPARATION: 9'**　　　**SERVES: 8**

## INGREDIENTS

- » 1-pound tomatillos
- » 2 small jalapeño peppers
- » 1 small onion
- » ½ cup chopped fresh cilantro
- » 1 teaspoon ground coriander
- » 1 teaspoon sea salt
- » 1½ cups water

## DIRECTIONS

1. Cut tomatillos in half and place in the Instant Pot®. Add enough water to cover.

2. Close lids, set steam release to Sealing, press the Manual button, and set time to 2 minutes. Once timer beeps, release pressure naturally, for 20 minutes. Press the Cancel and open lid.

3. Drain off excess water and transfer tomatillos to a food processor or blender, and add jalapeños, onion, cilantro, coriander, salt, and water. Pulse until well combined, about 20 pulses.

4. Wrap and cool for 2 hours before serving.

## NUTRITIONS:
27 Calories, 1g Fat, 1g Protein

# 39. GREEK EGGPLANT DIP

**COOKING: 3'**　　　**PREPARATION: 16'**　　　**SERVES: 8**

## INGREDIENTS

» 1 cup water
» 1 large eggplant
» 1 clove garlic
» ½ teaspoon salt
» 1 tablespoon red wine vinegar
» ½ cup extra-virgin olive oil
» 2 tablespoons minced fresh parsley

## DIRECTIONS

1. Add water to the Instant Pot®, add the rack to the pot, and place the steamer basket on the rack.

2. Place eggplant in steamer basket. Close, set steam release to Sealing, turn on Manual button, and set time to 3 minutes. When the timer stops, quick-release the pressure. Click Cancel button and open.

3. Situate eggplant to a food processor and add garlic, salt, and vinegar. Pulse until smooth, about 20 pulses.

4. Slowly add oil to the eggplant mixture while the food processor runs continuously until oil is completely incorporated. Stir in parsley. Serve at room temperature.

**NUTRITIONS:**
134 Calories, 14g Fat,1g Protein

# 40. BABA GHANOUSH

**COOKING: 1'**　　　**PREPARATION: 9'**　　　**SERVES: 8**

## INGREDIENTS

» 2 tablespoons extra-virgin olive oil
» 1 large eggplant
» 3 cloves garlic
» ½ cup water
» 3 tablespoons fresh flat-leaf parsley
» ½ teaspoon salt
» ¼ teaspoon smoked paprika
» 2 tablespoons lemon juice
» 2 tablespoons tahini

## DIRECTIONS

1. Press the Sauté button on the Instant Pot® and add 1 tablespoon oil. Add eggplant and cook until it begins to soften, about 5 minutes. Add garlic and cook 30 seconds.

2. Add water and close lid, click steam release to Sealing, select Manual, and time to 6 minutes. Once the timer rings, quick-release the pressure. Select Cancel and open lid.

3. Strain cooked eggplant and garlic and add to a food processor or blender along with parsley, salt, smoked paprika, lemon juice, and tahini. Add remaining 1 tablespoon oil and process. Serve warm or at room temperature.

**NUTRITIONS:**
79 Calories, 6g Fat, 2g Protein

# 41. CHICKPEA, PARSLEY, AND DILL DIP

**COOKING: 22'**  **PREPARATION: 11'**  **SERVES: 6**

## INGREDIENTS

- »  8 cups water
- »  1 cup dried chickpeas
- »  3 tablespoons olive oil
- »  2 garlic cloves
- »  2 tablespoons fresh parsley
- »  2 tablespoons fresh dill
- »  1 tablespoon lemon juice
- »  ¼ teaspoon salt

## DIRECTIONS

1. Add 4 cups water and chickpeas to the Instant Pot®. Cover, place steam release to Sealing. Set Manual, and time to 1 minute. When the timer beeps, quick-release the pressure until the float valve drops, press the Cancel button, and open lid.

2. Drain water, rinse chickpeas, and return to pot with 4 cups fresh water. Set aside to soak for 1 hour.

3. Add 1 tablespoon oil to pot. Close, adjust steam release to Sealing, click Manual, and the time to 20 minutes. When alarm beeps, let pressure release for 20 minutes. Click the Cancel, open and drain chickpeas.

4. Place chickpeas to a food processor or blender, and add garlic, parsley, dill, lemon juice, and remaining 2 tablespoons water. Blend for about 30 seconds.

5. With the processor or blender lid still in place, slowly add remaining 2 tablespoons oil while still blending, then add salt. Serve warm or at room temperature.

**NUTRITIONS:**
76 Calories, 4g Fat, 2g Protein

# 42. INSTANT POT® SALSA

**COOKING: 22'**  **PREPARATION: 9'**  **SERVES: 12**

## INGREDIENTS

- »  12 cups seeded diced tomatoes
- »  6 ounces tomato paste
- »  2 medium yellow onions
- »  6 small jalapeño peppers
- »  4 cloves garlic
- »  ¼ cup white vinegar
- »  ¼ cup lime juice
- »  2 tablespoons granulated sugar
- »  2 teaspoons salt
- »  ¼ cup chopped fresh cilantro

## DIRECTIONS

1. Place tomatoes, tomato paste, onions, jalapeños, garlic, vinegar, lime juice, sugar, and salt in the Instant Pot® and stir well. Close it, situate steam release to Sealing. Click Manual button, and time to 20 minutes.

2. Once timer beeps, quick-release the pressure. Open, stir in cilantro, and press the Cancel button.

3. Let salsa cool to room temperature, about 40 minutes, then transfer to a storage container and refrigerate overnight.

**NUTRITIONS:**
68 Calories, 0.1g Fat, 2g Protein

# 43. SFOUGATO

**COOKING: 13'**  **PREPARATION: 9'**  **SERVES: 4**

## INGREDIENTS

- » ½ cup crumbled feta cheese
- » ¼ cup bread crumbs
- » 1 medium onion
- » 4 tablespoons all-purpose flour
- » 2 tablespoons fresh mint
- » ½ teaspoon salt
- » ½ teaspoon ground black pepper
- » 1 tablespoon dried thyme
- » 6 large eggs, beaten
- » 1 cup water

## DIRECTIONS

1. In a medium bowl, mix cheese, bread crumbs, onion, flour, mint, salt, pepper, and thyme. Stir in eggs.

2. Spray an 8" round baking dish with nonstick cooking spray. Pour egg mixture into dish.

3. Place rack in the Instant Pot® and add water. Fold a long piece of foil in half lengthwise. Lay foil over rack to form a sling and top with dish. Cover loosely with foil. Seal lid, put steam release in Sealing, select Manual, and time to 8 minutes.

4. When the timer alarms, release the pressure. Uncover. Let stand 5 minutes, then remove dish from pot.

**NUTRITIONS:**
274 Calories, 14g Fat, 17g Protein

# 44. SKORDALIA

**COOKING: 11'**  **PREPARATION: 7'**  **SERVES: 16**

## INGREDIENTS

- » 1-pound russet potatoes
- » 3 cups plus ¼ cup water
- » 2 teaspoons salt
- » 8 cloves garlic
- » ¾ cup blanched almonds
- » ½ cup extra-virgin olive oil
- » 2 tablespoons lemon juice
- » 2 tablespoons white wine vinegar
- » ½ teaspoon ground black pepper

## DIRECTIONS

1. Place potatoes, 3 cups water, and 1 teaspoon salt in the Instant Pot® and stir well. Close, set steam release to Sealing, click Manual button, and set to 10 minutes.

2. While potatoes cook, place garlic and remaining 1 teaspoon salt on a cutting board. With the side of a knife, press garlic and salt until it forms a paste. Transfer garlic paste into a food processor along with almonds and olive oil. Purée into a paste. Set aside.

3. When the timer beeps, quick-release the pressure. Select Cancel button and open lid. Drain potatoes and transfer to a medium bowl. Add garlic mixture and mash with a potato masher until smooth. Stir in lemon juice, vinegar, and pepper. Stir in ¼ cup water a little at a time until mixture is thin enough for dipping. Serve warm or at room temperature.

**NUTRITIONS:**
115 Calories, 10g Fat, 2g Protein

# 45. PINTO BEAN DIP WITH AVOCADO PICO

**COOKING: 52'**          **PREPARATION: 6'**          **SERVES: 16**

## INGREDIENTS

- » 1 cup dried pinto beans
- » 4 cups water
- » 4 tablespoons cilantro, divided
- » 3 tablespoons extra-virgin olive oil
- » 1 teaspoon ground cumin
- » 1 clove garlic, peeled and minced
- » ½ teaspoon salt
- » 1 medium avocado
- » 1 large ripe tomato
- » 1 small jalapeño pepper
- » ½ medium white onion
- » 2 teaspoons lime juice

## NUTRITIONS:

59 Calories, 4g Fat, 1g Protein

## DIRECTIONS

1. Place beans, water, and 2 tablespoons cilantro in the Instant Pot®. Close lid, place steam release to Sealing, click Bean and set default time of 30 minutes.

2. When the timer rings, let pressure release naturally. Open then check the beans are tender. Drain off excess water. Crush beans with fork. Add oil, cumin, garlic, and salt and mix well.

3. Toss remaining 2 tablespoons cilantro with avocado, tomato, jalapeño, onion, and lime juice. Spoon topping over bean dip. Serve.

# CHAPTER 5
# APPETIZER AND SNACK RECIPES PART 4

# 46. POWER PODS & HEARTY HAZELNUTS WITH MUSTARD-Y MIX

## COOKING: 15'     PREPARATION: 15'     SERVES: 4

## INGREDIENTS

- » 1-lb. green beans, trimmed
- » 3-tbsp extra-virgin olive oil (divided)
- » 2-tsp whole grain mustard
- » 1-tbsp red wine vinegar
- » ¼-tsp salt
- » ¼-tsp ground pepper
- » ¼-cup toasted hazelnuts, chopped

## DIRECTIONS

1. Preheat your grill to high heat.
2. In a big mixing bowl, toss the green beans with a tablespoon of olive oil. Place the beans in a grill basket. Grill for 8 minutes until charring a few spots, stirring occasionally.
3. Combine and whisk together the remaining oil, mustard, vinegar, salt, and pepper in the same mixing bowl. Add the grilled beans and toss to coat evenly.
4. To serve, top the side dish with hazelnuts.

**NUTRITIONS:**
181 Calories, 15g Fats, 3g Protein

# 47. PEPPERY POTATOES

## COOKING: 18'     PREPARATION: 10'     SERVES: 4

## INGREDIENTS

- » 4-pcs large potatoes, cubed
- » 4-tbsp extra-virgin olive oil (divided)
- » 3-tbsp garlic, minced
- » ½-cup coriander or cilantro, finely chopped
- » 2-tbsp fresh lemon juice
- » 1¾-tbsp paprika
- » 2-tbsp parsley, minced

## DIRECTIONS

1. Place the potatoes in a microwave-safe dish. Pour over a tablespoon of olive oil. Cover the dish tightly with plastic wrap. Heat the potatoes for seven minutes in your microwave to par-cook them.
2. Cook 2 tablespoons of olive oil in a pan placed over medium-low heat. Add the garlic and cover. Cook for 3 minutes. Add the coriander, and cook 2 minutes. Transfer the garlic-coriander sauce in a bowl, and set aside.
3. In the same pan placed over medium heat, heat 1 tablespoon of olive oil. Add the par-cooked potatoes. Do not stir! Cook for 3 minutes until browned, flipping once with a spatula. Continue cooking until browning all the sides.
4. Take out the potatoes and place them on a dish. Pour over the garlic-coriander sauce and lemon juice. Add the paprika, parsley, and salt. Toss gently to coat evenly.

**NUTRITIONS:**
316.2 Calories, 14.2g Fats, 4.5g Protein

# 48. TURKEY SPHEROIDS WITH TZATZIKI SAUCE

**COOKING: 20'**  **PREPARATION: 10'**  **SERVES: 8**

## INGREDIENTS

### For Meatballs:
» 2-lbs ground turkey
» 2-tsp salt
» 2-cups zucchini, grated
» 1-tbsp lemon juice
» 1-cup crumbled feta cheese
» 1½-tsp pepper
» 1½-tsp garlic powder
» 1½-tbsp oregano
» ¼-cup red onion, finely minced

### For Tzatziki Sauce:
» 1-tsp garlic powder
» 1-tsp dill
» 1-tbsp white vinegar
» 1-tbsp lemon juice
» 1-cup sour cream
» ½-cup grated cucumber
» Salt and pepper

**NUTRITIONS:**
280 Calories, 16g Fats, 26.6g Protein

## DIRECTIONS

1. Preheat your oven to 350 °F.

### For the Meatballs:

2. Incorporate all the meatball ingredients in a large mixing bowl. Mix well until fully combined. Form the turkey mixture into spheroids, using ¼-cup of the mixture per spheroid.

3. Heat a non-stick skillet placed over high heat. Add the meatballs, and sear for 2 minutes.

4. Transfer the meatballs in a baking sheet. Situate the sheet in the oven, and bake for 15 minutes.

### For the Tzatziki Sauce:

5. Combine and whisk together all the sauce ingredients in a medium-sized mixing bowl. Mix well until fully combined. Refrigerate the sauce until ready to serve and eat.

# 49. CHEESY CAPRESE SALAD SKEWERS

**COOKING: 0'**  **PREPARATION: 15'**  **SERVES: 10**

## INGREDIENTS

» 8-oz cherry tomatoes, sliced in half
» A handful of fresh basil leaves, rinsed and drained
» 1-lb fresh mozzarella, cut into bite-sized slices
» Balsamic vinegar
» Extra virgin olive oil
» Freshly ground black pepper

## DIRECTIONS

1. Sandwich a folded basil leaf and mozzarella cheese between the halves of tomato onto a toothpick.

2. Drizzle with olive oil and balsamic vinegar each skewer. To serve, sprinkle with freshly ground black pepper.

**NUTRITIONS:**
94 Calories, 3.7g Fats, 2.1g Protein

# 50. LEAFY LACINATO TUSCAN TREAT

**COOKING: 0'**     **PREPARATION: 10'**     **SERVES: 1**

## INGREDIENTS

- » 1-tsp Dijon mustard
- » 1-tbsp light mayonnaise
- » 3-pcs medium-sized Lacinato kale leaves
- » 3-oz. cooked chicken breast, thinly sliced
- » 6-bulbs red onion, thinly sliced
- » 1-pc apple, cut into 9-slices

## DIRECTIONS

1. Mix the mustard and mayonnaise until fully combined.
2. Spread the mixture generously on each of the kale leaves. Top each leaf with 1-oz. chicken slices, 3-apple slices, and 2-red onion slices. Roll each kale leaf into a wrap.

**NUTRITIONS:**
370 Calories, 14g Fats, 29g Protein

# 51. GREEK GUACAMOLE HYBRID HUMMUS

**COOKING: 0'**     **PREPARATION: 10'**     **SERVES: 1**

## INGREDIENTS

- » 1-15 oz. canned chickpeas
- » 1-pc ripe avocado
- » ¼-cup tahini paste
- » 1-cup fresh cilantro leaves
- » ¼-cup lemon juice
- » 1-tsp ground cumin
- » ¼-cup extra-virgin olive oil
- » 1-clove garlic
- » ½ tsp salt

## DIRECTIONS

1. Drain the chickpeas and reserve 2-tablespoons of the liquid. Pour the reserved liquid in your food processor and add in the drained chickpeas.
2. Add the avocado, tahini, cilantro, lemon juice, cumin, oil, garlic, and salt. Puree the mixture into a smooth consistency.
3. Serve with pita chips, veggie chips, or crudités.

**NUTRITIONS:**
156 Calories, 12g Fats, 3g Protein

# 52. PORTABLE PACKED PICNIC PIECES

**COOKING: 0'**　　　　**PREPARATION: 5'**　　　　**SERVES: 1**

## INGREDIENTS

- » 1-slice of whole-wheat bread, cut into bite-size pieces
- » 10-pcs cherry tomatoes
- » ¼-oz. aged cheese, sliced
- » 6-pcs oil-cured olives

## NUTRITIONS:
197 Calories, 9g Fats, 7g Protein

## DIRECTIONS

1. Pack each of the ingredients in a portable container to serve you while snacking on the go.

# 53. PERFECT PIZZA & PASTRY

**COOKING: 15'**　　　　**PREPARATION: 35'**　　　　**SERVES: 10**

## INGREDIENTS

### For Pizza Dough:
- » 2-tsp honey
- » ¼-oz. active dry yeast
- » 1¼-cups warm water (about 120 °F)
- » 2-tbsp olive oil
- » 1-tsp sea salt
- » 3-cups whole grain flour + ¼-cup, as needed for rolling

### For Pizza Topping:
- » 1-cup pesto sauce (refer to Perky Pesto recipe)
- » 1-cup artichoke hearts
- » 1-cup wilted spinach leaves
- » 1-cup sun-dried tomato
- » ½-cup Kalamata olives
- » 4-oz. feta cheese
- » 4-oz. mixed cheese of equal parts low-fat mozzarella, asiago, and provolone

### Optional:
- » Bell pepper
- » Chicken breast, strips
- » Fresh basil
- » Pine nuts

## NUTRITIONS:
242.8 Calories, 15g Fats, 14g Protein

## DIRECTIONS

### For the Pizza Dough:
1. Preheat your oven to 350 °F.
2. Combine the honey and yeast with the warm water in your food processor with a dough attachment. Blend the mixture until fully combined. Allow the mixture to rest for 5 minutes to ensure the activity of the yeast through the appearance of bubbles on the surface.
3. Pour in the olive oil. Add the salt, and blend for half a minute. Add gradually 3 cups of flour, about half a cup at a time, blending for a couple of minutes between each addition.
4. Let your processor knead the mixture for 10 minutes until smooth and elastic, sprinkling it with flour whenever necessary to prevent the dough from sticking to the processor bowl's surfaces.
5. Take the dough from the bowl. Let it stand for 15 minutes, covered with a moist, warm towel.
6. 6.Using a rolling pin, roll out the dough to a half-inch thickness, dusting it with flour as needed. Poke holes indiscriminately on the dough using a fork to prevent crust bubbling.
7. Place the perforated, rolled dough on a pizza stone or baking sheet. Bake for 5 minutes.

### For Pizza Topping:
8. Lightly brush the baked pizza shell with olive oil.
9. Pour over the pesto sauce and spread thoroughly over the pizza shell's surface, leaving out a half-inch space around its edge as the crust.
10. Top the pizza with artichoke hearts, wilted spinach leaves, sun-dried tomatoes, and olives. Cover the top with the cheese.
11. Place the pizza directly on the oven rack. Bake for 10 minutes. Set aside for 5 minutes before slicing.

# 54. MARGHERITA MEDITERRANEAN MODEL

**COOKING: 15'**  **PREPARATION: 15'**  **SERVES: 10**

## INGREDIENTS

- » 1-batch pizza shell
- » 2-tbsp olive oil
- » ½-cup crushed tomatoes
- » 3-Roma tomatoes, sliced ¼-inch thick
- » ½-cup fresh basil leaves, thinly sliced
- » 6-oz. block mozzarella
- » ½-tsp sea salt

## DIRECTIONS

1. Preheat your oven to 450 °F.
2. Lightly brush the pizza shell with olive oil. Thoroughly spread the crushed tomatoes over the pizza shell, leaving a half-inch space around its edge as the crust.
3. Top the pizza with the Roma tomato slices, basil leaves, and mozzarella slices. Sprinkle salt over the pizza.
4. Place the pizza directly on the oven rack. Bake for 15 minutes. Put aside for 5 minutes before slicing.

**NUTRITIONS:**
251 Calories, 8g Fats, 9g Protein

# 55. FOWL & FETA FETTUCCINI

**COOKING: 30'**  **PREPARATION: 5'**  **SERVES: 6**

## INGREDIENTS

- » 2-tbsp extra-virgin olive oil
- » 1½-lb chicken breasts
- » ¼-tsp freshly ground black pepper
- » 1-tsp kosher salt
- » 2-cups water
- » 2-14.5-oz. cans tomatoes with garlic, oregano and basil
- » 1-lb whole-wheat fettuccini pasta
- » 4-oz. reduced-fat feta cheese
- » Fresh basil leaves, finely chopped (optional)

## DIRECTIONS

1. Heat up olive oil for 1 minute in your Dutch oven placed over high heat for 1 minute. Add the chicken, and sprinkle over with freshly ground black pepper and half a teaspoon of kosher salt. Cook the chicken for 8 minutes, flipping once. Sprinkle over with the remaining salt after flipping each chicken on its side. Cook further for 5 minutes until the chicken cooks through.
2. Pour in the water, and add the tomatoes. Stir in the fettuccini pasta, cook for 5 minutes, uncovered. Cover the dish, and cook further for 10 minutes.
3. Uncover the dish, and stir the pasta. Add 3-oz. of the feta cheese, and stir again. Cook further for 5 minutes, uncovered.
4. To serve, sprinkle over with the chopped basil and the remaining feta cheese.

**NUTRITIONS:**
390 Calories, 11g Fats, 19g Protein

# 56. VERY VEGAN PATRAS PASTA

**COOKING: 10'**     **PREPARATION: 5'**     **SERVES: 6**

## INGREDIENTS

- » 4-quarts salted water
- » 10-oz. gluten-free and whole grain pasta
- » 5-cloves garlic, minced
- » 1-cup hummus
- » Salt and pepper
- » 1/3cup water
- » ½-cup walnuts
- » ½-cup olives
- » 2-tbsp dried cranberries (optional)

## DIRECTIONS

1. Bring the salted water to a boil for cooking the pasta.
2. In the meantime, prepare for the hummus sauce. Combine the garlic, hummus, salt, and pepper with water in a mixing bowl. Add the walnuts, olive, and dried cranberries, if desired. Set aside.
3. Put pasta in the boiling water. Cook the pasta according to the package's specifications. Drain the pasta.
4. Transfer the pasta to a large serving bowl and combine with the sauce.

## NUTRITIONS:
329 Calories, 12.6g Fats, 12g Protein

# 57. SCRUMPTIOUS SHRIMP PAPPARDELLE PASTA

**COOKING: 20'**     **PREPARATION: 10'**     **SERVES: 4**

## INGREDIENTS

- » 3-quarts salted water
- » 1-lb. jumbo shrimp
- » ½-tsp kosher salt
- » ¼-tsp black pepper
- » 3-tbsp olive oil
- » 2-cups zucchini
- » 1-cup grape tomatoes
- » 1/8 tsp red pepper flakes
- » 2-cloves garlic
- » 1 tsp zest of 1-pc lemon
- » 2-tbsp lemon juice
- » 1-tbsp Italian parsley, chopped
- » 8-oz. fresh pappardelle pasta

## DIRECTIONS

1. Bring the salted water to a boil for cooking the pasta.
2. In the meantime, prepare for the shrimp. Combine the shrimp with salt and pepper. Set aside.
3. Heat a tablespoon of oil in a large sauté pan placed over medium heat. Add the zucchini slices and sauté for 4 minutes.
4. Add the grape tomatoes and sauté for 2 minutes. Stir in the salt to combine with the vegetables. Transfer the cooked vegetables to a medium-sized bowl. Set aside.
5. In the same sauté pan, pour in the remaining oil. Switch the heat to medium-low. Add the red pepper flakes and garlic. Cook for 2 minutes.
6. Add the seasoned shrimp, and keep the heat on medium-low. Cook the shrimp for 3 minutes on each side until they turn pinkish.
7. Stir in the zest of lemon and the lemon juice. Mix cooked vegetables back to the pan. Stir to combine with the shrimp. Set aside.
8. Situate pasta in the boiling water. Cook following the manufacturer's specifications until al dente texture. Drain the pasta.
9. Transfer the cooked pasta in a large serving bowl and combine with the lemony-garlic shrimp and vegetables.

## NUTRITIONS:
68 Calories, 0.1g Fat, 2g Protein

# 58. MIXED MUSHROOM PALERMITANI PASTA

**COOKING: 5'**         **PREPARATION: 30'**         **SERVES: 8**

## INGREDIENTS

- » 5-quarts salted water
- » 3-tbsp olive oil
- » 26-oz. assorted wild mushrooms
- » 4-cloves garlic, minced
- » 1-bulb red onion, diced
- » 1-tsp sea salt
- » 2-tbsp sherry cooking wine
- » 2½-tsp fresh thyme, diced
- » 1-lb. linguine pasta
- » ¾-cup reserved liquid from cooked pasta
- » 6-oz. goat cheese
- » ¼-cup hazelnuts

## DIRECTIONS

1. Bring the salted water to a boil for cooking the pasta.
2. In the meantime, heat the olive oil in a large skillet placed over medium-high heat. Add the mushrooms and sauté for 10 minutes until they brown.
3. Add the garlic, onions, and salt. Sauté for 4 minutes.
4. Stir in the wine, and cook down until the liquid evaporates. Sprinkle with thyme, and set aside.
5. Cook pasta in the boiling water in accordance with the manufacturer's specifications.
6. Before draining the pasta completely, reserve ¾-cup of the pasta liquid.
7. Transfer the cooked pasta in a large serving bowl and combine with the mushroom mixture, pasta liquid, and goat cheese. Toss gently to combine fully until the goat cheese melts completely.
8. To serve, top the pasta with chopped hazelnuts.

**NUTRITIONS:**
331 Calories, 12g Fats, 13g Protein

# 59. MEDITERRANEAN MACARONI WITH SEASONED SPINACH

**COOKING: 20'**         **PREPARATION: 5'**         **SERVES: 4**

## INGREDIENTS

- » 2-tbsp olive oil
- » 2-cloves garlic
- » 1-pc yellow onion
- » 10-oz. fresh baby spinach
- » 2-pcs fresh tomatoes
- » ¼-cup skim mozzarella cheese
- » ½-cup crumbled feta cheese
- » ½-cup white cheddar cheese, cubed
- » 1-cup low-sodium vegetable broth
- » 2-cups elbow whole-grain macaroni
- » 1-cup unsweetened almond milk
- » ½-tsp organic Italian Seasoning

## DIRECTIONS

1. Heat up olive oil in a large pan placed over medium-high heat. Add the garlic, onions, and a pinch of salt, and sauté for 3 minutes.
2. Add the spinach, tomatoes, cheese, vegetable broth, macaroni, milk, and seasonings. Mix well until fully combined. Bring the mixture to a boil, stirring frequently.
3. Lower heat to medium-low, and cover the pan. Cook further for 15 minutes, stirring every 3 minutes to prevent the pasta mixture from sticking on the pan's surfaces.
4. Remove the pasta from the heat and stir. To serve, garnish the pasta with parsley.

**NUTRITIONS:**
544 Calories, 23g Fats, 22g Protein

# 60. FRITTATA FILLED WITH ZESTY ZUCCHINI & TOMATO TOPPINGS

**COOKING: 10'**      **PREPARATION: 15'**      **SERVES: 4**

## INGREDIENTS

- » 8-pcs eggs
- » ¼-tsp red pepper, crushed
- » ¼-tsp salt
- » 1-tbsp olive oil
- » 1-pc small zucchini
- » ½-cup red or yellow cherry tomatoes
- » 1/3-cup walnuts, coarsely chopped
- » 2-oz. bite-sized fresh mozzarella balls (bocconcini)

## NUTRITIONS:

281 Calories, 14g Fats, 17g Protein

## DIRECTIONS

1. Preheat your broiler. Meanwhile, whisk together the eggs, crushed red pepper, and salt in a medium-sized bowl. Set aside.

2. In a 10-inch broiler-proof skillet placed over medium-high heat, heat the olive oil. Arrange the slices of zucchini in an even layer on the bottom of the skillet. Cook for 3 minutes, turning them once, halfway through.

3. Top the zucchini layer with cherry tomatoes. Pour the egg mixture over vegetables in skillet. Top with walnuts and mozzarella balls.

4. Switch to medium heat. Cook for 5 minutes. By using a spatula, lift the frittata for the uncooked portions of the egg mixture to flow underneath.

5. Place the skillet on the broiler. Broil the frittata 4-inches from the heat for 5 minutes until the top is set. To serve, cut the frittata into wedges.

# CHAPTER 6
# BREAKFAST RECIPES

# 61. AVOCADO EGG SCRAMBLE

**COOKING: 15'**  **PREPARATION: 8'**  **SERVES: 4**

## INGREDIENTS

- » 4 eggs, beaten
- » 1 white onion, diced
- » 1 tablespoon avocado oil
- » 1 avocado, finely chopped
- » ½ teaspoon chili flakes
- » 1 oz Cheddar cheese, shredded
- » ½ teaspoon salt
- » 1 tablespoon fresh parsley

## DIRECTIONS

1. Pour avocado oil in the skillet and bring it to boil.
2. Then add diced onion and roast it until it is light brown.
3. Meanwhile, mix up together chili flakes, beaten eggs, and salt.
4. Pour the egg mixture over the cooked onion and cook the mixture for 1 minute over the medium heat.
5. After this, scramble the eggs well with the help of the fork or spatula. Cook the eggs until they are solid but soft.
6. After this, add chopped avocado and shredded cheese.
7. Stir the scramble well and transfer in the serving plates.
8. Sprinkle the meal with fresh parsley.

**NUTRITIONS:**
236 Calories, 20g Fat, 8.6g Protein

# 62. BREAKFAST TOSTADAS

**COOKING: 6'**  **PREPARATION: 15'**  **SERVES: 6**

## INGREDIENTS

- » ½ white onion, diced
- » 1 tomato, chopped
- » 1 cucumber, chopped
- » 1 tablespoon fresh cilantro, chopped
- » ½ jalapeno pepper, chopped
- » 1 tablespoon lime juice
- » 6 corn tortillas
- » 1 tablespoon canola oil
- » 2 oz Cheddar cheese, shredded
- » ½ cup white beans, canned, drained
- » 6 eggs
- » ½ teaspoon butter
- » ½ teaspoon Sea salt

## DIRECTIONS

1. Make Pico de Galo: in the salad bowl combine together diced white onion, tomato, cucumber, fresh cilantro, and jalapeno pepper.
2. Then add lime juice and a ½ tablespoon of canola oil. Mix up the mixture well. Pico de Galo is cooked.
3. After this, preheat the oven to 390F.
4. Line the tray with baking paper.
5. Arrange the corn tortillas on the baking paper and brush with remaining canola oil from both sides.
6. Bake for 10 minutes.
7. Chill the cooked crunchy tortillas well.
8. Meanwhile, toss the butter in the skillet.
9. Crack the eggs in the melted butter and sprinkle them with sea salt.
10. Fry the eggs for 3-5 minutes over the medium heat.
11. After this, mash the beans until you get puree texture.
12. Spread the bean puree on the corn tortillas.
13. Add fried eggs.
14. Then top the eggs with Pico de Galo and shredded Cheddar cheese.

**NUTRITIONS:**
246 Calories, 11g fat, 14g protein

# 63. PARMESAN OMELET

**COOKING: 5'**     **PREPARATION: 10'**     **SERVES: 2**

## INGREDIENTS

- » 1 tablespoon cream cheese
- » 2 eggs, beaten
- » ¼ teaspoon paprika
- » ½ teaspoon dried oregano
- » ¼ teaspoon dried dill
- » 1 oz Parmesan, grated
- » 1 teaspoon coconut oil

## DIRECTIONS

1. Mix up together cream cheese with eggs, dried oregano, and dill.
2. Preheat coconut oil in the skillet.
3. Place egg mixture in the skillet and flatten it.
4. Add grated Parmesan and close the lid.
5. Cook omelet for 10 minutes over the low heat.
6. Then transfer the cooked omelet in the serving plate and sprinkle with paprika.

**NUTRITIONS:**
148 Calories, 12g fat, 11g protein

# 64. MENEMEN

**COOKING: 15'**     **PREPARATION: 6'**     **SERVES: 4**

## INGREDIENTS

- » 2 tomatoes, chopped
- » 2 eggs, beaten
- » 1 bell pepper, chopped
- » 1 teaspoon tomato paste
- » ¼ cup of water
- » 1 teaspoon butter
- » ½ white onion, diced
- » ½ teaspoon chili flakes
- » 1/3 teaspoon sea salt

## DIRECTIONS

1. Melt butter in the pan.
2. Add bell pepper and cook it for 3 minutes over the medium heat. Stir it from time to time.
3. After this, add diced onion and cook it for 2 minutes more.
4. Stir the vegetables and add tomatoes.
5. Cook them for 5 minutes over the medium-low heat.
6. Then add water and tomato paste. Stir well.
7. Add beaten eggs, chili flakes, and sea salt.
8. Stir well and cook Menemen for 4 minutes over the medium-low heat.
9. The cooked meal should be half runny.

**NUTRITIONS:**
67 Calories, 3.4g fat, 3.8g protein

# 65. WATERMELON PIZZA

**COOKING: 0'**          **PREPARATION: 10'**          **SERVES: 3**

## INGREDIENTS

- » 9 oz watermelon slice
- » 1 tablespoon Pomegranate sauce
- » 2 oz Feta cheese, crumbled
- » 1 tablespoon fresh cilantro, chopped

## DIRECTIONS

1. Place the watermelon slice in the plate and sprinkle with crumbled Feta cheese.
2. Add fresh cilantro.
3. After this, sprinkle the pizza with Pomegranate juice generously.
4. Cut the pizza into the servings.

**NUTRITIONS:**
143 Calories, 6.2g fat, 5.1g protein

# 66. HAM MUFFINS

**COOKING: 15'**          **PREPARATION: 10'**          **SERVES: 1**

## INGREDIENTS

- » 3 oz ham, chopped
- » 4 eggs, beaten
- » 2 tablespoons coconut flour
- » ½ teaspoon dried oregano
- » ¼ teaspoon dried cilantro

## DIRECTIONS

1. Spray the muffin's molds with cooking spray from inside.
2. In the bowl mix up together beaten eggs, coconut flour, dried oregano, cilantro, and ham.
3. When the liquid is homogenous, pour it in the prepared muffin molds.
4. Bake the muffins for 15 minutes at 360F.
5. Chill the cooked meal well and only after this remove from the molds.

**NUTRITIONS:**
128 Calories, 7.2g fat, 10g protein

# 67. MORNING PIZZA WITH SPROUTS

**COOKING: 20'**          **PREPARATION: 15'**          **SERVES: 6**

## INGREDIENTS

- » ½ cup wheat flour, whole grain
- » 2 tablespoons butter, softened
- » ¼ teaspoon baking powder
- » ¾ teaspoon salt
- » 5 oz chicken fillet, boiled
- » 2 oz Cheddar cheese, shredded
- » 1 teaspoon tomato sauce
- » 1 oz bean sprouts

## DIRECTIONS

1. Make the pizza crust: mix up together wheat flour, butter, baking powder, and salt. Knead the soft and non-sticky dough. Add more wheat flour if needed.
2. Leave the dough for 10 minutes to chill.
3. Then place the dough on the baking paper. Cover it with the second baking paper sheet.
4. Roll up the dough with the help of the rolling pin to get the round pizza crust.
5. After this, remove the upper baking paper sheet.
6. Transfer the pizza crust in the tray.
7. Spread the crust with tomato sauce.
8. Then shred the chicken fillet and arrange it over the pizza crust.
9. Add shredded Cheddar cheese.
10. Bake pizza for 20 minutes at 355F.
11. Then top the cooked pizza with bean sprouts.

**NUTRITIONS:**
157 Calories, 8.8g fat, 10.5g protein

# 68. BANANA QUINOA

**COOKING: 12'**          **PREPARATION: 10'**          **SERVES: 4**

## INGREDIENTS

- » 1 cup quinoa
- » 2 cup milk
- » 1 teaspoon vanilla extract
- » 1 teaspoon honey
- » 2 bananas, sliced
- » ¼ teaspoon ground cinnamon

## DIRECTIONS

1. Pour milk in the saucepan and add quinoa.
2. Close the lid and cook it over the medium heat for 12 minutes or until quinoa will absorb all liquid.
3. Then chill the quinoa for 10-15 minutes and place in the serving mason jars.
4. Add honey, vanilla extract, and ground cinnamon.
5. Stir well.
6. Top quinoa with banana and stirs it before serving.

**NUTRITIONS:**
279 Calories, 5.3g fat, 10.7g protein

# 69. AVOCADO MILK SHAKE

**COOKING: 0'**  **PREPARATION: 1"**  **SERVES: 2**

## INGREDIENTS

- » 1 avocado, peeled, pitted
- » 2 tablespoons of liquid honey
- » ½ teaspoon vanilla extract
- » ½ cup heavy cream
- » 1 cup milk
- » 1/3 cup ice cubes

## DIRECTIONS

1. Chop the avocado and put in the food processor.
2. Add liquid honey, vanilla extract, heavy cream, milk, and ice cubes.
3. Blend the mixture until it smooth.
4. Pour the cooked milkshake in the serving glasses.

**NUTRITIONS:**
291 Calories, 22g fat, 4.4g protein

# 70. EGG CASSEROLE WITH PAPRIKA

**COOKING: 28'**  **PREPARATION: 10'**  **SERVES: 4**

## INGREDIENTS

- » 2 eggs, beaten
- » 1 red bell pepper, chopped
- » 1 chili pepper, chopped
- » ½ red onion, diced
- » 1 teaspoon canola oil
- » ½ teaspoon salt
- » 1 teaspoon paprika
- » 1 tablespoon fresh cilantro, chopped
- » 1 garlic clove, diced
- » 1 teaspoon butter, softened
- » ¼ teaspoon chili flakes

## DIRECTIONS

1. Brush the casserole mold with canola oil and pour beaten eggs inside.
2. After this, toss the butter in the skillet and melt it over the medium heat.
3. Add chili pepper and red bell pepper.
4. After this, add red onion and cook the vegetables for 7-8 minutes over the medium heat. Stir them from time to time.
5. Transfer the vegetables in the casserole mold.
6. Add salt, paprika, cilantro, diced garlic, and chili flakes. Stir gently with the help of a spatula to get a homogenous mixture.
7. Bake the casserole for 20 minutes at 355F in the oven.
8. Then chill the meal well and cut into servings. Transfer the casserole in the serving plates with the help of the spatula.

**NUTRITIONS:**
68 Calories, 4.5g fat, 3.4g protein

# 71. CAULIFLOWER FRITTERS

**COOKING: 10'**　　　**PREPARATION: 10'**　　　**SERVES: 4**

## INGREDIENTS

- » 1 cup cauliflower, shredded
- » 1 egg, beaten
- » 1 tablespoon wheat flour, whole grain
- » 1 oz Parmesan, grated
- » ½ teaspoon ground black pepper
- » 1 tablespoon canola oil

## DIRECTIONS

1. In the mixing bowl mix up together shredded cauliflower and egg.
2. Add wheat flour, grated Parmesan, and ground black pepper.
3. Stir the mixture with the help of the fork until it is homogenous and smooth.
4. Pour canola oil in the skillet and bring it to boil.
5. Make the fritters from the cauliflower mixture with the help of the fingertips or use spoon and transfer in the hot oil.
6. Roast the fritters for 4 minutes from each side over the medium-low heat.

**NUTRITIONS:**
167 Calories, 12.3g fat, 8.8g protein

# 72. CREAMY OATMEAL WITH FIGS

**COOKING: 20'**　　　**PREPARATION: 10'**　　　**SERVES: 5**

## INGREDIENTS

- » 2 cups oatmeal
- » 1 ½ cup milk
- » 1 tablespoon butter
- » 3 figs, chopped
- » 1 tablespoon honey

## DIRECTIONS

1. Pour milk in the saucepan.
2. Add oatmeal and close the lid.
3. Cook the oatmeal for 15 minutes over the medium-low heat.
4. Then add chopped figs and honey.
5. Add butter and mix up the oatmeal well.
6. Cook it for 5 minutes more.
7. Close the lid and let the cooked breakfast rest for 10 minutes before serving.

**NUTRITIONS:**
222 Calories, 6g fat, 7.1g protein

# 73. BAKED OATMEAL WITH CINNAMON

**COOKING: 25'**   **PREPARATION: 10'**   **SERVES: 4**

## INGREDIENTS

- » 1 cup oatmeal
- » 1/3 cup milk
- » 1 pear, chopped
- » 1 teaspoon vanilla extract
- » 1 tablespoon Splenda
- » 1 teaspoon butter
- » ½ teaspoon ground cinnamon
- » 1 egg, beaten

## DIRECTIONS

1. In the big bowl mix up together oatmeal, milk, egg, vanilla extract, Splenda, and ground cinnamon.
2. 2.  Melt butter and add it in the oatmeal mixture.
3. 3.  Then add chopped pear and stir it well.
4. 4.  Transfer the oatmeal mixture in the casserole mold and flatten gently. Cover it with the foil and secure edges.
5. 5.  Bake the oatmeal for 25 minutes at 350F.

**NUTRITIONS:**
151 Calories, 3.9g fat, 4.9g protein

# 74. ALMOND CHIA PORRIDGE

**COOKING: 30'**   **PREPARATION: 10'**   **SERVES: 5**

## INGREDIENTS

- » 3 cups organic almond milk
- » 1/3 cup chia seeds, dried
- » 1 teaspoon vanilla extract
- » 1 tablespoon honey
- » ¼ teaspoon ground cardamom

## DIRECTIONS

1. Pour almond milk in the saucepan and bring it to boil.
2. Then chill the almond milk to the room temperature (or appx. For 10-15 minutes).
3. Add vanilla extract, honey, and ground cardamom. Stir well.
4. After this, add chia seeds and stir again.
5. Close the lid and let chia seeds soak the liquid for 20-25 minutes.
6. Transfer the cooked porridge into the serving ramekins.

**NUTRITIONS:**
150 Calories, 7.3g fat, 3.7g protein

# 75. COCOA OATMEAL

**COOKING: 15'**  **PREPARATION: 10'**  **SERVES: 2**

## INGREDIENTS

- » 1 ½ cup oatmeal
- » 1 tablespoon cocoa powder
- » ½ cup heavy cream
- » ¼ cup of water
- » 1 teaspoon vanilla extract
- » 1 tablespoon butter
- » 2 tablespoons Splenda

## DIRECTIONS

1. Mix up together oatmeal with cocoa powder and Splenda.
2. Transfer the mixture in the saucepan.
3. Add vanilla extract, water, and heavy cream. Stir it gently with the help of the spatula.
4. Close the lid and cook it for 10-15 minutes over the medium-low heat.
5. Remove the cooked cocoa oatmeal from the heat and add butter. Stir it well.

**NUTRITIONS:**
230 Calories, 10.6g fat, 4.6g protein

# CHAPTER 7
# BREAKFAST RECIPES PART 2

# 76. BERRY BREAKFAST SMOOTHIE

**COOKING: 0'**      **PREPARATION: 3'**      **SERVES: 1**

## INGREDIENTS

» 1/2 cup vanilla low-fat Greek yogurt
» 1/4 cup low-fat milk
» 1/2 cup blueberries or strawberries
» 6 to 8 ice cubes

## DIRECTIONS

1. 1. Place the Greek yogurt, milk, and berries in a blender and blend until the berries are liquefied. Mix in ice cubes and blend on high. Serve immediately.

**NUTRITIONS:**
98 calories, 10g fats, 7g protein

# 77. MEDITERRANEAN OMELET

**COOKING: 6'**      **PREPARATION: 15'**      **SERVES: 6**

## INGREDIENTS

» 2 teaspoons extra-virgin olive oil
» 1 garlic clove
» 1/2 red bell pepper
» 1/2 yellow bell pepper
» 1/4 cup thinly sliced red onion
» 2 tablespoons chopped fresh basil
» 2 tablespoons chopped fresh parsley
» 1/2 teaspoon salt
» 1/2 teaspoon black pepper
» 4 large eggs, beaten

## DIRECTIONS

1. In a big, heavy skillet, cook 1 teaspoon of the olive oil over medium heat. Add the garlic, peppers, and onion to the pan and sauté, stirring frequently, for 5 minutes.
2. Add the basil, parsley, salt, and pepper, increase the heat to medium-high, and sauté for 2 minutes. Slide the vegetable mixture onto a plate and return the pan to the heat.
3. Heat the remaining 1 teaspoon olive oil in the same pan and pour in the beaten eggs, tilting the pan to coat evenly. Cook the eggs just until the edges are bubbly and all but the center is dry, 3 to 5 minutes.
4. Either flip the omelet or use a spatula to turn it over.
5. Spoon the vegetable mixture onto one-half of the omelet and use a spatula to fold the empty side over the top. Slide the omelet onto a platter or cutting board.
6. To serve, cut the omelet in half and garnish with fresh parsley.

**NUTRITIONS:**
197 calories, 18g fats, 6g protein

# 78. HEARTY BERRY BREAKFAST OATS

**COOKING: 2'**          **PREPARATION: 11'**          **SERVES: 2**

## INGREDIENTS

- » 11/2 cups whole-grain rolled oats
- » 3/4 cup fresh blueberries, raspberries, or blackberries, or a combination
- » 2 teaspoons honey
- » 2 tablespoons walnut pieces

## DIRECTIONS

1. Prepare the whole-grain oats according to the package directions and divide between 2 deep bowls.

2. In a small microwave-safe bowl, heat the berries and honey for 30 seconds. Top each bowl of oatmeal with the fruit mixture. Sprinkle the walnuts over the fruit and serve hot.

**NUTRITIONS:**
204 calories, 17g fat, 4g protein

# 79. GARDEN SCRAMBLE

**COOKING: 13'**          **PREPARATION: 9'**          **SERVES: 4**

## INGREDIENTS

- » 1 teaspoon extra-virgin olive oil
- » 1/2 cup diced yellow squash
- » 1/2 cup diced green bell pepper
- » 1/4 cup diced sweet white onion
- » 6 cherry tomatoes, halved
- » 1 tablespoon chopped fresh basil
- » 1 tablespoon chopped fresh parsley
- » 1/2 teaspoon salt
- » 1/4 teaspoon freshly ground black pepper
- » 8 large eggs, beaten

## DIRECTIONS

1. In a large nonstick skillet, cook olive oil over medium heat. Add the squash, pepper, and onion and sauté for 4 minutes.

2. Add the tomatoes, basil, and parsley and season. Sauté for 1 minute, then pour the beaten eggs over the vegetables. Close and reduce the heat to low.

3. Cook for 6 minutes, making sure that the center is no longer runny.

4. To serve, slide the frittata onto a platter and cut into wedges.

**NUTRITIONS:**
211 calories, 17g fats, 5g protein

# 80. SUMMER DAY FRUIT SALAD

**COOKING: 0'**          **PREPARATION: 16'**          **SERVES: 8**

## INGREDIENTS

- » 2 cups cubed honeydew melon
- » 2 cups cubed cantaloupe
- » 2 cups red seedless grapes
- » 1 cup sliced fresh strawberries
- » 1 cup fresh blueberries
- » Zest and juice of 1 large lime
- » 1/2 cup unsweetened toasted coconut flakes
- » 1/4 cup honey
- » 1/4 teaspoon salt
- » 1/2 cup extra-virgin olive oil

## DIRECTIONS

1. Combine all of the fruits, the lime zest, and the coconut flakes in a large bowl and stir well to blend. Set aside.

2. In a blender, mix lime juice, honey, and salt and blend on low. Once the honey is incorporated, slowly add the olive oil and blend until opaque.

3. Drizzle dressing over the fruit and mix well. Cover and chill for at least 4 hours before serving.

**NUTRITIONS:**
196 calories, 16g fats, 3g protein

# 81. EGG, PANCETTA, AND SPINACH BENEDICT

**COOKING: 24'**          **PREPARATION: 16'**          **SERVES: 2**

## INGREDIENTS

- » 1/4 cup diced pancetta
- » 2 cups baby spinach leaves
- » 1/4 teaspoon freshly ground black pepper
- » 1/4 teaspoon salt, or to taste
- » 2 large eggs
- » Extra-virgin olive oil (optional)
- » 1 whole-grain English muffin, toasted

## DIRECTIONS

1. In a medium, heavy skillet, brown the pancetta over medium-low heat for about 5 minutes, stirring frequently, until crisp on all sides.

2. Stir in the spinach, pepper, and salt if desired (it may not need any, depending on how salty the pancetta is). Cook, stirring occasionally, until the spinach is just wilted, about 5 minutes. Transfer the mixture to a medium bowl.

3. Crack the eggs into the same pan (add olive oil if the pan looks dry), and cook until the whites are just opaque, 3 to 4 minutes. Carefully flip the eggs and continue cooking for 30 seconds to 1 minute until done to your preferred degree for over-easy eggs.

4. Situate muffin half on each of 2 plates and top each with half of the spinach mixture and 1 egg, yolk side up. Pierce the yolks just before serving.

**NUTRITIONS:**
391 calories, 21g fats, 15g protein

# 82. PEACH SUNRISE SMOOTHIE

**COOKING: 0'**　　　　**PREPARATION: 6'**　　　　**SERVES: 2**

## INGREDIENTS

» 1 large unpeeled peach, pitted and sliced (about 1/2 cup)
» 6 ounces vanilla or peach low-fat Greek yogurt
» 2 tablespoons low-fat milk
» 6 to 8 ice cubes

## DIRECTIONS

1. Incorporate all ingredients in a blender and blend until thick and creamy. Serve immediately.

**NUTRITIONS:**

98 calories, 16g fats, 3g protein

# 83. OAT AND FRUIT PARFAIT

**COOKING: 0'**　　　　**PREPARATION: 11'**　　　　**SERVES: 2**

## INGREDIENTS

» 1/2 cup whole-grain rolled oats
» 1/2 cup walnut pieces
» 1 teaspoon honey
» 1 cup sliced fresh strawberries
» 11/2 cups (12 ounces) vanilla low-fat Greek yogurt
» Fresh mint leaves for garnish

## DIRECTIONS

1. Preheat the oven to 300°F.
2. Spread the oats and walnuts in a single layer on a baking sheet.
3. Toast the oats and nuts just until you begin to smell the nuts, 10 to 12 minutes. Remove the pan from the oven and set aside.
4. In a small microwave-safe bowl, heat the honey just until warm, about 30 seconds. Add the strawberries and stir to coat.
5. Place 1 tablespoon of the strawberries in the bottom of each of 2 dessert dishes or 8-ounce glasses. Add a portion of yogurt and then a portion of oats and repeat the layers until the containers are full, ending with the berries. Serve immediately or chill until ready to eat.

**NUTRITIONS:**

108 calories, 10g fats, 3g protein

# 84. SAVORY AVOCADO SPREAD

**COOKING: 0'**  **PREPARATION: 17"**  **SERVES: 4**

## INGREDIENTS

- » 1 ripe avocado
- » 1 teaspoon lemon juice
- » 6 boneless sardine filets
- » 1/4 cup diced sweet white onion
- » 1 stalk celery, diced
- » 1/2 teaspoon salt
- » 1/4 teaspoon black pepper

## DIRECTIONS

1. In a blender, pulse avocado, lemon juice, and sardine filets
2. Spoon the mixture into a small bowl and add the onion, celery, salt, and pepper. Mix well with a fork and serve as desired.

**NUTRITIONS:**

109 calories, 15g fats, 6g protein

# 85. CHEESY STUFFED TOMATOES

**COOKING: 22'**  **PREPARATION: 6'**  **SERVES: 2**

## INGREDIENTS

- » 4 large, ripe tomatoes
- » 1 tablespoon extra-virgin olive oil
- » 2 garlic cloves, minced
- » 1/2 cup diced yellow onion
- » 1/2-pound cremini mushrooms
- » 1 tablespoon chopped fresh basil
- » 1 tablespoon chopped fresh oregano
- » 1/2 teaspoon salt
- » 1/4 teaspoon freshly ground black pepper
- » 1 cup shredded part-skim mozzarella cheese
- » 1 tablespoon grated Parmesan cheese

## DIRECTIONS

1. Preheat the oven to 375°F. Line a baking sheet with aluminum foil.
2. Cut sliver from the bottom of each tomato so they will stand upright without wobbling. Cut a 1/2-inch slice from the top of each tomato and use a spoon to gently remove most of the pulp, placing it in a medium bowl. Place the tomatoes on the baking sheet.
3. In a skillet, cook olive oil over medium heat. Sauté the garlic, onion, mushrooms, basil, and oregano for 5 minutes, and season with salt and pepper.
4. Transfer the mixture to the bowl and blend well with the tomato pulp. Stir in the mozzarella cheese.
5. Fill each tomato loosely with the mixture, top with Parmesan cheese, and bake until the cheese is bubbly, 15 to 20 minutes. Serve immediately.

**NUTRITIONS:**

201 calories, 19g fats, 6g protein

# 86. FRESH TOMATO PASTA BOWL

**COOKING: 26'**　　　**PREPARATION: 7'**　　　**SERVES: 4**

## INGREDIENTS

- » 8 ounces whole-grain linguine
- » 1 tablespoon extra-virgin olive oil
- » 2 garlic cloves, minced
- » 1/4 cup chopped yellow onion
- » 1 teaspoon chopped fresh oregano
- » 1/2 teaspoon salt
- » 1/4 teaspoon freshly ground black pepper
- » 1 teaspoon tomato paste
- » 8 ounces cherry tomatoes, halved
- » 1/2 cup grated Parmesan cheese
- » 1 tablespoon chopped fresh parsley

## DIRECTIONS

1. Boil water at high heat and cook the linguine according to the package instructions until al dente. Strain, reserving 1/2 cup of the pasta water. Do not rinse the pasta.
2. In a large, heavy skillet, heat the olive oil over medium-high heat. Sauté the garlic, onion, and oregano for 5 minutes.
3. Add the salt, pepper, tomato paste, and 1/4 cup of the reserved pasta water. Stir well and cook for 1 minute.
4. Stir in the tomatoes and cooked pasta, tossing everything well to coat. Add more pasta water if needed.
5. To serve, mound the pasta in shallow bowls and top with Parmesan cheese and parsley.

**NUTRITIONS:**
391 calories, 28g fats, 9g protein

# 87. GARLICKY BROILED SARDINES

**COOKING: 31'**　　　**PREPARATION: 6'**　　　**SERVES: 4**

## INGREDIENTS

- » 4 (3.25-ounce) cans sardines packed in water or olive oil
- » 2 tablespoons extra-virgin olive oil
- » 4 garlic cloves, minced
- » 1/2 teaspoon red pepper flakes
- » 1/2 teaspoon salt
- » 1/4 teaspoon black pepper

## DIRECTIONS

1. Preheat the broiler. Line a baking dish with aluminum foil. Lay sardines in a single layer on the foil.
2. Combine the olive oil (if using), garlic, and red pepper flakes in a small bowl and spoon over each sardine. Season with salt and pepper.
3. Broil just until sizzling, 2 to 3 minutes.
4. To serve, place 4 sardines on each plate and top with any remaining garlic mixture that has collected in the baking dish.

**NUTRITIONS:**
308 calories, 17g fats, 9g protein

# 88. HEART-HEALTHFUL TRAIL MIX

**COOKING: 32'**      **PREPARATION: 8'**      **SERVES: 12**

## INGREDIENTS

- » 1 cup raw almonds
- » 1 cup walnut halves
- » 1 cup pumpkin seeds
- » 1 cup dried apricots, cut into thin strips
- » 1 cup dried cherries, roughly chopped
- » 1 cup golden raisins
- » 2 tablespoons extra-virgin olive oil
- » 1 teaspoon salt

## DIRECTIONS

1. Preheat the oven to 300°F. Line a baking sheet with aluminum foil.

2. In a large bowl, mix almonds, walnuts, pumpkin seeds, apricots, cherries, and raisins. Pour the olive oil over all and toss well with clean hands. Add salt and toss again to distribute.

3. Pour the nut mixture onto the baking sheet in a single layer and bake until the fruits begin to brown, about 30 minutes. Chill on the baking sheet to room temperature.

4. Store in a large airtight container or zipper-top plastic bag.

**NUTRITIONS:**

109 calories, 7g fats, 1g protein

# 89. CITRUS-KISSED MELON

**COOKING: 0'**      **PREPARATION: 11'**      **SERVES: 4**

## INGREDIENTS

- » 2 cups cubed melon
- » 2 cups cubed cantaloupe
- » 1/2 cup freshly squeezed orange juice
- » 1/4 cup freshly squeezed lime juice
- » 1 tablespoon orange zest

## DIRECTIONS

1. In a large bowl, incorporate melon cubes. In a bowl, blend the orange juice, lime juice, and orange zest and pour over the fruit.

2. Cover and chill for at least 4 hours, stirring occasionally. Serve chilled.

**NUTRITIONS:**

101 calories, 11g fats, 2g protein

# 90. CAFÉ COOLER

**COOKING: 0'**  **PREPARATION: 16'**  **SERVES: 4**

## INGREDIENTS

- » Ice cubes
- » 2 cups low-fat milk
- » 1/2 teaspoon ground cinnamon
- » 1/2 teaspoon pure vanilla extract
- » 1 cup espresso, cooled to room temperature
- » 4 teaspoons sugar (optional)

## DIRECTIONS

1. Fill four tall glasses with ice cubes.
2. In a blender, combine the milk, cinnamon, and vanilla and blend until frothy.
3. Pour the milk over the ice cubes and top each drink with one-quarter of the espresso. If using sugar, stir it into the espresso until it has dissolved. Serve immediately, with chilled teaspoons for stirring.

## NUTRITIONS:
93 calories, 7g fats, 1g protein

# CHAPTER 8
# BREAKFAST RECIPES PART 3

# 91. SPRING CAPONATA WITH OLIVES AND POMEGRANATE

**COOKING: 21'**   **PREPARATION: 7'**   **SERVES: 4**

## INGREDIENTS

- »   3 ½ oz almonds
- »   10 ½ oz olives
- »   2oz celery stalk
- »   100 ml olive oil
- »   2 oz capers
- »   1 ½ oz sugar
- »   5oz raisins
- »   50ml white wine vinegar
- »   Grenades 1 piece
- »   Ground black pepper to taste

## DIRECTIONS

1. Boil a liter of salted water in a saucepan and add celery chopped into small pieces in it for two minutes. Drain the water, cool the celery so that it does not lose its green color.

2. Pour almonds into a frying pan and put in the oven for five minutes, preheated to 180 degrees.

3. Take out seeds from the olives and chop the flesh roughly.

4. Rinse the salted capers and chop them roughly. Roasted nuts in the oven are also roughly chopped.

5. Heat olive oil in a large saucepan, add sugar, capers, raisins, vinegar, a pinch of black pepper, olives, and simmer over medium heat for five minutes. Then pour celery into a stewpan and simmer for another two to three minutes. When serving, mix with pomegranate seeds and almonds.

**NUTRITIONS:**
650 Calories, 45.8g Fat, 8g Protein

# 92. SMOKED SALMON APPETIZER WITH FRESH CUCUMBER

**COOKING: 0'**   **PREPARATION: 10'**   **SERVES: 4**

## INGREDIENTS

- »   2 ½ tbsp sour cream 10%
- »   16 slices rye bread
- »   3 tbsp Greek yogurt
- »   Dill to taste
- »   16 pieces smoked salmon
- »   16 pieces cucumbers

## DIRECTIONS

1. Blend sour cream and yogurt.

2. Put slices of rye bread on the dish (you can cut circles or squares out of them).

3. On each put a mug of cucumber, a little sauce, and a slice of fish. Garnish with dill branches on top.

**NUTRITIONS:**
225 Calories, 9g Fat, 24g Protein

# 93. CYPRIOT TOMATO SALAD

**COOKING: 0'**     **PREPARATION: 13'**     **SERVES: 4**

## INGREDIENTS

- » **4 pieces tomatoes**
- » **50 ml sesame oil**
- » **1 tbsp red wine vinegar**
- » **2 tbsp - dried oregano**
- » **coarse sea salt to taste**
- » **9 oz feta cheese**

## DIRECTIONS

1. Cut the tomatoes into slices and put on a plate.
2. Sprinkle with sesame oil and vinegar, sprinkle with salt and oregano.
3. Cut the cheese and put it on the tomatoes.
4. Allow the dish to stand for 30 minutes so that the tomatoes absorb spices and aromas.

**NUTRITIONS:**
80 Calories, 7g Fat, 3g Protein

# 94. TANGERINE AND OLIVE SALAD

**COOKING: 0'**     **PREPARATION: 16'**     **SERVES: 4**

## INGREDIENTS

- » ½ lb. tangerines
- » 50 ml extra virgin olive oil
- » 3 ½ oz Kalamata olives
- » ½ tsp Ground cumin
- » 1 tbsp White wine vinegar
- » ¼ tsp paprika
- » 1/8 tsp Cayenne pepper
- » 1-piece Lettuce
- » 2 oz Parsley
- » Salt to taste
- » Ground black pepper to taste

## DIRECTIONS

1. 1. Remove the peel from the tangerines and remove the membranes between the slices (this can be done with a sharp knife, trying to touch the pulp as little as possible, or by hand, if the fruit is easy to peel). Put the naked slices in a wide bowl.
2. 2. Olives (first, they will need to be removed from the seeds) cut in half and add to the tangerines.
3. 3. Beat vinegar, oil, cumin, and paprika with a whisk in a separate bowl until smooth. Add the resulting dressing to a bowl.
4. 4. Wash and dry lettuce with your hands to tear into small flakes and arrange on four plates, put tangerines with olives on top, and sprinkle salad with chopped parsley.

**NUTRITIONS:**
173 Calories, 15.4g Fat, 1.4g Protein

# 95. FARFALLE WITH AVOCADO

**COOKING: 6'**     **PREPARATION: 13'**     **SERVES: 4**

## INGREDIENTS

- » 10 ½ oz Farfalle pasta
- » 5 oz Champignons
- » 1 bunch Radish
- » 1-piece Avocado
- » 1 oz Parsley
- » 6 oz Canned Tuna
- » 6 tbsp vegetable broth
- » 1 tbsp mustard
- » Salt to taste
- » Ground black pepper to taste

## DIRECTIONS

1. Boil the pasta.
2. Cut the champignons into thin plates and fry. Cut the radish into 6-8 slices. Cut avocado into slices. Finely chop the parsley.
3. Mix the broth with mustard, salt, and pepper, pour pasta on it.
4. Add tuna (previously draining the liquid), champignons, radishes, avocados, parsley. Mix everything and let it brew for half an hour in a cool place.

**NUTRITIONS:**
125 Calories, 3.2g Fat, 7g Protein

# 96. SALAD OF SQUID, APPLES, AND GREEN PEAS

**COOKING: 4'**     **PREPARATION: 13'**     **SERVES: 2**

## INGREDIENTS

- » 7 oz squids
- » 2 chicken egg
- » ½ apple
- » 8 ½ oz canned Green Peas
- » Mayonnaise to taste
- » Ground black pepper to taste
- » Salt to taste
- » Lemon juice to taste

## DIRECTIONS

1. Squids boiled in salted water (cook 3 minutes after boiling) cut into strips.
2. Finely chopped boiled eggs and apples.
3. Stir everything. Add peas and pepper. Season to taste with mayonnaise (can be sour cream); add lemon juice if desired.

**NUTRITIONS:**
303 Calories, 7.4g Fat, 45g Protein

# 97. THREE BEAN SALAD WITH FRENCH SAUCE

**COOKING: 4'**         **PREPARATION: 11'**         **SERVES: 4**

## INGREDIENTS

- » 3 ½ oz Green beans
- » 7 oz Beans fava
- » 11 oz Lima Beans
- » 11oz Kidney Beans
- » 1 Red onion
- » 1 tsp Italian parsley
- » 2 tbsp French sauce

## DIRECTIONS

1. Boil lightly salted water in a small saucepan. Put in it chopped green beans and fava beans (after defrosting them).
2. Cook for 1 minute, then drain the water. Fill with cold water, cool, and drain again.
3. Finely chop the small onion and parsley. Remove the beans from cans and drain the water.
4. Stir all the ingredients in a bowl, fill with sauce.

**NUTRITIONS:**
81 Calories, 5.5 Fat, 0.8g Protein

# 98. SANDWICH WITH TONGUE, ARUGULA AND CHAMPIGNONS

**COOKING: 0'**         **PREPARATION: 16'**         **SERVES: 2**

## INGREDIENTS

- » 1-piece pitta bread
- » 1-piece Tomatoes flame
- » 1 bunch Arugula
- » 5oz Fresh champignons
- » 1 tsp Truffle oil
- » 2 tbsp Olive Oil
- » Dried thyme to taste
- » Ground black pepper to taste
- » Salt to taste
- » 3 ½ oz veal tongue

## DIRECTIONS

1. Cut the tongue into long thin slices and fry in olive oil, salt, pepper, and add thyme to taste.
2. Lightly fry the champignons in olive oil, put in a clean bowl, trying to leave excess oil in a pan. Drizzle with truffle oil to give mushrooms a flavor.
3. Put the arugula, thin slices of tomato, mushrooms, and tongue evenly on the unfolded pita bread.
4. Wrap tightly, if necessary, cut off excess pita bread along the edges. Cut into two and serve.

**NUTRITIONS:**
200 Calories, 13.6g Fat, 7.5g Protein

# 99. PINEAPPLE RASPBERRY SMOOTHIE

**COOKING: 0'**     **PREPARATION: 20'**     **SERVES: 4**

## INGREDIENTS

- » 1 ½ lb. pineapple
- » 10 ½ oz frozen raspberries
- » 300 ml vanilla rice milk
- » 3 tbsp buckwheat flakes
- » Mint to taste

## DIRECTIONS

1. Piece of pineapple peel and remove the core. Cut into medium pieces.
2. Raspberries can be put frozen can be thawed overnight on the top shelf of the refrigerator.
3. Take 200 ml of rice milk (in the absence of it, of course, you can replace it with non-fat milk), buckwheat flakes, slices of mandarin and pineapple, and beat at high speed in a blender.
4. Let stand for about 10-15 minutes. During this time, buckwheat flakes will swell.
5. Add another 100 ml of rice drink and punch in the blender again. If the smoothie is still thick, bring the water or rice drink to the desired concentration.
6. Garnish with fresh mint leaves.

**NUTRITIONS:**
45 Calories, 0.3g Fa, 8g Protein

# 100. MORNING CAKE WITH OATMEAL, BANANAS, AND BLUEBERRIES

**COOKING: 33'**     **PREPARATION: 18'**     **SERVES: 4**

## INGREDIENTS

- » 2 pieces Bananas
- » 1 cup Blueberries
- » 3 tbsp Honey
- » 1oz walnuts
- » 1 cup oatmeal
- » 200 ml milk
- » 1/3 tsp cinnamon
- » 1 chicken egg
- » 1 tsp vanilla
- » 1 tsp powdered sugar

## DIRECTIONS

1. Set the oven to 375 F. Cover the bottom dish and sides of the foil
2. Cut the bananas into rings and put them in the prepared dishes. There we add half the blueberries, 1/4 tsp of cinnamon, 1 tbsp of honey, and cover with foil. Bake for 15 minutes
3. Then, in a bowl, mix the oatmeal, half the walnuts, the baking powder for the dough, and the remaining cinnamon; mix everything. In a separate bowl, beat the remaining honey, milk, eggs, and vanilla.
4. Get bananas with blueberries from the oven, sprinkle with an oatmeal mixture. Then evenly pour the mixture from milk. Sprinkle with the remaining blueberries and walnuts.
5. Bake the cake for about 30 minutes. For decoration, sprinkle with powdered sugar. Serve warm.

**NUTRITIONS:**
83 Calories, 2.2g Fat, 2.5g Protein

# 101. PITA CHICKEN SALAD

**COOKING: 4'**     **PREPARATION: 18'**     **SERVES: 4**

## INGREDIENTS

- Olive oil 1 tablespoon
- 1-piece chicken breast
- 2 pieces pita
- Dried basil to taste
- 3 tbsp natural yogurt
- 1 tbsp lemon juice
- 1 clove garlic
- 1 bunch (7 oz) green salad
- 1 tomato
- 2 chives
- 1 cucumber
- Salt to taste
- Ground black pepper to taste

## DIRECTIONS

1. Rub the chicken slices with salt, pepper, and dried basil, fry in a pan until cooked.
2. Put chicken, salad, slices of tomato, cucumber, and onion in half the pits.
3. Mix yogurt with lemon juice and garlic, add to the salad in Pita.

**NUTRITIONS:**

94 Calories, 1.8g Fat, 6g Protein

# 102. SALAD WITH SPINACH, TOMATOES, AND POACHED EGG

**COOKING: 5'**     **PREPARATION: 13'**     **SERVES: 2**

## INGREDIENTS

- 3 oz spinach
- 2 tomatoes
- 2 chicken egg
- 2oz Feta cheese
- 2 tsp lemon juice
- 1 tbsp vegetable oil
- 2 tbsp agave syrup
- 1 ½ tsp sour cream 15%
- 1 tbsp dill
- 1 ½ oz Red onion

## DIRECTIONS

1. Pour vegetable oil onto the cling film.
2. Gently break the egg so that the yolk remains intact.
3. Collect the film with the egg in a bag, squeeze out the air, tie and cook for 5 minutes.
4. Mix lemon juice, agave syrup (1 tbsp.) And vegetable oil, let the dressing rest.
5. Cut the tomatoes into a cube and the onion into strips, fill with salt and pepper dressing.
6. Add spinach leaves, mix.
7. Top with feta cheese and poached egg.
8. Mix sour cream with chopped dill and syrup (1 tbsp.).
9. Pour over the salad dressing with the prepared sauce.

**NUTRITIONS:**

200 Calories, 12g Fat , 7.5g Protein

# 103. POTATO SCALLOPS WITH TRUFFLE OIL

**COOKING: 24'**  **PREPARATION: 8'**  **SERVES: 1**

## INGREDIENTS

- » 4 oz scallops
- » 3 oz potato
- » ½ oz Parmesan cheese
- » ½ tsp lime zest
- » ½ oz butter
- » 1 tbsp olive oil
- » 1 ½ tsp truffle oil
- » 1 tsp arugula
- » 2/3 oz cherry Tomatoes
- » 1 chive
- » ½ tsp thyme
- » Sea salt to taste
- » Ground black pepper to taste

## DIRECTIONS

1. Fry scallops on both sides in olive oil with thyme. Salt, pepper.
2. Separately, boil the potatoes and rub through a sieve. Add the zest of lime, grated Parmesan cheese, and butter. Salt, pepper.
3. Lightly warm the arugula and cherry tomatoes in olive oil.
4. Put mashed potatoes through the ring on a plate, scallops symmetrically put on it, arugula and cherry on the scallops, garnish with thyme and onion, pour with truffle oil.

**NUTRITIONS:**
279 Calories, 59.8g Fat, 24.5g Protein

# 104. MEDITERRANEAN PASTA WITH BASIL

**COOKING: 19'**  **PREPARATION: 12'**  **SERVES: 4**

## INGREDIENTS

- » 2 red bell peppers
- » 2 red onions
- » 2 chili peppers
- » 3 cloves garlic
- » 1 tsp brown sugar
- » 2 tbsp olive oil
- » 2 lb. tomatoes
- » 2/3 lb. pasta
- » 1 tbsp fresh basil leaves
- » 2 tbsp grated Parmesan cheese

## DIRECTIONS

1. Preheat the oven to 390 F degrees. Put pepper, onion, chili, and garlic in a deep pan. Sprinkle with sugar, drizzle with olive oil, and season with salt and ground black pepper to taste.
2. Bake in the oven for 15 minutes, add chopped tomatoes and cook for another 15 minutes.
3. While the vegetables are baking, prepare the pasta following the instructions on the package.
4. Take out the vegetables from the oven and mix the pasta to them. Sprinkle top with parmesan and basil leaves.

**NUTRITIONS:**
136 Calories, 3.2g Fat, 4g Protein

# 105. PITA WITH GREENS, FRIED ONIONS, AND BACON

**COOKING: 3'**     **PREPARATION: 8'**     **SERVES: 2**

## INGREDIENTS

» 2 pitas
» 3 ½ oz bacon
» 1 ½ oz red onion
» 1 bunch green salad
» 3 ½ oz tomatoes
» 2 cloves garlic
» Sea salt to taste
» Ground black pepper to taste
» 2 tbsp vegetable oil
» ½ lemon

## NUTRITIONS:

470 Calories, 21g Fat, 14.5g Protein

## DIRECTIONS

1. Cut onion and tomato into slices, finely chop the garlic.
2. Heat oil and fry the onion and bacon until golden brown.
3. Add garlic, fry for about a minute.
4. Put lettuce leaves on Pita, put tomatoes, fried onions, and bacon on top.
5. Before serving, sprinkle with lemon juice, salt, pepper to taste.

# CHAPTER 9
# BREAKFAST RECIPES PART 4

# 106. BANANA OATS

**COOKING: 0'**　　　**PREPARATION: 11'**　　　**SERVES: 2**

## INGREDIENTS

- » 1 banana, peeled and sliced
- » ¾ c. almond milk
- » ½ c. cold-brewed coffee
- » 2 pitted dates
- » 2 tbsps. cocoa powder
- » 1 c. rolled oats
- » 1 ½ tbsps. chia seeds

## DIRECTIONS

1. Using a blender, add in all ingredients.
2. Process well for 5 minutes and serve.

**NUTRITIONS:**
288 Calories, 4.4g Fat, 7.7g Protein

# 107. BREAKFAST SANDWICH

**COOKING: 20'**　　　**PREPARATION: 3'**　　　**SERVES: 4**

## INGREDIENTS

- » 4 multigrain sandwich thins
- » 4 tsps. olive oil
- » 4 eggs
- » 1 tbsp. rosemary, fresh
- » 2 c. baby spinach leaves, fresh
- » 1 tomato, sliced
- » 1 tbsp. of feta cheese
- » Pinch of kosher salt
- » Ground black pepper

## DIRECTIONS

1. Set oven to 375 F/190 C.
2. Brush the thins' sides with 2 tsps. of olive oil and set on a baking sheet.
3. Set in the oven and toast for 5 minutes or until the edges are lightly brown.
4. In a skillet, add in the rest of the olive oil and rosemary to heat over high heat.
5. Break and place whole eggs one at a time into the skillet.
6. Break yolks up with a spatula. Flip the egg and cook on another side until done. Remove eggs from heat.
7. Place toasted sandwich thins on 4 separate plates. Divine spinach among the thins.
8. Top each thin with two tomato slices, cooked egg, and 1 tbsp. of feta cheese.
9. Lightly sprinkle with salt and pepper for flavoring.
10. Place remaining sandwich thin halves over the top and they are ready to serve.

**NUTRITIONS:**
241 Calories, 12.2g Fat, 13g Protein

# 108. BREAKFAST COUSCOUS

**COOKING: 8'**   **PREPARATION: 9'**   **SERVES: 4**

## INGREDIENTS

- » **3 c. low-fat milk**
- » **1 c. whole-wheat couscous, uncooked**
- » **1 cinnamon stick**
- » **½ chopped apricot, dried**
- » **¼ c. currants, dried**
- » **6 tsps. brown sugar**
- » **¼ tsp. salt**
- » **4 tsps. melted butter**

## DIRECTIONS

1. Take a large saucepan and combine milk and cinnamon stick and heat over medium.
2. Heat for 3 minutes or until microbubbles forms around edges of the pan. Do not boil.
3. Remove from heat, stir in the couscous, apricots, currants, salt, and 4 tsps. brown sugar.
4. Wrap mixture and allow it to sit for 15 minutes. Remove and throw away the cinnamon stick.
5. Divide couscous among 4 bowls, and top each with 1 tsp. melted butter and ½ tsp. brown sugar. Ready to serve.

**NUTRITIONS:**
306 Calories, 6g Fat, 11g Protein

# 109. AVOCADO AND APPLE SMOOTHIE

**COOKING: 0'**   **PREPARATION: 6'**   **SERVES: 2**

## INGREDIENTS

- » 3 c. spinach
- » 1 cored green apple, chopped
- » 1 pitted avocado, peeled and chopped
- » 3 tbsps. chia seeds
- » 1 tsp. honey
- » 1 frozen banana, peeled
- » 2 c. coconut water

## DIRECTIONS

1. Using your blender, add in all the ingredients.
2. Process well for 5 minutes to obtain a smooth consistency and serve in glasses.

**NUTRITIONS:**
208 Calories, 10.1g Fat, 2.1g Protein

# 110. MINI FRITTATAS

**COOKING: 20'**  **PREPARATION: 9'**  **SERVES: 8**

## INGREDIENTS

- » 1 chopped yellow onion
- » 1 c. grated parmesan
- » 1 chopped yellow bell pepper
- » 1 chopped red bell pepper
- » 1 chopped zucchini
- » Salt and black pepper
- » A drizzle of olive oil
- » 8 whisked eggs
- » 2 tbsps. chopped chives

## DIRECTIONS

1. Set a pan over medium-high heat. Add in oil to warm. Stir in all ingredients except chives and eggs. Sauté for around 5 minutes.
2. Put the eggs on a muffin pan and top by the chives.
3. Set oven to 350 F/176 C. Place the muffin pan into the oven to bake for about 10 minutes.
4. Serve the eggs on a plate with sautéed vegetables.

**NUTRITIONS:**
55 Calories, 3g Fat, 4.2g Protein

# 111. SUN-DRIED TOMATOES OATMEAL

**COOKING: 4'**  **PREPARATION: 20'**  **SERVES: 4**

## INGREDIENTS

- » 3 c. water
- » 1 c. almond milk
- » 1 tbsp. olive oil
- » 1 c. steel-cut oats
- » ¼ c. chopped tomatoes, sun-dried
- » A pinch of red pepper flakes

## DIRECTIONS

1. Using a pan, add water and milk to mix. Set on medium heat and allow to boil.
2. Set up another pan on medium-high heat. Warm oil and add oats to cook for 2 minutes. Transfer to the first pan plus tomatoes then stir. Let simmer for approximately 20 minutes.
3. Set in serving bowls and top with red pepper flakes. Enjoy.

**NUTRITIONS:**
170 Calories, 17.8g Fat, 1.5g Protein

# 112. BREAKFAST EGG ON AVOCADO

**COOKING: 9'**         **PREPARATION: 15'**         **SERVES: 6**

## INGREDIENTS

- » 1 tsp. garlic powder
- » ½ tsp. sea salt
- » ¼ c. shredded Parmesan cheese
- » ¼ tsp. black pepper
- » 3 pitted avocados, halved
- » 6 eggs

## DIRECTIONS

1. Prep muffin tins and preheat the oven to 350 F/176 C.
2. Split the avocado. To ensure that the egg would fit inside the cavity of the avocado, lightly scrape off 1/3 of the meat.
3. Place avocado on a muffin tin to ensure that it faces with the top-up. Evenly season each avocado with pepper, salt, and garlic powder.
4. Add one egg on each avocado cavity and garnish tops with cheese. Set in your oven to bake until the egg white is set, about 15 minutes. Serve and enjoy.

**NUTRITIONS:**
252 Calories, 20g Fat, 14g Protein

# 113. BREKKY EGG- POTATO HASH

**COOKING: 8'**         **PREPARATION: 25'**         **SERVES: 2**

## INGREDIENTS

- » 1 zucchini, diced
- » ½ c. chicken broth
- » ½ lb. or 220 g cooked chicken
- » 1 tbsp. olive oil
- » 4 oz. or 113g shrimp
- » Salt and black pepper
- » 1 diced sweet potato
- » 2 eggs
- » ¼ tsp. cayenne pepper
- » 2 tsps. garlic powder
- » 1 c. fresh spinach

## DIRECTIONS

1. In a skillet, add the olive oil.
2. Fry the shrimp, cooked chicken and sweet potato for 2 minutes.
3. Add the cayenne pepper, garlic powder and toss for 4 minutes.
4. Add the zucchini and toss for another 3 minutes.
5. Whisk the eggs in a bowl and add to the skillet.
6. Season using salt and pepper. Cover with the lid.
7. Cook for 1 more minute and mix in the chicken broth.
8. Cover and cook for another 8 minutes on high heat.
9. Add the spinach, toss for 2 more minutes and serve.

**NUTRITIONS:**
200 Calories, 13.6g Fat, 7.5g Protein

# 114. BASIL AND TOMATO SOUP

**COOKING: 7'**　　　　**PREPARATION: 25'**　　　　**SERVES: 2**

## INGREDIENTS

- » 2 tbsps. vegetable broth
- » 1 minced garlic clove
- » ½ c. white onion
- » 1 chopped celery stalk
- » 1 chopped carrot
- » 3 c. tomatoes, chopped
- » Salt and pepper
- » 2 bay leaves
- » 1 ½ c. unsweetened almond milk
- » 1/3 c. basil leaves

## DIRECTIONS

1. Cook vegetable broth in a large saucepan over medium heat.
2. Add in garlic and onions and cook for 4 minutes.
3. Add in carrots and celery. Cook for 1 more minute.
4. Mix in the tomatoes and bring to a boil. Simmer for 15 minutes.
5. Add the almond milk, basil and bay leaves.
6. Season and serve.

**NUTRITIONS:**
213 Calories, 3.9g Fat, 6.9g Protein

# 115. BUTTERNUT SQUASH HUMMUS

**COOKING: 15'**　　　　**PREPARATION: 16'**　　　　**SERVES: 4**

## INGREDIENTS

- » 2 lbs. or 900 g seeded butternut squash, peeled
- » 1 tbsp. olive oil
- » ¼ c. tahini
- » 2 tbsps. lemon juice
- » 2 minced cloves garlic
- » Salt and pepper

## DIRECTIONS

1. Heat the oven to 300 F/148 C.
2. Coat the butternut squash with olive oil.
3. Set in a baking dish to bake for 15 minutes in the oven.
4. Once the squash is cooked, place in a food processor together with the rest of the ingredients.
5. Pulse until smooth.
6. Serve with carrots and celery sticks
7. For further use of place in individual containers, put a label and store it in the fridge.
8. Allow warming at room temperature before heating in the microwave oven.

**NUTRITIONS:**
115 Calories, 5.8g Fat, 2.5g Protein

# 116. SAVORY MUFFINS

**COOKING: 15'** | **PREPARATION: 9'** | **SERVES: 6**

## INGREDIENTS

- » 9 ham slices
- » 1/3 c. chopped spinach
- » ¼ c. crumbled feta cheese
- » ½ c. chopped roasted red peppers
- » Salt and black pepper
- » 1½ tbsps. basil pesto
- » 5 whisked eggs

## DIRECTIONS

1. Grease a muffin tin. Use 1 ½ ham slices to line each of the muffin molds.
2. Except for black pepper, salt, pesto, and eggs, divide the rest of the ingredients into your ham cups.
3. Using a bowl, whisk together the pepper, salt, pesto, and eggs. Pour your pepper mixture on top.
4. Set oven to 400 F/204 C and bake for about 15 minutes.
5. Serve immediately.

**NUTRITIONS:**
109 Calories, 6.7g Fat, 9.3g Protein

# 117. FARRO SALAD

**COOKING: 5'** | **PREPARATION: 7'** | **SERVES: 2**

## INGREDIENTS

- » 1 tbsp. olive oil
- » Salt and black pepper
- » 1 bunch baby spinach, chopped
- » 1 pitted avocado, peeled and chopped
- » 1 minced garlic clove
- » 2 c. cooked farro
- » ½ c. cherry tomatoes, cubed

## DIRECTIONS

1. Adjust your heat to medium. Set oil in a pan and heat.
2. Toss in the rest of the ingredients. Cook the mixture for approximately 5 minutes.
3. Set in serving plates and enjoy.

**NUTRITIONS:**
157 Calories, 13.7g Fat, 3.6g Protein

# 118. CRANBERRY AND DATES SQUARES

**COOKING: 9'**  **PREPARATION: 30'**  **SERVES: 10**

## INGREDIENTS

- » 12 pitted dates, chopped
- » 1 tsp. vanilla extract
- » ¼ c. honey
- » ½ c. rolled oats
- » ¾ c. dried cranberries
- » ¼ c. melted almond avocado oil
- » 1 c. chopped walnuts, roasted
- » ¼ c. pumpkin seeds

## DIRECTIONS

1. Using a bowl, stir in all ingredients to mix.
2. Line a parchment paper on a baking sheet. Press the mixture on the setup.
3. Set in your freezer for about 30 minutes. Slice into 10 squares and enjoy.

**NUTRITIONS:**
263 Calories, 13.4g Fat, 3.5g Protein

# 119. LENTILS AND CHEDDAR FRITTATA

**COOKING: 17'**  **PREPARATION: 4'**  **SERVES: 4**

## INGREDIENTS

- » 1 chopped red onion
- » 2 tbsps. olive oil
- » 1 c. boiled sweet potatoes, chopped
- » ¾ c. chopped ham
- » 4 whisked eggs
- » ¾ c. cooked lentils
- » 2 tbsps. Greek yogurt
- » Salt and black pepper
- » ½ c. halved cherry tomatoes,
- » ¾ c. grated cheddar cheese

## DIRECTIONS

1. Adjust your heat to medium and set a pan in place. Add in oil to heat. Stir in onion and allow to sauté for about 2 minutes.
2. Except for cheese and eggs, toss in the other ingredients and cook for 3 more minutes.
3. Add in the eggs, top with cheese. Cook for 10 more minutes while covered.
4. Slice the frittata, set in serving bowls and enjoy.

**NUTRITIONS:**
274 Calories, 17.36g Fat, 11.4g Protein

# 120. TUNA SANDWICH

**COOKING: 5'**　　　**PREPARATION: 9'**　　　**SERVES: 2**

## INGREDIENTS

- » 6 oz. canned tuna, drained and flaked
- » 1 pitted avocado, peeled and mashed
- » 4 whole-wheat bread slices
- » Pinch salt and black pepper
- » 1 tbsp. crumbled feta cheese
- » 1 c. baby spinach

## DIRECTIONS

1. Using a bowl, stir in pepper, salt, tuna, and cheese to mix.
2. To the bread slices, apply a spread of the mashed avocado.
3. Equally, divide the tuna mixture and spinach onto 2 of the slices. Top with the remaining 2 slices. Serve.

**NUTRITIONS:**
283 Calories, 11.2g Fat, 4.5g Protein

# CHAPTER 10
# MAIN DISH RECIPES

# 121. CHICKEN SHAWARMA

**COOKING: 15'**     **PREPARATION: 8'**     **SERVINGS: 8**

## INGREDIENTS

- » 2 lb. chicken breast, sliced into strips
- » 1 teaspoon paprika
- » 1 teaspoon ground cumin
- » 1/4 teaspoon granulated garlic
- » 1/2 teaspoon turmeric
- » 1/4 teaspoon ground allspice

## DIRECTION

1. Season the chicken with the spices, and a little salt and pepper.
2. Pour 1 cup chicken broth to the skillet.
3. Seal the skillet.
4. Choose poultry setting.
5. Cook for 15 minutes.
6. Release the pressure naturally. Serve with flatbread.

**NUTRITIONS:**
481 calories, 21g fats, 9g Protein

# 122. HONEY BALSAMIC CHICKEN

**COOKING: 30'**     **PREPARATION: 7'**     **SERVINGS: 5**

## INGREDIENTS

- » 1/4 cup honey
- » 1/2 cup balsamic vinegar
- » 1/4 cup soy sauce
- » 2 cloves garlic minced
- » 10 chicken drumsticks

## DIRECTIONS

1. Mix the honey, vinegar, soy sauce and garlic in a bowl.
2. Soak the chicken in the sauce for 30 minutes.
3. Cover the skillet.
4. Set it to manual.
5. Cook at high pressure for 10 minutes.
6. Release the pressure quickly.
7. Choose the sauté button to thicken the sauce.

**NUTRITIONS:**
517 calories, 26g fats, 10g Protein

# 123. GARLIC AND LEMON CHICKEN DISH

**COOKING: 10'**    **PREPARATION: 11'**    **SERVINGS: 4**

## INGREDIENTS

- » 2-3 pounds chicken breast
- » 1 teaspoon salt
- » 1 onion, diced
- » 1 tablespoon ghee
- » 5 garlic cloves, minced
- » ½ cup organic chicken broth
- » 1 teaspoon dried parsley
- » 1 large lemon, juiced
- » 3-4 teaspoon arrowroot flour

## DIRECTIONS

1. Set your skillet to Sauté mode. Add diced up onion and cooking fat
2. Allow the onions to cook for 5 -10 minutes
3. Add the rest of the ingredients except arrowroot flour
4. Lock up the lid and set the skillet to poultry mode. Cook until the timer runs out
5. Allow the pressure to release naturally
6. Once done, remove ¼ cup of the sauce from the skillet and add arrowroot to make a slurry
7. Add the slurry to the skillet to make the gravy thick. Keep stirring well. Serve!

**NUTRITIONS:**
511 calories, 29g fats, 11g Protein

# 124. HIGH-QUALITY BELIZEAN CHICKEN STEW

**COOKING: 23'**    **PREPARATION: 7'**    **SERVINGS: 4**

## INGREDIENTS

- » 4 whole chicken
- » 1 tablespoon coconut oil
- » 2 tablespoons achiote seasoning
- » 2 tablespoons white vinegar
- » 3 tablespoons Worcestershire sauce
- » 1 cup yellow onion, sliced
- » 3 garlic cloves, sliced
- » 1 teaspoon ground cumin
- » 1 teaspoon dried oregano
- » ½ teaspoon black pepper
- » 2 cups chicken stock

## DIRECTIONS

1. Take a large sized bowl and add achiote paste, vinegar, Worcestershire sauce, oregano, cumin and pepper. Mix well and add chicken pieces and rub the marinade all over them
2. Allow the chicken to sit overnight. Set your skillet to Sauté mode and add coconut oil
3. Once hot, cook chicken pieces to the skillet in batches. Remove the seared chicken and transfer them to a plate
4. Add onions, garlic to the skillet and Sauté for 2-3 minutes. Add chicken pieces back to the skillet
5. Pour chicken broth to the bowl with marinade and stir well. Add the mixture to the skillet
6. Seal up the lid and cook for about 20 minutes at high pressure
7. Once done, release the pressure naturally. Season with a bit of salt and serve!

**NUTRITIONS:**
517 calories, 21g fats, 9g Protein

# 125. CRISPY MEDITERRANEAN CHICKEN THIGHS

**COOKING: 35'**  **PREPARATION: 9'**  **SERVINGS: 6**

## INGREDIENTS

- » 2 tablespoons extra-virgin olive oil
- » 2 teaspoons dried rosemary
- » 1½ teaspoons ground cumin
- » 1½ teaspoons ground coriander
- » ¾ teaspoon dried oregano
- » 1/8 teaspoon salt
- » 6 chicken thighs (about 3 pounds)

## DIRECTION

1. Preheat the oven to 450°F. Line a baking sheet with parchment paper.
2. Place the olive oil and spices into a large bowl and mix together, making a paste. Add the chicken and mix together until evenly coated. Place on the prepared baking sheet.
3. Bake for 30 to 35 minutes.

**NUTRITIONS:**
491 calories, 22g fats, 10g Protein

# 126. GREEK PENNE AND CHICKEN

**COOKING: 9'**  **PREPARATION: 11'**  **SERVINGS: 4**

## INGREDIENTS

- » 16-ounce package of Penne Pasta
- » 1-pound Chicken Breast Halves
- » 1/2 cup of Chopped Red Onion
- » 1 1/2 tablespoons of Butter
- » 2 cloves of Minced Garlic
- » 14-ounce can of Artichoke Hearts
- » 1 Chopped Tomato
- » 3 tablespoons of Chopped Fresh Parsley
- » 1/2 cup of Crumbled Feta Cheese
- » 2 tablespoons of Lemon Juice
- » 1 teaspoon of Dried Oregano
- » Ground Black Pepper
- » Salt

## DIRECTIONS

1. In a large sized skillet over a medium-high heat, melt your butter. Add your garlic and onion. Cook approximately 2 minutes. Add your chopped chicken and continue to cook until golden brown. Should take approximately 5 to 6 minutes. Stir occasionally.
2. Reduce your heat to a medium-low. Drain and chop your artichoke hearts. Add them to your skillet along with your chopped tomato, fresh parsley, feta cheese, dried oregano, lemon juice, and drained pasta. Cook for 2 to 3.
3. Season. Serve!

**NUTRITIONS:**
411 calories, 20g fats, 8g Protein

# 127. YOGURT-MARINATED CHICKEN KEBABS

**COOKING: 20'**          **PREPARATION:31'**          **SERVINGS: 4**

## INGREDIENTS

- » **½ cup plain Greek yogurt**
- » **1 tablespoon lemon juice**
- » **½ teaspoon ground cumin**
- » **½ teaspoon ground coriander**
- » **½ teaspoon kosher salt**
- » **¼ teaspoon cayenne pepper**
- » **1½ pound chicken breast**

**NUTRITIONS:**

391 calories, 22g fats, 9g Protein

## DIRECTIONS

1. In a huge bowl, mix yogurt, lemon juice, cumin, coriander, salt, and cayenne pepper. Mix together thoroughly and then add the chicken. Marinate for at least 30 minutes, and up to overnight in the refrigerator.

2. Bake for 20 minutes, turning the chicken over once halfway through the cooking time.

# 128. BRAISED CHICKEN WITH ROASTED BELL PEPPERS

**COOKING: 54'**          **PREPARATION:7'**          **SERVINGS: 8**

## INGREDIENTS

- » 2 tablespoons extra-virgin olive oil
- » 4 pounds bone-in chicken, breast and thighs, skin removed
- » 1½ teaspoon kosher salt, divided
- » ¼ teaspoon freshly ground black pepper
- » 1 onion, julienned
- » 6 garlic cloves, sliced
- » 1 cup white wine
- » 2 pounds tomatoes, chopped
- » ¼ teaspoon red pepper flakes
- » 3 bell peppers
- » 1/3 cup fresh parsley, chopped
- » 1 tablespoon lemon juice

## DIRECTIONS

1. Cook olive oil in a large Dutch oven or skillet over medium-high heat. Season the chicken with ¾ teaspoon of the salt and the pepper. Add half the chicken to the skillet and brown about 2 minutes on each side. Transfer to a plate, and repeat with the remaining half of the chicken.

2. Decrease heat to medium and add the onion. Sauté for about 5 minutes. Sauté garlic for 30 seconds. Add the wine, increase the heat to medium-high, and bring to a boil to deglaze the skillet, scraping up any brown bits on the bottom. Reduce the liquid by half, about 5 to 7 minutes. Add the tomatoes, red pepper flakes, and the remaining ¾ teaspoon salt and mix well. Add the chicken back to the skillet, cover, reduce the heat to low, and simmer for 40 minutes, turning the chicken halfway through the cooking time.

3. While the chicken cooks, prepare the roasted bell peppers. If you are using raw peppers, please refer to the roasting method here. If using jarred roasted red peppers, move on to step 4.

4. Chop the bell peppers into 1-inch pieces and set aside.

5. Once the chicken is cooked through, transfer it to a plate.

6. Increase the heat to high and bring the mixture to a boil. Reduce by half, about 10 minutes

7. Once is cool enough to handle, remove the meat from the bone and return it to the skillet with the bell peppers. Simmer 5 minutes to heat through. Stir in the parsley and lemon juice.

**NUTRITIONS:**

501 calories, 25g fats, 6g Protein

# 129. CHICKEN STEW WITH ARTICHOKES, CAPERS, AND OLIVES

**COOKING: 33'**     **PREPARATION:6'**     **SERVINGS: 4**

## INGREDIENTS

- » 1½ pounds boneless, skinless chicken thighs
- » 1 teaspoon kosher salt, divided
- » ¼ teaspoon freshly ground black pepper
- » 2 tablespoons olive oil
- » 1 onion, julienned
- » 4 garlic cloves, sliced
- » 1 teaspoon ground turmeric
- » 1 teaspoon ground cumin
- » ½ teaspoon ground coriander
- » ½ teaspoon ground cinnamon
- » ¼ teaspoon red pepper flakes
- » 1 dried bay leaf
- » 1¼ cups no-salt-added chicken stock
- » ¼ cup white wine vinegar
- » 2 tablespoons lemon juice
- » 1 tablespoon lemon zest
- » 1 (14-ounce) can artichoke hearts, drained
- » ¼ cup olives, pitted and chopped
- » 1 teaspoon capers, rinsed and chopped
- » 1 tablespoon fresh mint, chopped
- » 1 tablespoon fresh parsley, chopped

## DIRECTION

1. Season the chicken with ½ teaspoon of salt and pepper.
2. Cook olive oil in a large skillet over medium heat. sauté chicken for 3 minutes per side. Transfer to a plate and set aside.
3. Add the onion to the same pan and sauté until translucent, about 5 minutes. Add the garlic and sauté 30 seconds. Add the remaining ½ teaspoon salt, the turmeric, cumin, coriander, cinnamon, red pepper flakes, and bay leaf and sauté 30 seconds.
4. Add ¼ cup of the chicken stock and increase the heat to medium-high to deglaze the pan, scraping up any brown bits on the bottom. Add the remaining 1 cup stock, the lemon juice, and lemon zest. Cover, lower the heat to low, and simmer for 10 minutes.
5. Add the artichokes, olives, and capers and mix well. Add the reserved chicken and nestle it into the mixture. Simmer for 15 minutes. Garnish with the mint and parsley.

**NUTRITIONS:**
601 calories, 30g fats, 12g Protein

# 130. ZAATAR CHICKEN TENDERS

**COOKING: 15'**     **PREPARATION:8'**     **SERVINGS: 4**

## INGREDIENTS

- » Olive oil cooking spray
- » 1-pound chicken tenders
- » 1½ tablespoons zaatar
- » ½ teaspoon kosher salt
- » ¼ teaspoon freshly ground black pepper

## DIRECTIONS

1. In a large bowl, combine the chicken, zaatar, salt, and black pepper.
2. Mix together well, covering the chicken tenders fully.
3. Arrange in a single layer on the baking sheet and bake for 15 minutes, turning the chicken over once halfway through the cooking time.

**NUTRITIONS:**
304 calories, 19g fats, 7g Protein

# 131. LEMON CHICKEN WITH ARTICHOKES AND CRISPY KALE

**COOKING: 35'**           **PREPARATION:9'**           **SERVINGS: 4**

## INGREDIENTS

» **3 tablespoons extra-virgin olive oil, divided**
» **2 tablespoons lemon juice**
» **Zest of 1 lemon**
» **2 garlic cloves, minced**
» **2 teaspoons dried rosemary**
» **¼ teaspoon freshly ground black pepper**
» **1½ pounds boneless, skinless chicken breast**
» **2 (14-ounce) cans artichoke hearts, drained**
» **1 bunch (about 6 ounces) Lacinato kale**

## DIRECTIONS

1. In a bowl, combine 2 tablespoons of the olive oil, the lemon juice, lemon zest, garlic, rosemary, salt, and black pepper. Mix well and then add the chicken and artichokes. Marinate for at least 30 minutes, and up to 4 hours in the refrigerator.

2. Pull out chicken and artichokes from the marinade and spread them in a single layer on the baking sheet. Roast for 15 minutes, flip over, and roast another 15 minutes. Remove the baking sheet and put the chicken, artichokes, and juices on a platter or large plate. Tent with foil to keep warm.

3. Change the oven temperature to broil. In a large bowl, combine the kale with the remaining 1 tablespoon of the olive oil. Arrange the kale on the baking sheet and broil until golden brown in skillets and as crispy as you like, about 3 to 5 minutes.

4. Place the kale on top of the chicken and artichokes.

**NUTRITIONS:**
497 calories, 24g fats, 11g Protein

# 132. SUMAC CHICKEN WITH CAULIFLOWER AND CARROTS

**COOKING: 40'**           **PREPARATION:8'**           **SERVINGS: 4**

## INGREDIENTS

» 3 tablespoons extra-virgin olive oil
» 1 tablespoon ground sumac
» 1 teaspoon kosher salt
» ½ teaspoon ground cumin
» ¼ teaspoon freshly ground black pepper
» 1½ pounds bone-in chicken thighs and drumsticks
» 1 medium cauliflower, cut into 1-inch florets
» 2 carrots
» 1 lemon, cut into ¼-inch-thick slices
» 1 tablespoon lemon juice
» ¼ cup fresh parsley, chopped
» ¼ cup fresh mint, chopped

## DIRECTIONS

1. Set the oven to 425°F. Prep a baking sheet using foil.

2. In a large bowl, scourge the olive oil, sumac, salt, cumin, and black pepper. Add the chicken, cauliflower, and carrots and toss until thoroughly coated with the oil and spice mixture.

3. Arrange the cauliflower, carrots, and chicken in a single layer on the baking sheet. Top with the lemon slices. Roast for 40 minutes, tossing the vegetables once halfway through. Sprinkle the lemon juice over the chicken and vegetables and garnish with the parsley and mint.

**NUTRITIONS:**
401 calories, 24g fat, 11g Protein

# 133. HARISSA YOGURT CHICKEN THIGHS

**COOKING: 23'**     **PREPARATION:9'**     **SERVINGS: 4**

## INGREDIENTS

- » ½ cup plain Greek yogurt
- » 2 tablespoons harissa
- » 1 tablespoon lemon juice
- » ¼ teaspoon freshly ground black pepper
- » 1½ pounds boneless

## DIRECTION

1. Mix yogurt, harissa, lemon juice, salt, and black pepper. Add the chicken and mix together. Marinate for at least 15 minutes, and up to 4 hours in the refrigerator.
2. Remove the chicken thighs from the marinade and arrange in a single layer on the baking sheet. Roast for 20 minutes, turning the chicken over halfway.
3. Change the oven temperature to broil. Broil the chicken until golden brown in skillets, 2 to 3 minutes.

**NUTRITIONS:**
391 calories, 20g fats, 9g Protein

# 134. BRAISED CHICKEN WITH WILD MUSHROOMS

**COOKING: 28'**     **PREPARATION:11'**     **SERVINGS: 4**

## INGREDIENTS

- » 1/4 cup dried porcini or morel mushrooms
- » 1/4 cup olive oil
- » 2–3 slices low-salt turkey bacon, chopped
- » 1 chicken, cut into pieces
- » 1 small celery stalk, diced
- » 1 small dried red chili, chopped
- » 1/4 cup vermouth or white wine
- » 1/4 cup tomato puree
- » 1/4 cup low-salt chicken stock
- » 1/2 teaspoon arrowroot
- » 1/4 cup flat-leaf parsley, chopped
- » 4 teaspoons fresh thyme, chopped
- » 3 teaspoons fresh tarragon

## DIRECTIONS

1. Soak mushrooms onto boiling water over them for 20 minutes to soften.
2. Drain and chop, reserving the liquid.
3. Heat the olive oil on medium heat. Add the bacon and cook until browned and slightly crisp. Drain the bacon on a paper towel.
4. Season the chicken, and add to the oil and bacon drippings.
5. Cook for 10–15 minutes.
6. Add the celery and the chopped chili, and cook for 3–5 minutes.
7. Deglaze the pan with the wine, using a wooden spoon to scrape up the brown bits stuck to the bottom.
8. Add the tomato puree, chicken stock, arrowroot, and mushroom liquid. Cover and simmer on low for 45 minutes.
9. Add the fresh chopped herbs and cook an additional 10 minutes, until the sauce thickens.
10. Season with freshly ground pepper and sea salt to taste. Serve with wilted greens or crunchy green beans.

**NUTRITIONS:**
501 calories, 21g fats, 12g Protein

# 135. BRAISED DUCK WITH FENNEL ROOT

**COOKING: 45'**  **PREPARATION:13'**  **SERVINGS: 6**

## INGREDIENTS

- » **1/4 cup olive oil**
- » **1 whole duck, cleaned**
- » **3 teaspoon fresh rosemary**
- » **2 garlic cloves, minced**
- » **3 fennel bulbs, cut into chunks**
- » **1/2 cup sherry**

## DIRECTIONS

1. Preheat the oven to 375 degrees.
2. Cook olive oil in a Dutch oven.
3. Season the duck, including the cavity, with the rosemary, garlic, sea salt, and freshly ground pepper.
4. Place the duck in the oil, and cook it for 10–15 minutes, turning as necessary to brown all sides.
5. Add the fennel bulbs and cook an additional 5 minutes.
6. Pour the sherry over the duck and fennel, cover and cook in the oven for 30–45 minutes, or until internal temperature of the duck is 140–150 degrees at its thickest part.
7. Allow duck to sit for 15 minutes before serving.

## NUTRITIONS:

571 calories, 24g fats, 15g Protein

# CHAPTER 11
# MAIN DISH RECIPES PART 2

# 136. TURKEY BURGERS WITH MANGO SALSA

**COOKING: 10'**          **PREPARATION:15'**          **SERVES: 6**

## INGREDIENTS

- » 1½ pounds ground turkey breast
- » 1 teaspoon sea salt, divided
- » ¼ teaspoon freshly ground black pepper
- » 2 tablespoons extra-virgin olive oil
- » 2 mangos, peeled, pitted, and cubed
- » ½ red onion, finely chopped
- » Juice of 1 lime
- » 1 garlic clove, minced
- » ½ jalapeño pepper, seeded and finely minced
- » 2 tablespoons chopped fresh cilantro leaves

## DIRECTION

1. Form the turkey breast into 4 patties and season with ½ teaspoon of sea salt and the pepper.

2. In a nonstick skillet over medium-high heat, heat the olive oil until it shimmers.

3. Add the turkey patties and cook for about 5 minutes per side until browned.

4. While the patties cook, mix together the mango, red onion, lime juice, garlic, jalapeño, cilantro, and remaining ½ teaspoon of sea salt in a small bowl. Spoon the salsa over the turkey patties and serve.

**NUTRITIONS:**
384 calories, 3g Protein, 16g Fat

# 137. HERB-ROASTED TURKEY BREAST

**COOKING: 90'**          **PREPARATION:15'**          **SERVES: 6**

## INGREDIENTS

- » 2 tablespoons extra-virgin olive oil
- » 4 garlic cloves, minced
- » Zest of 1 lemon
- » 1 tablespoon fresh thyme leaves
- » 1 tablespoon fresh rosemary leaves
- » 2 tablespoons fresh Italian parsley leaves
- » 1 teaspoon ground mustard
- » 1 teaspoon sea salt
- » ¼ teaspoon black pepper
- » 1 (6-pound) bone-in, skin-on turkey breast
- » 1 cup dry white wine

## DIRECTION

1. Preheat the oven to 325°F.

2. Scourge olive oil, garlic, lemon zest, thyme, rosemary, parsley, mustard, sea salt, and pepper. Lay out herb mixture evenly over the surface of the turkey breast, and loosen the skin and rub underneath as well. Place the turkey breast in a roasting pan on a rack, skin-side up.

3. Pour the wine in the pan. Roast for 1 to 1½ hour. Take out from the oven and rest for 20 minutes, tented with aluminum foil to keep it warm, before carving.

**NUTRITIONS:**
392 calories, 84 Protein, 6g Fat

# 138. CHICKEN SAUSAGE AND PEPPERS

**COOKING: 20'**          **PREPARATION:10'**          **SERVES: 6**

## INGREDIENTS

» 2 tablespoons extra-virgin olive oil
» 6 Italian chicken sausage links
» 1 onion
» 1 red bell pepper
» 1 green bell pepper
» 3 garlic cloves, minced
» ½ cup dry white wine
» ½ teaspoon sea salt
» ¼ teaspoon freshly ground black pepper
» Pinch red pepper flakes

## DIRECTION

1. In a skillet at medium-high heat, cook olive oil.

2. Add the sausages and cook for 5 to 7 minutes, turning occasionally, until browned, and they reach an internal temperature of 165°F. With tongs, remove the sausage from the pan and set aside on a platter, tented with aluminum foil to keep warm.

3. Put skillet back to the heat and add the onion, red bell pepper, and green bell pepper. Cook for 5 to 7 minutes.

4. Cook garlic 30 seconds, stirring constantly.

5. Stir in the wine, sea salt, pepper, and red pepper flakes. Scrape and fold in any browned bits from the bottom. Simmer for about 4 minutes more. Spoon the peppers over the sausages and serve.

**NUTRITIONS:**
173 Calories, 22g Protein, 5g Fat

# 139. CHICKEN PICCATA

**COOKING: 15'**          **PREPARATION:10'**          **SERVES: 6**

## INGREDIENTS

» ½ cup whole-wheat flour
» ½ teaspoon sea salt
» 1/8 teaspoon freshly ground black pepper
» 1½ pounds boneless
» 3 tablespoons extra-virgin olive oil
» 1 cup unsalted chicken broth
» ½ cup dry white wine
» Juice of 1 lemon
» Zest of 1 lemon
» ¼ cup capers, drained and rinsed
» ¼ cup chopped fresh parsley leaves

## DIRECTION

1. In a shallow dish, whisk the flour, sea salt, and pepper. Dredge the chicken in the flour and tap off any excess.

2. In a pan over medium-high heat, cook olive oil.

3. Add the chicken and cook for about 4 minutes. Remove the chicken from the pan and set aside, tented with aluminum foil to keep warm.

4. Return back to the heat and mix broth, wine, lemon juice, and lemon zest, and capers. Simmer for 3 to 4 minutes, stirring. Remove the skillet from the heat and return the chicken to the pan. Turn to coat. Stir in the parsley and serve.

**NUTRITIONS:**
153 Calories, 8g Protein, 9g Fat

# 140. ONE-PAN TUSCAN CHICKEN

**COOKING: 25'**  **PREPARATION:10'**  **SERVES: 6**

## INGREDIENTS

» ¼ cup extra-virgin olive oil, divided
» 1-pound boneless chicken
» 1 onion
» 1 red bell pepper
» 3 garlic cloves
» ½ cup dry white wine
» 2 (14-ounce) can tomatoes
» 1 (14-ounce) can white beans
» 1 tablespoon dried Italian seasoning
» ½ teaspoon sea salt
» 1/8 teaspoon freshly ground black pepper
» 1/8 teaspoon red pepper flakes
» ¼ cup chopped fresh basil leaves

## DIRECTION

1. In a huge skillet over medium-high heat, preheat 2 tablespoons of olive oil.
2. Add the chicken and cook for about 6 minutes, stirring. Take out the chicken and set aside on a platter, tented with aluminum foil to keep warm.
3. Return the skillet to the heat and heat the remaining 2 tablespoons of olive oil.
4. Add the onion and red bell pepper. Cook for about 5 minutes.
5. Cook garlic for 30 seconds.
6. Stir in the wine. Cook for 1 minute, stirring.
7. Add the crushed and chopped tomatoes, white beans, Italian seasoning, sea salt, pepper, and red pepper flakes. Bring to a simmer and reduce the heat to medium. Cook for 5 minutes, stirring occasionally.
8. Take chicken and any juices that have collected back to the skillet. Cook for 1 to 2 minutes. Pull out from the heat and stir in the basil before serving.

## NUTRITIONS:
271 Calories, 14g Protein, 0.1g Fat

# 141. CHICKEN KAPAMA

**COOKING: 2 HOURS**  **PREPARATION:10'**  **SERVES: 4**

## INGREDIENTS

» 1 (32-ounce) can chopped tomatoes
» ¼ cup dry white wine
» 2 tablespoons tomato paste
» 3 tablespoons extra-virgin olive oil
» ¼ teaspoon red pepper flakes
» 1 teaspoon ground allspice
» ½ teaspoon dried oregano
» 2 whole cloves
» 1 cinnamon stick
» ½ teaspoon sea salt
» 1/8 teaspoon black pepper
» 4 boneless, skinless chicken breast halves

## DIRECTION

1. In pot over medium-high heat, mix the tomatoes, wine, tomato paste, olive oil, red pepper flakes, allspice, oregano, cloves, cinnamon stick, sea salt, and pepper. Bring to a simmer, stirring occasionally. Adjust heat to medium-low and simmer for 30 minutes, stirring occasionally. Remove and discard the whole cloves and cinnamon stick from the sauce and let the sauce cool.
2. Preheat the oven to 350°F.
3. Situate chicken in a 9-by-13-inch baking dish. Drizzle sauce over the chicken and cover the pan with aluminum foil. Bake for 45 minutes.

## NUTRITIONS:
220 Calories, 8g Protein, 14g Fat

# 142. SPINACH AND FETA-STUFFED CHICKEN BREASTS

**COOKING: 45'**     **PREPARATION:10'**     **SERVES: 4**

## INGREDIENTS

- » 2 tablespoons extra-virgin olive oil
- » 1-pound fresh baby spinach
- » 3 garlic cloves, minced
- » Zest of 1 lemon
- » ½ teaspoon sea salt
- » 1/8 teaspoon freshly ground black pepper
- » ½ cup crumbled feta cheese
- » 4 chicken breast halves

## DIRECTION

1. Preheat the oven to 350°F.
2. Preheat oil and skillet over medium-high heat
3. Cook spinach for 3 to 4 minutes.
4. Cook garlic, lemon zest, sea salt, and pepper. Cool slightly and mix in the cheese.
5. Spread the spinach and cheese mixture in an even layer over the chicken pieces and roll the breast around the filling. Hold closed with toothpicks or butcher's twine. Place the breasts in a 9-by-13-inch baking dish and bake for 30 to 40 minutes. Take away from the oven and let rest for 5 minutes before slicing and serving.

**NUTRITIONS:**
263 Calories, 17g Protein, 20g Fat

# 143. ROSEMARY BAKED CHICKEN DRUMSTICKS

**COOKING: 1 HOUR**     **PREPARATION:5'**     **SERVES: 6**

## INGREDIENTS

- » 2 tablespoons chopped fresh rosemary leaves
- » 1 teaspoon garlic powder
- » ½ teaspoon sea salt
- » 1/8 teaspoon freshly ground black pepper
- » Zest of 1 lemon
- » 12 chicken drumsticks

## DIRECTION

1. Preheat the oven to 350°F.
2. Blend rosemary, garlic powder, sea salt, pepper, and lemon zest.
3. Situate drumsticks in a 9-by-13-inch baking dish and sprinkle with the rosemary mixture. Bake for about 1 hour.

**NUTRITIONS:**
163 Calories, 26g Protein, 6g Fat

# 144. CHICKEN WITH ONIONS, POTATOES, FIGS, AND CARROTS

**COOKING: 45'**    **PREPARATION:5'**    **SERVES: 4**

## INGREDIENTS

- » 2 cups fingerling potatoes, halved
- » 4 fresh figs, quartered
- » 2 carrots, julienned
- » 2 tablespoons extra-virgin olive oil
- » 1 teaspoon sea salt, divided
- » ¼ teaspoon freshly ground black pepper
- » 4 chicken leg-thigh quarters
- » 2 tablespoons chopped fresh parsley leaves

## DIRECTION

1. Preheat the oven to 425°F.
2. In a small bowl, toss the potatoes, figs, and carrots with the olive oil, ½ teaspoon of sea salt, and the pepper. Spread in a 9-by-13-inch baking dish.
3. Rub chicken with the remaining ½ teaspoon of sea salt. Place it on top of the vegetables. Bake for 35 to 45 minutes.
4. Sprinkle with the parsley and serve.

**NUTRITIONS:**
429 Calories, 52g Protein, 12g Fat

# 145. CHICKEN GYROS WITH TZATZIKI

**COOKING: 80'**    **PREPARATION:10'**    **SERVES: 6**

## INGREDIENTS

- » 1-pound ground chicken breast
- » 1 onion
- » 2 tablespoons dried rosemary
- » 1 tablespoon dried marjoram
- » 6 garlic cloves, minced
- » ½ teaspoon sea salt
- » ¼ teaspoon freshly ground black pepper
- » Tzatziki Sauce

## DIRECTION

1. Preheat the oven to 350°F.
2. In a stand mixer, blend chicken, onion, rosemary, marjoram, garlic, sea salt, and pepper.
3. Press the mixture into a loaf pan. Bake for about 1 hour. Pull out from the oven and set aside for 20 minutes before slicing.
4. Slice the gyro and spoon the tzatziki sauce over the top.

**NUTRITIONS:**
289 Calories, 50g Protein, 1g Fat

# 146. EGGPLANT CASSEROLE

**COOKING: 45'**　　　**PREPARATION:10'**　　　**SERVES: 8**

## INGREDIENTS

» 5 tablespoons extra-virgin olive oil
» 1 eggplant
» 1 onion
» 1 green bell pepper
» 1-pound ground turkey
» 3 garlic cloves, minced
» 2 tablespoons tomato paste
» 1 (14-ounce) can chopped tomatoes
» 1 tablespoon Italian seasoning
» 2 teaspoons Worcestershire sauce
» 1 teaspoon dried oregano
» ½ teaspoon ground cinnamon
» 1 cup unsweetened nonfat plain Greek yogurt
» 1 egg, beaten
» ¼ teaspoon freshly ground black pepper
» ¼ teaspoon ground nutmeg
» ¼ cup grated Parmesan cheese
» 2 tablespoons chopped fresh parsley leaves

## DIRECTION

1. Preheat the oven to 400°F.
2. Preheat skillet over medium-high heat, pour 3 tablespoons
3. Add the eggplant slices and brown for 3 to 4 minutes per side. Transfer to paper towels to drain.
4. Return to the heat and pour remaining 2 tablespoons of olive oil. Add the onion and green bell pepper. Cook for 5 minutes. Remove from the pan and set aside.
5. Put back to the heat and add the turkey. Cook for about 5 minutes
6. Cook garlic.
7. Stir in the tomato paste, tomatoes, Italian seasoning, Worcestershire sauce, oregano, and cinnamon. Return the onion and bell pepper to the pan. Cook for 5 minutes, stirring.
8. Scourge yogurt, egg, pepper, nutmeg, and cheese.
9. In a 9-by-13-inch baking dish, spread half the meat mixture. Layer with half the eggplant. Add the remaining meat mixture and the remaining eggplant. Spread with the yogurt mixture. Bake for about 20 minutes.

## NUTRITIONS:

338 Calories, 28g Protein, 20g Fat

# 147. DIJON AND HERB PORK TENDERLOIN

**COOKING: 30'**　　　**PREPARATION:10'**　　　**SERVES: 6**

## INGREDIENTS

» ½ cup fresh Italian parsley leaves
» 3 tablespoons fresh rosemary leaves
» 3 tablespoons fresh thyme leaves
» 3 tablespoons Dijon mustard
» 1 tablespoon extra-virgin olive oil
» 4 garlic cloves, minced
» ½ teaspoon sea salt
» ¼ teaspoon freshly ground black pepper
» 1 (1½-pound) pork tenderloin

## DIRECTION

1. Preheat the oven to 400°F.
2. In a blender, pulse parsley, rosemary, thyme, mustard, olive oil, garlic, sea salt, and pepper. Spread the mixture evenly over the pork and place it on a rimmed baking sheet.
3. Bake for about 20 minutes. Remove from the oven and set aside for 10 minutes before slicing and serving.

## NUTRITIONS:

393 Calories, 74g Protein, 12g Fat

# 148. STEAK WITH RED WINE-MUSHROOM SAUCE

**COOKING: 20'**　　　　**PREPARATION:10'**　　　　**SERVES: 4**

## INGREDIENTS

- » For marinade and steak
- » 1 cup dry red wine
- » 3 garlic cloves, minced
- » 2 tablespoons extra-virgin olive oil
- » 1 tablespoon low-sodium soy sauce
- » 1 tablespoon dried thyme
- » 1 teaspoon Dijon mustard
- » 2 tablespoons extra-virgin olive oil
- » 1½ pounds skirt steak
- » For mushroom sauce
- » 2 tablespoons extra-virgin olive oil
- » 1-pound cremini mushrooms
- » ½ teaspoon sea salt
- » 1 teaspoon dried thyme
- » 1/8 teaspoon black pepper
- » 2 garlic cloves, minced
- » 1 cup dry red wine

## DIRECTION

1. For marinade and steak
2. In a small bowl, whisk the wine, garlic, olive oil, soy sauce, thyme, and mustard. Pour into a resealable bag and add the steak. Refrigerate the steak to marinate for 4 to 8 hours. Remove the steak from the marinade and pat it dry with paper towels.
3. In a big skillet over medium-high heat, warm up olive oil.
4. Cook steak for 4 minutes per side. Pull out steak from the skillet and put it on a plate tented with aluminum foil to keep warm, while you prepare the mushroom sauce.
5. When the mushroom sauce is ready, slice the steak against the grain into ½-inch-thick slices.
6. For mushroom sauce
7. Preheat skillet over medium-high heat, heat the olive oil.
8. Add the mushrooms, sea salt, thyme, and pepper. Cook for about 6 minutes.
9. Cook garlic for 30 seconds.
10. Stir in the wine, and use the side of a wooden spoon to scrape and fold in any browned bits from the bottom of the skillet. Cook for about 4 minutes. Serve the mushrooms spooned over the steak.

**NUTRITIONS:**

405 Calories, 33g Protein, 22g Fat

# 149. GREEK MEATBALLS

**COOKING: 25'**　　　　**PREPARATION:20'**　　　　**SERVES: 4**

## INGREDIENTS

- » 2 whole-wheat bread slices
- » 1¼ pounds ground turkey
- » 1 egg
- » ¼ cup seasoned whole-wheat bread crumbs
- » 3 garlic cloves, minced
- » ¼ red onion, grated
- » ¼ cup chopped fresh Italian parsley leaves
- » 2 tablespoons chopped fresh mint leaves
- » 2 tablespoons chopped fresh oregano leaves
- » ½ teaspoon sea salt
- » ¼ teaspoon freshly ground black pepper

## DIRECTION

1. Prep baking sheet with foil.
2. Run the bread under water to wet it, and squeeze out any excess. Tear the wet bread into small pieces and place it in a medium bowl.
3. Add the turkey, egg, bread crumbs, garlic, red onion, parsley, mint, oregano, sea salt, and pepper. Mix well. Form the mixture into ¼-cup-size balls. Place the meatballs on the prepared sheet and bake for about 25 minutes

**NUTRITIONS:**

350 Calories, 42g Protein, 18g Fat

# 150. LAMB WITH STRING BEANS

## COOKING: 1 HOUR          PREPARATION:10'          SERVES: 6

## INGREDIENTS

- » ¼ cup extra-virgin olive oil
- » 6 lamb chops
- » 1 teaspoon sea salt
- » ½ teaspoon black pepper
- » 2 tablespoons tomato paste
- » 1½ cups hot water
- » 1-pound green beans
- » 1 onion
- » 2 tomatoes

## DIRECTION

1. In a skillet at medium-high heat, pour 2 tablespoons of olive oil.

2. Season the lamb chops with ½ teaspoon of sea salt and 1/8 teaspoon of pepper. Cook the lamb in the hot oil for about 4 minutes. Transfer the meat to a platter and set aside.

3. Put back to the heat then put the 2 tablespoons of olive oil. Heat until it shimmers.

4. Blend tomato paste in the hot water. Mix to the hot skillet along with the green beans, onion, tomatoes, and the remaining ½ teaspoon of sea salt and ¼ teaspoon of pepper. Bring to a simmer.

5. Return the lamb chops to the pan. Bring to a boil and reduce the heat to medium-low. Simmer for 45 minutes until the beans are soft, adding additional water as needed to adjust the thickness of the sauce.

## NUTRITIONS:

439 Calories, 50g Protein, 22g Fat

# CHAPTER 12
## MAIN DISH RECIPES PART 3

# 151. GREEK LAMB CHOP

**COOKING: 8'**     **PREPARATION:10'**     **SERVES: 8**

## INGREDIENTS

- » 8 trimmed lamb loin chops
- » 2 tbsp lemon juice
- » 1 tbsp dried oregano
- » 1 tbsp minced garlic
- » ½ tsp salt
- » ¼ tsp black pepper

## DIRECTION

1. Preheat the broiler
2. Combine oregano, garlic, lemon juice, salt and pepper and rub on both sides of the lamb. Place the lamb on a broiler pan coated with cooking spray and cook for 4 min on each side.

**NUTRITIONS:**
457 Calories, 49g Protein, 20g Fat

# 152. SKILLET BRAISED COD WITH ASPARAGUS AND POTATOES

**COOKING: 20'**     **PREPARATION:20'**     **SERVES: 4**

## INGREDIENTS

- » 4 skinless cod fillets
- » 1-pound asparagus
- » 12 oz halved small purple potatoes
- » Finely grated zest of ½ lemon
- » Juice of ½ lemon
- » ½ cup white wine
- » ¼ cup torn fresh basil leaves
- » 1 ½ tbsp olive oil
- » 1 tbsp capers
- » 3 cloves sliced garlic

## DIRECTION

1. Take a large and tall pan on the sides and heat the oil over medium-high.
2. Season the cod abundantly with salt and pepper and put in the pan, with the hot oil, for 1 min. Carefully flip for 1 more min and after transferring the cod to a plate. Set aside.
3. Add the lemon zest, capers and garlic to the pan and mix to coat with the remaining oil in the pan and cook about 1 min. Add the wine and deglaze the pan. Add lemon juice, potatoes, ½ tsp salt, ¼ tsp pepper and 2 cup of water and bring to a boil, reduce heat and simmer until potatoes are tender, for 10 to 12 min.
4. Mix the asparagus and cook for 2 min. Bring back the cod filets and any juices accumulated in the pan. Cook until the asparagus are tender, for about 3 min.
5. Divide the cod fillets into shallow bowls and add the potatoes and asparagus. Mix the basil in the broth left in the pan and pour over the cod.

**NUTRITIONS:**
461 Calories, 40g Protein, 16g Fat

    **THE COMPLETE MEDITERRANEAN DIET COOKBOOK 2021**

# 153. SAVORY VEGETABLE PANCAKES

**COOKING: 40'**  **PREPARATION:10'**  **SERVES: 7**

## INGREDIENTS

- » 8 peeled carrots
- » 2 cloves garlic
- » 1 zucchini
- » 1 bunch green onions
- » ½ bunch parsley
- » 1 recipe pancake batter

## DIRECTION

1. Grate chop the zucchini and carrots using grater. Finely chop the onions, mince the garlic and roughly chop the parsley.

2. Prepare pancakes with your favorite recipe or buy them in the store, but use ¼ cup of liquid less than required, zucchini will add a large amount of liquid to the mix. Fold the vegetables in the prepared pancake batter.

3. Heat a pan over medium-high heat and brush it gently with olive oil. Use a 1/3 measuring cup to scoop the batter on the heated pan. Cook 3 to 4 min, until the outer edge has set, then turn over. Cook for another 2 min and remove from the heat.

4. Season the pancakes with plenty of salt. Serve with butter, sour cream or even a salted jam.

**NUTRITIONS:**
291 Calories, 24g Protein, 10g Fat

# 154. MEDITERRANEAN TUNA NOODLE CASSEROLE

**COOKING: 40'**  **PREPARATION:15'**  **SERVES: 5**

## INGREDIENTS

- » 10 oz dried egg noodles
- » 9 oz halved frozen artichoke hearts
- » 6 oz drained olive oil packed tuna
- » 4 sliced scallions
- » 1-pound sliced ¼ inch thick small red potatoes
- » 2 cup milk
- » ¾ cup finely grated Parmesan cheese
- » ¾ cup drained capers
- » ½ cup finely chopped flat-leaf parsley
- » ½ cup sliced black olives
- » ¼ cup flour
- » 4 tbsp unsalted butter
- » 2 tsp Kosher salt, divided

## DIRECTION

1. Place a grill in the middle of the oven and heat to 400° F. Lightly coat a 2-quart baking tray with oil. Set aside.

2. Bring a large pan of salt water to a boil. Add the noodles and cook for 2 min less than recommended in the package directions. Strain noodles. Season immediately with olive oil so that they don't pile up. Set aside.

3. Fill the pan with water again and bring to a boil. Add the potato slices and cook for 4 min. Drain well, then bring them back to the pan.

4. Cook butter in a small saucepan over medium heat, while the noodles and potatoes are cooking. When it melts and expands, add the flour and cook for about 5 min mixing constantly, until the sauce thickens slightly, about 5 min. Add 1 tsp salt and pepper to taste.

5. Add the egg noodles to the potato pan, then pour the sauce over it. Add and mix the remaining 1 tsp of salt, capers, olive oil, tuna, artichoke hearts, shallots, parsley and ½ cup of Parmesan. Taste and season with more salt as needed.

6. Transfer to the baking tray and distribute it in a uniform layer. Season with the remaining ¼ cup of Parmesan and bake, uncovered, about 25 min.

**NUTRITIONS:**
457 Calories, 37g Protein, 21g Fat

# 155. ACQUAPAZZA SNAPPER

**COOKING: 35'**       **PREPARATION:10'**       **SERVES: 4**

## INGREDIENTS

» 1 ½ pounds cut into 4 pieces red snapper fillets
» 1 ½ coarsely chopped ripe tomatoes
» 3 cups water
» 2 tbsp olive oil
» 1 tbsp chopped thyme leaves
» 1 tbsp chopped oregano leaves
» ¼ tsp red pepper flakes
» 3 cloves minced garlic

## DIRECTION

1. Cook oil in a casserole large enough to hold all 4 pieces of snapper fillets in a single layer over medium heat. Cook garlic and red pepper flakes

2. Add the water, tomatoes, thyme, oregano and simmer. Cover, reduce over medium-low heat and simmer for 15 min. Remove the lid and continue to simmer for another 10 min so that the liquid decreases slightly, pressing occasionally on the tomatoes. Taste and season with salt as needed.

3. Put the snapper fillets in the casserole with the skin facing down, if there is skin. Season with salt, and cook for 8 to 10 min.

4. Place the snapper fillets on 4 large, shallow bowls and put the broth around it. Serve immediately.

**NUTRITIONS:**
501 Calories, 52g Protein, 26g Fat

# 156. EGGPLANT BROWN RICE BOWL

**COOKING: 40'**       **PREPARATION:20'**       **SERVES: 4**

## INGREDIENTS

» 2 pounds cut into ½ inch-thick rounds eggplants
» 15 oz drained and rinsed garbanzo beans
» 4 cup cooked brown rice
» ½ cup tahini
» ½ cup coarsely chopped cilantro
» ¼ cup coarsely chopped mint leaves
» ¼ cup pomegranate arils
» 4 tbsp olive oil
» 1 tbsp zaatar
» 1 ½ tsp maple syrup
» 1 tsp squeezed lemon juice
» ½ tsp ground turmeric
» 1 clove minced garlic

## DIRECTION

1. Situate rack in the middle of the oven and preheat to 400° F.

2. Place the eggplant on a rimmed baking sheet. Season with 3 tbsp of olive oil, then sprinkle with zaatar and a large pinch of salt. Using your hands, mix until the eggplant is well coated. Place the eggplants in a single layer. Cook for 15 min. Flip the eggplants and cook for another 10 min. Remove from the oven and season with a pinch of salt and black pepper. Set aside.

3. Put the tahini and 1/3 cup of water in a small bowl and blend until smooth and thick. Add 1 tbsp of olive oil, maple syrup, turmeric, squeezed lemon juice, garlic and season with salt.

4. Divide the rice into 4 bowls. Complete with the garbanzo beans and eggplants. Sprinkle with the mint, pomegranate arils and cilantro. Season generously the turmeric tahini on top.

**NUTRITIONS:**
307 Calories, 31g Protein, 18g Fat

# 157. EXTRA-CRISPY VEGGIE-PACKED PIZZA

**COOKING: 18'**　　　　**PREPARATION:15'**　　　　**SERVES: 4**

## INGREDIENTS

- » 1 (5 oz) thin whole-wheat pizza crust
- » 2 ½ oz crumbled feta cheese
- » 2 oz baby spring mix
- » 2 thinly sliced tomatoes
- » 1 cup shaved zucchini strips
- » ½ cup thinly sliced red onion
- » ¼ cup chopped basil
- » ¼ cup basil pesto
- » 1 tbsp canola oil
- » 1 tbsp white wine vinegar
- » ½ tsp kosher salt, divided
- » ¼ tsp black pepper
- » 1/8 tsp crushed red pepper

## DIRECTION

1. Set oven to 400°F with the rack in the upper position. Combine the oil, vinegar, black pepper and ¼ tsp of salt in a bowl. Mix the zucchini in the mixture and let stand at room temperature for 10 min.

2. Meantime, place pizza crust on a baking tray, spread the basil pesto on the crust. Season the cheese over the pesto and garnish with the tomatoes and red pepper. Cook on the grill above 400°F for 6 min. Raise the grill and continue to cook for about 2 min. Pull out from the oven and leave to cool for 2 min.

3. Add the spring mixture, basil and onion to the zucchini mixture. Put the prepared mixture evenly on the pizza and season with the remaining ¼ tsp of salt.

**NUTRITIONS:**
399 Calories, 31g Protein, 19g Fat

# 158. GREEK TURKEY BURGERS

**COOKING: 10'**　　　　**PREPARATION:15'**　　　　**SERVES: 4**

## INGREDIENTS

- » 4 Whole-Wheat hamburger buns
- » 1 pound 93% lean ground turkey
- » 2 cups arugula
- » ½ cup sliced cucumber
- » ½ cup thinly sliced red onion
- » 1/3 cup chopped kalamata olives
- » 1/3 cup plain whole-milk Greek yogurt
- » ¼ cup canola mayonnaise
- » 1 tbsp lemon juice
- » 2 tsp dried oregano
- » 1 tsp ground cumin
- » ¼ tsp kosher salt
- » ¼ tsp black pepper, divided

## DIRECTION

1. Combine turkey, oregano, cumin, mayonnaise, salt and 1/8 tsp of pepper. Form the mixture into 4 patties.

2. Heat a big cast-iron pan at high heat. Slightly coat the pan with cooking spray and add the turkey patties. Cook for about 4 to 5 min per side.

3. Combine the yogurt, lemon juice, olives and the remaining 1/8 tsp of pepper in a small bowl. Sprinkle the yogurt mixture on the cut sides of the top and bottom buns. Divide the arugula between the lower halves of the sandwiches, garnish with cooked patties, cucumber and red onion. Wrap with the top halves of the rolls and serve.

**NUTRITIONS:**
459 Calories, 48g Protein, 19g Fat

# 159. BEEF AND LAMB KOFTA LETTUCE WRAPS

**COOKING: 40'**  **PREPARATION:20'**  **SERVES: 4**

## INGREDIENTS

- » 12 Boston lettuce leaves
- » 1 slice torn into pieces whole-grain bread
- » 1 large egg
- » 1 package (about 8.8 oz) precooked brown rice
- » 8 oz ground sirloin
- » 6 oz lean ground lamb
- » ¾ cup 2% reduced-fat Greek yogurt
- » 5 tbsp grated red onion divided
- » 3 tbsp diced English cucumber
- » 2 tbsp chopped parsley
- » 1 tbsp olive oil, divided
- » 1 tbsp chopped mint
- » 1 tsp paprika
- » ¾ tsp kosher salt, divided
- » ½ tsp ground allspice
- » ½ tsp ground cinnamon
- » ½ tsp ground black pepper, divided

## DIRECTION

1. Put the bread in a mini kitchen robot and blend until large crumbs are formed. Combine bread, sirloin, lamb, egg, allspice, mint, parsley, cinnamon, 2 tbsp of onion, ½ tsp of salt and ¼ tsp of black pepper. Form the mixture into 12 patties. Preheat nonstick pan over medium-high heat and add 1 tsp of oil. Place the patties on the pan, cook 2 to 3 min on each side.

2. Combine the yogurt, the remaining ¼ tsp of pepper, ¼ tsp of salt, the cucumber and the 3 tbsp of onion in a medium bowl and mix.

3. Cook the rice according to package directions. Season with paprika and the remaining 2 tsp of oil.

4. Place the lettuce leaves on a large serving plate and put the rice, patties and yogurt mixture.

## NUTRITIONS:

471 Calories, 47g Protein, 16g Fat

# 160. CHICKEN SOUVLAKI

**COOKING: 10'**  **PREPARATION:25'**  **SERVES: 4**

## INGREDIENTS

- » 4 pocketless pitas
- » 2 cut into thin wedges tomatoes
- » 1 cut into thin wedges small onion
- » 1 halved cucumber
- » 1 1/3pound chicken breasts
- » 2 cups plain yogurt
- » 1/3 cup black olives
- » 6 tbsp butter
- » 2 tbsp olive oil
- » 1 tbsp dried oregano
- » 1 ½ tsp lemon juice
- » 1 ¼ tsp salt
- » ¼ tsp dried dill
- » 1 clove minced garlic

## DIRECTION

1. Put the yogurt in a colander lined with a paper towel and place it on a bowl, leave to drain in the refrigerator for 15 min. In a medium glass bowl combine the cucumber with 1 tsp of salt, let it rest for about 15 min. Squeeze the cucumber to remove the liquid. Return the cucumber to the bowl and add the drained yogurt, garlic, dill and 1/8 tsp of pepper.

2. Preheat the grill or the broiler. In a small glass bowl combine the oil oregano, lemon juice, the remaining ¼ tsp of salt and the remaining ¼ tsp of pepper. Dip the chicken cubes into the oil mixture and thread them onto the skewers. Grill the chicken over high heat, flipping once until cooked, about 5 min in total. Transfer the chicken to a plate.

3. Spread both sides of the pitas with butter and grill, flipping once for about 4 min in total. Cut into quarters.

4. Place the pitas on plates and garnish with the onion, tomatoes and chicken skewers with any sauce accumulated. Serve with the tzatziki and olives.

## NUTRITIONS:

460 Calories, 40g Protein, 18g Fat

# 161. SPICY CHICKEN SHAWARMA

**COOKING: 6'**　　　　**PREPARATION:15'**　　　　**SERVES: 4**

## INGREDIENTS

» 1-pound chicken breast
» 4 (6-inch) halved pitas
» ½ cup chopped plum tomato
» ½ cup chopped cucumber
» ¼ cup chopped red onion
» 5 tbsp plain low-fat Greek-style yogurt, divided
» 2 tbsp lemon juice, divided
» 2 tbsp finely chopped parsley
» 2 tbsp extra-virgin olive oil
» 1 tbsp tahini
» ½ tsp salt
» ½ tsp crushed red pepper
» ¼ tsp ground cumin
» ¼ tsp ground ginger
» 1/8 tsp ground coriander

## DIRECTION

1. Combine the parsley, salt, red pepper, ginger, cumin, coriander, 1 tbsp of yogurt, 1 tbsp of juice and 2 cloves of garlic. Add the chicken, stir to coat. Preheat oil in nonstick pan over medium-high heat. Add the chicken mixture to the pan and cook for 6 min

2. In the meantime, combine the remaining 1 tbsp of lemon juice, the remaining ¼ cup of yogurt and the remaining 1 clove of garlic and the tahini, mixing well. Put 1 ½ tsp of the tahini mixture inside each half of the pita, divide the chicken between the halves of the pita. Fill each half of the pita with 1 tbsp of cucumber, 1 tbsp of tomato and 1 ½ tsp of onion.

## NUTRITIONS:

440 Calories, 37g Protein, 19g Fat

# 162. LEMON CHICKEN PITA BURGERS WITH SPICED YOGURT SAUCE

**COOKING: 6'**　　　　**PREPARATION:15'**　　　　**SERVES: 4**

## INGREDIENTS

» 4 (6-inch) cut in half pitas
» 2 lightly beaten large egg whites
» 1-pound ground chicken
» 2 cups shredded lettuce
» ½ cup diced tomato
» ½ cup chopped green onions
» ½ cup plain low-fat yogurt
» 1/3 cup Italian-seasoned breadcrumbs
» 1 tbsp olive oil
» 1 tbsp Greek seasoning blend
» 2 tsp grated lemon zest, divided
» 1 ½ tsp chopped oregano
» ½ tsp coarsely ground black pepper

## DIRECTION

1. Combine the chicken, eggs, onion, black pepper, breadcrumbs, Greek seasoning blend and 1 tsp of zest, mixing well. Split mixture into 8 equal portions and make patties ¼-inch thick.

2. Heat the oil in a large nonstick pan over medium-high heat. Put on the patties and cook for 2 min per side. Cover, lower the heat to medium and cook for 4 min.

3. Combine oregano, yogurt and the remaining zest. Fill each half of the pita with 1 patty, 1 tbsp of yogurt mix, 1 tbsp of tomato and ¼ cup of lettuce.

## NUTRITIONS:

391 Calories, 40g Protein, 20g Fat

# 163. LAMB CHOP WITH PISTACHIO GREMOLATA

**COOKING: 8'**     **PREPARATION:10'**     **SERVES: 4**

## INGREDIENTS

- » 8 trimmed lamb loin chops
- » 2 tbsp chopped flat-leaf parsley
- » 2 tbsp finely chopped pistachios
- » 1 tbsp chopped cilantro
- » 2 tsp grated lemon zest
- » ½ tsp salt
- » ½ tsp ground cumin
- » ¼ tsp ground coriander
- » ¼ tsp black pepper
- » 1/8 tsp salt
- » 1/8 ground cinnamon
- » 1 clove minced garlic

## DIRECTION

1. Heat nonstick pan at medium-high heat. Combine the cumin, coriander, cinnamon, salt and black pepper and season evenly on both sides of the lamb. Coat the pan with cooking spray and add the lamb, cook for 4 min per side.

2. In the meantime, combine the pistachios, cilantro, parsley, lemon zest, salt and garlic, season over the lamb.

**NUTRITIONS:**
409 Calories, 41g Protein, 22g Fat

# 164. PITA SALAD WITH CUCUMBER, FENNEL AND CHICKEN

**COOKING: 12'**     **PREPARATION:10'**     **SERVES: 4**

## INGREDIENTS

- » 2 (6-inch) pitas
- » ½ halved lengthwise and thinly sliced English cucumber
- » 2 cups thinly sliced fennel bulb
- » 1 cup shredded skinless, boneless rotisserie chicken breast
- » ½ cup chopped flat-leaf parsley
- » ¼ cup vertically sliced red onion
- » ¼ cup lemon juice
- » 3 tbsp extra-virgin olive oil
- » 1 tbsp white wine vinegar
- » ½ tsp chopped oregano
- » ½ tsp salt, divided
- » ¼ tsp black pepper, divided

## DIRECTION

1. Preheat the oven to 350°F.

2. Situate pitas on a baking tray and bake for 12 min, cool down 1 min. Cut into small pieces and combine with fennel, chicken, parsley and red onion. Season with ¼ tsp of salt and 1/8 tsp of pepper.

3. Add the juice, oregano, vinegar, the remaining ¼ tsp of salt and 1/8 tsp of pepper. Gradually add the oil, mixing with a whisk. Season with dressing over the pita mixture to coat and serve.

**NUTRITIONS:**
413 Calories, 38g Protein, 17g Fat

# 165. HALIBUT WITH LEMON-FENNEL SALAD

**COOKING: 5'**          **PREPARATION:15'**          **SERVES: 4**

## INGREDIENTS

- » 4 halibut fillets
- » 2 cups thinly sliced fennel bulb
- » ¼ cup thinly vertically sliced red onion
- » 2 tbsp lemon juice
- » 1 tbsp thyme leaves
- » 1 tbsp chopped flat-leaf parsley
- » 5 tsp extra-virgin olive oil, divided
- » 1 tsp coriander
- » ½ tsp salt
- » ½ tsp cumin
- » ¼ tsp ground black pepper
- » 2 cloves minced garlic

## DIRECTION

1. Combine the coriander, cumin, salt and black pepper in a small bowl. Combine 2 tsp of olive oil, garlic and 1 ½ tsp of spice mixture in another small bowl, evenly rub the garlic mixture on the halibut. Heat 1 tsp of oil in a large nonstick pan over medium-high heat. Cook the halibut to the pan for 5 min.

2. Combine the remaining 2 tsp of oil, ¾ tsp of spice mixture, the fennel bulb, onion, lemon juice, thyme leaves and parsley in a bowl, mix well to coat, and serve salad with halibut.

## NUTRITIONS:

427 Calories, 39g Protein, 20g Fat

# CHAPTER 13
# MAIN DISH RECIPES PART 4

# 166. TUSCAN BEEF STEW

**COOKING: 4 HOURS**  **PREPARATION:10'**  **SERVES: 8**

## INGREDIENTS

- » 2 pounds beef stew meat
- » 4 carrots
- » 2 (14½-ounce) cans tomatoes
- » 1 medium onion
- » 1 package McCormick Slow Cookers Hearty Beef Stew Seasoning
- » ½ cup water
- » ½ cup dry red wine
- » 1 teaspoon rosemary leaves
- » 8 slices Italian bread

## DIRECTION

1. Place the cubed beef in the slow cooker along with the carrots, diced tomatoes, and onion wedges.
2. Mix the seasoning package in the ½ cup of water and stir well, making sure there are no lumps remaining.
3. Add the red wine to the water and stir slightly. Add the rosemary leaves to the water-and-wine mixture and then pour over the meat, stirring to ensure the meat is completely covered.
4. Turn the slow cooker to low and cook for 8 hours, or cook for 4 hours on high.
5. Serve with toasted Italian bread.

**NUTRITIONS:**
329 Calories, 15g fat, 25.6g Protein

# 167. MEDITERRANEAN BEEF STEW

**COOKING: 8 HOURS**  **PREPARATION:25'**  **SERVES: 6**

## INGREDIENTS

- » 1 tablespoon olive oil
- » 8 ounces sliced mushrooms
- » 1 onion
- » 2 pounds chuck roast
- » 1 cup beef stock
- » 1 (14½-ounce) can tomatoes with juice
- » ½ cup tomato sauce
- » ¼ cup balsamic vinegar
- » 1 can black olives
- » ½ cup garlic cloves
- » 2 tablespoons fresh rosemary
- » 2 tablespoons fresh parsley
- » 1 tablespoon capers

## DIRECTION

1. Heat a skillet over high heat. Add 1 tablespoon of olive oil. Once heated, cook cubed roast.
2. Once cooked, stir rest of the olive oil (if needed), then toss in the onions and mushrooms. When they have softened, transfer to the slow cooker.
3. Add the beef stock to the skillet to deglaze the pan, then pour it over the meat in the slow cooker.
4. Mix rest of the ingredients to the slow cooker to coat.
5. Set the temperature on your slow cooker to low and cook for 8 hours.

**NUTRITIONS:**
471 Calories, 23.4g fat, 47.1g Protein

# 168. CABBAGE ROLL CASSEROLE WITH VEAL

**COOKING: 4-8 HOURS**     **PREPARATION:5'**     **SERVES: 6**

## INGREDIENTS

- » 1-pound raw ground veal
- » 1 head of cabbage
- » 1 medium green pepper
- » 1 medium onion, chopped
- » 1 (15-ounce) can tomatoes
- » 2 (15-ounce) cans tomato sauce
- » 1 teaspoon minced garlic
- » 1 tablespoon Worcestershire sauce
- » 1 tablespoon beef bouillon
- » ½ teaspoon salt
- » ½ teaspoon pepper
- » 1 cup uncooked brown rice

## DIRECTION

1. Situate all the ingredients to your slow cooker
2. Stir well to combine.
3. Set your slow cooker to high and cook for 4 hours, or cook for 8 hours on low.

**NUTRITIONS:**

335 Calories, 18g fat, 22.9g Protein

# 169. SLOW COOKED DAUBE PROVENCAL

**COOKING: 4-8 HOURS**     **PREPARATION:15'**     **SERVES: 8-10**

## INGREDIENTS

- » 1 tablespoon olive oil
- » 10 garlic cloves, minced
- » 2 pounds boneless chuck roast
- » 1½ teaspoons salt
- » ½ teaspoon black pepper
- » 1 cup dry red wine
- » 2 cups carrots, chopped
- » 1½ cups onion, chopped
- » ½ cup beef broth
- » 1 (14-ounce) can diced tomatoes
- » 1 tablespoon tomato paste
- » 1 teaspoon fresh rosemary, chopped
- » 1 teaspoon fresh thyme, chopped
- » ½ teaspoon orange zest, grated
- » ½ teaspoon ground cinnamon
- » ¼ teaspoon ground cloves
- » 1 bay leaf

## DIRECTION

1. Preheat skillet and then add the olive oil. Cook minced garlic and onions
2. Add the cubed meat, salt, and pepper and cook until the meat has browned.
3. Transfer the meat to the slow cooker.
4. Put beef broth to the skillet and let simmer for about 3 minutes to deglaze the pan, then pour into slow cooker over the meat.
5. Add the rest of the ingredients to the slow cooker and stir well to combine.
6. Set your slow cooker to low and cook for 8 hours, or set to high and cook for 4 hours.
7. Serve with a side of egg noodles, rice or some crusty Italian bread.

**NUTRITIONS:**

547 Calories, 30.5g fat, 45.2g Protein

# 170. OSSO BUCCO

**COOKING: 8 HOURS**    **PREPARATION:30'**    **SERVES: 2-4**

## INGREDIENTS

- » 4 beef shanks or veal shanks
- » 1 teaspoon sea salt
- » ½ teaspoon ground black pepper
- » 3 tablespoons whole wheat flour
- » 1–2 tablespoons olive oil
- » 2 medium onions, diced
- » 2 medium carrots, diced
- » 2 celery stalks, diced
- » 4 garlic cloves, minced
- » 1 (14-ounce) can diced tomatoes
- » 2 teaspoons dried thyme leaves
- » ½ cup beef or vegetable stock

**NUTRITIONS:**

589 Calories, 21.3g fat, 74.7g Protein

## DIRECTION

1. Season the shanks on both sides, then dip in the flour to coat.
2. Heat a large skillet over high heat. Add the olive oil. When the oil is hot, add the shanks and brown evenly on both sides. When browned, transfer to the slow cooker.
3. Pour the stock into the skillet and let simmer for 3–5 minutes while stirring to deglaze the pan.
4. Add the rest of the ingredients to the slow cooker and pour the stock from the skillet over the top.
5. Click slow cooker to low and cook for 8 hours.
6. Serve the Osso Bucco over quinoa, brown rice, or even cauliflower rice.

# 171. SLOW COOKER BEEF BOURGUIGNON

**COOKING: 6-8 HOURS**    **PREPARATION:5'**    **SERVES: 6-8**

## INGREDIENTS

- » 1 tablespoon extra-virgin olive oil
- » 6 ounces bacon
- » 3 pounds beef brisket
- » 1 large carrot
- » 1 large white onion
- » 6 cloves garlic
- » ½ teaspoon coarse salt
- » ½ teaspoon pepper
- » 2 tablespoons whole wheat
- » 12 small pearl onions
- » 3 cups red wine
- » 2 cups beef stock
- » 2 tablespoons tomato paste
- » 1 beef bouillon cube
- » 1 teaspoon fresh thyme
- » 2 tablespoons fresh parsley
- » 2 bay leaves
- » 2 tablespoons butter
- » 1-pound mushrooms

## DIRECTION

1. Preheat skillet over medium-high heat, pour olive oil. When the oil has heated, cook the bacon until it is crisp, then place it in your slow cooker. Save the bacon fat in the skillet.
2. Dry the beef with a paper towel and cook it in the same skillet with the bacon fat until all sides have the same brown coloring.
3. Transfer to the slow cooker.
4. Add the onions and carrots to the slow cooker and season with the salt and pepper. Stir to combine the ingredients and make sure everything is seasoned.
5. Pour the red wine into the skillet and simmer for 4–5 minutes to deglaze the pan, then whisk in the flour, stirring until smooth.
6. When the liquid has thickened, pour it into the slow cooker and stir to coat everything with the wine mixture. Add the tomato paste, bouillon cube, thyme, parsley, 4 cloves of garlic, and bay leaf.
7. Set your slow cooker to high and cook for 6 hours, or set to low and cook for 8 hours.
8. Before serving, melt the butter in a skillet over medium heat. When the oil is hot, add the remaining 2 cloves of garlic and cook for about 1 minute before adding the mushrooms.
9. Cook the mushrooms until soft, then add to the slow cooker and mix to combine.
10. Serve with mashed potatoes, rice or noodles.

**NUTRITIONS:**

672 Calories, 32g fat, 56g Protein

# 172. BALSAMIC BEEF

**COOKING: 8 HOURS** **PREPARATION:5'** **SERVES: 8**

## INGREDIENTS

- » 2 pounds boneless chuck roast
- » 1 tablespoon olive oil
- » Rub
- » 1 teaspoon garlic powder
- » ½ teaspoon onion powder
- » 1 teaspoon sea salt
- » ½ teaspoon black pepper
- » Sauce
- » ½ cup balsamic vinegar
- » 2 tablespoons honey
- » 1 tablespoon honey mustard
- » 1 cup beef broth
- » 1 tablespoon tapioca

## DIRECTION

1. Incorporate all of the ingredients for the rub.
2. In a separate bowl, mix the balsamic vinegar, honey, honey mustard, and beef broth.
3. Coat the roast in olive oil, then rub in the spices from the rub mix.
4. Place the roast in the slow cooker and then pour the sauce over the top.
5. Select slow cooker to low and cook for 8 hours.
6. If you want to thicken, pour the liquid into a saucepan and heat to boiling on the stovetop. Stir in the flour until smooth and let simmer until the sauce thickens.

**NUTRITIONS:**
306 Calories, 19g fat, 25g Protein

# 173. VEAL POT ROAST

**COOKING: 5 HOURS** **PREPARATION:20'** **SERVES: 6-8**

## INGREDIENTS

- » 2 tablespoons olive oil
- » Salt and pepper
- » 3-pound boneless veal roast
- » 4 medium carrots, peeled
- » 2 parsnips, peeled and halved
- » 2 white turnips, peeled and quartered
- » 10 garlic cloves, peeled
- » 2 sprigs fresh thyme
- » 1 orange, scrubbed and zested
- » 1 cup chicken or veal stock

## DIRECTION

1. Heat a large skillet over medium-high heat.
2. Coat veal roast all over with olive oil, then season with salt and pepper.
3. When the skillet is hot, add the veal roast and sear on all sides.
4. Once roast is cooked on all sides, transfer it to the slow cooker.
5. Toss the carrots, parsnips, turnips, and garlic into the skillet. Stir and cook for about 5 minutes—not all the way through, just to get some of the brown bits from the veal and give them a bit of color.
6. Transfer the vegetables to the slow cooker, placing them all around the meat.
7. Top the roast with the thyme and the zest from the orange. Slice orange in half and squeeze the juice over the top of the meat.
8. Add the chicken stock, then cook the roast on low for 5 hours.

**NUTRITIONS:**
426 Calories, 12.8g fat, 48.8g Protein

# 174. MEDITERRANEAN RICE AND SAUSAGE

**COOKING: 8 HOURS**　　　**PREPARATION:15'**　　　**SERVES: 6**

## INGREDIENTS

- » 1½ pounds Italian sausage, crumbled
- » 1 medium onion, chopped
- » 2 tablespoons steak sauce
- » 2 cups long grain rice, uncooked
- » 1 (14-ounce) can diced tomatoes with juice
- » ½ cup water
- » 1 medium green pepper, diced

## DIRECTION

1. Spray your slow cooker with olive oil or nonstick cooking spray.
2. Add the sausage, onion, and steak sauce to the slow cooker.
3. Cook on low for 8 to 10 hours.
4. After 8 hours, add the rice, tomatoes, water and green pepper. Stir to combine thoroughly.
5. Cook for 20 to 25 minutes.

**NUTRITIONS:**
650 Calories, 36g fat, 22g Protein

# 175. SPANISH MEATBALLS

**COOKING: 5 HOURS**　　　**PREPARATION:20'**　　　**SERVES: 6**

## INGREDIENTS

- » 1-pound ground turkey
- » 1-pound ground pork
- » 2 eggs
- » 1 (20-ounce) can diced tomatoes
- » ¾ cup sweet onion, minced, divided
- » ¼ cup plus 1 tablespoon breadcrumbs
- » 3 tablespoons fresh parsley, chopped
- » 1½ teaspoons cumin
- » 1½ teaspoons paprika (sweet or hot)

## DIRECTION

1. Spray the slow cooker with olive oil.
2. In a mixing bowl, mix ground meat, eggs, about half of the onions, the breadcrumbs, and the spices.
3. Wash your hands and mix together until everything is well combined. Shape into meatballs.
4. Mix 2 tablespoons of olive oil over medium heat. When the skillet and oil are hot, add the meatballs and brown on all sides. When they are done, transfer them to the slow cooker.
5. Add the rest of the onions and the tomatoes to the skillet and allow them to cook for a few minutes, scraping the brown bits from the meatballs up to add flavor.
6. Pour the tomatoes over the meatballs in the slow cooker and cook on low for 5 hours.

**NUTRITIONS:**
372 Calories, 21.7g fat, 28.5g Protein

# 176. LAMB SHANKS WITH RED WINE

**COOKING: 5 HOURS**   **PREPARATION:20'**   **SERVES: 4**

## INGREDIENTS

» 2 tablespoons olive oil
» 2 tablespoons flour
» 4 lamb shanks, trimmed
» 1 onion, chopped
» 2 garlic cloves, crushed
» 2/3 cup red wine
» 3 cups tomato sauce

## DIRECTION

1. Heat a skillet over high heat. Add the olive oil.
2. Season the lamb shanks then roll in the flour. Shake off excess flour and place the shanks in the skillet to brown on all sides.
3. Spray the slow cooker with olive oil and place the browned shanks in the slow cooker.
4. Add the crushed garlic to the red wine. Mix with the tomato sauce and then pour the mixture over the lamb shanks and cook on low for 5–6 hours

**NUTRITIONS:**
354 Calories, 12g fat, 42g Protein

# 177. LEG OF LAMB WITH ROSEMARY AND GARLIC

**COOKING: 8 HOURS**   **PREPARATION:15'**   **SERVES: 4**

## INGREDIENTS

» 3–4-pound leg of lamb
» 4 garlic cloves, sliced thin
» 5–8 sprigs fresh rosemary (more if desired)
» 2 tablespoons olive oil
» 1 lemon, halved
» ¼ cup flour

## DIRECTION

1. Put skillet over high heat and pour olive oil.
2. When the olive oil is hot, add the leg of lamb and sear on both sides until brown.
3. Spray the slow cooker with olive oil and then transfer the lamb to the slow cooker.
4. Squeeze the lemon over the meat and then place in the pot next to the lamb.
5. Take a sharp knife and make small incisions in the meat, then stuff the holes you created with rosemary and garlic.
6. Place any remaining rosemary and garlic on top of the roast.
7. Cook on low for 8 hours.

**NUTRITIONS:**
-6557 Calories, 39g fat, 46g Protein

# 178. LEMON HONEY LAMB SHOULDER

**COOKING: 8 HOURS**  **PREPARATION:10'**  **SERVES: 4**

## INGREDIENTS

- » 3 cloves garlic, thinly sliced
- » 1 tablespoon fresh rosemary, chopped
- » 1 teaspoon lemon zest, grated
- » ½ teaspoon each salt and pepper
- » 4–5-pound boneless lamb shoulder roast
- » 3 tablespoons lemon juice
- » 1 tablespoon honey
- » 6 shallots, quartered
- » 2 teaspoons cornstarch

## DIRECTION

1. Stir garlic, rosemary, lemon zest, salt, and pepper.
2. Rub the spice mixture into the lamb shoulder. Make sure to coat the whole roast.
3. Spray the slow cooker with olive oil and add the lamb.
4. Mix together the honey and lemon juice and then pour over the meat.
5. Arrange the shallots beside the meat in the slow cooker.
6. Cook on low for 8 hours.
7. Serve. You can make a gravy by transferring the juice from the slow cooker to a medium saucepan. Thoroughly mix the cornstarch into a little water until smooth. Then mix into the juice and bring to a simmer. Simmer until mixture thickens.

**NUTRITIONS:**
240 Calories, 11g fat, 31g Protein

# 179. ITALIAN SHREDDED PORK STEW

**COOKING: 8 HOURS**  **PREPARATION:20'**  **SERVES: 8**

## INGREDIENTS

- » 2 medium sweet potatoes
- » 2 cups fresh kale, chopped
- » 1 large onion, chopped
- » 4 cloves garlic, minced
- » 1 2½–3½ pound boneless pork shoulder butt roast
- » 1 (14-ounce) can cannellini beans
- » 1½ teaspoons Italian seasoning
- » ½ teaspoon salt
- » ½ teaspoon pepper
- » 3 (14½-ounce) cans chicken broth
- » Sour cream (optional)

## DIRECTION

1. Coat slow cooker with nonstick cooking spray or olive oil.
2. Place the cubed sweet potatoes, kale, garlic and onion into the slow cooker.
3. Add the pork shoulder on top of the potatoes.
4. Add the beans, Italian seasoning salt, and pepper.
5. Pour the chicken broth over the meat.
6. Cook on low for 8 hours.
7. Serve with sour cream, if desired.

**NUTRITIONS:**
283 Calories, 13g fat, 24g Protein

# 180. PARMESAN HONEY PORK LOIN ROAST

**COOKING: 5 HOURS**     **PREPARATION:10'**     **SERVES: 8**

## INGREDIENTS

» 3-pound pork loin
» 2/3 cup grated parmesan cheese
» ½ cup honey
» 3 tablespoons soy sauce
» 1 tablespoon oregano
» 1 tablespoon basil
» 2 tablespoons garlic, chopped
» 2 tablespoons olive oil
» ½ teaspoon salt
» 2 tablespoons cornstarch
» ¼ cup chicken broth

## DIRECTION

1. Spray your slow cooker with olive oil or nonstick cooking spray.
2. Place the pork loin in the slow cooker.
3. In a small mixing bowl, combine the cheese, honey, soy sauce, oregano, basil, garlic, olive oil, and salt. Stir with a fork to combine well, then pour over the pork loin.
4. Cook in low for 5–6 hours.
5. Remove the pork loin and put on a serving platter.
6. Pour the juices from the slow cooker into a small saucepan.
7. Create a slurry by mixing the cornstarch into the chicken broth and whisking until smooth.
8. Bring the contents of the saucepan to a boil, then whisk in the slurry and let simmer until thickened. Pour over the pork loin and serve.

## NUTRITIONS:
449 Calories, 15g fat, 55g Protein

# CHAPTER 14
# SIDE RECIPES

# 181. PASSION FRUIT AND SPICY COUSCOUS

**COOKING: 15'**  **PREPARATION:15'**  **SERVES: 4**

## INGREDIENTS

- » 1 pinch of salt
- » 1 pinch of allspice
- » 1 teaspoon of mixed spice
- » 1 cup of boiling water
- » 2 teaspoons of extra-virgin olive oil
- » ½ cup of full-fat Greek yogurt
- » ½ cup of honey
- » 1 cup of couscous
- » 1 teaspoon of orange zest
- » 2 oranges, peeled and sliced
- » 2 tablespoons of passion fruit pulp
- » ½ cup of blueberries
- » ½ cup of walnuts, roasted and unsalted
- » 2 tablespoons of fresh mint

## DIRECTION

1. In a mixing bowl, combine the salt, allspice, mixed spice, honey, couscous, and boiling water. Cover the bowl and allow to rest for five to ten minutes, or until the water has been absorbed. Using a fork, give the mixture a good stir, then add the diced walnuts.

2. In a separate bowl, combine the passion fruit, yogurt, and orange zest.

3. To serve, dish the couscous up into four bowls, add the yogurt mixture, and top with the sliced orange, blueberries, and mint leaves.

**NUTRITIONS:**

100 calories, 10.5g fat, 2.1g Protein

# 182. SPRING SANDWICH

**COOKING: 25'**  **PREPARATION:10'**  **SERVES: 4**

## INGREDIENTS

- » 1 pinch of salt
- » 1 pinch of black pepper
- » 4 teaspoons of extra-virgin olive oil
- » 4 eggs
- » 4 multigrain sandwich thins
- » 1 onion, finely diced
- » 1 tomato, sliced thinly
- » 2 cups of fresh baby spinach leaves
- » 4 tablespoons of crumbled feta
- » 1 sprig of fresh rosemary

## DIRECTION

1. Preheat your oven to 375 F.

2. Slice the multigrain sandwich thins open and brush each side with one teaspoon of olive oil. Place them into the oven and toast for five minutes. Remove and set aside.

3. Situate non-stick skillet over medium heat, add the remaining 2 teaspoons of olive oil and strip the leaves of rosemary off into the pan. Add in the eggs, one by one.

4. Cook until the eggs have whitened, and the yolks stay runny. Flip once using a spatula and then remove from the heat.

5. Place the multigrain thins onto serving plates, then place the spinach leaves on top, followed by sliced tomato, one egg, and a sprinkling of feta cheese. Add salt and pepper, then close your sandwich using the remaining multigrain thins.

**NUTRITIONS:**

150 calories, 15g fat, 3g Protein

# 183. SPRINGTIME QUINOA SALAD

**COOKING: 25'**          **PREPARATION:10'**          **SERVES: 4**

## INGREDIENTS

- » for vinaigrette:
- » 1 pinch of salt
- » 1 pinch of black pepper
- » ½ teaspoon of dried thyme
- » ½ teaspoon of dried oregano
- » ¼ cup of extra-virgin olive oil
- » 1 tablespoon of honey
- » juice of 1 lemon
- » 1 clove of garlic, minced
- » 2 tablespoons of fresh basil, diced
- » for salad:
- » 1 ½ cups of cooked quinoa
- » 4 cups of mixed leafy greens
- » ½ cup of kalamata olives, halved and pitted
- » ¼ cup of sun-dried tomatoes, diced
- » ½ cup of almonds, raw, unsalted and diced

## DIRECTION

1. Combine all the vinaigrette ingredients together, either by hand or using a blender or food processor. Set the vinaigrette aside in the refrigerator.
2. In a large salad bowl, combine the salad ingredients.
3. Drizzle the vinaigrette over the salad, then serve.

**NUTRITIONS:**
201 calories, 13g fat, 4g Protein

# 184. SEAFOOD SOUVLAKI BOWL

**COOKING: 20'**          **PREPARATION:20'**          **SERVES: 4**

## INGREDIENTS

- » 1 pinch of salt
- » 1 pinch of black pepper
- » 1 tablespoon of fresh oregano
- » 1 tablespoon of paprika
- » 1 tablespoon of fresh dill
- » 3 tablespoons of extra-virgin olive oil
- » 2 tablespoons of balsamic vinegar
- » 6 tablespoons of freshly squeezed lemon juice
- » 2 cloves of garlic, minced
- » 1 lb. of fresh salmon, cut into 4 fillets
- » 1 pinch of salt
- » 1 pinch of black pepper
- » 2 tablespoons of extra-virgin olive oil
- » Juice of 1 lemon
- » 2 red bell peppers, diced
- » 1 large cucumber, diced
- » 1 zucchini, sliced
- » 1 cup of cherry tomatoes, halved
- » ½ cup of kalamata olives, pitted and halved
- » 1 cup of dry pearled couscous
- » 8 oz. of feta, cubed

## DIRECTION

1. Cook the couscous following the package instructions and set aside.
2. In a medium mixing bowl, add all the souvlaki ingredients apart from the fish. Combine well, then coat each fish fillet. Allow the fillets to rest in the bowl for 15 minutes.
3. In a separate mixing bowl, combine the sliced bell peppers and zucchini. Add two tablespoons of olive oil, salt, and pepper. Combine and set aside.
4. In a medium skillet over medium heat, cook the salmon until tender, then remove from the heat.
5. Add the sliced peppers and zucchini to the skillet and cook for three minutes until you see charring, then remove from the heat.
6. To serve, dish the couscous up into four serving bowls and top with the lemon juice. Add the cooked salmon, charred vegetables, cucumber, tomatoes, olives, and feta.

**NUTRITIONS:**
159 calories, 11g fat, 2g Protein

# 185. SPAGHETTI NICOISE

**COOKING: 20'**  **PREPARATION:15'**  **SERVES: 4**

## INGREDIENTS

- » 1 pinch of salt
- » 1 pinch of black pepper
- » ½ teaspoon of chili flakes
- » 8 oz. of spaghetti
- » 14 oz. of canned tuna chunks in oil
- » 1/3 cup of kalamata olives
- » 8 oz. of cherry tomatoes
- » 3 oz. of arugula
- » ½ cup of pine nuts
- » 1 pinch of salt
- » 1 pinch of black pepper
- » 2 tablespoons of extra-virgin olive oil
- » 1 tablespoon of Dijon mustard
- » ¼ cup of lemon juice
- » 1 tablespoon of lemon zest
- » 1 clove of garlic, minced
- » 1 tablespoon of capers

## DIRECTION

1. Stir all the ingredients for the dressing.
2. Cook the pasta according the package instructions.
3. Boil the eggs, deshell and cut them in half. Set this aside.
4. Rinse and drain cooked pasta.
5. Add the remaining ingredients, give it a toss, top with the eggs, and then drizzle with the mustard dressing.

**NUTRITIONS:**
287 calories, 14g fat, 4g Protein

# 186. TOMATO POACHED FISH WITH HERBS AND CHICKPEAS

**COOKING: 20'**  **PREPARATION:20'**  **SERVES: 2**

## INGREDIENTS

- » 1 pinch of salt
- » 1 pinch of black pepper
- » 4 sprigs of fresh oregano
- » 4 sprigs of fresh dill
- » 1 ½ cups of water
- » 1 cup of white wine
- » 2 tablespoons of extra-virgin olive oil
- » 1 tablespoon of tomato paste
- » 2 cloves of garlic
- » 2 shallots
- » 1 lemon
- » zest of 1 lemon
- » 14 oz. can of chickpeas
- » 8 oz. of cherry tomatoes
- » 1 Fresno pepper
- » 1 lb. of cod

## DIRECTION

1. Situate saucepan over high heat, cook olive oil, garlic, and shallots for two minutes.
2. Add the salt, pepper, tomato paste, cherry tomatoes, chickpeas, and Fresno pepper.
3. Stir in the water and wine. Place the fish into the center of the pan, ensuring it is submerged in the liquid. Sprinkle the lemon zest over the broth, then add the lemon slices and fresh herbs.
4. Place a lid onto the saucepan and allow the broth to simmer for five to ten minutes, depending on the thickness of the cut of fish.
5. When cooked, remove from the heat and serve over basmati rice. Top with a few toasted pistachios for added texture.

**NUTRITIONS:**
351 calories, 21g fat, 9g Protein

# 187. GARLIC PRAWN AND PEA RISOTTO

**COOKING: 30'**     **PREPARATION:15'**     **SERVES: 4**

## INGREDIENTS

- » 1 pinch of salt
- » 1 pinch of black pepper
- » 1 red chili
- » 3 tablespoons of extra-virgin olive oil
- » oz. of butter
- » Juice of 1 lemon
- » Zest of 1 lemon
- » 50 Fl oz. of fish stock
- » 1 cup of white wine
- » 1 clove of garlic, finely diced
- » 1 onion, diced
- » 7 oz. of frozen peas
- » 14 oz. of raw prawns
- » oz. of Arborio rice

## DIRECTION

1. Rinse the prawns under running water and then remove their heads and shells. Keep these aside and keep the prawn meat aside.
2. Situate saucepan over medium heat, add one tablespoon of olive oil, garlic, half of the finely diced chili, prawn heads, and shells. Cook until the shells change color. Boil stock, then turn the heat down to a simmer.
3. In a separate medium saucepan over medium heat, add half the butter and the onions. Cook until the onions have softened. Add the risotto into the pan and stir continuously until you notice that the rice has become transparent in appearance.
4. Stir wine to the rice and cook
5. Begin to ladle the stock over the rice, one spoonful at a time. Ensure that the ladle of stock has evaporated before continuing to add the next. Stir in the peas and prawns.
6. Continue adding stock until the rice has reached an al dente texture, soft with a starchy center, around 20 to 30 minutes. Continue to cook until the prawn meat has changed color.
7. Remove the risotto from the heat, then add the remaining chili, olive oil, and lemon juice.
8. Top with salt, pepper, lemon zest and serve.

**NUTRITIONS:**
341 calories, 16g fat, 7g Protein

# 188. HONEY AND VANILLA CUSTARD CUPS WITH CRUNCHY FILO PASTRY

**COOKING: 2 HOURS**     **PREPARATION:25'**     **SERVES: 4**

## INGREDIENTS

- » 1 vanilla bean, cut lengthways
- » 2 cups of full-fat milk
- » 1/3 cup of honey
- » 1 tablespoon of brown sugar
- » 2 tablespoons of custard powder
- » 4 to 6 ripe figs, quartered
- » 1 sheet of filo pastry
- » 2 tablespoons of raw pistachios

## DIRECTION

1. Situate saucepan over medium heat, simmer vanilla bean, milk, and honey
2. In a heatproof dish, combine the sugar and custard powder. Transfer the milk mixture into the bowl containing the custard powder. Using a whisk, combine well and then transfer back into the saucepan.
3. Bring to a boil, constantly whisking until the custard thickens. Remove the vanilla bean.
4. Pour the custard into cups and allow to chill in the refrigerator for 2 hours.
5. Heat your oven to 350 F and line a baking tray with parchment.
6. Put the pastry sheet onto an even surface and spray lightly with olive oil cooking spray.
7. Sprinkle half the pistachios over the pastry and then fold the pastry in half. Heat up 2 tablespoons of honey in the microwave, then coat the pastry.
8. Place the pastry into the oven and allow to bake for 10 minutes. Remove from heat and allow it to cool.
9. Gently break the filo pastry into pieces, then top the custard with the shards and fresh-cut figs.

**NUTRITIONS:**
307 calories, 17g fat, 4g Protein

# 189. MEDITERRANEAN TOSTADAS

**COOKING: 10'**     **PREPARATION:15'**     **SERVES: 4**

## INGREDIENTS

- » 1 pinch salt
- » 1 pinch black pepper
- » 1 pinch oregano
- » 1 pinch garlic powder
- » 4 tostadas
- » 1 tablespoon of extra-virgin olive oil
- » ½ cup of milk
- » ½ cup of roasted red pepper hummus
- » 8 eggs, beaten
- » ½ cup of green onion, finely diced
- » ½ cup of red bell peppers, finely diced
- » ½ cup of diced cucumber
- » ½ cup of diced tomato
- » ¼ cup of crumbled feta
- » 1 handful of fresh basil

## DIRECTION

1. Position non-stick skillet over medium heat, cook olive oil and red peppers. Cook until these have softened, then add the salt, pepper, oregano, garlic powder, milk, eggs, and onion.
2. Gently stir the mixture until you reach a scrambled egg consistency.
3. Once cooked through, remove from the heat.
4. Place a tostada onto each place, and top with the hummus, egg, tomato, cucumber, feta, and fresh basil leaves.

## NUTRITIONS:

251 calories, 19g fat, 6g Protein

# 190. VEGETABLE RATATOUILLE

**COOKING: 40'**     **PREPARATION:15'**     **SERVES: 8**

## INGREDIENTS

- » 1 pinch salt
- » 1 pinch black pepper
- » 1 pinch brown sugar
- » ¼ cup extra-virgin olive oil
- » ¼ cup of white wine
- » 3 cloves of garlic
- » 1 onion, diced
- » 1 lb. of eggplant
- » 1 cup of zucchini
- » 1 ½ cups of canned tomato
- » 1 red bell pepper, diced
- » 1 green bell pepper, diced
- » ½ cup of fresh basil

## DIRECTION

1. Place saucepan over medium heat, cook olive oil and finely diced garlic and onion.
2. Add the cubed eggplant and continue to cook for a further 5 minutes.
3. Add the salt, pepper, and diced bell peppers. Allow to cook for another 3 minutes.
4. Add the sliced zucchini to the saucepan and cook for 3 minutes.
5. Mix white wine and canned tomatoes.
6. Allow to simmer for another five minutes. Taste the ratatouille.
7. Pull away from the heat, add the basil, and serve with a side portion of barley or brown rice.

## NUTRITIONS:

401 calories, 19g fat, 7g Protein

# 191. CITRUS CUPS

**COOKING: 15'**      **PREPARATION:15'**      **SERVES: 4**

## INGREDIENTS

- » ½ cup of water
- » 1 tablespoon of orange juice
- » 3 cups of full-fat Greek yogurt
- » 1 vanilla bean
- » 1 ruby grapefruit
- » 2 mandarins
- » 1 orange
- » 6 strips of mandarin rind
- » 1/3 cup of powdered sugar
- » 1 small handful of fresh mint leaves

## DIRECTION

1. Slice open the vanilla bean lengthways and transfer the seeds into a medium saucepan. Add the pod to the saucepan as well, followed by the water, sugar, and mandarin rind.

2. Bring the mixture to a boil, then turn down to a simmer and cook for five minutes or until the syrup has thickened.

3. Allow to cool, remove the pod, and stir in the orange juice.

4. Pour the syrup over the sliced citrus fruits and allow to rest.

5. Dish the yogurt up into four bowls, top with the citrus and syrup, sprinkle with a bit of mint, then serve.

**NUTRITIONS:**
217 calories, 16g fat, 4g Protein

# 192. MIXED BERRY PANCAKES AND RICOTTA

**COOKING: 25'**      **PREPARATION:15'**      **SERVES: 4**

## INGREDIENTS

- » 1 pinch of salt
- » ½ cup of milk
- » 1 tablespoon of canola oil
- » 2 eggs
- » 1 ½ tablespoon of coarse brown sugar
- » 1 teaspoon of baking powder
- » ¼ teaspoon of baking soda
- » 1 1/3 cup of all-purpose flour
- » ½ cup of ricotta cheese
- » 1 cup of mixed berries

## DIRECTION

1. In a mixing bowl, combine the salt, sugar, baking powder, baking soda, and flour.

2. In a separate mixing bowl, combine the ricotta, eggs, oil, and milk.

3. Combine the wet mixture with the dry mixture. Mix well. Put aside for 10 minutes.

4. Place a large, non-stick frying pan over medium heat. When the pan is hot to the touch, spoon even amounts of the batter into the pan, making sure that the batter dollops do not touch.

5. When they begin to bubble through, flip them over and cook for a further minute or two.

6. Follow this process until all the batter has been made into pancakes.

7. Evenly divide the pancakes between four plates. Top with mixed berries and drizzle with maple syrup and a few extra dollops of ricotta.

**NUTRITIONS:**
281 calories, 19g fat, 5g Protein

# 193. MEDITERRANEAN FRITTATA

**COOKING: 25'**　　　　**PREPARATION:5'**　　　　**SERVES: 4**

## INGREDIENTS

» 1 pinch of salt
» 1 pinch of black pepper
» 1 tablespoon of extra-virgin olive oil
» 2 egg whites
» 6 eggs
» 1 cup of goat cheese
» 1 cup of Parmesan, shredded
» 8 oz. of mixed mushrooms
» 1 leek, diced
» 1 lb. of asparagus, finely sliced
» ½ cup of fresh basil leaves

## DIRECTION

1. Preheat your oven to 400 F.

2. Scourge egg whites and eggs, salt, pepper, Parmesan cheese, and basil leaves. Set this aside.

3. In a large skillet, preferably non-stick, add the olive oil and leeks over medium heat. Cook until the leeks have softened, then add in the mushrooms, asparagus, stir to combine and cook for a further 5 minutes.

4. Put egg mixture to the skillet, using a spatula to spread the eggs evenly over the mixture. Allow to cook for two minutes and then top with the goat cheese.

5. Place the skillet into the oven and allow to bake for five minutes

6. Remove from the oven and serve.

**NUTRITIONS:**
317 calories, 11g fat, 3g Protein

# 194. CAPONATA

**COOKING: 70'**　　　　**PREPARATION:30'**　　　　**SERVES: 6**

## INGREDIENTS

» 1 pinch of salt
» 1 pinch of black pepper
» Fl oz. of extra-virgin olive oil
» Fl oz. of red wine vinegar
» 2 shallots, diced
» 4 sticks of celery, diced
» 4 plum tomatoes, diced
» 3 eggplants
» 2 teaspoons of capers
» oz. of raisins
» ½ cup of pine nuts, raw
» ½ cup of fresh basil leaves
» Extra-virgin olive oil
» 1 clove of garlic
» 8 slices of ciabatta

## DIRECTION

1. Place casserole over medium heat, cook olive oil and cubed eggplant

2. Remove the eggplant and set aside.

3. Add the diced shallots to the casserole and cook until softened. Follow by adding the plum tomatoes.

4. Allow the tomatoes to break down and return the eggplant cubes to this mixture.

5. Add the salt, pepper, vinegar, celery, capers, and raisins.

6. Set heat to low, cover and simmer for 40 minutes. Once the vegetables have cooked through, remove from the heat and set aside.

7. Coat the sliced ciabatta with olive oil and place onto a griddle pan over medium heat. Remove once charred on both sides. Rub the ciabatta slices with garlic cloves to enhance their flavor.

8. Top the caponata with the pine nuts and basil leaves, and serve with the sliced ciabatta on the side.

**NUTRITIONS:**
311 calories, 12g fat, 2g Protein

# 195. FRESH DELI PASTA

**COOKING: 30'**　　　　**PREPARATION:15'**　　　　**SERVES: 4**

## INGREDIENTS

- » 1 pinch of salt
- » 1 pinch of black pepper
- » 2 tablespoons of extra-virgin olive oil
- » 2 teaspoons of white wine vinegar
- » 1 clove of garlic
- » 1 tomato, diced
- » 10 sun-dried tomatoes
- » 7 oz. of frozen peas
- » oz. of pasta of your choice
- » oz. of prosciutto
- » ½ cup of fresh basil leaves

## DIRECTION

1. In a large saucepan, cover the pasta with water and add a pinch of salt. Bring to a boil and allow to cook for 10 minutes, then add the frozen peas and cook for another 2 minutes.

2. Once the pasta is tender, drain it by placing it into a colander and running cold water over it. Give the colander a few shakes and set aside.

3. Pulse salt, pepper, olive oil, vinegar, garlic, 10 leaves of basil, tomato, and 5 of the sun-dried tomatoes into a blender.

4. Add the cooked pasta and peas to the serving bowl, add the remaining basil leaves, and lightly tear the prosciutto over the pasta.

5. Toss then serve.

## NUTRITIONS:
341 calories, 11g fat, 3g Protein

# CHAPTER 15
# SIDE RECIPES PART 2

# 196. BALSAMIC ASPARAGUS

**COOKING: 15'**    **PREPARATION:10'**    **SERVINGS: 4**

## INGREDIENTS

- » 3 tablespoons olive oil
- » 3 garlic cloves
- » 2 tablespoons shallot
- » 2 teaspoons balsamic vinegar
- » 1 and ½ pound asparagus

## DIRECTION

1. Preheat pan with the oil over medium-high heat, add the garlic and the shallot and sauté for 3 minutes.
2. Add the rest of the ingredients, cook for 12 minutes more, divide between plates and serve.

**NUTRITIONS:**
100 calories, 10.5g fat, 2.1g Protein

# 197. LIME CUCUMBER MIX

**COOKING: 0'**    **PREPARATION:10'**    **SERVINGS: 8**

## INGREDIENTS

- » 4 cucumbers
- » ½ cup green bell pepper
- » 1 yellow onion
- » 1 chili pepper
- » 1 garlic clove
- » 1 teaspoon parsley
- » 2 tablespoons lime juice
- » 1 tablespoon dill
- » 1 tablespoon olive oil

## DIRECTION

1. Incorporate cucumber with the bell peppers and the rest of the ingredients, toss and serve as a side dish.

**NUTRITIONS:**
123 calories, 4.3g fat, 2g Protein

# 198. WALNUTS CUCUMBER MIX

**COOKING: 0'**     **PREPARATION:5'**     **SERVINGS: 2**

## INGREDIENTS

- » 2 cucumbers
- » 1 tablespoon olive oil
- » 1 red chili pepper
- » 1 tablespoon lemon juice
- » 3 tablespoons walnuts
- » 1 tablespoon balsamic vinegar
- » 1 teaspoon chives

## DIRECTION

1. Mix cucumbers with the oil and the rest of the ingredients, toss and serve

**NUTRITIONS:**
121 calories, 2.3g fat, 2.4g Protein

# 199. CHEESY BEET SALAD

**COOKING: 1 HOUR**     **PREPARATION:10'**     **SERVINGS: 4**

## INGREDIENTS

- » 4 beets
- » 3 tablespoons olive oil
- » ¼ cup lime juice
- » 8 slices goat cheese
- » 1/3 cup walnuts
- » 1 tablespoon chives

## DIRECTION

1. In a roasting pan, combine the beets with the oil, salt and pepper, toss and bake at 400 degrees F for 1 hour.
2. Cool the beets down, transfer them to a bowl, add the rest of the ingredients, toss and serve as a side salad.

**NUTRITIONS:**
156 calories, 4.2g fat, 4g Protein

# 200. ROSEMARY BEETS

**COOKING: 20'**  **PREPARATION:10'**  **SERVINGS: 4**

## INGREDIENTS

- » 4 medium beets
- » 1/3 cup balsamic vinegar
- » 1 teaspoon rosemary, chopped
- » 1 garlic clove, minced
- » ½ teaspoon Italian seasoning
- » 1 tablespoon olive oil

## DIRECTION

1. Place pan with the oil over medium heat, add the beets and the rest of the ingredients, toss, and cook for 20 minutes.
2. Divide the mix between plates and serve.

**NUTRITIONS:**
165 calories, 3.4g fat, 2.3g Protein

# 201. SQUASH AND TOMATOES MIX

**COOKING: 20'**  **PREPARATION:10'**  **SERVINGS: 6**

## INGREDIENTS

- » 5 medium squash
- » 3 tablespoons olive oil
- » 1 cup pine nuts
- » ¼ cup goat cheese
- » 6 tomatoes
- » ½ yellow onion
- » 2 tablespoons cilantro
- » 2 tablespoons lemon juice

## DIRECTION

1. Put pan with the oil over medium heat, cook onion and pine nuts for 3 minutes.
2. Add the squash and the rest of the ingredients, cook everything for 15 minutes, divide between plates and serve.

**NUTRITIONS:**
200 calories, 4.5g fat, 4g Protein

# 202. BALSAMIC EGGPLANT MIX

**COOKING: 20'**          **PREPARATION:10'**          **SERVINGS: 6**

## INGREDIENTS

- » 1/3 cup chicken stock
- » 2 tablespoons balsamic vinegar
- » 1 tablespoon lime juice
- » 2 big eggplants
- » 1 tablespoon rosemary
- » ¼ cup cilantro
- » 2 tablespoons olive oil

## DIRECTION

1. In a roasting pan, combine the eggplants with the stock, the vinegar and the rest of the ingredients, introduce the pan in the oven and bake at 390 degrees F for 20 minutes.
2. Divide the mix between plates and serve.

**NUTRITIONS:**
201 calories, 4.5g fat, 3g Protein

# 203. SAGE BARLEY MIX

**COOKING: 45'**          **PREPARATION:10'**          **SERVINGS: 4**

## INGREDIENTS

- » 1 tablespoon olive oil
- » 1 red onion, chopped
- » 1 tablespoon leaves
- » 1 garlic clove, minced
- » 14 ounces barley
- » ½ tablespoon parmesan
- » 6 cups veggie stock

## DIRECTION

1. Preheat pan with the oil over medium heat, sauté onion and garlic for 5 minutes.
2. Add the sage, barley and the rest of the ingredients except the parmesan, stir, bring to a simmer and cook for 40 minutes,
3. Add the parmesan, stir, divide between plates.

**NUTRITIONS:**
210 calories, 6.5g fat, 3.4g Protein

# 204. HICKPEAS AND BEETS MIX

**COOKING: 25'**     **PREPARATION:10'**     **SERVINGS: 4**

## INGREDIENTS

- » 3 tablespoons capers
- » Juice of 1 lemon
- » Zest of 1 lemon, grated
- » 1 red onion, chopped
- » 3 tablespoons olive oil
- » 14 ounces canned chickpeas
- » 8 ounces beets
- » 1 tablespoon parsley

## DIRECTION

1. Situate pan with the oil over medium heat, add the onion, lemon zest, lemon juice and the capers and sauté for 5 minutes.
2. Add the rest of the ingredients, stir and cook over medium-low heat for 20 minutes more.
3. Divide the mix between plates and serve.

**NUTRITIONS:**
199 calories, 4.5g fat, Protein

# 205. CREAMY SWEET POTATOES MIX

**COOKING: 1 HOUR**     **PREPARATION:10'**     **SERVINGS: 4**

## INGREDIENTS

- » 4 tablespoons olive oil
- » 1 garlic clove, minced
- » 4 medium sweet potatoes
- » 1 red onion, sliced
- » 3 ounces baby spinach
- » Zest and juice of 1 lemon
- » 1 and ½ tablespoons Greek yogurt
- » 2 tablespoons tahini paste

## DIRECTION

1. Situate potatoes on a baking sheet lined with parchment paper, bake at 350 degrees F for 1 hour.
2. Peel the potatoes, cut them into wedges and put them in a bowl.
3. Add the garlic, the oil and the rest of the ingredients, toss, divide the mix between plates and serve.

**NUTRITIONS:**
214 calories, 5.6g fat, 3.1g Protein

# 206. CABBAGE AND MUSHROOMS MIX

**COOKING: 15'**  **PREPARATION:10'**  **SERVINGS: 2**

## INGREDIENTS

- » 1 yellow onion, sliced
- » 2 tablespoons olive oil
- » 1 tablespoon balsamic vinegar
- » ½ pound white mushrooms
- » 1 green cabbage head
- » 4 spring onions

## DIRECTION

1. Position pan with the oil over medium heat, add the yellow onion and the spring onions and cook for 5 minutes.

2. Add the rest of the ingredients, cook everything for 10 minutes, divide between plates and serve.

**NUTRITIONS:**
199 calories, 4.5g fat, 2.2g Protein

# 207. LEMON MUSHROOM RICE

**COOKING: 30'**  **PREPARATION:10'**  **SERVINGS: 4**

## INGREDIENTS

- » 2 cups chicken stock
- » 1 yellow onion, chopped
- » ½ pound white mushrooms
- » 2 garlic cloves, minced
- » 8 ounces wild rice
- » Juice and zest of 1 lemon
- » 1 tablespoon chives, chopped
- » 6 tablespoons goat cheese

## DIRECTION

1. Heat up a pot with the stock over medium heat, add the rice, onion and the rest of the ingredients except the chives and the cheese, bring to a simmer and cook for 25 minutes.

2. Add the remaining ingredients, cook everything for 5 minutes, divide between plates and serve.

**NUTRITIONS:**
222 calories, 5.5g fat, 5.6g Protein

# 208. PAPRIKA AND CHIVES POTATOES

**COOKING: 68'**     **PREPARATION:10'**     **SERVINGS: 4**

## INGREDIENTS

- » 4 potatoes
- » 1 tablespoon olive oil
- » 1 celery stalk, chopped
- » 2 tomatoes, chopped
- » 1 teaspoon sweet paprika
- » 2 tablespoons chives, chopped

## DIRECTION

1. Situate potatoes on a baking sheet lined with parchment paper bake at 350 degrees F for 1 hour.
2. Cool the potatoes down, peel and cut them into larger cubes.
3. Preheat pan with the oil over medium heat, add the celery and the tomatoes and sauté for 2 minutes.
4. Add the potatoes and the rest of the ingredients, toss, cook everything for 6 minutes, divide the mix between plates and serve.

**NUTRITIONS:**
233 calories, 8.7g fat, 6.4g Protein

# 209. BULGUR, KALE AND CHEESE MIX

**COOKING: 10'**     **PREPARATION:10'**     **SERVINGS: 6**

## INGREDIENTS

- » 4 ounces bulgur
- » 4 ounces kale
- » 1 tablespoon mint
- » 3 spring onions
- » 1 cucumber
- » A pinch of allspice
- » 2 tablespoons olive oil
- » Zest and juice of ½ lemon
- » 4 ounces feta cheese

## DIRECTION

1. Put bulgur in a bowl, cover with hot water, aside for 10 minutes and fluff with a fork.
2. Warmup pan with the oil over medium heat, add the onions and the allspice and cook for 3 minutes.
3. Add the bulgur and the rest of the ingredients, cook everything for 5-6 minutes more, divide between plates and serve.

**NUTRITIONS:**
200 calories, 6.7g fat, 4.5g Protein

# 210. SPICY GREEN BEANS MIX

**COOKING: 15'**  **PREPARATION:5'**  **SERVINGS: 4**

## INGREDIENTS

- » 4 teaspoons olive oil
- » 1 garlic clove, minced
- » ½ teaspoon hot paprika
- » ¾ cup veggie stock
- » 1 yellow onion, sliced
- » 1-pound green beans
- » ½ cup goat cheese, shredded
- » 2 teaspoon balsamic vinegar

## NUTRITIONS:

188 calories, 4g fat, 4.4g Protein

## DIRECTION

1. Put pan with the oil over medium heat, add the garlic, stir and cook for 1 minute.

2. Add the green beans and the rest of the ingredients, toss, cook everything for 15 minutes more, divide between plates and serve.

# CHAPTER 16
# SIDE RECIPES PART 3

# 211. PISTACHIO ARUGULA SALAD

**COOKING: 0'**  **PREPARATION: 20'**  **SERVES: 6**

## INGREDIENTS

- » ¼ cup olive oil
- » 6 cups kale, chopped rough
- » 2 cups arugula
- » ½ teaspoon smoked paprika
- » 2 tablespoons lemon juice, fresh
- » 1/3 cup pistachios, unsalted & shelled
- » 6 tablespoons parmesan, grated

## DIRECTION

1. Get out a large bowl and combine your oil, lemon juice, kale and smoked paprika. Massage it into the leaves for about fifteen seconds. You then need to allow it to sit for ten minutes.

2. Mix everything together before serving with grated cheese on top.

**NUTRITIONS:**
150 Calories, 5g Protein, 12g Fat

# 212. POTATO SALAD

**COOKING: 13'**  **PREPARATION: 9'**  **SERVES: 6**

## INGREDIENTS

- » 2 lbs. golden potatoes
- » 3 tablespoons olive oil
- » 3 tablespoons lemon juice, fresh
- » 1 tablespoon olive brine
- » ¼ teaspoon sea salt, fine
- » ½ cup olives, sliced
- » 1 cup celery, sliced
- » 2 tablespoons oregano
- » 2 tablespoons mint leaves

## DIRECTION

1. Boil potatoes in saucepan before turning the heat down to medium-low. Cook for fifteen more minutes.

2. Get out a small bowl and whisk your oil, lemon juice, olive brine and salt together.

3. Drain your potatoes using a colander and transfer it to a serving bowl. Pour in three tablespoons of dressing over your potatoes, and mix well with oregano, and min along with the remaining dressing.

**NUTRITIONS:**
175 Calories, 3g Protein, 7g Fat

# 213. RAISIN RICE PILAF

**COOKING: 8'**          **PREPARATION:13'**          **SERVES: 5**

## INGREDIENTS

- » 1 tablespoon olive oil
- » 1 teaspoon cumin
- » 1 cup onion, chopped
- » ½ cup carrot, shredded
- » ½ teaspoon cinnamon
- » 2 cups instant brown rice
- » 1 ¾ cup orange juice
- » 1 cup golden raisins
- » ¼ cup water
- » ½ cup pistachios, shelled
- » fresh chives, chopped for garnish

## DIRECTION

1. Place a medium saucepan over medium-high heat before adding in your oil. Add n your onion, and stir often so it doesn't burn. Cook for about five minutes and then add in your cumin, cinnamon and carrot. Cook for about another minute.

2. Add in your orange juice, water and rice. Boil before covering your saucepan. Turn the heat down to medium-low and then allow it to simmer for six to seven minutes.

3. Stir in your pistachios, chives and raisins. Serve warm.

**NUTRITIONS:**
320 Calories, 6g Protein, 7g Fat

# 214. LEBANESE DELIGHT

**COOKING: 25'**          **PREPARATION:7'**          **SERVES: 5**

## INGREDIENTS

- » 1 tablespoon olive oil
- » 1 cup vermicelli
- » 3 cups cabbage, shredded
- » 3 cups vegetable broth, low sodium
- » ½ cup water
- » 1 cup instant brown rice
- » ¼ teaspoon sea salt, fine
- » 2 cloves garlic
- » ¼ teaspoon crushed red pepper
- » ½ cup cilantro fresh & chopped
- » lemon slices to garnish

## DIRECTION

1. Get out a saucepan and then place it over medium-high heat. Add in your oil and once it's hot you will need to add in your pasta. Cook for three minutes or until your pasta is toasted. You will have to stir often in order to keep it from burning.

2. Ad in your cabbage, cooking for another four minutes. Continue to stir often.

3. Add in your water and rice. Season with salt, red pepper and garlic before bringing it all to a boil over high heat. Stir, and then cover. Once it's covered turn the heat down to medium-low. Allow it all to simmer for ten minutes.

4. Remove the pan from the burner and then allow it to sit without lifting the lid for five minutes. Take the garlic cloves out and then mash them using a fork. Place them back in, and stir them into the rice. Stir in your cilantro as well and serve warm. Garnish with lemon wedges if desired.

**NUTRITIONS:**
259 Calories, 7g Protein, 4g Fat

# 215. MEDITERRANEAN SWEET POTATO

**COOKING: 25'**          **PREPARATION:6'**          **SERVES: 4**

## INGREDIENTS

- » 4 sweet potatoes
- » 15 ounce can chickpeas, rinsed & drained
- » ½ tablespoon olive oil
- » ½ teaspoon cumin
- » ½ teaspoon coriander
- » ½ teaspoon cinnamon
- » 1 pinch sea salt, fine
- » ½ teaspoon paprika
- » ¼ cup hummus
- » 1 tablespoon lemon juice, fresh
- » 2-3 teaspoon dill, fresh
- » 3 cloves garlic, minced
- » unsweetened almond milk as needed

## DIRECTION

1. Set oven to 400, and then get out a baking sheet. Line it with foil.
2. Wash your sweet potatoes before halving them lengthwise.
3. Take your olive oil, cumin, chickpeas, coriander, sea salt and paprika on your baking sheet. Rub the sweet potatoes with olive oil, placing them face down over the mixture.
4. Roast for twenty to twenty-five minutes.
5. Mix your dill, lemon juice, hummus, garlic and a dash of almond milk.
6. Smash the insides of the sweet potato down, topping with chickpea mixture and sauce before serving.

**NUTRITIONS:**
313 Calories, 8.6g Protein, 9g fats

# 216. FLAVORFUL BRAISED KALE

**COOKING: 32'**          **PREPARATION:7'**          **SERVES: 6**

## INGREDIENTS

- » 1 lb. Kale
- » 1 Cup Cherry Tomatoes, Halved
- » 2 Teaspoons Olive Oil
- » 4 Cloves Garlic, Sliced Thin
- » ½ Cup Vegetable Stock
- » ¼ Teaspoon Sea Salt, Fine
- » 1 Tablespoon Lemon Juice, Fresh
- » 1/8 Teaspoon Black Pepper

## DIRECTION

1. Preheat olive oil in a frying pan using medium heat, and add in your garlic. Sauté for a minute or two until lightly golden.
2. Mix your kale and vegetable stock with your garlic, adding it to your pan.
3. Cover the pan and then turn the heat down to medium-low.
4. Allow it to cook until your kale wilts and part of your vegetable stock should be dissolved.
5. Stir in your tomatoes and cook without a lid until your kale is tender, and then remove it from heat.
6. Mix in your salt, pepper and lemon juice before serving warm.

**NUTRITIONS:**
70 Calories, 4g Protein, 0.5g Fat

# 217. BEAN SALAD

**COOKING: 0'**          **PREPARATION: 16'**          **SERVES: 6**

## INGREDIENTS

- » 1 can garbanzo beans, rinsed & drained
- » 2 tablespoons balsamic vinegar
- » ¼ cup olive oil
- » 4 cloves garlic, chopped fine
- » 1/3 cup parsley, fresh & chopped
- » ¼ cup olive oil
- » 1 red onion, diced
- » 6 lettuce leaves
- » ½ cup celery, chopped fine/black pepper to taste

## DIRECTION

1. Make the vinaigrette dressing by whipping together your garlic, parsley, vinegar and pepper in a bowl.
2. Add the olive oil to this mixture and whisk before setting it aside.
3. Add in your onion and beans, and then pour your dressing on top. Toss then cover it. Chill before serving
4. Place a lettuce leaf on the plate when serving and spoon the mixture in. garnish with celery.

**NUTRITIONS:**
218 Calories, 7g Protein, 0.1g Fat

# 218. BASIL TOMATO SKEWERS

**COOKING: 0'**          **PREPARATION: 14'**          **SERVES: 2**

## INGREDIENTS

- » 16 mozzarella balls, fresh & small
- » 16 basil leaves, fresh
- » 16 cherry tomatoes
- » olive oil to drizzle
- » sea salt & black pepper to taste

## DIRECTION

1. Start by threading your basil, cheese and tomatoes together on small skewers.
2. Drizzle with oil before seasoning. Serve.

**NUTRITIONS:**
46 Calories, 7.6g Protein, 0.9g Fat

# 219. OLIVES WITH FETA

**COOKING: 0'**          **PREPARATION:5'**          **SERVES: 4**

## INGREDIENTS

» ½ Cup Feta Cheese
» 1 Cup Kalamata Olives
» 2 Cloves Garlic, Sliced
» 2 Tablespoons Olive Oil
» 1 Lemon, Zested & Juiced
» 1 Teaspoon Rosemary, Fresh & Chopped
» Crushed Red Pepper
» Black Pepper to Taste

## DIRECTION

1. Mix everything together and serve over crackers.

**NUTRITIONS:**
71 Calories, 4g Protein, 2.6g Fat

# 220. BLACK BEAN MEDLEY

**COOKING: 0'**          **PREPARATION:5'**          **SERVES: 4**

## INGREDIENTS

» 4 plum tomatoes, chopped
» 14.5 ounces black beans, canned & drained
» ½ red onion, sliced
» ¼ cup dill, fresh & chopped
» 1 lemon, juiced
» 2 tablespoons olive oil
» ¼ cup feta cheese, crumbled
» sea salt to taste

## DIRECTION

1. Mix everything in a bowl except for your feta and salt. Top the beans with salt and feta.

**NUTRITIONS:**
121 Calories, 6g Protein, 5g Fat

THE COMPLETE MEDITERRANEAN DIET COOKBOOK 2021

# 221. MEDITERRANEAN QUICHE

**COOKING: 25'**     **PREPARATION: 7'**     **SERVES: 6**

## INGREDIENTS

- » ½ cup sundried tomatoes
- » 2 cloves garlic, minced
- » 1 onion, diced
- » 2 tablespoons butter
- » 1 prepared pie crust
- » boiling water
- » 1 red pepper, diced
- » 2 cups spinach, fresh
- » ¼ cup kalamata olives
- » 1 teaspoon oregano
- » 1 teaspoon parsley
- » 1/3 cup feta cheese, crumbled
- » 4 eggs, large
- » 1 ¼ cup milk
- » sea salt & black pepper to taste
- » 1 cup cheddar cheese, shredded & divided

## DIRECTION

1. Add your tomatoes to boiling water and allow it to cook for five minutes before draining.
2. Chop the tomatoes before setting them to the side, and adjust the oven to 375.
3. Spread the pie crust into a nine-inch pie pan, and heat the butter and add in your garlic and onion.
4. Cook for three minutes before adding in your red pepper, and then cook for another three minutes.
5. Add in your parsley and oregano before adding in your spinach and olives. Cook for about another five minutes. Take it off heat, and then add in your feta cheese and tomatoes.
6. Spread your mixture into the prepared pie crust, and then beat the egg and milk. Season with salt and pepper and then add in half a cup of cheese.
7. Pour this mixture over your spinach, and then bake for fifty-five minutes. It should be golden, and serve warm.

## NUTRITIONS:
417 Calories, 14.5g Protein, 13.3g Fat

---

# 222. GRILLED FISH WITH LEMONS

**COOKING: 20'**     **PREPARATION: 8'**     **SERVES: 4**

## INGREDIENTS

- » 3-4 Lemons
- » 1 Tablespoon Olive Oil
- » Sea Salt & Black Pepper to Taste
- » 4 Catfish Fillets, 4 Ounces Each
- » Nonstick Cooking Spray

## DIRECTION

1. Pat your fillets dry using a paper towel and let them come to room temperature. This may take ten minutes. Coat the cooking grate of your grill with nonstick cooking spray while it's cold. Once it's coated preheat it to 400 degrees.
2. Cut one lemon in half, setting it to the side. Slice your remaining half of the lemon into ¼ inch slices. Get out a bowl and squeeze a tablespoon of juice from your reserved half. Add your oil to the bowl, mixing well.
3. Brush your fish down with the oil and lemon mixture.
4. Place your lemon slices on the grill and then put our fillets on top. Grill with your lid closed. Turn the fish halfway through if they're more than a half an inch thick.

## NUTRITIONS:
147 Calories, 22g Protein, 1g Fat

# 223. PESTO WALNUT NOODLES

**COOKING: 25'**  **PREPARATION: 7'**  **SERVES: 4**

## INGREDIENTS

» 4 Zucchini, Made into Zoodles
» ¼ Cup Olive Oil, Divided
» ½ Teaspoon Crushed Red Pepper
» 2 Cloves Garlic, Minced & Divided
» ¼ Teaspoon Black Pepper
» ¼ Teaspoon sea Salt
» 2 Tablespoons Parmesan Cheese, Grated & Divided
» 1 Cup Basil, Fresh & Packed
» ¾ Cup Walnut Pieces, Divided

## DIRECTION

1. Start by making your zucchini noodles by using a spiralizer to get ribbons. Combine your zoodles with a minced garlic clove and tablespoon of oil. Season with salt and pepper and crushed red pepper. Set it to the side.

2. Get out a large skillet and heat a ½ a tablespoon of oil over medium-high heat. Add in half of your zoodles, cooking for five minutes. Repeat with another ½ a tablespoon of oil and your remaining zoodles.

3. Make your pesto while your zoodles cook. Put your garlic clove, a tablespoon or parmesan, basil leaves and ¼ cup of walnuts in your food processor. Season with salt and pepper if desired, and drizzle the remaining two tablespoons of oil in until completely blended.

4. Add the pesto to your zoodles, topping with remaining walnuts and parmesan to serve.

**NUTRITIONS:**
301 Calories, 7g Protein, 28g Fat

# 224. TOMATO TABBOULEH

**COOKING: 30'**  **PREPARATION: 6'**  **SERVES: 4**

## INGREDIENTS

» 8 beefsteak tomatoes
» ½ cup water
» 3 tablespoons olive oil, divided
» ½ cup whole wheat couscous, uncooked
» 1 ½ cups parsley, fresh & minced
» 2 scallions chopped
» 1/3 cup mint, fresh & minced
» sea salt & black pepper to taste
» 1 lemon
» 4 teaspoons honey, raw
» 1/3 cup almonds, chopped

## DIRECTION

1. Set oven to 400 degrees. Take your tomato and slice the top off each one before scooping the flesh out. Put the tops flesh and seeds in a mixing bowl.

2. Get out a baking dish before adding in a tablespoon of oil to grease it. Place your tomatoes in the dish, and then cover your dish with foil.

3. Now you will make your couscous while your tomatoes cook. Bring the water to a boil using a saucepan and then add the couscous in and cover. Remove it from heat, and allow it to sit for five minutes. Fluff it with a fork.

4. Chop your tomato flesh and tops up, and then drain the excess water using a colander. Measure a cup of your chopped tomatoes and place them back in the mixing bowl. Mix with mint scallions, pepper, salt and parsley.

5. Zest lemon, and then half the lemon. Squeeze the lemon juice in, and mix well.

6. Add your tomato mix to the couscous.

7. Carefully remove your tomatoes from the oven and then divide your tabbouleh among your tomatoes. Cover the pan with foil and then put it in the oven. Cook for another eight to ten minutes.

8. Drizzle with honey and top with almonds before serving.

**NUTRITIONS:**
314 Calories, 8g Protein, 15g Fat

# 225. LEMON FARO BOWL

**COOKING: 25'**　　　　**PREPARATION:9'**　　　　**SERVES: 6**

## INGREDIENTS

- » 1 ½ tablespoon olive oil
- » 1 cup onion, chopped
- » 2 cloves garlic, minced
- » 1 carrot, shredded
- » 2 cups vegetable broth, low sodium
- » 1 cup pearled faro
- » 2 avocados, peeled, pitted & sliced
- » 1 lemon, small

## DIRECTION

1. Situate saucepan over medium-high heat. Add in a tablespoon of oil and then throw in your onion once the oil is hot. Cook for about five minutes, stirring frequently to keep it from burning.

2. Add in your carrot and garlic. Allow it to cook for about another minute while you continue to stir.

3. Add in your broth and faro. Boil and adjust your heat to high to help. Once it boils, lower it to medium-low and cover your saucepan. Let it simmer for twenty minutes.

4. Pour the faro into a bowl and add in your avocado and zest. Drizzle with your remaining oil and add in your lemon wedges.

## NUTRITIONS:

279 Calories, 7g Protein, 14g Fat

# CHAPTER 17
# SEAFOOD RECIPES

# 226. BAKED BEAN FISH MEAL

**COOKING: 10'**         **PREPARATION:10'**         **SERVINGS: 4**

## INGREDIENTS

- » 1 tablespoon balsamic vinegar
- » 2 ½ cups green beans
- » 1-pint cherry or grape tomatoes
- » 4 (4-ounce each) fish fillets, such as cod or tilapia
- » 2 tablespoons olive oil

## DIRECTION

1. Preheat an oven to 400 degrees. Grease two baking sheets with some olive oil or olive oil spray. Arrange 2 fish fillets on each sheet. In a mixing bowl, pour olive oil and vinegar. Combine to mix well with each other.

2. Mix green beans and tomatoes. Combine to mix well with each other. Combine both mixtures well with each other. Add mixture equally over fish fillets. Bake for 6-8 minutes, until fish opaque and easy to flake. Serve warm.

**NUTRITIONS:**
229 Calories, 13g Fat, 2.5g Protein

# 227. MUSHROOM COD STEW

**COOKING: 20'**         **PREPARATION:10'**         **SERVINGS: 6**

## INGREDIENTS

- » 2 tablespoons extra-virgin olive oil
- » 2 garlic cloves, minced
- » 1 can tomato
- » 2 cups chopped onion
- » ¾ teaspoon smoked paprika
- » a (12-ounce) jar roasted red peppers
- » 1/3 cup dry red wine
- » ¼ teaspoon kosher or sea salt
- » ¼ teaspoon black pepper
- » 1 cup black olives
- » 1 ½ pounds cod fillets, cut into 1-inch pieces
- » 3 cups sliced mushrooms

## DIRECTION

1. Get medium-large cooking pot, warm up oil over medium heat. Add onions and stir-cook for 4 minutes.

2. Add garlic and smoked paprika; cook for 1 minute, stirring often. Add tomatoes with juice, roasted peppers, olives, wine, pepper, and salt; stir gently.

3. Boil mixture. Add the cod and mushrooms; turn down heat to medium. Close and cook until the cod is easy to flake, stir in between. Serve warm.

**NUTRITIONS:**
238 Calories, 7g Fat, 3.5g Protein

# 228. SPICED SWORDFISH

**COOKING: 15'**  **PREPARATION:10'**  **SERVINGS: 4**

## INGREDIENTS

- » 4 (7 ounces each) swordfish steaks
- » 1/2 teaspoon ground black pepper
- » 12 cloves of garlic, peeled
- » 3/4 teaspoon salt
- » 1 1/2 teaspoon ground cumin
- » 1 teaspoon paprika
- » 1 teaspoon coriander
- » 3 tablespoons lemon juice
- » 1/3 cup olive oil

## DIRECTION

1. Take a blender or food processor, open the lid and add all the ingredients except for swordfish. Close the lid and blend to make a smooth mixture. Pat dry fish steaks; coat evenly with the prepared spice mixture.

2. Add them over an aluminum foil, cover and refrigerator for 1 hour. Preheat a griddle pan over high heat, pour oil and heat it. Add fish steaks; stir-cook for 5-6 minutes per side until cooked through and evenly browned. Serve warm.

**NUTRITIONS:**
255 Calories, 12g Fat, 0.5g Protein

# 229. ANCHOVY PASTA MANIA

**COOKING: 20'**  **PREPARATION:10'**  **SERVINGS: 4**

## INGREDIENTS

- » 4 anchovy fillets, packed in olive oil
- » ½ pound broccoli, cut into 1-inch florets
- » 2 cloves garlic, sliced
- » 1-pound whole-wheat penne
- » 2 tablespoons olive oil
- » ¼ cup Parmesan cheese, grated
- » Salt and black pepper, to taste
- » Red pepper flakes, to taste

## DIRECTION

1. Cook pasta as directed over pack; drain and set aside. Take a medium saucepan or skillet, add oil. Heat over medium heat.

2. Add anchovies, broccoli, and garlic, and stir-cook until veggies turn tender for 4-5 minutes. Take off heat; mix in the pasta. Serve warm with Parmesan cheese, red pepper flakes, salt, and black pepper sprinkled on top.

**NUTRITIONS:**
328 Calories, 8g Fat, 7g Protein

# 230. SHRIMP GARLIC PASTA

**COOKING: 15'**     **PREPARATION:10'**     **SERVINGS: 4**

## INGREDIENTS

- » 1-pound shrimp
- » 3 garlic cloves, minced
- » 1 onion, finely chopped
- » 1 package whole wheat or bean pasta
- » 4 tablespoons olive oil
- » Salt and black pepper, to taste
- » ¼ cup basil, cut into strips
- » ¾ cup chicken broth, low-sodium

## DIRECTION

1. Cook pasta as directed over pack; rinse and set aside. Get medium saucepan, add oil then warm up over medium heat. Add onion, garlic and stir-cook until become translucent and fragrant for 3 minutes.

2. Add shrimp, black pepper (ground) and salt; stir-cook for 3 minutes until shrimps are opaque. Add broth and simmer for 2-3 more minutes. Add pasta in serving plates; add shrimp mixture over; serve warm with basil on top.

**NUTRITIONS:**
605 Calories, 17g Fat, 19g Protein

# 231. VINEGAR HONEYED SALMON

**COOKING: 5'**     **PREPARATION:10'**     **SERVINGS: 4**

## INGREDIENTS

- » 4 (8-ounce) salmon filets
- » 1/2 cup balsamic vinegar
- » 1 tablespoon honey
- » Black pepper and salt, to taste
- » 1 tablespoon olive oil

## DIRECTION

1. Combine honey and vinegar. Combine to mix well with each other.

2. Season fish fillets with the black pepper (ground) and sea salt; brush with honey glaze. Take a medium saucepan or skillet, add oil.

3. Heat over medium heat. Add salmon fillets and stir-cook until medium rare in center and lightly browned for 3-4 minutes per side. Serve warm.

**NUTRITIONS:**
481 Calories, 16g Fat, 1.5g Protein

# 232. ORANGE FISH MEAL

**COOKING: 5'**     **PREPARATION:10'**     **SERVINGS: 4**

## INGREDIENTS

- » ¼ teaspoon kosher or sea salt
- » 1 tablespoon extra-virgin olive oil
- » 1 tablespoon orange juice
- » 4 (4-ounce) tilapia fillets, with or without skin
- » ¼ cup chopped red onion
- » 1 avocado, pitted, skinned, and sliced

## DIRECTION

1. Take a baking dish of 9-inch; add olive oil, orange juice, and salt. Combine well. Add fish fillets and coat well.

2. Add onions over fish fillets. Cover with a plastic wrap. Microwave for 3 minutes until fish is cooked well and easy to flake. Serve warm with sliced avocado on top.

**NUTRITIONS:**
231 Calories, 9g Fat, 2.5g Protein

# 233. SHRIMP ZOODLES

**COOKING: 5'**     **PREPARATION:10'**     **SERVINGS: 2**

## INGREDIENTS

- » 2 tablespoons chopped parsley
- » 2 teaspoons minced garlic
- » 1 teaspoon salt
- » ½ teaspoon black pepper
- » 2 medium zucchinis, spiralized
- » 3/4 pounds medium shrimp, peeled & deveined
- » 1 tablespoon olive oil
- » 1 lemon, juiced and zested

## DIRECTION

1. Take a medium saucepan or skillet, add oil, lemon juice, lemon zest. Heat over medium heat. Add shrimps and stir-cook 1 minute per side.

2. Sauté garlic and red pepper flakes for 1 more minute. Add Zoodles and stir gently; cook for 3 minutes until cooked to satisfaction. Season well, serve warm with parsley on top.

**NUTRITIONS:**
329 Calories, 12g Fat, 3g Protein

# 234. ASPARAGUS TROUT MEAL

**COOKING: 20'**  **PREPARATION:10'**  **SERVINGS: 4**

## INGREDIENTS

- » 2 pounds trout fillets
- » 1-pound asparagus
- » 1 tablespoon olive oil
- » 1 garlic clove, finely minced
- » 1 scallion, thinly sliced
- » 4 medium golden potatoes
- » 2 Roma tomatoes, chopped
- » 8 pitted kalamata olives, chopped
- » 1 large carrot, thinly sliced
- » 2 tablespoons dried parsley
- » ¼ cup ground cumin
- » 2 tablespoons paprika
- » 1 tablespoon vegetable bouillon seasoning
- » ½ cup dry white wine

## DIRECTION

1. In a mixing bowl, add fish fillets, white pepper and salt. Combine to mix well with each other. Take a medium saucepan or skillet, add oil.

2. Heat over medium heat. Add asparagus, potatoes, garlic, white part scallion, and stir-cook until become softened for 4-5 minutes. Add tomatoes, carrot and olives; stir-cook for 6-7 minutes until turn tender. Add cumin, paprika, parsley, bouillon seasoning, and salt. Stir mixture well.

3. Mix in white wine and fish fillets. Over low heat, cover and simmer mixture for about 6 minutes until fish is easy to flake, stir in between. Serve warm with green scallions on top.

**NUTRITIONS:**
303 Calories, 17g Fat, 6g Protein

# 235. KALE OLIVE TUNA

**COOKING: 15'**  **PREPARATION:10'**  **SERVINGS: 6**

## INGREDIENTS

- » 1 cup chopped onion
- » 3 garlic cloves, minced
- » 1 (2.25-ounce) can sliced olives
- » 1-pound kale, chopped
- » 3 tablespoons extra-virgin olive oil
- » ¼ cup capers
- » ¼ teaspoon crushed red pepper
- » 2 teaspoons sugar
- » 1 (15-ounce) can cannellini beans
- » 2 (6-ounce) cans tuna in olive oil, un-drained
- » ¼ teaspoon black pepper
- » ¼ teaspoon kosher or sea salt

## DIRECTION

1. Soak kale in boiling water for 2 minutes; drain and set aside. Take a medium-large cooking pot or stock pot, heat oil over medium heat.

2. Add onion and stir-cook until become translucent and softened. Add garlic and stir-cook until become fragrant for 1 minute.

3. Add olives, capers, and red pepper, and stir-cook for 1 minute. Mix in cooked kale and sugar. Over low heat, cover and simmer mixture for about 8-10 minutes, stir in between.

4. Add tuna, beans, pepper, and salt. Stir well and serve warm.

**NUTRITIONS:**
242 Calories, 11g Fat, 7g Protein

# 236. TANGY ROSEMARY SHRIMPS

**COOKING: 10'**          **PREPARATION:10'**          **SERVINGS: 6**

## INGREDIENTS

- » 1 large orange, zested and peeled
- » 3 garlic cloves, minced
- » 1 ½ pounds raw shrimp, shells and tails removed
- » 3 tablespoons olive oil
- » 1 tablespoon chopped thyme
- » 1 tablespoon chopped rosemary
- » ¼ teaspoon black pepper
- » ¼ teaspoon kosher or sea salt

## DIRECTION

1. Take a zip-top plastic bag, add orange zest, shrimps, 2 tablespoons olive oil, garlic, thyme, rosemary, salt, and black pepper. Shake well and set aside to marinate for 5 minutes.

2. Take a medium saucepan or skillet, add 1 tablespoon olive oil. Heat over medium heat. Add shrimps and stir-cook for 2-3 minutes per side until totally pink and opaque.

3. Slice orange into bite-sized wedges and add in a serving plate. Add shrimps and combine well. Serve fresh.

**NUTRITIONS:**
187 Calories, 7g Fat, 0.5g Protein

# 237. ASPARAGUS SALMON

**COOKING: 15'**          **PREPARATION:10'**          **SERVINGS: 2**

## INGREDIENTS

- » 8.8-ounce bunch asparagus
- » 2 small salmon fillets
- » 1 ½ teaspoon salt
- » 1 teaspoon black pepper
- » 1 tablespoon olive oil
- » 1 cup hollandaise sauce, low-carb

## DIRECTION

1. Season well the salmon fillets. Take a medium saucepan or skillet, add oil. Heat over medium heat.

2. Add salmon fillets and stir-cook until evenly seared and cooked well for 4-5 minutes per side. Add asparagus and stir cook for 4-5 more minutes. Serve warm with hollandaise sauce on top.

**NUTRITIONS:**
565 Calories, 7g Fat, 2.5g Protein

# 238. TUNA NUTTY SALAD

**COOKING: 0'**　　　**PREPARATION:10'**　　　**SERVINGS: 4**

## INGREDIENTS

» 1 tablespoon chopped tarragon
» 1 stalk celery, trimmed and finely diced
» 1 medium shallot, diced
» 3 tablespoons chopped chives
» 1 (5-ounce) can tuna (covered in olive oil)
» 1 teaspoon Dijon mustard
» 2-3 tablespoons mayonnaise
» 1/4 teaspoon salt
» 1/8 teaspoon pepper
» 1/4 cup pine nuts, toasted

## DIRECTION

1. In a large salad bowl, add tuna, shallot, chives, tarragon, and celery. Combine to mix well with each other. In a mixing bowl, add mayonnaise, mustard, salt, and black pepper.

2. Combine to mix well with each other. Add mayonnaise mixture to salad bowl; toss well to combine. Add pine nuts and toss again. Serve fresh.

**NUTRITIONS:**
236 Calories, 14g Fat, 1g Protein

# 239. CREAMY SHRIMP SOUP

**COOKING: 35'**　　　**PREPARATION:10'**　　　**SERVINGS: 6**

## INGREDIENTS

» 1-pound medium shrimp
» 1 leek, both whites and light green parts, sliced
» 1 medium fennel bulb, chopped
» 2 tablespoons olive oil
» 3 stalks celery, chopped
» 1 clove garlic, minced
» Sea salt and ground pepper to taste
» 4 cups vegetable or chicken broth
» 1 tablespoon fennel seeds
» 2 tablespoons light cream
» Juice of 1 lemon

## DIRECTION

1. Take a medium-large cooking pot or Dutch oven, heat oil over medium heat. Add celery, leek, and fennel and stir-cook for about 15 minutes, until vegetables are softened and browned. Add garlic; season with black pepper and sea salt to taste. Add fennel seed and stir.

2. Pour broth and bring to a boil. Over low heat, simmer mixture for about 20 minutes, stir in between. Add shrimp and cook until just pink for 3 minutes. Mix in cream and lemon juice; serve warm.

**NUTRITIONS:**
174 Calories, 5g Fat, 2g Protein

# 240. SPICED SALMON WITH VEGETABLE QUINOA

**COOKING: 10'**     **PREPARATION:30'**     **SERVINGS: 4**

## INGREDIENTS

» 1 cup uncooked quinoa
» 1 teaspoon of salt, divided in half
» ¾ cup cucumbers, seeds removed, diced
» 1 cup of cherry tomatoes, halved
» ¼ cup red onion, minced
» 4 fresh basil leaves, cut in thin slices
» Zest from one lemon
» ¼ teaspoon black pepper
» 1 teaspoon cumin
» ½ teaspoon paprika
» 4 (5-oz.) salmon fillets
» 8 lemon wedges
» ¼ cup fresh parsley, chopped

## NUTRITIONS:

385 Calories, 12.5g Fat, 35.5g Protein

## DIRECTION

1. Directions:

2. To a medium-sized saucepan, add the quinoa, 2 cups of water, and ½ teaspoons of the salt. Heat these until the water is boiling, then lower the temperature until it is simmering. Cover the pan and let it cook 20 minutes or as long as the quinoa package instructs. Turn off the burner under the quinoa and allow it to sit, covered, for at least another 5 minutes before serving.

3. Right before serving, add the onion, tomatoes, cucumbers, basil leaves, and lemon zest to the quinoa and use a spoon to stir everything together gently. In the meantime (while the quinoa cooks), prepare the salmon. Turn on the oven broiler to high and make sure a rack is in the lower part of the oven. To a small bowl, add the following components: black pepper, ½ teaspoon of the salt, cumin, and paprika. Stir them together.

4. Place foil over the top of a glass or aluminum baking sheet, then spray it with nonstick cooking spray. Place salmon fillets on the foil. Rub the spice mixture over each fillet (about ½ teaspoons of the spice mixture per fillet). Add the lemon wedges to the pan edges near the salmon.

5. Cook the salmon under the broiler for 8-10 minutes. Your goal is for the salmon to flake apart easily with a fork. Sprinkle the salmon with the parsley, then serve it with the lemon wedges and vegetable parsley. Enjoy!

# CHAPTER 18
# SEAFOOD RECIPES PART 2

# 241. BAKED COD WITH VEGETABLES

**COOKING: 25'**  **PREPARATION:15'**  **SERVES: 2**

## INGREDIENTS

» 1 pound (454 g) thick cod fillet, cut into 4 even portions
» ¼ teaspoon onion powder (optional)
» ¼ teaspoon paprika
» 3 tablespoons extra-virgin olive oil
» 4 medium scallions
» ½ cup fresh chopped basil, divided
» 3 tablespoons minced garlic (optional)
» 2 teaspoons salt
» 2 teaspoons freshly ground black pepper
» ¼ teaspoon dry marjoram (optional)
» 6 sun-dried tomato slices
» ½ cup dry white wine
» ½ cup crumbled feta cheese
» 1 (15-ounce / 425-g) can oil-packed artichoke hearts, drained
» 1 lemon, sliced
» 1 cup pitted kalamata olives
» 1 teaspoon capers (optional)
» 4 small red potatoes, quartered

## NUTRITIONS:
1168 calories, 60g fat, 64g Protein

## DIRECTION

1. Set oven to 375°F (190°C).
2. Season the fish with paprika and onion powder (if desired).
3. Heat an ovenproof skillet over medium heat and sear the top side of the cod for about 1 minute until golden. Set aside.
4. Heat the olive oil in the same skillet over medium heat. Add the scallions, ¼ cup of basil, garlic (if desired), salt, pepper, marjoram (if desired), tomato slices, and white wine and stir to combine. Boil then removes from heat.
5. Evenly spread the sauce on the bottom of skillet. Place the cod on top of the tomato basil sauce and scatter with feta cheese. Place the artichokes in the skillet and top with the lemon slices.
6. Scatter with the olives, capers (if desired), and the remaining ¼ cup of basil. Pullout from the heat and transfer to the preheated oven. Bake for 15 to 20 minutes
7. Meanwhile, place the quartered potatoes on a baking sheet or wrapped in aluminum foil. Bake in the oven for 15 minutes.
8. Cool for 5 minutes before serving.

# 242. SLOW COOKER SALMON IN FOIL

**COOKING: 2 HOURS**  **PREPARATION:5'**  **SERVES: 2**

## INGREDIENTS

» 2 (6-ounce / 170-g) salmon fillets
» 1 tablespoon olive oil
» 2 cloves garlic, minced
» ½ tablespoon lime juice
» 1 teaspoon finely chopped fresh parsley
» ¼ teaspoon black pepper

## DIRECTION

1. Spread a length of foil onto a work surface and place the salmon fillets in the middle.
2. Blend olive oil, garlic, lime juice, parsley, and black pepper. Brush the mixture over the fillets. Fold the foil over and crimp the sides to make a packet.
3. Place the packet into the slow cooker, cover, and cook on High for 2 hours
4. Serve hot.

## NUTRITIONS:
446 calories, 21g fat, 65g Protein

# 243. DILL CHUTNEY SALMON

**COOKING: 3'**     **PREPARATION:5'**     **SERVES: 2**

## INGREDIENTS

- » Chutney:
- » ¼ cup fresh dill
- » ¼ cup extra virgin olive oil
- » Juice from ½ lemon
- » Sea salt, to taste
- » Fish:
- » 2 cups water
- » 2 salmon fillets
- » Juice from ½ lemon
- » ¼ teaspoon paprika
- » Salt and freshly ground pepper to taste

## DIRECTION

1. Pulse all the chutney ingredients in a food processor until creamy. Set aside.
2. Add the water and steamer basket to the Instant Pot. Place salmon fillets, skin-side down, on the steamer basket. Drizzle the lemon juice over salmon and sprinkle with the paprika.
3. Secure the lid. Select the Manual mode and set the cooking time for 3 minutes at High Pressure.
4. Once cooking is complete, do a quick pressure release. Carefully open the lid.
5. Season the fillets with pepper and salt to taste. Serve topped with the dill chutney.

**NUTRITIONS:**
636 calories, 41g fat, 65g Protein

# 244. GARLIC-BUTTER PARMESAN SALMON AND ASPARAGUS

**COOKING: 15'**     **PREPARATION:10'**     **SERVES: 2**

## INGREDIENTS

- » 2 (6-ounce / 170-g) salmon fillets, skin on and patted dry
- » Pink Himalayan salt
- » Freshly ground black pepper, to taste
- » 1 pound (454 g) fresh asparagus, ends snapped off
- » 3 tablespoons almond butter
- » 2 garlic cloves, minced
- » ¼ cup grated Parmesan cheese

## DIRECTION

1. Prep oven to 400°F (205°C). Line a baking sheet with aluminum foil.
2. Season both sides of the salmon fillets.
3. Situate salmon in the middle of the baking sheet and arrange the asparagus around the salmon.
4. Heat the almond butter in a small saucepan over medium heat.
5. Cook minced garlic
6. Drizzle the garlic-butter sauce over the salmon and asparagus and scatter the Parmesan cheese on top.
7. Bake in the preheated oven for about 12 minutes. You can switch the oven to broil at the end of cooking time for about 3 minutes to get a nice char on the asparagus.
8. Let cool for 5 minutes before serving.

**NUTRITIONS:**
435 calories, 26g fat, 42g Protein

# 245. LEMON ROSEMARY ROASTED BRANZINO

**COOKING: 30'**     **PREPARATION:15'**     **SERVES: 2**

## INGREDIENTS

- » 4 tablespoons extra-virgin olive oil, divided
- » 2 (8-ounce) Branzino fillets
- » 1 garlic clove, minced
- » 1 bunch scallions
- » 10 to 12 small cherry tomatoes, halved
- » 1 large carrot, cut into ¼-inch rounds
- » ½ cup dry white wine
- » 2 tablespoons paprika
- » 2 teaspoons kosher salt
- » ½ tablespoon ground chili pepper
- » 2 rosemary sprigs or 1 tablespoon dried rosemary
- » 1 small lemon, thinly sliced
- » ½ cup sliced pitted kalamata olives

## DIRECTION

1. Heat a large ovenproof skillet over high heat until hot, about 2 minutes. Add 1 tablespoon of olive oil and heat
2. Add the Branzino fillets, skin-side up, and sear for 2 minutes. Flip the fillets and cook. Set aside.
3. Swirl 2 tablespoons of olive oil around the skillet to coat evenly.
4. Add the garlic, scallions, tomatoes, and carrot, and sauté for 5 minutes
5. Add the wine, stirring until all ingredients are well combined. Carefully place the fish over the sauce.
6. Preheat the oven to 450ºF (235ºC).
7. Brush the fillets with the remaining 1 tablespoon of olive oil and season with paprika, salt, and chili pepper. Top each fillet with a rosemary sprig and lemon slices. Scatter the olives over fish and around the skillet.
8. Roast for about 10 minutes until the lemon slices are browned. Serve hot.

**NUTRITIONS:**
724 calories, 43g fat, 57g Protein

# 246. GRILLED LEMON PESTO SALMON

**COOKING: 10'**     **PREPARATION:5'**     **SERVES: 2**

## INGREDIENTS

- » 10 ounces (283 g) salmon fillet
- » 2 tablespoons prepared pesto sauce
- » 1 large fresh lemon, sliced
- » Cooking spray

## DIRECTION

1. Preheat the grill to medium-high heat. Spray the grill grates with cooking spray.
2. Season the salmon well. Spread the pesto sauce on top.
3. Make a bed of fresh lemon slices about the same size as the salmon fillet on the hot grill, and place the salmon on top of the lemon slices. Put any additional lemon slices on top of the salmon.
4. Grill the salmon for 10 minutes.
5. Serve hot.

**NUTRITIONS:**
Cooking spray 316 calories, 21g fat, 29g Protein

# 247. STEAMED TROUT WITH LEMON HERB CRUST

**COOKING: 15'**     **PREPARATION:10'**     **SERVES: 2**

## INGREDIENTS

- » 3 tablespoons olive oil
- » 3 garlic cloves, chopped
- » 2 tablespoons fresh lemon juice
- » 1 tablespoon chopped fresh mint
- » 1 tablespoon chopped fresh parsley
- » ¼ teaspoon dried ground thyme
- » 1 teaspoon sea salt
- » 1 pound (454 g) fresh trout (2 pieces)
- » 2 cups fish stock

## DIRECTION

1. Blend olive oil, garlic, lemon juice, mint, parsley, thyme, and salt. Brush the marinade onto the fish.
2. Insert a trivet in the Instant Pot. Fill in the fish stock and place the fish on the trivet.
3. Secure the lid. Select the Steam mode and set the cooking time for 15 minutes at High Pressure.
4. Once cooking is complete, do a quick pressure release. Carefully open the lid. Serve warm.

**NUTRITIONS:**
477 calories, 30g fat, 52g Protein

# 248. ROASTED TROUT STUFFED WITH VEGGIES

**COOKING: 25'**     **PREPARATION:10'**     **SERVES: 2**

## INGREDIENTS

- » 2 (8-ounce) whole trout fillets
- » 1 tablespoon extra-virgin olive oil
- » ¼ teaspoon salt
- » 1/8 teaspoon black pepper
- » 1 small onion, thinly sliced
- » ½ red bell pepper
- » 1 poblano pepper
- » 2 or 3 shiitake mushrooms, sliced
- » 1 lemon, sliced

## DIRECTION

1. Set oven to 425ºF (220ºC). Coat baking sheet with nonstick cooking spray.
2. Rub both trout fillets, inside and out, with the olive oil. Season with salt and pepper.
3. Mix together the onion, bell pepper, poblano pepper, and mushrooms in a large bowl. Stuff half of this mix into the cavity of each fillet. Top the mixture with 2 or 3 lemon slices inside each fillet.
4. Place the fish on the prepared baking sheet side by side. Roast in the preheated oven for 25 minutes
5. Pullout from the oven and serve on a plate.

**NUTRITIONS:**
453 calories, 22g fat, 49g Protein

# 249. LEMONY TROUT WITH CARAMELIZED SHALLOTS

**COOKING: 20'**     **PREPARATION:10'**     **SERVES: 2**

## INGREDIENTS

- » Shallots:
- » 1 teaspoon almond butter
- » 2 shallots, thinly sliced
- » Dash salt
- » Trout:
- » 1 tablespoon almond butter
- » 2 (4-ounce / 113-g) trout fillets
- » 3 tablespoons capers
- » ¼ cup freshly squeezed lemon juice
- » ¼ teaspoon salt
- » Dash freshly ground black pepper
- » 1 lemon, thinly sliced

## DIRECTION

1. For Shallots
2. Situate skillet over medium heat, cook the butter, shallots, and salt for 20 minutes, stirring every 5 minutes.
3. For Trout
4. Meanwhile, in another large skillet over medium heat, heat 1 teaspoon of almond butter.
5. Add the trout fillets and cook each side for 3 minutes, or until flaky. Transfer to a plate and set aside.
6. In the skillet used for the trout, stir in the capers, lemon juice, salt, and pepper, then bring to a simmer. Whisk in the remaining 1 tablespoon of almond butter. Spoon the sauce over the fish.
7. Garnish the fish with the lemon slices and caramelized shallots before serving.

**NUTRITIONS:**
344 calories, 18g fat, 21g Protein

# 250. EASY TOMATO TUNA MELTS

**COOKING: 4'**     **PREPARATION:5'**     **SERVES: 2**

## INGREDIENTS

- » 1 (5-oz) can chunk light tuna packed in water
- » 2 tablespoons plain Greek yogurt
- » 2 tablespoons finely chopped celery
- » 1 tablespoon finely chopped red onion
- » 2 teaspoons freshly squeezed lemon juice
- » 1 large tomato, cut into ¾-inch-thick rounds
- » ½ cup shredded Cheddar cheese

## DIRECTION

1. Preheat the broiler to High.
2. Stir together the tuna, yogurt, celery, red onion, lemon juice, and cayenne pepper in a medium bowl.
3. Place the tomato rounds on a baking sheet. Top each with some tuna salad and Cheddar cheese.
4. Broil for 3 to 4 minutes until the cheese is melted and bubbly. Cool for 5 minutes before serving.

**NUTRITIONS:**
244 calories, 10g fat, 30g Protein

# 251. MACKEREL AND GREEN BEAN SALAD

**COOKING: 10'**  **PREPARATION:10'**  **SERVES: 2**

## INGREDIENTS

- » 2 cups green beans
- » 1 tablespoon avocado oil
- » 2 mackerel fillets
- » 4 cups mixed salad greens
- » 2 hard-boiled eggs, sliced
- » 1 avocado, sliced
- » 2 tablespoons lemon juice
- » 2 tablespoons olive oil
- » 1 teaspoon Dijon mustard
- » Salt and black pepper, to taste

## DIRECTION

1. Cook the green beans in pot of boiling water for about 3 minutes. Drain and set aside.
2. Melt the avocado oil in a pan over medium heat. Add the mackerel fillets and cook each side for 4 minutes.
3. Divide the greens between two salad bowls. Top with the mackerel, sliced egg, and avocado slices.
4. Scourge lemon juice, olive oil, mustard, salt, and pepper, and drizzle over the salad. Add the cooked green beans and toss to combine, then serve.

## NUTRITIONS:
737 calories, 57g fat, 34g Protein

# 252. HAZELNUT CRUSTED SEA BASS

**COOKING: 15'**  **PREPARATION:10'**  **SERVES: 2**

## INGREDIENTS

- » 2 tablespoons almond butter
- » 2 sea bass fillets
- » 1/3 cup roasted hazelnuts
- » A pinch of cayenne pepper

## DIRECTION

1. Ready oven to 425ºF (220ºC). Line a baking dish with waxed paper.
2. Brush the almond butter over the fillets.
3. Pulse the hazelnuts and cayenne in a food processor. Coat the sea bass with the hazelnut mixture, then transfer to the baking dish.
4. Bake in the preheated oven for about 15 minutes. Cool for 5 minutes before serving.

## NUTRITIONS:
468 calories, 31g fat, 40g Protein

# 253. SHRIMP AND PEA PAELLA

**COOKING: 60'**  **PREPARATION: 20'**  **SERVES: 2**

## INGREDIENTS

- » 2 tablespoons olive oil
- » 1 garlic clove, minced
- » ½ large onion, minced
- » 1 cup diced tomato
- » ½ cup short-grain rice
- » ½ teaspoon sweet paprika
- » ½ cup dry white wine
- » 1¼ cups low-sodium chicken stock
- » 8 ounces (227 g) large raw shrimp
- » 1 cup frozen peas
- » ¼ cup jarred roasted red peppers

## DIRECTION

1. Heat the olive oil in a large skillet over medium-high heat.
2. Add the garlic and onion and sauté for 3 minutes, or until the onion is softened.
3. Add the tomato, rice, and paprika and stir for 3 minutes to toast the rice.
4. Add the wine and chicken stock and stir to combine. Bring the mixture to a boil.
5. Cover and set heat to medium-low, and simmer for 45 minutes
6. Add the shrimp, peas, and roasted red peppers. Cover and cook for an additional 5 minutes. Season with salt to taste and serve.

**NUTRITIONS:**
646 calories, 27g fat, 42g Protein

# 254. GARLIC SHRIMP WITH ARUGULA PESTO

**COOKING: 5'**  **PREPARATION: 20'**  **SERVES: 2**

## INGREDIENTS

- » 3 cups lightly packed arugula
- » ½ cup lightly packed basil leaves
- » ¼ cup walnuts
- » 3 tablespoons olive oil
- » 3 medium garlic cloves
- » 2 tablespoons grated Parmesan cheese
- » 1 tablespoon freshly squeezed lemon juice
- » 1 (10-ounce) package zucchini noodles
- » 8 ounces (227 g) cooked, shelled shrimp
- » 2 Roma tomatoes, diced

## DIRECTION

1. Process the arugula, basil, walnuts, olive oil, garlic, Parmesan cheese, and lemon juice in a food processor until smooth, scraping down the sides as needed. Season
2. Heat a skillet over medium heat. Add the pesto, zucchini noodles, and cooked shrimp. Toss to combine the sauce over the noodles and shrimp, and cook until heated through.
3. Season well. Serve topped with the diced tomatoes.

**NUTRITIONS:**
435 calories, 30.2g fat, 33g Protein

THE COMPLETE MEDITERRANEAN DIET COOKBOOK 2021

# 255. BAKED OYSTERS WITH VEGETABLES

**COOKING: 17'**   **PREPARATION:30'**   **SERVES: 2**

## INGREDIENTS

- » 2 cups coarse salt, for holding the oysters
- » 1 dozen fresh oysters, scrubbed
- » 1 tablespoon almond butter
- » ¼ cup finely chopped scallions
- » ½ cup finely chopped artichoke hearts
- » ¼ cup finely chopped red bell pepper
- » 1 garlic clove, minced
- » 1 tablespoon finely chopped fresh parsley
- » Zest and juice of ½ lemon

## NUTRITIONS:

135 calories, 7g fat, 6g Protein

## DIRECTION

1. Pour the salt into a baking dish and spread to fill the bottom of the dish evenly.
2. Using a shucking knife, insert the blade at the joint of the shell, where it hinges open and shut. Firmly apply pressure to pop the blade in, and work the knife around the shell to open. Discard the empty half of the shell. Using the knife, gently loosen the oyster, and remove any shell particles. Sprinkle salt in the oysters
3. Set oven to 425°F (220°C).
4. Heat the almond butter in a large skillet over medium heat. Add the scallions, artichoke hearts, and bell pepper, and cook for 5 to 7 minutes. Cook garlic
5. Takeout from the heat and stir in the parsley, lemon zest and juice, and season to taste with salt and pepper.
6. Divide the vegetable mixture evenly among the oysters. Bake in the preheated oven for 10 to 12 minutes.

# CHAPTER 19
# SEAFOOD RECIPES PART 3

# 256. GRILLED WHOLE SEA BASS

**COOKING: 15'**　　　**PREPARATION:5'**　　　**SERVES: 2**

## INGREDIENTS

- » 1 (1-pound) whole lavraki
- » ¼ cup extra-virgin olive oil
- » 1 bunch fresh thyme
- » ¼ cup chopped fresh parsley
- » 2 teaspoons minced garlic
- » 1 small lemon, cut into ¼-inch rounds

## DIRECTION

1. Preheat a grill to high heat.
2. Rub the olive oil all over the fish's surface and in its middle cavity.
3. Season liberally with salt and pepper.
4. Stuff the inner cavity with the thyme, parsley, garlic, and lemon slices.
5. Set the lavraki on the grill (see Cooking tip). Cook for 6 minutes per side.
6. Remove the head, backbone, and tail. Carve 2 fillets from each side for serving.

**NUTRITIONS:**
480 Calories, 34g Fat, 43g Protein

# 257. PAN-COOKED FISH WITH TOMATOES

**COOKING: 45'**　　　**PREPARATION:20'**　　　**SERVES: 8**

## INGREDIENTS

- » 1½ cups extra-virgin olive oil
- » 1½ cups tomato juice
- » 2 (12-ounce) cans organic tomato paste
- » 2 teaspoons sea salt
- » 2 teaspoons cane sugar
- » 1 teaspoon black pepper
- » 1 teaspoon dried Greek oregano
- » 3 pounds fresh white fish fillets
- » 2 large sweet onions
- » 1 cup white wine
- » 1½ cups bread crumbs
- » 4 garlic cloves
- » ½ cup fresh parsley
- » 4 large, firm tomatoes

## DIRECTION

1. Preheat the oven to 325°F.
2. Blend olive oil, tomato juice, tomato paste, salt, sugar, pepper, and oregano. Rub small amount of the mixture onto the bottom of 9-by-13-inch roasting pan.
3. Lay the fresh fish fillets side by side on top of the tomato mixture.
4. Cover with the onion slices, overlapping them.
5. Sprinkle the wine evenly over each piece of fish.
6. Pour half of the tomato and olive oil mixture over the fish.
7. Blend bread crumbs, garlic, and parsley. Spread over the fish.
8. Lay the tomato slices, overlapping them, over the fish. Drizzle remaining tomato mixture over the top.
9. Bake for 40 to 45 minutes.

**NUTRITIONS:**
908 Calories, 55g Fat, 51g Protein

# 258. FISH STEAMED IN PARCHMENT WITH VEGGIES

**COOKING: 20'**          **PREPARATION:25'**          **SERVES: 4**

## INGREDIENTS

- » Juice of 2 lemons
- » 4 tablespoons extra-virgin olive oil
- » 2 teaspoons sea salt
- » 1 teaspoon freshly ground black pepper
- » 4 (6- to 8-ounce) fish fillets
- » ½ pound tomatoes, chopped
- » ½ cup chopped scallion
- » ¼ cup chopped Kalamata olives
- » 1 tablespoon capers, drained
- » ¼ cup white wine vinegar
- » 2 garlic cloves, minced
- » 1 fennel bulb

## DIRECTION

1. Preheat the oven to 375°F.
2. Scourge lemon juice, 2 tablespoons of olive oil, salt, and pepper.
3. Add the fish and marinate in the refrigerator for 10 minutes.
4. In a medium bowl, combine the tomatoes, scallion, olives, capers, vinegar, remaining 2 tablespoons of olive oil, and garlic.
5. Fold 4 (12-by-16-inch) pieces of parchment paper in half and cut out a half heart shape, keeping as much of the parchment as possible. Unfold the hearts and place ¼ of the fennel close to the center crease to make a bed for the fish. Top with 1 fish fillet and ¼ of the tomato mixture.
6. Fold the parchment back over the fish and, starting at the bottom end, start folding the edges, overlapping to seal the packet. Bake for 20 minutes.

**NUTRITIONS:**
277 Calories, 16g Fat, 27g Protein

# 259. SWORDFISH SOUVLAKI

**COOKING: 10'**          **PREPARATION:25'**          **SERVES: 4**

## INGREDIENTS

- » ½ cup freshly squeezed lemon juice
- » ½ cup extra-virgin olive oil
- » 1 teaspoon kosher salt
- » 1 teaspoon freshly ground black pepper
- » 1 teaspoon dried Greek oregano
- » 2 pounds swordfish steaks
- » 8 ounces cherry tomatoes
- » 1 red onion, quartered

## DIRECTION

1. Scourge lemon juice, olive oil, salt, pepper, and oregano.
2. Add the fish and marinate in the refrigerator for 10 to 15 minutes.
3. Heat a grill to medium-high heat.
4. Skewer the swordfish, tomatoes, and red onion, alternating 1 to 2 pieces of fish for each tomato and onion quarter. Grill the kebabs for 10 minutes.
5. Alternatively, broil the skewers carefully for 3 to 5 minutes per side, checking frequently.
6. Serve with a squeeze of lemon and Avocado Skordalia / Avocado Garlic Spread.

**NUTRITIONS:**
493 Calories, 34g Fat, 42g Protein

# 260. STUFFED MONKFISH

**COOKING: 8'**     **PREPARATION:20'**     **SERVES: 4**

## INGREDIENTS

» 4 (6-ounce) fresh white fish fillets
» 6 tablespoons extra-virgin olive oil, divided
» ½ teaspoon sea salt
» ½ teaspoon freshly ground black pepper
» ¼ cup feta cheese
» ¼ cup minced green olives
» ¼ cup minced orange pulp
» 1 tablespoon orange zest
» ½ teaspoon dried dill
» ¼ cup chopped fresh Greek basil

## DIRECTION

1. Blend fish with 2 tablespoons of olive oil, salt, and pepper.
2. In another bowl, mix together the feta, olives, and orange pulp. Spoon the mixture onto the fish fillets and spread it to coat them. Roll the fillets, inserting 2 toothpicks through to the other side to hold them together.
3. In heavy-bottomed skillet over medium-high heat, heat the remaining olive oil for about 15 seconds.
4. Add the rolled fillets and cook for 6 to 8 minutes, depending on their thickness, rolling onto each side as they cook.
5. Top each piece with the orange zest, dill, and basil, equally divided.

**NUTRITIONS:**
365 Calories, 25g Fat, 29g Protein

# 261. SHRIMP SANTORINI

**COOKING: 30'**     **PREPARATION:20'**     **SERVES: 4**

## INGREDIENTS

» 1-pound shrimp
» 5 tablespoons extra-virgin olive oil
» 2 teaspoons kosher salt
» 2 teaspoons freshly ground black pepper
» 1 onion, chopped
» 4 garlic cloves, minced
» 2 pounds tomatoes, chopped or grated
» ½ teaspoon red pepper flakes
» ½ teaspoon dried Greek oregano
» 6 ounces feta cheese
» 3 tablespoons chopped fresh parsley

## DIRECTION

1. Preheat the oven to 400°F.
2. Throw shrimp with 1 tablespoon of olive oil and the salt, and season with black pepper.
3. Using medium oven-safe skillet over medium heat, cook 4 tablespoons of olive oil.
4. Add the onion and season with salt. Cook for 3 to 5 minutes.
5. Add the garlic and black pepper. Cook for 4 minutes.
6. Cook tomatoes, red pepper flakes, and oregano for 10 minutes.
7. Arrange the shrimp and olives (if using) over the tomato mixture in one layer.
8. Crumble the feta over the surface.
9. Bake for 10 to 12 minutes.
10. Remove from the oven and garnish with parsley.

**NUTRITIONS:**
458 Calories, 29g Fat, 35g Protein

# 262. GREEK-STYLE SHRIMP COCKTAIL

**COOKING: 5'**   **PREPARATION:15'**   **SERVES: 4**

## INGREDIENTS

- » 1 pound (20- to 30-count) wild shrimp
- » 1 egg
- » 1 tablespoon Greek oregano or dill
- » 2 teaspoons minced Kalamata olives
- » 1 garlic clove, minced
- » 1 teaspoon mustard
- » ½ cup walnut oil
- » ¼ teaspoon sea salt
- » ¼ teaspoon freshly ground black pepper

## DIRECTION

1. Boil 8 cups of water in pot over high heat.
2. Add the shrimp and boil for 2 to 3 minutes, until pink. Drain and cool.
3. In a food processor, combine the egg, oregano, olives, garlic, and mustard. Blend to combine.
4. With the processor running on low speed, very gradually add the walnut oil through the feed tube on your food processor.
5. When it has thickened to a mayonnaise-like texture, blend in the salt and pepper. Serve.

**NUTRITIONS:**
257 Calories, 13g Fat, 31g Protein

# 263.FRIED CALAMARI

**COOKING: 2'**   **PREPARATION:20'**   **SERVES: 6**

## INGREDIENTS

- » 2 eggs
- » 1 cup organic cornmeal
- » 1 teaspoon sea salt
- » ½ teaspoon dried dill
- » 1-pound calamari rings and tentacles
- » ½ cup Kalamata olives, pitted
- » 1 lemon, cut into wedges and seeded
- » 2 cups extra-virgin olive oil

## DIRECTION

1. Beat the eggs in a flat shallow dish with a fork.
2. In another flat shallow dish, mix the cornmeal, salt, and dill with a fork.
3. Prepare the calamari, olives, and lemon slices for frying by lightly coating each piece with egg and dredging through the seasoned cornmeal.
4. With a skillet over medium heat, heat the olive oil
5. Add the calamari, lemon, and olives to the pan. Fry for about 2 minutes
6. Remove the items with a slotted spoon and place on paper towel to drain any excess oil.

**NUTRITIONS:**
374 Calories, 19g Fat, 23g Protein

# 264. STUFFED SQUID

**COOKING: 45'**  **PREPARATION:20'**  **SERVES: 4**

## INGREDIENTS

- » For squid
- » 1 tablespoon extra-virgin olive oil
- » 1 onion, chopped
- » 1 teaspoon sea salt
- » 1 teaspoon freshly ground black pepper
- » 3 garlic cloves, minced
- » 1-pound small squid
- » ½ pound cherry tomatoes, halved
- » ¼ cup basmati or long-grain rice, rinsed
- » ¼ cup pine nuts, toasted
- » ¼ cup fresh basil
- » For sauce
- » ¼ cup extra-virgin olive oil
- » 1 onion, chopped
- » 1 teaspoon sea salt
- » 1 teaspoon black pepper
- » 2 garlic cloves, chopped
- » ¼ cup dry white wine
- » 1 (28-ounce) can diced tomatoes
- » ¼ cup fresh basil, cut into chiffonade
- » Juice of 1 lemon
- » Lemon slices, for serving

## NUTRITIONS:
429 Calories, 25g Fat, 22g Protein

## DIRECTION

1. Situate pot over medium-high heat, heat the olive oil.
2. Sauté onion, salt, and pepper for 5 minutes.
3. Add the garlic. Cook for 1 minute
4. If the squid came with tentacles, chop them up and put them in the pot now.
5. Add the cherry tomatoes, rice, and pine nuts. Cook for 3 minutes
6. Fold the fresh basil into the mixture.
7. Prick the squid bodies all over with a toothpick and snip off the very end of the cavity.
8. Stuff each squid with filling so it is ¼-to-½ full. The rice will expand when the squid cooks in the sauce, so make sure there's room.
9. For sauce and cook the squid
10. In the same pot in which you cooked the stuffing, heat the olive oil over medium-high heat.
11. Add the onion, salt, and pepper. Cook for 3 to 5 minutes
12. Add the garlic. Cook for about 1 minute.
13. Stir white wine to deglaze the pan
14. Stir in the tomatoes. Cook for 10 minutes.
15. Add the basil.
16. Add the stuffed squid in even layers to the pot. Cover the pot and simmer for 30 minutes. Check the squid by piercing it with a knife—if there is too much resistance, cook for 15 minutes more.
17. When the squid is cooked through, squeeze the lemon into the pot and serve with additional lemon slices.

# 265. OCTOPUS WITH FIGS AND PEACHES

**COOKING: 10'**  **PREPARATION:15'**  **SERVES: 4**

## INGREDIENTS

- » 1-pound octopus tentacles
- » ¼ cup extra-virgin olive oil
- » 1 teaspoon sea salt
- » 1 teaspoon black pepper
- » 1 teaspoon granulated garlic
- » ½ teaspoon dried Greek oregano
- » 1 cup fig balsamic vinegar
- » 6 fresh figs, halved
- » 2 large peaches, quartered
- » ¼ cup chopped fresh parsley

## NUTRITIONS:
304 Calories, 14g Fat, 21g Protein

## DIRECTION

1. In a large bowl, thoroughly mix the octopus, olive oil, salt, pepper, garlic, and oregano to coat well. Marinate in the refrigerator for 2 hours. Bring to room temperature before cooking.
2. In an 8- to 10-inch heavy-bottomed deep skillet over medium-high heat, bring the fig balsamic vinegar to a boil. Reduce the heat to a rolling simmer. Stir with the flat side of a metal spatula so any thickened vinegar is mixed into the liquid instead of sticking to the pan. After about 4 minutes, when the vinegar is foamy on top, add the octopus and stir quickly, cooking for only 2 to 3 minutes
3. Add the figs and peaches to the vinegar remaining in the skillet. Cook for about 1 minute, stirring them into the caramelized vinegar just until coated and soft. Transfer to the serving bowl and gently stir to combine.
4. Top with the parsley.

# 266. OCTOPUS WITH POTATOES

**COOKING: 35'**     **PREPARATION:10'**     **SERVES: 4**

## INGREDIENTS

- » 2 pounds octopus, cleaned
- » 1-pound baby potatoes
- » 1 fennel bulb, quartered
- » 1 bay leaf
- » 10 peppercorns
- » Juice of 2 lemons
- » ¼ cup extra-virgin olive oil
- » 1 teaspoon kosher salt
- » 1 teaspoon freshly ground black pepper
- » 3 garlic cloves
- » 1 cup chopped scallions
- » ¼ cup chopped fresh parsley

## DIRECTION

1. Place 8-quart pot over medium-high heat, mix octopus, potatoes, fennel, bay leaf, and peppercorns. Cover with water. Cover the pot, bring to a boil, reduce the heat to low, and simmer. Don't overcook the octopus or it will be rubbery.
2. Preheat a grill to high heat.
3. Remove the octopus and cut it into 2- to 3-inch pieces and place them on the grill for 1 to 2 minutes per side.
4. In a medium bowl, whisk the lemon juice, olive oil, salt, pepper, and garlic.
5. Remove the potatoes from the pot and add to the dressing, along with the scallions and parsley, and toss to combine.
6. Add the grilled octopus to the bowl and toss with the rest of the ingredients. Turn out onto a platter and serve.

**NUTRITIONS:**

392 Calories, 15g Fat, 43g Protein

# 267. FETA CRAB CAKES

**COOKING: 15'**     **PREPARATION:30'**     **SERVES: 4**

## INGREDIENTS

- » 1-pound crabmeat
- » ½ cup minced scallion
- » 1/3 cup bread crumbs
- » ¼ cup feta cheese
- » 2 eggs
- » 2 garlic cloves
- » 1 small Anaheim or pasilla chili
- » 1 medium firm tomato
- » 2 tablespoons minced fresh fennel
- » 2 tablespoons minced fresh parsley
- » ½ teaspoon dried dill
- » ½ teaspoon dried Greek oregano
- » ½ teaspoon sea salt
- » ½ teaspoon freshly ground black pepper
- » ¼ teaspoon ground nutmeg
- » 3 tablespoons extra-virgin olive oil

## DIRECTION

1. Blend crabmeat, scallion, bread crumbs, feta, eggs, garlic, chili, tomato, fennel, parsley, dill, oregano, salt, pepper, and nutmeg. Mix thoroughly. Split mixture into 8 equal portions and form each into a 2½-inch patty about ½ inch thick, creating a definitive edge for easier flipping when cooking.
2. Situate skillet over medium-high heat, heat the olive oil. Place the crab cakes in the heated pan and brown for 7 to 8 minutes per side.

**NUTRITIONS:**

315 Calories, 16g Fat, 15g Protein

# 268. STEAMED MUSSELS WITH WHITE WINE AND FENNEL

**COOKING: 30'** **PREPARATION:20'** **SERVES: 4**

## INGREDIENTS

- » ¼ cup extra-virgin olive oil
- » 1 onion, chopped
- » 1 teaspoon sea salt
- » 4 garlic cloves, minced
- » 1 teaspoon red pepper flakes
- » 1 fennel bulb
- » 1 cup dry white wine
- » 4 pounds mussels
- » Juice of 2 lemons

## DIRECTION

1. Position 8-quart pot over medium-high heat, heat the olive oil.
2. Add the onion and salt. Cook for 5 minutes, until translucent.
3. Add garlic and red pepper flakes. Cook for 1 minute.
4. Stir in the chopped fennel. Cook for 3 minutes.
5. Stir in the wine and simmer for about 7 minutes.
6. Carefully pour the mussels into the pot. Reduce the heat to medium, give everything a good stir, cover the pot, and cook for 5 to 7 minutes.
7. Remove the opened mussels and divide them among 4 bowls. Re-cover the pot and cook any unopened mussels for 3 minutes more. Divide any additional opened mussels among the bowls. Discard any unopened mussels. Evenly distribute the broth into the bowls. Garnish with the fennel leaves.

**NUTRITIONS:**
578 Calories, 23g Fat, 55g Protein

# 269. SEAFOOD RICE

**COOKING: 40'** **PREPARATION:10'** **SERVES: 6**

## INGREDIENTS

- » 1 tablespoon extra-virgin olive oil
- » 1½ pounds seafood
- » 1 onion, chopped
- » 1 teaspoon sea salt
- » 4 garlic cloves, minced
- » 1 cup chopped celery
- » 2 medium tomatoes
- » ½ cup dry white wine
- » 2 cups arborio rice
- » ¼ cup chopped fresh parsley
- » ¼ cup chopped fresh dill
- » 4¼ cups chicken broth

## DIRECTION

1. Put skillet over medium-high heat, heat 1 tablespoon of olive oil.
2. Add the squid and cook for about 2 minutes. Remove the squid and set aside.
3. Add the remaining 1 teaspoon of olive oil to the skillet to heat.
4. Add the onion and salt. Cook for 5 minutes.
5. Cook garlic.
6. Add the celery and tomatoes. Cook for 3 minutes.
7. Pour in the wine and cook for about 3 minutes, stirring frequently.
8. Stir in the rice, parsley, dill, and 4 cups of broth. Cover the skillet and simmer for 15 minutes.
9. Top the rice mixture with the shrimp and mussels, cover the skillet, and simmer for 5 minutes more, until the shrimp are just cooked.
10. Return the squid to the skillet. Discard any unopened mussels. Side with the lemon wedges

**NUTRITIONS:**
246 Calories, 5g Fat, 28g Protein

# 270. MIXED SEAFOOD WITH WINE AND CAPERS

**COOKING: 10'**  **PREPARATION:25'**  **SERVES: 4**

## INGREDIENTS

- » 1 (1-pound) bag frozen mixed seafood
- » ½ cup white wine
- » ¼ cup extra-virgin olive oil
- » ½ teaspoon sea salt
- » ½ teaspoon freshly ground black pepper
- » ½ cup capers, drained
- » ¼ cup chopped fresh parsley

## NUTRITIONS:

235 Calories, 14g Fat, 17g Protein

## DIRECTION

1. Thaw the frozen seafood by rinsing in a colander under cold running water for several minutes, turning so that it will thaw evenly. Put aside for 5 minutes, and squeeze out excess water completely.

2. In a small bowl, whisk the white wine, olive oil, salt, and pepper.

3. In a 10-inch skillet over medium-high heat, bring the white wine mixture to a simmer.

4. Add the seafood and stir in the capers. Cook for 5 minutes.

5. Sprinkle with the parsley and serve.

# CHAPTER 20
# VEGETABLE RECIPES

# 271. GREEK STUFFED COLLARD GREENS

**COOKING: 20'**  **PREPARATION:10'**  **SERVES: 4**

## INGREDIENTS

- » 1 (28-ounce) can low-sodium crushed tomatoes
- » 8 collard green leaves
- » 2 (10-ounce) bags frozen grain medley
- » 2 tablespoons grated Parmesan cheese

## DIRECTION

1. Preheat the oven to 400°F. Pour the tomatoes into a baking pan and set aside.

2. Fill a large stockpot about three-quarters of the way with water and bring to a boil. Add the collard greens and cook for 2 minutes. Drain in a colander. Put the greens on a clean towel or paper towels and blot dry.

3. To assemble the stuffed collards, lay one leaf flat on the counter vertically. Add about ½ cup of the lentils and rice mixture to the middle of the leaf, and spread it evenly along the middle of the leaf. Fold one long side of the leaf over the rice filling, then fold over the other long side so it is slightly overlapping. Take the bottom end, where the stem was, and gently but firmly roll up until you have a slightly square package. Carefully transfer the stuffed leaf to the baking pan, and place it seam-side down in the crushed tomatoes. Repeat with the remaining leaves.

4. Sprinkle the leaves with the grated cheese, and cover the pan with aluminum foil. Bake for 20 minutes, or until the collards are tender-firm, and serve.

**NUTRITIONS:**
205 Calories, 8g Fat, 6g Protein

# 272. WALNUT PESTO ZOODLES

**COOKING: 10'**  **PREPARATION:15'**  **SERVES: 4**

## INGREDIENTS

- » 4 medium zucchinis
- » ¼ cup extra-virgin olive oil, divided
- » 2 garlic cloves
- » ½ teaspoon crushed red pepper
- » ¼ teaspoon black pepper, divided
- » ¼ teaspoon kosher or sea salt
- » 2 tablespoons grated Parmesan cheese
- » 1 cup packed fresh basil leaves
- » ¾ cup walnut pieces, divided

## DIRECTION

1. Make the zucchini noodles (zoodles) using a spiralizer or your vegetable peeler to make ribbons. Mix zoodles with 1 tablespoon of oil, 1 minced garlic clove, all the crushed red pepper, 1/8 teaspoon of black pepper, and 1/8 teaspoon of salt. Set aside.

2. In a large skillet over medium-high heat, heat ½ tablespoon of oil. Add half of the zoodles to the pan and cook for 5 minutes, stirring every minute or so. Pour the cooked zoodles into a large serving bowl, and repeat with another ½ tablespoon of oil and the remaining zoodles. Add those zoodles to the serving bowl when they are done cooking.

3. While the zoodles are cooking, make the pesto. Using a high-powered blender, add the 2 tablespoons of oil first and then the rest of the pesto ingredients. Pulse until the pesto is completely blended.

4. Add the pesto to the zoodles along with the remaining 1 tablespoon of Parmesan and the remaining ½ cup of walnuts. Mix together well and serve.

**NUTRITIONS:**
301 Calories, 28g Fat, 7g Protein

# 273. CAULIFLOWER STEAKS WITH EGGPLANT RELISH

**COOKING: 25'**  **PREPARATION:5'**  **SERVES: 4**

## INGREDIENTS

- » 2 small heads cauliflower
- » ¼ teaspoon kosher or sea salt
- » ¼ teaspoon smoked paprika
- » extra-virgin olive oil, divided
- » 1 recipe Eggplant Relish Spread

## DIRECTION

1. Situate large, rimmed baking sheet in the oven. Set oven to 400°F with the pan inside.

2. Stand one head of cauliflower on a cutting board, stem-end down. With a long chef's knife, slice down through the very center of the head, including the stem. Starting at the cut edge, measure about 1 inch and cut one thick slice from each cauliflower half, including as much of the stem as possible, to make two cauliflower "steaks." Reserve the remaining cauliflower for another use. Repeat with the second cauliflower head.

3. Dry each steak well with a clean towel. Sprinkle the salt and smoked paprika evenly over both sides of each cauliflower steak.

4. Put skillet over medium-high heat, cook 2 tablespoons of oil. When the oil is very hot, add two cauliflower steaks to the pan and cook for about 3 minutes. Flip and cook for 2 more minutes. Transfer the steaks to a plate. Wipe out the pan to remove most of the hot oil. Repeat the cooking process with the remaining 2 tablespoons of oil and the remaining two steaks.

5. Using oven mitts, carefully remove the baking sheet from the oven and place the cauliflower on the baking sheet. Roast in the oven for 13 minutes. Serve with the Eggplant Relish Spread.

**NUTRITIONS:**
282 calories, 22g Fat, 8g Protein

# 274. MEDITERRANEAN LENTIL SLOPPY JOES

**COOKING: 15'**  **PREPARATION:5'**  **SERVES: 4**

## INGREDIENTS

- » 1 tablespoon extra-virgin olive oil
- » 1 cup chopped onion
- » 1 cup chopped bell pepper
- » 2 garlic cloves
- » 1 (15-ounce) can lentils, drained and rinsed
- » 1 (14.5-ounce) can low-sodium tomatoes
- » 1 teaspoon ground cumin
- » 1 teaspoon dried thyme
- » ¼ teaspoon kosher or sea salt
- » 4 whole-wheat pita breads, split open
- » 1½ cups chopped seedless cucumber
- » 1 cup chopped romaine lettuce

## DIRECTION

1. In a saucepan at medium-high heat, sauté onion and bell pepper for 4 minutes. Cook garlic and stir in lentils, tomatoes (with their liquid), cumin, thyme, and salt.

2. Turn the heat to medium and cook, stirring occasionally, for 10 minutes.

3. Stuff the lentil mixture inside each pita. Lay the cucumbers and lettuce on top of mixture and serve.

**NUTRITIONS:**
334 Calories, 5g Fat, 16g Protein

# 275. GORGONZOLA SWEET POTATO BURGERS

**COOKING: 15'**       **PREPARATION:10'**       **SERVES: 4**

## INGREDIENTS

- » 1 large sweet potato (about 8 ounces)
- » 2 tablespoons extra-virgin olive oil, divided
- » 1 cup chopped onion (about ½ medium onion)
- » 1 cup old-fashioned rolled oats
- » 1 large egg
- » 1 tablespoon balsamic vinegar
- » 1 tablespoon dried oregano
- » 1 garlic clove
- » ¼ teaspoon kosher or sea salt
- » ½ cup crumbled Gorgonzola

## DIRECTION

1. Prick sweet potato all over and microwave on high for 4 to 5 minutes. Cool slightly, then slice in half.

2. While the sweet potato is cooking, in a large skillet over medium-high heat, heat 1 tablespoon of oil. Cook onion

3. Using a spoon, carefully scoop the sweet potato flesh out of the skin and put the flesh in a food processor. Blend onion, oats, egg, vinegar, oregano, garlic, and salt. Add the cheese and pulse four times to barely combine. With your hands, form the mixture into four (½-cup-size) burgers. Place the burgers on a plate, and press to flatten each to about ¾-inch thick.

4. Clean out the skillet with a paper towel, then heat the remaining 1 tablespoon of oil over medium-high heat until very hot, about 2 minutes. Add the burgers to the hot oil, then turn the heat down to medium. Cook the burgers for 5 minutes, flip with a spatula, then cook an additional 5 minutes. Enjoy as is or serve on salad greens or whole-wheat rolls.

**NUTRITIONS:**
223 Calories, 13g Fat, 7g Protein

# 276. ZUCCHINI-EGGPLANT GRATIN

**COOKING: 20'**       **PREPARATION:10'**       **SERVES: 6**

## INGREDIENTS

- » 1 large eggplant
- » 2 large zucchinis
- » ¼ teaspoon black pepper
- » ¼ teaspoon kosher or sea salt
- » 3 tablespoons extra-virgin olive oil
- » 1 tablespoon all-purpose flour
- » ¾ cup 2% milk
- » 1/3 cup Parmesan cheese
- » 1 cup chopped tomato
- » 1 cup diced or shredded fresh mozzarella
- » ¼ cup fresh basil leaves

## DIRECTION

1. Preheat the oven to 425°F.

2. Mix eggplant, zucchini, pepper, and salt.

3. Situate skillet over medium-high heat, heat 1 tablespoon of oil. Add half the veggie mixture to the skillet. Stir a few times, then cover and cook for 5 minutes, stirring occasionally. Pour the cooked veggies into a baking dish. Situate skillet back on the heat, add 1 tablespoon of oil, and repeat with the remaining veggies. Add the veggies to the baking dish.

4. While the vegetables are cooking, heat the milk in the microwave for 1 minute. Set aside.

5. Place a medium saucepan over medium heat. Add the remaining tablespoon of oil and flour, and whisk together for about 1 minute

6. Slowly pour the warm milk into the oil mixture, whisking the entire time. Add 1/3 cup of Parmesan cheese, and whisk until melted. Pour the cheese sauce over the vegetables in the baking dish and mix well.

7. Gently mix in the tomatoes and mozzarella cheese. Roast in the oven for 10 minutes, or until the gratin is almost set and not runny. Garnish with the fresh basil leaves and the remaining 2 tablespoons of Parmesan cheese before serving.

**NUTRITIONS:**
207 Calories, 14g Fat, 11g Protein

# 277. GRILLED STUFFED PORTOBELLO MUSHROOMS

**COOKING: 25'**          **PREPARATION:5'**          **SERVES: 6**

## INGREDIENTS

» 3 tablespoons extra-virgin olive oil
» 1 cup diced onion
» 2 garlic cloves
» 3 cups chopped mushrooms
» 2 small zucchinis
» 1 cup chopped tomato
» 1 teaspoon dried oregano
» ¼ teaspoon crushed red pepper
» ¼ teaspoon kosher or sea salt
» 6 large portobello mushrooms
» 4 ounces fresh mozzarella cheese
» Additional dried oregano, for serving (optional)

## NUTRITIONS:

171 Calories, 12g Fat, 9g Protein

## DIRECTION

1. Position skillet over medium heat, heat 2 tablespoons of oil. Add the onion and cook for 4 minutes, stirring occasionally. Stir in the garlic and cook for 1 minute, stirring often.

2. Stir in the mushrooms, zucchini, tomato, oregano, crushed red pepper, and salt. Cook for 10 minutes, stirring occasionally. Remove from the heat.

3. While the veggies are cooking, heat the grill or grill pan to medium-high heat.

4. Brush the remaining tablespoon of oil over the portobello mushroom caps. Place the mushrooms bottom-side (where the stem was removed) down on the grill or pan. Cover and cook for 5 minutes.

5. Flip the mushroom caps over, and spoon about ½ cup of the cooked vegetable mixture into each cap. Top each with about 2½ tablespoons of mozzarella and additional oregano, if desired.

6. Cover and grill for 4 to 5 minutes.

7. Remove each portobello with a spatula, and let them sit for about 5 minutes to cool slightly before serving.

# 278. STUFFED TOMATOES WITH TABBOULEH

**COOKING: 20'**          **PREPARATION:10'**          **SERVES: 4**

## INGREDIENTS

» 8 medium beefsteak tomatoes
» 3 tablespoons extra-virgin olive oil
» ½ cup water
» ½ cup whole-wheat couscous
» 1½ cups minced fresh curly parsley
» 1/3 cup minced fresh mint
» 2 scallions
» ¼ teaspoon black pepper
» ¼ teaspoon kosher or sea salt
» 1 medium lemon
» 4 teaspoons honey
» 1/3 cup chopped almonds

## DIRECTION

1. Preheat the oven to 400°F.

2. Cut top off each tomato and set aside. Spoon out all the flesh inside, and put the tops, flesh, and seeds in a large mixing bowl.

3. Grease a baking dish with 1 tablespoon of oil. Place the carved-out tomatoes in the baking dish, and cover with aluminum foil. Roast for 10 minutes.

4. While the tomatoes are cooking, make the couscous by bringing the water to boil in a medium saucepan. Pour in the couscous, remove from the heat, and cover. Let sit for 5 minutes, then stir with a fork.

5. While the couscous is cooking, chop up the tomato flesh and tops. Drain off the excess tomato water using a colander. Measure out 1 cup of the chopped tomatoes (reserve any remaining chopped tomatoes for another use). Add the cup of tomatoes back into the mixing bowl. Mix in the parsley, mint, scallions, pepper, and salt.

6. Using a Micro plane or citrus grater, zest the lemon into the mixing bowl. Halve the lemon, and squeeze the juice through a strainer (to catch the seeds) from both halves into the bowl with the tomato mixture. Mix well.

7. When the couscous is ready, add it to the tomato mixture and mix well.

8. With oven mitts, carefully remove the tomatoes from the oven. Divide the tabbouleh evenly among the tomatoes and stuff them, using a spoon to press the filling down so it all fits. Wrap with the foil and return it to the oven. Cook for another 8 to 10 minutes. Before serving, top each tomato with a drizzle of ½ teaspoon of honey and about 2 teaspoons of almonds.

## NUTRITIONS:

314 Calories, 15g Fat, 8g Protein

# 279. POLENTA WITH MUSHROOM BOLOGNESE

**COOKING: 25'**     **PREPARATION:5'**     **SERVES: 4**

## INGREDIENTS

- » 2 (8-ounce) packages white button mushrooms
- » 3 tablespoons extra-virgin olive oil, divided
- » 1½ cups onion
- » ½ cup carrot
- » 4 garlic cloves
- » 1 (18-ounce) tube plain polenta
- » ¼ cup tomato paste
- » 1 tablespoon dried oregano
- » ¼ teaspoon ground nutmeg
- » ¼ teaspoon kosher or sea salt
- » ¼ teaspoon freshly ground black pepper
- » ½ cup dry red wine
- » ½ cup whole milk
- » ½ teaspoon sugar

## DIRECTION

1. Situate half the mushrooms in a food processor bowl and pulse about 15 times. Do with the remaining mushrooms and set aside.

2. Situate stockpot over medium-high heat, heat 2 tablespoons of oil. Cook onion and carrot then mushrooms and garlic for 10 minutes.

3. While cooking, add the remaining 1 tablespoon of oil to skillet at medium-high heat. Put 4 slices of polenta to the skillet and cook for 3 to 4 minutes. Remove the polenta from the skillet, place it on a shallow serving dish, and cover with aluminum foil to keep warm. Repeat with the remaining 4 slices of polenta.

4. To the mushroom mixture in the stockpot, add the tomato paste, oregano, nutmeg, salt, and pepper and stir. Continue cooking for another 2 to 3 minutes. Add the wine and cook for 1 to 2 minutes. Lower the heat to medium.

5. Meanwhile, in a small, microwave-safe bowl, mix the milk and sugar together and microwave on high for 30 to 45 seconds. Simmer the milk into the mushroom mixture. Drizzle the mushroom veggie sauce over the warm polenta slices.

## NUTRITIONS:
300 Calories, 12g Fat, 9g Protein

# 280. NORTH AFRICAN PEANUT STEW OVER CAULIFLOWER RICE

**COOKING: 25'**     **PREPARATION:5'**     **SERVES: 4**

## INGREDIENTS

- » 1 cup frozen corn
- » 2 tablespoons extra-virgin olive oil
- » 1 cup chopped onion
- » 2 medium Yukon Gold potatoes
- » 1 large sweet potato
- » 3 garlic cloves
- » 1½ teaspoons ground cumin
- » 1 teaspoon ground allspice
- » 1 teaspoon freshly grated ginger root
- » ½ teaspoon crushed red pepper
- » ¼ teaspoon kosher or sea salt
- » ½ cup water
- » 1 (28-ounce) can diced tomatoes, undrained
- » 1 (12-ounce) package frozen plain cauliflower rice
- » 1 (15-ounce) can lentils, undrained
- » 1/3 cup creamy peanut butter

## DIRECTION

1. Put the corn on the counter to partially thaw while making the stew.

2. In a large stockpot over medium-high heat, heat the oil. Add the onion, potatoes, and sweet potatoes. Cook for 7 minutes. Move the potatoes to the edges of the pot, and add the garlic, cumin, allspice, ginger, crushed red pepper, and salt. Cook for 1 minute, stirring constantly. Stir in the water and cook for 1 more minute, scraping up the crispy bits from the bottom of the pan.

3. Add the tomatoes with their juices to the stockpot. Cook for 15 minutes uncovered, stirring occasionally.

4. While the tomatoes are cooking, cook the cauliflower rice according to the package directions.

5. Into the tomato mixture, stir in the lentils, partially thawed corn, and peanut butter. Adjust to medium heat and cook for 1 to 2 minutes. Serve over the cauliflower rice with hot peppers, peanuts, and fresh cilantro, if desired.

## NUTRITIONS:
467 Calories, 20g Fat, 21g Protein

# 281. ITALIAN BAKED BEANS

**COOKING: 15'**  **PREPARATION:5'**  **SERVES: 6**

## INGREDIENTS

- » 2 teaspoons extra-virgin olive oil
- » ½ cup minced onion
- » 1 (12-ounce) can low-sodium tomato paste
- » ¼ cup red wine vinegar
- » 2 tablespoons honey
- » ¼ teaspoon ground cinnamon
- » ½ cup water
- » 2 (15-ounce) cans cannellini

## DIRECTION

1. Position saucepan over medium heat, heat the oil. Cook onion. Add the tomato paste, vinegar, honey, cinnamon, and water, and mix well. Turn the heat to low.

2. Drain and rinse one can of the beans in a colander and add to the saucepan. Pour the entire second can of beans (including the liquid) into the saucepan. Let it cook for 10 minutes, stirring occasionally, and serve.

**NUTRITIONS:**
236 Calories, 3g Fat, 10g Protein

# 282. CANNELLINI BEAN LETTUCE WRAPS

**COOKING: 10'**  **PREPARATION:10'**  **SERVES: 4**

## INGREDIENTS

- » 1 tablespoon extra-virgin olive oil
- » ½ cup diced red onion
- » ¾ cup chopped fresh tomatoes
- » ¼ teaspoon freshly ground black pepper
- » 1 (15-ounce) can cannellini beans
- » ¼ cup curly parsley
- » ½ cup Lemony Garlic Hummus
- » 8 romaine lettuce leaves

## DIRECTION

1. Position skillet over medium heat, heat the oil. Add the onion and cook for 3 minutes, stirring occasionally. Add the tomatoes and pepper and cook for 3 more minutes, stirring occasionally. Add the beans and cook for 3 more minutes, stirring occasionally. Pullout from the heat, and mix in the parsley.

2. Spread 1 tablespoon of hummus over each lettuce leaf. Evenly spread the warm bean mixture down the center of each leaf. Fold one side of the lettuce leaf over the filling lengthwise, then fold over the other side to make a wrap and serve.

**NUTRITIONS:**
211 Calories, 8g Fat, 10g Protein

# 283. ISRAELI EGGPLANT, CHICKPEA, AND MINT SAUTÉ

**COOKING: 20'**          **PREPARATION:5'**          **SERVES: 6**

## INGREDIENTS

- » 1 medium globe eggplant
- » 1 tablespoon extra-virgin olive oil
- » 2 tablespoons lemon juice
- » 2 tablespoons balsamic vinegar
- » 1 teaspoon ground cumin
- » ¼ teaspoon salt
- » 1 (15-ounce) can chickpeas
- » 1 cup sliced sweet onion
- » ¼ cup mint leaves
- » 1 tablespoon sesame seeds
- » 1 garlic clove

## DIRECTION

1. Place one oven rack about 4 inches below the broiler element. Turn the broiler to the highest setting to preheat. Grease rimmed baking sheet using nonstick cooking spray.
2. Slice eggplant lengthwise into four slabs (½- to 5/8-inch thick). Place the eggplant slabs on the prepared baking sheet. Put aside.
3. Scourge oil, lemon juice, vinegar, cumin, and salt. Brush 2 tablespoons of the lemon dressing over both sides of the eggplant slabs.
4. Broil the eggplant under the heating element for 4 minutes, flip them, then broil for 4 minutes.
5. While the eggplant is broiling, combine the chickpeas, onion, mint, sesame seeds, and garlic. Add the reserved dressing, and gently mix.
6. When done, situate slabs from the baking sheet to a cooling rack and cool for 3 minutes. When slightly cooled, cut each slab crosswise into ½-inch strips.
7. Toss eggplant to the mixture and serve warm.

**NUTRITIONS:**
159 Calories, 4g Fat, 6g Protein

# 284. MEDITERRANEAN LENTILS AND RICE

**COOKING: 25'**          **PREPARATION:5'**          **SERVES: 4**

## INGREDIENTS

- » 2¼ cups low-sodium vegetable broth
- » ½ cup lentils
- » ½ cup uncooked instant brown rice
- » ½ cup diced carrots
- » ½ cup diced celery
- » 1 (2.25-ounce) can sliced olives
- » ¼ cup diced red onion
- » ¼ cup chopped fresh curly-leaf parsley
- » 1½ tablespoons extra-virgin olive oil
- » 1 tablespoon freshly squeezed lemon juice
- » 1 garlic clove
- » ¼ teaspoon kosher or sea salt
- » ¼ teaspoon black pepper

## DIRECTION

1. Position saucepan over high heat, bring the broth and lentils to a boil, cover, and lower the heat to medium-low. Cook for 8 minutes.
2. Raise the heat to medium, and stir in the rice. Cover the pot and cook the mixture for 15 minutes. Take away pot from the heat and let it sit, covered, for 1 minute, then stir.
3. While the lentils and rice are cooking, mix together the carrots, celery, olives, onion, and parsley in a large serving bowl.
4. In a small bowl, whisk together the oil, lemon juice, garlic, salt, and pepper. Set aside.
5. When cooked, put them to the serving bowl. Pour the dressing on top, and mix everything together. Serve.

**NUTRITIONS:**
230 Calories, 8g Fat, 8g Protein

# 285. BROWN RICE PILAF WITH GOLDEN RAISINS

**COOKING: 15'**　　　　**PREPARATION:5'**　　　　**SERVES: 6**

## INGREDIENTS

- » 1 tablespoon extra-virgin olive oil
- » 1 cup chopped onion
- » ½ cup shredded carrot
- » 1 teaspoon ground cumin
- » ½ teaspoon ground cinnamon
- » 2 cups instant brown rice
- » 1¾ cups 100% orange juice
- » ¼ cup water
- » 1 cup golden raisins
- » ½ cup shelled pistachios

## NUTRITIONS:

320 Calories, 7g Fat, 6g Protein

## DIRECTION

1. Put saucepan on medium-high heat, cook onion for 5 minutes. Sauté carrot, cumin, and cinnamon.

2. Stir in the rice, orange juice, and water. Bring to a boil, cover, then lower the heat to medium-low. Simmer for 7 minutes.

3. Stir in the raisins, pistachios, and chives (if using) and serve.

# CHAPTER 21
## VEGETABLE RECIPES PART 2

# 286. VEGETARIAN QUINOA PILAF

**COOKING: 35'**       **PREPARATION:9'**       **SERVINGS: 1**

## INGREDIENTS

» 3 TB. extra-virgin olive oil
» 2 portobello mushrooms, sliced
» 1 medium red onion, finely chopped
» 1 TB. minced garlic
» 1 (16-oz.) can diced tomatoes, with juice
» 2 cups water
» 2 tsp. salt
» 1 TB. dried oregano
» 1 TB. turmeric
» 1 tsp. paprika
» 1 tsp. ground black pepper
» 2 cups red or yellow quinoa
» 1/2 cup fresh parsley, chopped

## DIRECTION

1. In a huge, 3-quart pot over medium heat, cook extra-virgin olive oil. Cook portobello mushrooms
2. Cook red onion and garlic, stir for 5 minutes.
3. Add tomatoes with juice, water, salt, oregano, turmeric, paprika, and black pepper. Stir, and simmer for 5 minutes.
4. Add red quinoa to the pot, and stir. Cover, reduce heat to low, and cook for 20 minutes.
5. Remove from heat, fluff with a fork, cover, and let sit for 10 minutes.
6. Spoon quinoa onto a plate, sprinkle with parsley, and serve warm.

## NUTRITIONS:
305 Calories, 8g Fat, 4g Protein

# 287. ROASTED AND CURRIED CAULIFLOWER

**COOKING: 50'**       **PREPARATION:8'**       **SERVES: 6**

## INGREDIENTS

» 1 lime (juiced)
» 1 medium head of cauliflower
» 1 tsp cayenne pepper
» 1 tsp sea salt
» 1 tsp smoked paprika
» 1 ½ cups full fat Greek yogurt
» ½ tsp black pepper
» 2 tbsp yellow curry powder
» 2 tsp lime zest
» 1 clove garlic
» 1 tbsp cilantro
» 1/2 cup pine nuts
» 1/4 cup olive oil
» 1/4 cup sun-dried tomatoes
» 2 tbsp feta cheese (crumbled)

## DIRECTION

1. Prep baking sheet with parchment paper and preheat the oven to 3750F.
2. Mix well lime zest, curry, black pepper, yogurt, paprika, sea salt, and lime in a bowl. Rub all over the cauliflower.
3. Place cauliflower on the prepared pan and po in the oven. Bake for about 45 minutes.
4. Meanwhile, make the topping ingredients by pulsing sun dried tomatoes, half of pine nits, and garlic in a food processor. Process until chunky.
5. Transfer mixture in a bowl and fold in remaining topping ingredients.
6. One cauliflower is done, remove from the oven and let it cool enough to handle. Break into bite sized pieces and drizzle topping ingredients over it.
7. Serve and enjoy.

## NUTRITIONS:
384 Calories, 15g Protein, 30g Fat

# 288. EASY AND HEALTHY BAKED VEGETABLES

**COOKING: 75'**          **PREPARATION:9'**          **SERVES: 6**

## INGREDIENTS

- » 2 lbs. Brussels sprouts, trimmed
- » 3 lbs. Butternut Squash
- » 1 lb. Pork breakfast sausage
- » 1 tbsp fat from fried sausage

## DIRECTION

1. Grease a 9x inch baking pan and preheat oven to 3500F.
2. With medium high fire, situate nonstick saucepan and cook sausage. Break up sausages and cook until browned.
3. In a greased pan mix browned sausage, squash, sprouts, sea salt and fat. Toss to mix well. Pop into the oven and cook for an hour.
4. Remove from oven and serve warm.

**NUTRITIONS:**
364 Calories, 19g Protein, 17g Fat

# 289. GREEN BEANS AND TOMATOES

**COOKING: 30'**          **PREPARATION:7'**          **SERVES: 2**

## INGREDIENTS

- » 1/4 cup extra-virgin olive oil
- » 2 medium white onions, chopped
- » 11/2 tsp. salt
- » 3 medium tomatoes, chopped
- » 1/4 cup minced garlic
- » 1/2 tsp. ground black pepper
- » 1/2 tsp. cayenne

## DIRECTION

1. 4 cups green beans, trimmed and cut into in. pieces
2. In a big, 3-quart pot over medium heat, cook extra-virgin olive oil. Sauté white onions for 5 minutes.
3. Add salt, tomatoes, and garlic, and cook for 10 minutes.
4. Add black pepper, cayenne, and green beans, and toss together. Cover and cook for 10 minutes.
5. Serve with pita bread.

**NUTRITIONS:**
341 Calories, 10g Fat, 4g Protein

# 290. CRUNCHY KALE CHIPS

**COOKING: 2 HOURS**    **PREPARATION:11'**    **SERVES: 8**

## INGREDIENTS

- » 2 tbsp filtered water
- » ½ tsp sea salt
- » 1 tbsp raw honey
- » 2 tbsp nutritional yeast
- » 1 lemon, juiced
- » 1 cup sweet potato
- » 1 cup fresh cashews
- » 2 bunches green curly kale

## DIRECTION

1. Prepare a baking sheet by covering with an unbleached parchment paper. Preheat oven to 00F.
2. In a large mixing bowl, place kale.
3. In a food processor, process remaining ingredients until smooth. Pour over kale.
4. With your hands, coat kale with marinade.
5. Evenly spread kale onto parchment paper and pop in the oven. Dehydrate for 2 hours and turn leaves after the first hour of baking.
6. Remove from oven; let it cool completely before serving.

**NUTRITIONS:**
209 Calories, 7g Protein, 15.9g Fat

# 291. ZUCCHINI LASAGNA

**COOKING: 45'**    **PREPARATION:13'**    **SERVES: 4**

## INGREDIENTS

- » 2 zucchinis, trimmed
- » 1 cup Mozzarella, shredded
- » ½ cup tomato sauce
- » 1 onion, chopped
- » 1 tablespoon olive oil
- » ½ cup potato, boiled, mashed
- » 1 teaspoon Italian seasonings
- » ¼ cup tomato sauce
- » 1 teaspoon butter, softened

## DIRECTION

1. Heat up olive oil in the skillet.
2. Add onion and roast it until light brown.
3. Meanwhile, slice the zucchini lengthwise.
4. Grease the casserole mold with butter from inside.
5. Put ½ part of sliced zucchini in the casserole mold to get the layer.
6. Then add the layer of cooked onion and a ½ cup of Mozzarella cheese.
7. After this, make the layer from the remaining zucchini.
8. Top the vegetables with a layer of mashed potatoes and Mozzarella.
9. Pour the tomato sauce over the cheese and cover the surface of the mold with foil. Secure the edges.
10. Bake the lasagna for 30 minutes at 365F.
11. Then discard the foil and cook lasagna for 10 minutes more.

**NUTRITIONS:**
103 calories, 6.3g fat, 4.1g Protein

# 292. GARLIC PARMESAN ARTICHOKES

**COOKING: 10'**  **PREPARATION: 9'**  **SERVES: 4**

## INGREDIENTS

- » 4 artichokes, wash, trim, and cut top
- » 1/2 cup vegetable broth
- » 1/4 cup parmesan cheese, grated
- » 1 tbsp olive oil
- » 2 tsp garlic, minced
- » Salt

## DIRECTION

1. Pour broth into the instant pot then place steamer rack in the pot.
2. Place artichoke steam side down on steamer rack into the pot.
3. Sprinkle garlic and grated cheese on top of artichokes and season with salt. Drizzle oil over artichokes.
4. Seal pot with lid and cook on high for 10 minutes.
5. Once done, release pressure using quick release. Remove lid.
6. Serve and enjoy.

**NUTRITIONS:**
132 Calories, 5.2g Fat, 7.9g Protein

# 293. ROASTED BRUSSELS SPROUTS AND PECANS

**COOKING: 3 HOURS**  **PREPARATION: 9'**  **SERVING; 7**

## INGREDIENTS

- » 1 ½ pounds fresh Brussels sprouts
- » 4 tablespoons olive oil
- » 4 cloves of garlic, minced
- » 3 tablespoons water
- » Salt and pepper to taste
- » ½ cup chopped pecans

## DIRECTION

1. Place all ingredients in the Instant Pot.
2. Combine all ingredients until well combined.
3. Close the lid and make sure that the steam release vent is set to "Venting."
4. Press the "Slow Cook" button and adjust the cooking time to 3 hours.
5. Sprinkle with a dash of lemon juice if desired.

**NUTRITIONS:**
161 Calories, 4.1g Protein, 13g Fat

# 294. PARMESAN VEGGIES MIX

**COOKING: 40'**  **PREPARATION:8'**  **SERVES: 4**

## INGREDIENTS

- » 1 zucchini, sliced
- » 1 carrot, sliced
- » 1 eggplant, sliced
- » 1 red onion, sliced
- » 1 sweet pepper, sliced
- » ½ cup cream
- » 1 teaspoon dried oregano
- » 1 teaspoon ground black pepper
- » 1 teaspoon dried basil
- » 2 oz Parmesan, grated
- » 1 teaspoon butter, softened

## DIRECTION

1. Mix up together cream, dried oregano, ground black pepper, and dried basil.
2. Grease the springform pan with butter and arrange all vegetable one-by-one in it.
3. Then pour cream mixture over the vegetables.
4. Top the ratatouille with Parmesan and cover with foil. Secure the edges.
5. Bake the meal for 40 minutes at 36.
6. The remove the foil from the meal and chill it for 10 minutes before serving.

**NUTRITIONS:**
139 calories, 6.1g fat, 7.4g Protein

# 295. ALMOND KALE

**COOKING: 10'**  **PREPARATION:7'**  **SERVES: 2**

## INGREDIENTS

- » 2 cups kale, chopped
- » 1 tablespoon butter
- » 1 cup of water
- » 1 tablespoon almond, chopped
- » 1 teaspoon cumin seeds
- » ½ teaspoon salt

## DIRECTION

1. Bring the water to boil.
2. Add kale in the hot water and boil the greens for 3 minutes.
3. After this, drain the water.
4. Melt the butter in the skillet.
5. Add cumin seeds and roast them for 1 minute over the medium heat or until they start to give a smell.
6. Add boiled kale and mix up.
7. After this, sprinkle the kale with salt and almonds. Mix up well.
8. Roast the kale for 2 minutes.

**NUTRITIONS:**
105 calories, 7.5g fat, 2.9g Protein

# 296. TOMATO BASIL CAULIFLOWER RICE

**COOKING: 10'**  **PREPARATION:13'**  **SERVES: 4**

## INGREDIENTS

» Dried parsley for garnish
» ¼ cup tomato paste
» ½ teaspoon garlic, minced
» ½ teaspoon onion powder
» ½ teaspoon marjoram
» 1 ½ teaspoon dried basil
» 1 teaspoon dried oregano
» 1 large head of cauliflower
» 1 teaspoon oil

## DIRECTION

1. Slice cauliflower into florets and put in the food processor.
2. Pulse until it has a coarse consistency similar with rice. Set aside.
3. In a skillet, heat the oil and sauté the garlic and onion for three minutes. Add the rest of the ingredients. Cook for 8 minutes.

**NUTRITIONS:**
106 Calories, 3.3g Protein, 5g Fat

# 297. ALLSPICE OKRA

**COOKING: 20'**  **PREPARATION:7'**  **SERVES: 2**

## INGREDIENTS

» 1 teaspoon allspices
» ¼ teaspoon ground cumin
» 1/3 teaspoon garlic, diced
» 1/3 cup crushed tomatoes
» 2 cups okra, chopped
» 1 teaspoon tomato paste
» ½ teaspoon salt
» 1 cup of water
» ½ teaspoon sunflower oil

## DIRECTION

1. Heat up sunflower oil in the saucepan and add okra.
2. Sprinkle the vegetables with allspices and roast for 3 minutes.
3. After this, add ground cumin, garlic, and crushed tomatoes.
4. Bring the mixture to boil and add water.
5. Close the lid and simmer Baima for 10 minutes over the medium heat.
6. Then remove the cooked meal from the heat and let it rest for 10-15 minutes before serving.

**NUTRITIONS:**
62 calories, 1.6g fat, 2.5g Protein

# 298. GARLICKY ROSEMARY POTATOES

**COOKING: 2'**      **PREPARATION:9'**      **SERVES: 4**

## INGREDIENTS

» 1-pound potatoes
» 2 garlic cloves
» ½ teaspoon salt
» 1 tablespoon olive oil
» 2 sprigs of rosemary

## DIRECTION

1. Situate trivet or steamer basket in the Instant Pot and pour in a cup of water.
2. In a baking dish that can fit inside the Instant Pot, combine all ingredients and toss to coat everything.
3. Cover the baking dish with aluminum foil and place on the steamer basket.
4. Cover and press the Steam button.
5. Adjust the cooking time to 30 minutes
6. Do quick pressure release.
7. Once cooled, evenly divide into serving size, keep in your preferred container, and refrigerate until ready to eat.

**NUTRITIONS:**

119 Calories, 2.39g Protein, 3.48g Fat

# 299. CREAMY CARROT CHOWDER

**COOKING: 40'**      **PREPARATION:11'**      **SERVES: 8**

## INGREDIENTS

» 8 fresh mint sprigs
» ½ cup 2% Greek Style Plain yogurt
» 1 tsp fresh ginger
» 2 cups chicken broth
» 1 lb. baby carrots
» 1/3 cup sliced shallots
» 2 tsp sesame oil

## DIRECTION

1. On medium fire, place a medium heavy bottom pot and heat oil.
2. Sauté shallots until tender around minutes.
3. Add carrots and sauté for another 4 minutes.
4. Pour broth, cover and bring to a boil. Once soup is boiling, slow fire to a simmer and cook carrots until tender around 22 minutes.
5. Add ginger and continue cooking while covered for another eight minutes.
6. Turn off fire and let it cool for 10 minutes.
7. Pour mixture into blender and puree. If needed, puree carrots in batches then return to pot.
8. Heat pureed carrots until heated through around 2 minutes.
9. Turn off fire and evenly pour into 8 serving bowls.
10. Serve and enjoy.

**NUTRITIONS:**

47 Calories, 2.2g Protein, 1.6g Fat "300. Cauliflower Hash Brown"

# 300. CAULIFLOWER HASH BROWN

**COOKING: 6'**      **PREPARATION:11'**      **SERVES: 6**

## INGREDIENTS

» 12 eggs, beaten
» ½ cup coconut milk
» ½ teaspoon dry mustard
» Salt and pepper to taste
» 1 head cauliflower, shredded
» 2 cups shredded cheese

## DIRECTION

1. Place all ingredients in a mixing bowl until well combined.
2. Put enough oil for frying in a skillet and heat over medium flame.
3. Add a large dollop of cauliflower mixture in the skillet and flatten with the back of a fork.
4. Fry until golden brown.
5. Place in a plate lined with a kitchen towel to absorb excess oil.
6. Place in individual containers.
7. Put a label and store in the fridge.
8. Allow to thaw at room temperature before heating in the microwave oven.

## NUTRITIONS:

340 Calories, 22.8g Protein, 25g Fat

# CHAPTER 22
# VEGETABLE RECIPES PART 3

# 301. MEDITERRANEAN VEGGIE BOWL

**COOKING: 20'**     **PREPARATION:10'**     **SERVES: 4**

## INGREDIENTS

- » 2 cups water
- » 1 cup quinoa
- » 1½ teaspoons salt, divided
- » 1-pint (2 cups) cherry tomatoes
- » 1 large bell pepper
- » 1 large cucumber
- » 1 cup Kalamata olives
- » ½ cup freshly squeezed lemon juice
- » 1 cup extra-virgin olive oil
- » ½ teaspoon black pepper

## DIRECTION

1. Situate medium pot over medium heat, boil the water. Add the bulgur (or quinoa) and 1 teaspoon of salt. Cover and cook for 15 to 20 minutes.
2. To arrange the veggies in your 4 bowls, visually divide each bowl into 5 sections. Place the cooked bulgur in one section. Follow with the tomatoes, bell pepper, cucumbers, and olives.
3. Scourge lemon juice, olive oil, remaining ½ teaspoon salt, and black pepper.
4. Evenly spoon the dressing over the 4 bowls.
5. Serve immediately or cover and refrigerate for later.

**NUTRITIONS:**

772 Calories, 6g Protein, 68g Fat

# 302. GRILLED VEGGIE AND HUMMUS WRAP

**COOKING: 10'**     **PREPARATION:15'**     **SERVES: 6**

## INGREDIENTS

- » Situate medium pot over medium heat, boil the water. Add the bulgur (or quinoa) and 1 teaspoon of salt. Cover and cook for 15 to 20 minutes.
- » To arrange the veggies in your 4 bowls, visually divide each bowl into 5 sections. Place the cooked bulgur in one section. Follow with the tomatoes, bell pepper, cucumbers, and olives.
- » Scourge lemon juice, olive oil, remaining ½ teaspoon salt, and black pepper.
- » Evenly spoon the dressing over the 4 bowls.
- » Serve immediately or cover and refrigerate for later.

## DIRECTION

1. Preheat a grill, large grill pan, or lightly oiled large skillet on medium heat.
2. Slice the eggplant and onion into circles. Rub vegetables with olive oil and sprinkle with salt.
3. Cook the vegetables on both sides, about 3 to 4 minutes each side.
4. To make the wrap, lay the lavash or pita flat. Spread about 2 tablespoons of hummus on the wrap.
5. Evenly divide the vegetables among the wraps, layering them along one side of the wrap. Gently fold over the side of the wrap with the vegetables, tucking them in and making a tight wrap.
6. Lay the wrap seam side-down and cut in half or thirds.

**NUTRITIONS:**

362 Calories, 15g Protein, 26g Fat

# 303. SPANISH GREEN BEANS

**COOKING: 20'**　　　　**PREPARATION:10'**　　　　**SERVES: 4**

## INGREDIENTS

- ¼ cup extra-virgin olive oil
- 1 large onion, chopped
- 4 cloves garlic, finely chopped
- 1-pound green beans
- 1½ teaspoons salt, divided
- 1 (15-ounce) can diced tomatoes
- ½ teaspoon freshly ground black pepper

## DIRECTION

1. Position large pot over medium heat, cook olive oil, onion, and garlic.
2. Cut the green beans into 2-inch pieces.
3. Add the green beans and 1 teaspoon of salt to the pot and toss everything together; cook for 3 minutes.
4. Add the diced tomatoes, remaining ½ teaspoon of salt, and black pepper to the pot; continue to cook for another 12 minutes, stirring occasionally.

**NUTRITIONS:**
200 Calories, 4g Protein, 14g Fat

# 304. RUSTIC CAULIFLOWER AND CARROT HASH

**COOKING: 10'**　　　　**PREPARATION:10'**　　　　**SERVES: 4**

## INGREDIENTS

- 3 tablespoons extra-virgin olive oil
- 1 large onion
- 1 tablespoon garlic
- 2 cups carrots
- 4 cups cauliflower pieces
- 1 teaspoon salt
- ½ teaspoon ground cumin

## DIRECTION

1. Preheat a pan over medium heat, cook the olive oil, onion, garlic, and carrots for 3 minutes.
2. Cut the cauliflower into 1-inch or bite-size pieces. Add the cauliflower, salt, and cumin to the skillet and toss to combine with the carrots and onions.
3. Cover and cook for 3 minutes.
4. Toss the vegetables and continue to cook for 4 minutes.
5. Serve warm.

**NUTRITIONS:**
159 Calories, 3g Protein, 11g Fat

# 305. ROASTED CAULIFLOWER AND TOMATOES

**COOKING: 25'**      **PREPARATION:5'**      **SERVES: 4**

## INGREDIENTS

- » 4 cups cauliflower
- » 6 tablespoons extra-virgin olive oil
- » 1 teaspoon salt
- » 4 cups cherry tomatoes
- » ½ teaspoon black pepper
- » ½ cup grated Parmesan cheese

## DIRECTION

1. Preheat the oven to 425°F.
2. Add the cauliflower, 3 tablespoons of olive oil, and ½ teaspoon of salt to a large bowl and toss to coat evenly. Pour onto a baking sheet and spread the cauliflower out in an even layer.
3. In another large bowl, add the tomatoes, remaining 3 tablespoons of olive oil, and ½ teaspoon of salt, and toss to coat evenly. Pour onto a different baking sheet.
4. Put the sheet of cauliflower and the sheet of tomatoes in the oven to roast for 17 to 20 minutes until the cauliflower is lightly browned and tomatoes are plump.
5. Using a spatula, spoon the cauliflower into a serving dish, and top with tomatoes, black pepper, and Parmesan cheese. Serve warm.

**NUTRITIONS:**
294 Calories, 9g Protein, 26g Fat

# 306. ROASTED ACORN SQUASH

**COOKING: 35'**      **PREPARATION:10'**      **SERVES: 6**

## INGREDIENTS

- » 2 acorn squash, medium to large
- » 2 tablespoons extra-virgin olive oil
- » 1 teaspoon salt, plus more for seasoning
- » 5 tablespoons unsalted butter
- » ¼ cup chopped sage leaves
- » 2 tablespoons fresh thyme leaves
- » ½ teaspoon freshly ground black pepper

## DIRECTION

1. Preheat the oven to 400°F.
2. Cut the acorn squash in half lengthwise. Spoon out the seeds and cut it horizontally into ¾-inch-thick slices.
3. In a large bowl, drizzle the squash with the olive oil, sprinkle with salt, and toss together to coat.
4. Lay the acorn squash flat on a baking sheet.
5. Put the baking sheet in the oven and bake the squash for 20 minutes. Flip squash over with a spatula and bake for another 15 minutes.
6. Cook butter in a medium saucepan over medium heat.
7. Heat sage and thyme to the melted butter for 30 seconds.
8. Transfer the cooked squash slices to a plate. Spoon the butter/herb mixture over the squash. Season with salt and black pepper. Serve warm.

**NUTRITIONS:**
188 Calories, 1g Protein, 15g Fat

# 307. SAUTEED GARLIC SPINACH

**COOKING: 10'**     **PREPARATION:5'**     **SERVES: 4**

## INGREDIENTS

- » Ingredients:
- » ¼ cup extra-virgin olive oil
- » 1 large onion, thinly sliced
- » 3 cloves garlic, minced
- » 6 (1-pound) bags of baby spinach, washed
- » ½ teaspoon salt
- » 1 lemon, cut into wedges

## DIRECTION

1. Cook the olive oil, onion, and garlic in a large skillet for 2 minutes over medium heat.
2. Add one bag of spinach and ½ teaspoon of salt. Cover the skillet and let the spinach wilt for 30 seconds. Repeat (omitting the salt), adding 1 bag of spinach at a time.
3. Once all the spinach has been added, remove the cover and cook for 3 minutes, letting some of the moisture evaporate.
4. Serve with squeeze of lemon over the top.

**NUTRITIONS:**

301 Calories, 17g Protein, 14g Fat

# 308. GARLICKY SAUTEED ZUCCHINI WITH MINT

**COOKING: 10'**     **PREPARATION:5'**     **SERVES: 4**

## INGREDIENTS

- » 3 large green zucchinis
- » 3 tablespoons extra-virgin olive oil
- » 1 large onion, chopped
- » 3 cloves garlic, minced
- » 1 teaspoon salt
- » 1 teaspoon dried mint

## DIRECTION

1. Cut the zucchini into ½-inch cubes.
2. Position skillet over medium heat, cook the olive oil, onions, and garlic for 3 minutes, stirring constantly.
3. Add the zucchini and salt to the skillet and toss to combine with the onions and garlic, cooking for 5 minutes.
4. Add the mint to the skillet, tossing to combine. Cook for another 2 minutes. Serve warm.

**NUTRITIONS:**

147 Calories, 4g Protein, 11g Fat

# 309. STEWED OKRA

**COOKING: 25'**  **PREPARATION:5'**  **SERVES: 4**

## INGREDIENTS

» ¼ cup extra-virgin olive oil
» 1 large onion, chopped
» 4 cloves garlic, finely chopped
» 1 teaspoon salt
» 1 pound fresh or frozen okra, cleaned
» 1 (15-ounce) can plain tomato sauce
» 2 cups water
» ½ cup fresh cilantro, finely chopped
» ½ teaspoon freshly ground black pepper

## DIRECTION

1. Situate pot over medium heat, stir and cook the olive oil, onion, garlic, and salt for 1 minute.
2. Stir in the okra and cook for 3 minutes.
3. Add the tomato sauce, water, cilantro, and black pepper; stir, cover, and let cook for 15 minutes, stirring occasionally.
4. Serve warm.

**NUTRITIONS:**
201 Calories, 4g Protein, 14g Fat

# 310. SWEET VEGGIE-STUFFED PEPPERS

**COOKING: 30'**  **PREPARATION:20'**  **SERVES: 6**

## INGREDIENTS

» 6 large bell peppers, different colors
» 3 tablespoons extra-virgin olive oil
» 1 large onion, chopped
» 3 cloves garlic, minced
» 1 carrot, chopped
» 1 (16-ounce) can garbanzo beans
» 3 cups cooked rice
» 1½ teaspoons salt
» ½ teaspoon freshly ground black pepper

## DIRECTION

1. Preheat the oven to 350°F.
2. Make sure to choose peppers that can stand upright. Cut off the pepper cap and remove the seeds, reserving the cap for later. Stand the peppers in a baking dish.
3. In a skillet over medium heat, sauté olive oil, onion, garlic, and carrots for 3 minutes.
4. Stir in the garbanzo beans. Cook for another 3 minutes.
5. Remove the pan from the heat and spoon the cooked ingredients to a large bowl.
6. Add the rice, salt, and pepper; toss to combine.
7. Stuff each pepper to the top and then put the pepper caps back on.
8. Cover the baking dish with aluminum foil and bake for 25 minutes.
9. Remove the foil and bake for another 5 minutes.
10. Serve warm.

**NUTRITIONS:**
301 Calories, 8g Protein, 9g Fat

# 311. MOUSSAKA

**COOKING: 40'**       **PREPARATION:55'**       **SERVES: 6**

## INGREDIENTS

» 2 large eggplants
» 2 teaspoons salt, divided
» ¼ cup extra-virgin olive oil
» 2 large onions, sliced
» 10 cloves garlic, sliced
» 2 (15-ounce) cans diced tomatoes
» 1 (16-oz) can garbanzo beans
» 1 teaspoon dried oregano
» ½ teaspoon freshly ground black pepper

## DIRECTION

1. Slice the eggplant horizontally into ¼-inch-thick round disks. Sprinkle the eggplant slices with 1 teaspoon of salt and place in a colander for 30 minutes. This will draw out the excess water from the eggplant.

2. Preheat the oven to 450°F. Pat the slices of eggplant dry with a paper towel and spray each side with an olive oil spray or lightly brush each side with olive oil.

3. Situate eggplant in a single layer on a baking sheet. Put in the oven and bake for 10 minutes. Then, using a spatula, flip the slices over and bake for another 10 minutes.

4. In a large skillet add the olive oil, onions, garlic, and remaining 1 teaspoon of salt. Cook for 4 minutes. Add the tomatoes, garbanzo beans, oregano, and black pepper. Simmer for 11 minutes, stirring occasionally.

5. Using a deep casserole dish, begin to layer, starting with eggplant, then the sauce. Repeat until all ingredients have been used. Bake in the oven for 20 minutes.

6. Remove from the oven and serve warm.

## NUTRITIONS:
262 Calories, 8g Protein, 11g Fat

# 312. VEGETABLE-STUFFED GRAPE LEAVES

**COOKING: 45'**       **PREPARATION: 50'**       **SERVES: 8**

## INGREDIENTS

» 2 cups white rice
» 2 large tomatoes
» 1 large onion
» 1 green onion
» 1 cup fresh Italian parsley
» 3 cloves garlic, minced
» 2½ teaspoons salt
» ½ teaspoon black pepper
» 1 (16-ounce) jar grape leaves
» 1 cup lemon juice
» ½ cup extra-virgin olive oil
» 4 to 6 cups water

## DIRECTION

1. Mix rice, tomatoes, onion, green onion, parsley, garlic, salt, and black pepper.

2. Drain and rinse the grape leaves.

3. Prepare a large pot by placing a layer of grape leaves on the bottom. Lay each leaf flat and trim off any stems.

4. Place 2 tablespoons of the rice mixture at the base of each leaf. Fold over the sides, then roll as tight as possible. Situate rolled grape leaves in the pot, lining up each rolled grape leaf. Continue to layer in the rolled grape leaves.

5. Gently pour the lemon juice and olive oil over the grape leaves, and add enough water just to cover the grape leaves by 1 inch.

6. Lay a heavy plate that is smaller than the opening of the pot upside down over the grape leaves. Cover the pot and cook the leaves over medium-low heat for 45 minutes. Let stand for 20 minutes before serving.

7. Serve warm or cold.

## NUTRITIONS:
532 Calories, 12g Protein, 21g Fat

# 313. GRILLED EGGPLANT ROLLS

**COOKING: 10'**　　**PREPARATION: 30'**　　**SERVES: 6**

## INGREDIENTS

- » 2 large eggplants
- » 1 teaspoon salt
- » 4 ounces goat cheese
- » 1 cup ricotta
- » ¼ cup fresh basil, finely chopped
- » ½ teaspoon black pepper

## DIRECTION

1. Cutoff the tops of the eggplants and cut the eggplants lengthwise into ¼-inch-thick slices. Sprinkle the slices with the salt and place the eggplant in a colander for 15 to 20 minutes. The salt will draw out excess water from the eggplant.
2. In a large bowl, combine the goat cheese, ricotta, basil, and pepper.
3. Preheat a grill, grill pan, or lightly oiled skillet on medium heat. Dry eggplant slices using paper towel and lightly spray with olive oil spray. Place the eggplant on the grill, grill pan, or skillet and cook for 3 minutes on each side.
4. Remove the eggplant from the heat and let cool for 5 minutes.
5. To roll, lay one eggplant slice flat, place a tablespoon of the cheese mixture at the base of the slice, and roll up. Serve immediately or chill until serving.
6. Nutrition:

**NUTRITIONS:**
255 Calories, 15g Protein, 15g Fat

# 314. CRISPY ZUCCHINI FRITTERS

**COOKING: 20'**　　**PREPARATION: 15'**　　**SERVES: 6**

## INGREDIENTS

- » 2 large green zucchinis
- » 2 tablespoons Italian parsley
- » 3 cloves garlic, minced
- » 1 teaspoon salt
- » 1 cup flour
- » 1 large egg, beaten
- » ½ cup water
- » 1 teaspoon baking powder
- » 3 cups vegetable or avocado oil

## DIRECTION

1. Grate the zucchini into a large bowl.
2. Add the parsley, garlic, salt, flour, egg, water, and baking powder to the bowl and stir to combine.
3. In a large pot or fryer over medium heat, heat oil to 365°F.
4. Drop the fritter batter into the hot oil by spoonful. Turn the fritters over using a slotted spoon and fry until they are golden brown, about 2 to 3 minutes.
5. Remove the fritters from the oil and drain on a plate lined with paper towels.
6. Serve warm with Creamy Tzatziki dip.

**NUTRITIONS:**
446 Calories, 5g Protein, 38g Fat

# 315. CHEESY SPINACH PIES

**COOKING: 40'**      **PREPARATION:20'**      **SERVES: 6-8**

## INGREDIENTS

» 2 tablespoons extra-virgin olive oil
» 1 large onion, chopped
» 2 cloves garlic, minced
» 3 (1-pound) bags of baby spinach, washed
» 1 cup feta cheese
» 1 large egg, beaten
» Puff pastry sheets

## NUTRITIONS:
503 Calories, 16g Protein, 32g Fat

## DIRECTION

1. Preheat the oven to 375°F.

2. In a large skillet over medium heat, cook the olive oil, onion, and garlic for 3 minutes.

3. Add the spinach to the skillet one bag at a time, letting it wilt in between each bag. Toss using tongs. Cook for 4 minutes. Once the spinach is cooked, drain any excess liquid from the pan.

4. In a large bowl, combine the feta cheese, egg, and cooked spinach.

5. Lay the puff pastry flat on a counter. Cut the pastry into 3-inch squares.

6. Place a tablespoon of the spinach mixture in the center of a puff-pastry square. Fold over one corner of the square to the diagonal corner, forming a triangle. Crimp the edges of the pie by pressing down with the tines of a fork to seal them together. Repeat until all squares are filled.

7. Place the pies on a parchment-lined baking sheet and bake for 25 to 30 minutes or until golden brown. Serve warm or at room temperature.

# CHAPTER 23
# SOUP AND STEW RECIPES

# 316. MINESTRONE SOUP

**COOKING: 1 HOUR**  **PREPARATION:10'**  **SERVINGS: 4**

## INGREDIENTS

- » 1 small white onion
- » 4 cloves garlic
- » 1/2 cup carrots
- » 1 medium zucchini
- » 1 medium yellow squash
- » 2 tablespoons minced fresh parsley
- » 1/4 cup celery sliced
- » 3 tablespoons olive oil
- » 2 x 15 oz. cans cannellini beans
- » 2 x 15 oz. can red kidney beans
- » 1 x 14.5 oz. can fire-roasted diced tomatoes, drained
- » 4 cups vegetable stock
- » 2 cups of water
- » 1 1/2 teaspoons oregano
- » 1/2 teaspoon basil
- » 1/4 teaspoon thyme
- » 1 teaspoon salt
- » 1/2 teaspoon pepper
- » 3/4 cup small pasta shells
- » 4 cups fresh baby spinach
- » 1/4 cup Parmesan or Romano cheese

## DIRECTION

1. Grab a stockpot and place over medium heat. Add the oil then the onions, garlic, carrots, zucchini, squash, parsley, and celery. Cook for five minutes until the veggies are getting soft.

2. Pour in the stock, water, beans, tomatoes, herbs, and salt and pepper. Stir well. Decrease heat, cover, and simmer for 30 minutes.

3. Add the pasta and spinach, stir well then cover and cook for a further 20 minutes until the pasta is cooked through. Stir through the cheese then serve and enjoy.

## NUTRITIONS:

34 calories, 26.3 g Protein, 30.3 g Fat

# 317. CHICKEN WILD RICE SOUP

**COOKING: 15'**  **PREPARATION:10'**  **SERVINGS: 6**

## INGREDIENTS

- » 2/3 cup wild rice, uncooked
- » 1 tablespoon onion, chopped finely
- » 1 tablespoon fresh parsley, chopped
- » 1 cup carrots, chopped
- » 8-ounces chicken breast, cooked
- » 2 tablespoon butter
- » 1/4 cup all-purpose white flour
- » 5 cups low-sodium chicken broth
- » 1 tablespoon slivered almonds

## DIRECTION

1. Start by adding rice and 2 cups broth along with ½ cup water to a cooking pot. Cook the chicken until the rice is al dente and set it aside. Add butter to a saucepan and melt it.

2. Stir in onion and sauté until soft then add the flour and the remaining broth.

3. Stir it and then cook for it 1 minute then add the chicken, cooked rice, and carrots. Cook for 5 minutes on simmer. Garnish with almonds. Serve fresh.

## NUTRITIONS:

287 calories, 21g Protein, 35g Fat

# 318. CLASSIC CHICKEN SOUP

**COOKING: 25'**     **PREPARATION:10'**     **SERVINGS: 2**

## INGREDIENTS

- » 1 1/2 cups low-sodium vegetable broth
- » 1 cup of water
- » 1/4 teaspoon poultry seasoning
- » 1/4 teaspoon black pepper
- » 1 cup chicken strips
- » 1/4 cup carrot
- » 2-ounces egg noodles, uncooked

## DIRECTION

1. Gather all the ingredients into a slow cooker and toss it Cook soup on high heat for 25 minutes.
2. Serve warm.
3. Nutrition:
4. 103 calories
5. 8g protein
6. 11g fat

**NUTRITIONS:**
103 calories, 8g Protein, 11g Fat

# 319. CUCUMBER SOUP

**COOKING: 0'**     **PREPARATION:10'**     **SERVINGS: 4**

## INGREDIENTS

- » 2 medium cucumbers
- » 1/3 cup sweet white onion
- » 1 green onion
- » 1/4 cup fresh mint
- » 2 tablespoons fresh dill
- » 2 tablespoons lemon juice
- » 2/3 cup water
- » 1/2 cup half and half cream
- » 1/3 cup sour cream
- » 1/2 teaspoon pepper
- » Fresh dill sprigs for garnish

## DIRECTION

1. Situate all of the ingredients into a food processor and toss. Puree the mixture and refrigerate for 2 hours. Garnish with dill sprigs. Enjoy fresh.

**NUTRITIONS:**
77 calories, 2g Protein, 6g fats

# 320. SQUASH AND TURMERIC SOUP

**COOKING: 30'**  **PREPARATION:10'**  **SERVINGS: 4**

## INGREDIENTS

- » 4 cups low-sodium vegetable broth
- » 2 medium zucchini squash
- » 2 medium yellow crookneck squash
- » 1 small onion
- » 1/2 cup frozen green peas
- » 2 tablespoons olive oil
- » 1/2 cup plain nonfat Greek yogurt
- » 2 teaspoon turmeric

## DIRECTION

1. Warm the broth in a saucepan on medium heat. Toss in onion, squash, and zucchini. Let it simmer for approximately 25 minutes then add oil and green peas.

2. Cook for another 5 minutes then allow it to cool. Puree the soup using a handheld blender then add Greek yogurt and turmeric. Refrigerate it overnight and serve fresh.

**NUTRITIONS:**
100 calories, 4g Protein, 10g Fat

# 321. LEEK, POTATO, AND CARROT SOUP

**COOKING: 25'**  **PREPARATION:15'**  **SERVINGS: 4**

## INGREDIENTS

- » 1 - leek
- » ¾ - cup diced and boiled potatoes
- » ¾ - cup diced and boiled carrots
- » 1 - garlic clove
- » 1 - tablespoon oil
- » Crushed pepper to taste
- » 3 - cups low sodium chicken stock
- » Chopped parsley for garnish
- » 1 - bay leaf
- » ¼ - teaspoon ground cumin

## DIRECTION

1. Trim off and take away a portion of the coarse inexperienced portions of the leek, at that factor reduce daintily and flush altogether in virus water. Channel properly. Warmth the oil in an extensively based pot. Include the leek and garlic, and sear over low warmth for two-3 minutes, till sensitive.

2. Include the inventory, inlet leaf, cumin, and pepper. Heat the mixture, mix constantly. Include the bubbled potatoes and carrots and stew for 10-15minutes Modify the flavoring, eliminate the inlet leaf, and serve sprinkled generously with slashed parsley.

3. To make a pureed soup, manner the soup in a blender or nourishment processor till smooth Come again to the pan. Include ½ field milk. Bring to bubble and stew for 2-3minutes

**NUTRITIONS:**
315 calories, 8g fat, 15g Protein

# 322. BELL PEPPER SOUP

**COOKING: 35'**      **PREPARATION: 30'**      **SERVINGS: 4**

## INGREDIENTS

- » 4 - cups low-sodium chicken broth
- » 3 - red peppers
- » 2 - medium onions
- » 3 - tablespoon lemon juice
- » 1 - tablespoon finely minced lemon zest
- » A pinch cayenne peppers
- » ¼ - teaspoon cinnamon
- » ½ - cup finely minced fresh cilantro

## DIRECTION

1. In a medium stockpot, consolidate each one of the fixings except for the cilantro and warmth to the point of boiling over excessive warm temperature.

2. Diminish the warmth and stew, ordinarily secured, for around 30 minutes, till thickened. Cool marginally. Utilizing a hand blender or nourishment processor, puree the soup. Include the cilantro and tenderly heat.

## NUTRITIONS:
265 calories, 8g fat, 5g Protein

---

# 323. YUCATAN SOUP

**COOKING: 20'**      **PREPARATION: 10'**      **SERVINGS: 4**

## INGREDIENTS

- » ½ cup onion, chopped
- » 8 cloves garlic, chopped
- » 2 Serrano chili peppers, chopped
- » 1 medium tomato, chopped
- » 1 ½ cups chicken breast, cooked, shredded
- » 2 six-inch corn tortillas, sliced
- » 1 tablespoon olive oil
- » 4 cups chicken broth
- » 1 bay leaf
- » ¼ cup lime juice
- » ¼ cup cilantro, chopped
- » 1 teaspoon black pepper

## DIRECTION

1. Spread the corn tortillas in a baking sheet and bake them for 3 minutes at 400°F. Place a suitably-sized saucepan over medium heat and add oil to heat.

2. Toss in chili peppers, garlic, and onion, then sauté until soft. Stir in broth, tomatoes, bay leaf, and chicken.

3. Let this chicken soup cook for 10 minutes on a simmer. Stir in cilantro, lime juice, and black pepper. Garnish with baked corn tortillas. Serve.

## NUTRITIONS:
215 calories, 21g Protein, 32g Fat

# 324. ZESTY TACO SOUP

**COOKING: 7 HOURS**　　**PREPARATION:10'**　　**SERVINGS: 2**

## INGREDIENTS

» 1 ½ pounds chicken breast
» 15 ½ ounces canned dark red kidney beans
» 15 ½ ounces canned white corn
» 1 cup canned tomatoes
» ½ cup onion
» 15 ½ ounces canned yellow hominy
» ½ cup green bell peppers
» 1 garlic clove
» 1 medium jalapeno
» 1 tablespoon package McCormick
» 2 cups chicken broth

## DIRECTION

1. Add drained beans, hominy, corn, onion, garlic, jalapeno pepper, chicken, and green peppers to a Crockpot.

2. Cover the beans-corn mixture and cook for 1 hour on "high" temperature. Set heat to "low" and continue cooking for 6 hours. Shred the slow-cooked chicken and return to the taco soup. Serve warm.

**NUTRITIONS:**
191 calories, 21g Protein, 20g Fat

# 325. SOUTHWESTERN POSOLE

**COOKING: 53'**　　**PREPARATION:10'**　　**SERVINGS: 4**

## INGREDIENTS

» 1 tablespoon olive oil
» 1-pound pork loin, diced
» ½ cup onion, chopped
» 1 garlic clove, chopped
» 28 ounces canned white hominy
» 4 ounces canned diced green chilis
» 4 cups chicken broth
» ¼ teaspoon black pepper

## DIRECTION

1. Place a suitably-sized cooking pot over medium heat and add oil to heat. Toss in pork pieces and sauté for 4 minutes.

2. Stir in garlic and onion, then stir for 4 minutes, or until onion is soft. Add the remaining ingredients, then cover the pork soup. Cook this for 45 minutes, or until the pork is tender. Serve warm.

**NUTRITIONS:**
286 calories, 25g Protein, 15g Fat

# 326. SPRING VEGETABLE SOUP

**COOKING: 45'**  **PREPARATION: 10'**  **SERVINGS: 4**

## INGREDIENTS

- » 1 cup fresh green beans
- » ¾ cup celery
- » ½ cup onion
- » ½ cup carrots
- » ½ cup mushrooms
- » ½ cup of frozen corn
- » 1 medium Roma tomato
- » 2 tablespoons olive oil
- » ½ cup of frozen corn
- » 4 cups vegetable broth
- » 1 teaspoon dried oregano leaves
- » 1 teaspoon garlic powder

## DIRECTION

1. Place a suitably-sized cooking pot over medium heat and add olive oil to heat. Toss in onion and celery, then sauté until soft. Stir in the corn and rest of the ingredients and cook the soup to boil.

2. Now reduce its heat to a simmer and cook for 45 minutes. Serve warm.

**NUTRITIONS:**
115 calories, 3g Protein, 13g Fat

# 327. SEAFOOD CORN CHOWDER

**COOKING: 12'**  **PREPARATION: 10'**  **SERVINGS: 4**

## INGREDIENTS

- » 1 tablespoon butter
- » 1 cup onion
- » 1/3 cup celery
- » ½ cup green bell pepper
- » ½ cup red bell pepper
- » 1 tablespoon white flour
- » 14 ounces chicken broth
- » 2 cups cream
- » 6 ounces evaporated milk
- » 10 ounces surimi imitation crab chunks
- » 2 cups frozen corn kernels
- » ½ teaspoon black pepper
- » ½ teaspoon paprika

## DIRECTION

1. Place a suitably-sized saucepan over medium heat and add butter to melt. Toss in onion, green and red peppers, and celery, then sauté for 5 minutes. Stir in flour and whisk well for 2 minutes.

2. Pour in chicken broth and stir until it boils. Add evaporated milk, corn, surimi crab, paprika, black pepper, and creamer. Cook for 5 minutes then serves warm.

**NUTRITIONS:**
175 calories, 8g Protein, 7g Fat

# 328. BEEF SAGE SOUP

**COOKING: 20'**     **PREPARATION:10'**     **SERVINGS: 4**

## INGREDIENTS

» ½ pound ground beef
» ½ teaspoon ground sage
» ½ teaspoon black pepper
» ½ teaspoon dried basil
» ½ teaspoon garlic powder
» 4 slices bread, cubed
» 2 tablespoons olive oil
» 1 tablespoon herb seasoning blend
» 2 garlic cloves, minced
» 3 cups chicken broth
» 1 ½ cups water
» 4 tablespoons fresh parsley
» 2 tablespoons parmesan cheese

## DIRECTION

1. Preheat your oven to 375ºF. Mix beef with sage, basil, black pepper, and garlic powder in a bowl, then set it aside. Toss the bread cubes with olive oil in a baking sheet and bake them for 8 minutes.

2. Meanwhile, sauté the beef mixture in a greased cooking pot until it is browned. Stir in garlic and sauté for 2 minutes, then add parsley, water, and broth. Cover the beef soup and cook for 10 minutes on a simmer. Garnish the soup with parmesan cheese and baked bread. Serve warm.

**NUTRITIONS:**

336 calories, 26g Protein, 16g Fat

# 329. CABBAGE BORSCHT

**COOKING: 90'**     **PREPARATION:10'**     **SERVINGS: 6**

## INGREDIENTS

» 2 pounds beef steaks
» 6 cups cold water
» 2 tablespoons olive oil
» ½ cup tomato sauce
» 1 medium cabbage, chopped
» 1 cup onion, diced
» 1 cup carrots, diced
» 1 cup turnips, peeled and diced
» 1 teaspoon pepper
» 6 tablespoons lemon juice
» 4 tablespoons sugar

## DIRECTION

1. Start by placing steak in a large cooking pot and pour enough water to cover it. Cover the beef pot and cook it on a simmer until it is tender, then shred it using a fork. Add olive oil, onion, tomato sauce, carrots, turnips, and shredded steak to the cooking liquid in the pot.

2. Stir in black pepper, sugar, and lemon juice to season the soup. Cover the cabbage soup and cook on low heat for 1 ½ hour. Serve warm.

**NUTRITIONS:**

212 calories, 19g Protein, 10g Fat

# 331. GROUND BEEF SOUP

**COOKING: 30'**     **PREPARATION:10'**     **SERVINGS: 4**

## INGREDIENTS

- » 1-pound lean ground beef
- » ½ cup onion, chopped
- » 2 teaspoons lemon-pepper seasoning blend
- » 1 cup beef broth
- » 2 cups of water
- » 1/3 cup white rice, uncooked
- » 3 cups of frozen mixed vegetables
- » 1 tablespoon sour cream

## DIRECTION

1. Spray a saucepan with cooking oil and place it over medium heat. Toss in onion and ground beef, then sauté until brown. Stir in broth and rest of the ingredients, then boil it.

2. Reduce heat to a simmer, then cover the soup to cook for 30 minutes. Garnish with sour cream. Enjoy.

## NUTRITIONS:

223 calories, 20g Protein, 20g Fat

# CHAPTER 24
# SOUP AND STEW RECIPES PART 2

# 331. MEXICAN TORTILLA SOUP

**COOKING: 40'**  **PREPARATION: 7'**  **SERVES: 4**

## INGREDIENTS

- » 1-pound chicken breasts
- » 1 can (15 ounces) whole peeled tomatoes
- » 1 can (10 ounces) red enchilada sauce
- » 1 and 1/2 teaspoons minced garlic
- » 1 yellow onion, diced
- » 1 can (4 ounces) fire-roasted diced green chili
- » 1 can (15 ounces) black beans
- » 1 can (15 ounces) fire-roasted corn
- » 1 container (32 ounces) chicken stock
- » 1 teaspoon ground cumin
- » 2 teaspoons chili powder
- » 3/4 teaspoons paprika
- » 1 bay leaf
- » 1 tablespoon chopped cilantro

## DIRECTION

1. Set your Instant Pot on Sauté mode.
2. Toss olive oil, onion and garlic into the insert of the Instant Pot.
3. Sauté for 4 minutes then add chicken and remaining ingredients.
4. Mix well gently then seal and lock the lid.
5. Select Manual mode for 7 minutes at high pressure.
6. Once done, release the pressure completely then remove the lid.
7. Adjust seasoning as needed.
8. Garnish with desired toppings.

## NUTRITIONS:

390 Calories, 29.5g Protein, 26.5g Fat

# 332. CHICKEN NOODLE SOUP

**COOKING: 35'**  **PREPARATION: 9'**  **SERVES: 6**

## INGREDIENTS

- » 1 tablespoon olive oil
- » 1 1/2 cups carrots
- » 1 1/2 cup diced celery
- » 1 cup chopped yellow onion
- » 3 tablespoons minced garlic
- » 8 cups low-sodium chicken broth
- » 2 teaspoons minced fresh thyme
- » 2 teaspoons minced fresh rosemary
- » 1 bay leaf
- » 2 1/2 lbs. chicken thighs
- » 3 cups wide egg noodles, such as American beauty
- » 1 tablespoon fresh lemon juice
- » 1/4 cup chopped fresh parsley

## DIRECTION

1. Preheat olive oil in the insert of the Instant Pot on Sauté mode.
2. Add onion, celery, and carrots and sauté them for minutes.
3. Stir in garlic and sauté for 1 minute.
4. Add bay leaf, thyme, broth, rosemary, salt, and pepper.
5. Seal and secure the Instant Pot lid and select Manual mode for 10 minutes at high pressure.
6. Once done, release the pressure completely then remove the lid.
7. Add noodles to the insert and switch the Instant Pot to sauté mode.
8. Cook the soup for 6 minutes until noodles are all done.
9. Pullout chicken and shred it using a fork.
10. Return the chicken to the soup then add lemon juice and parsley.

## NUTRITIONS:

333 Calories, 44.7g Protein, 13.7g Fat, 333.

# 333. CHEESY BROCCOLI SOUP

**COOKING: 30'**　　　　**PREPARATION: 11'**　　　　**SERVES: 4**

## INGREDIENTS

- » ½ cup heavy whipping cream
- » 1 cup broccoli
- » 1 cup cheddar cheese
- » Salt, to taste
- » 1½ cups chicken broth

## DIRECTION

1. Cook chicken broth in a large pot and add broccoli.
2. Boil and stir in the rest of the ingredients.
3. Allow the soup to simmer on low heat for about 20 minutes.
4. Ladle out into a bowl and serve hot.

**NUTRITIONS:**

188 Calories, 15g Fats, 9.8g Protein, 334

# 334. RICH POTATO SOUP

**COOKING: 30'**　　　　**PREPARATION: 6'**　　　　**SERVES: 4**

## INGREDIENTS

- » 1 tablespoon butter
- » 1 medium onion, diced
- » 3 cloves garlic, minced
- » 3 cups chicken broth
- » 1 can/box cream of chicken soup
- » 7-8 medium-sized russet potatoes
- » 1 1/2 teaspoons salt
- » 1 cup milk
- » 1 tablespoon flour
- » 2 cups shredded cheddar cheese
- » Garnish:
- » 5-6 slices bacon, chopped
- » Sliced green onions
- » Shredded cheddar cheese

## DIRECTION

1. Heat butter in the insert of the Instant Pot on sauté mode.
2. Add onions and sauté for 4 minutes until soft.
3. Stir in garlic and sauté it for 1 minute.
4. Add potatoes, cream of chicken, broth, salt, and pepper to the insert.
5. Mix well then seal and lock the lid.
6. Cook this mixture for 10 minutes at Manual Mode with high pressure.
7. Meanwhile, mix flour with milk in a bowl and set it aside.
8. Once the instant pot beeps, release the pressure completely.
9. Remove the Instant Pot lid and switch the instant pot to Sauté mode.
10. Pour in flour slurry and stir cook the mixture for 5 minutes until it thickens.
11. Add 2 cups of cheddar cheese and let it melt.
12. Garnish it as desired.

**NUTRITIONS:**

784 Calories, 34g Protein, 46.5g Fat

# 335. MEDITERRANEAN LENTIL SOUP

**COOKING: 20'**　　　**PREPARATION:9'**　　　**SERVES: 4**

## INGREDIENTS

» 1 tablespoon olive oil
» 1/2 cup red lentils
» 1 medium yellow or red onion
» 2 garlic cloves
» 1/2 teaspoon ground cumin
» 1/2 teaspoon ground coriander
» 1/2 teaspoon ground sumac
» 1/2 teaspoon red chili flakes
» 1/2 teaspoon dried parsley
» 3/4 teaspoons dried mint flakes
» 2.5 cups water
» juice of 1/2 lime

## DIRECTION

1. Preheat oil in the insert of your Instant Pot on Sauté mode.
2. Add onion and sauté until it turns golden brown.
3. Toss in the garlic, parsley sugar, mint flakes, red chili flakes, sumac, coriander, and cumin.
4. Stir cook this mixture for 2 minutes.
5. Add water, lentils, salt, and pepper. Stir gently.
6. Seal and lock the Instant Pot lid and select Manual mode for 8 minutes at high pressure.
7. Once done, release the pressure completely then remove the lid.
8. Stir well then add lime juice.

**NUTRITIONS:**
525 Calories, 30g Protein, 19.3g Fat

# 336. SAUSAGE KALE SOUP WITH MUSHROOMS

**COOKING: 70'**　　　**PREPARATION:8'**　　　**SERVES: 6**

## INGREDIENTS

» 2 cups fresh kale
» 6.5 ounces mushrooms, sliced
» 6 cups chicken bone broth
» 1-pound sausage, cooked and sliced

## DIRECTION

1. Heat chicken broth with two cans of water in a large pot and bring to a boil.
2. Stir in the rest of the ingredients and allow the soup to simmer on low heat for about 1 hour.
3. Dish out and serve hot.

**NUTRITIONS:**
259 Calories, 20g Fats, 14g Protein

# 337. CLASSIC MINESTRONE

**COOKING: 25'**  **PREPARATION:12'**  **SERVES: 6**

## INGREDIENTS

- » 2 tablespoons olive oil
- » 3 cloves garlic
- » 1 onion, diced
- » 2 carrots
- » 2 stalks celery
- » 1 1/2 teaspoons dried basil
- » 1 teaspoon dried oregano
- » 1/2 teaspoon fennel seed
- » 6 cups low sodium chicken broth
- » 1 (28-ounce) can tomatoes
- » 1 (16-ounce) can kidney beans
- » 1 zucchini
- » 1 Parmesan rind
- » 1 bay leaf
- » 1 bunch kale leaves, chopped
- » 2 teaspoons red wine vinegar
- » 1/3 cup freshly grated Parmesan
- » 2 tablespoons chopped fresh parsley leaves

## DIRECTION

1. Preheat olive oil in the insert of the Instant Pot on Sauté mode.
2. Add carrots, celery, and onion, sauté for 3 minutes.
3. Stir in fennel seeds, oregano, and basil. Stir cook for 1 minute.
4. Add stock, beans, tomatoes, parmesan, bay leaf, and zucchini.
5. Secure and seal the Instant Pot lid then select Manual mode to cook for minutes at high pressure.
6. Once done, release the pressure completely then remove the lid.
7. Add kale and let it sit for 2 minutes in the hot soup.
8. Stir in red wine, vinegar, pepper, and salt.
9. Garnish with parsley and parmesan.

## NUTRITIONS:

805 Calories, 124 Protein, 34g Fat

# 338. TURKEY MEATBALL AND DITALINI SOUP

**COOKING: 40'**  **PREPARATION:15'**  **SERVES: 4**

## INGREDIENTS

- » meatballs:
- » 1 pound 93% lean ground turkey
- » 1/3 cup seasoned breadcrumbs
- » 3 tablespoons grated Pecorino Romano cheese
- » 1 large egg, beaten
- » 1 clove crushed garlic
- » 1 tablespoon fresh minced parsley
- » 1/2 teaspoon kosher salt
- » Soup:
- » 1 teaspoon olive oil
- » 1/2 cup onion
- » 1/2 cup celery
- » 1/2 cup carrot
- » 3 cloves garlic
- » 1 can San Marzano tomatoes
- » 4 cups reduced sodium chicken broth
- » 4 torn basil leaves
- » 2 bay leaves
- » 1 cup ditalini pasta
- » 1 cup zucchini, diced small
- » Parmesan rind, optional
- » Grated parmesan cheese, optional for serving

## DIRECTION

1. Thoroughly combine turkey with egg, garlic, parsley, salt, pecorino and breadcrumbs in a bowl.
2. Make 30 equal sized meatballs out of this mixture.
3. Preheat olive oil in the insert of the Instant Pot on Sauté mode.
4. Sear the meatballs in the heated oil in batches, until brown.
5. Set the meatballs aside in a plate.
6. Add more oil to the insert of the Instant Pot.
7. Stir in carrots, garlic, celery, and onion. Sauté for 4 minutes.
8. Add basil, bay leaves, tomatoes, and Parmesan rind.
9. Return the seared meatballs to the pot along with the broth.
10. Secure and sear the Instant Pot lid and select Manual mode for 15 minutes at high pressure.
11. Once done, release the pressure completely then remove the lid.
12. Add zucchini and pasta, cook it for 4 minutes on Sauté mode.
13. Garnish with cheese and basil.

## NUTRITIONS:

261 Calories, 37g Protein, 7g Fat

# 339. MINT AVOCADO CHILLED SOUP

**COOKING: 0'**　　　**PREPARATION:6'**　　　**SERVES: 2**

## INGREDIENTS

- » 1 cup coconut milk, chilled
- » 1 medium ripe avocado
- » 1 tablespoon lime juice
- » Salt, to taste
- » 20 fresh mint leaves

## DIRECTION

1. Put all the ingredients into an immersion blender and blend until a thick mixture is formed.
2. Allow to cool in the fridge for about 10 minutes and serve chilled.

**NUTRITIONS:**

286 Calories, 27g Fats, 4.2g Protein

# 340. SPLIT PEA SOUP

**COOKING: 30'**　　　**PREPARATION:11'**　　　**SERVES: 6**

## INGREDIENTS

- » 3 tablespoons butter
- » 1 onion diced
- » 2 ribs celery diced
- » 2 carrots diced
- » 6 oz. diced ham
- » 1 lb. dry split peas sorted and rinsed
- » 6 cups chicken stock
- » 2 bay leaves

## DIRECTION

1. Set your Instant Pot on Sauté mode and melt butter in it.
2. Stir in celery, onion, carrots, salt, and pepper.
3. Sauté them for 5 minutes then stir in split peas, ham bone, chicken stock, and bay leaves.
4. Seal and lock the Instant Pot lid then select Manual mode for 15 minutes at high pressure.
5. Once done, release the pressure completely then remove the lid.
6. Remove the ham bone and separate meat from the bone.
7. Shred meat and return it to the soup.
8. Adjust seasoning as needed then serve warm.

**NUTRITIONS:**

190 Calories, 8g Protein, 3.5g Fat

# 341. BUTTERNUT SQUASH SOUP

**COOKING: 40'**      **PREPARATION: 8'**      **SERVES: 4**

## INGREDIENTS

- » 1 tablespoon olive oil
- » 1 medium yellow onion chopped
- » 1 large carrot chopped
- » 1 celery rib chopped
- » 3 cloves of garlic minced
- » 2 lbs. butternut squash, peeled chopped
- » 2 cups vegetable broth
- » 1 green apple peeled, cored, and chopped
- » 1/4 teaspoon ground cinnamon
- » 1 sprig fresh thyme
- » 1 sprig fresh rosemary
- » 1 teaspoon kosher salt
- » 1/2 teaspoon black pepper
- » Pinch of nutmeg optional

## DIRECTION

1. Preheat olive oil in the insert of the Instant Pot on Sauté mode.
2. Add celery, carrots, and garlic, sauté for 5 minutes.
3. Stir in squash, broth, cinnamon, apple nutmeg, rosemary, thyme, salt, and pepper.
4. Mix well gently then seal and secure the lid.
5. Select Manual mode to cook for 10 minutes at high pressure.
6. Once done, release the pressure completely then remove the lid.
7. Puree the soup using an immersion blender.
8. Serve warm.

**NUTRITIONS:**
282 Calories, 13g Protein, 4.7g Fat

# 342. BEEF STROGANOFF SOUP

**COOKING: 35'**      **PREPARATION: 9'**      **SERVES: 6**

## INGREDIENTS

- » 1.5 pounds stew meat
- » 6 cups beef broth
- » 4 tablespoons Worcestershire sauce
- » 1/2 teaspoon Italian seasoning blend
- » 1 1/2 teaspoons onion powder
- » 2 teaspoons garlic powder
- » salt and pepper to taste
- » 1/2 cup sour cream
- » 8 ounces mushrooms, sliced
- » 8 ounces short noodles, cooked
- » 1/3 cup cold water
- » 1/4 cup corn starch

## DIRECTION

1. Add meat, 5 cups broth, Italian seasoning, Worcestershire sauce, garlic powder, salt, pepper, and onion powder to the insert of the Instant Pot.
2. Secure and seal the Instant Pot lid then select Manual mode for 1 hour at high pressure.
3. Once done, release the pressure completely then remove the lid.
4. Click Instant pot on Soup mode and add sour cream along with 1 cup broth.
5. Mix well then add mushrooms and mix well.
6. Whisk corn-starch with water and pour this mixture into the pot.
7. Cook this mixture until it thickens then add noodles, salt, and pepper.
8. Garnish with cheese parsley, black pepper.

**NUTRITIONS:**
320 Calories, 26.9g Protein, 13.7g Fat

# 343. CREAMY LOW CARB BUTTERNUT SQUASH SOUP

**COOKING: 70'**  **PREPARATION:12'**  **SERVES: 8**

## INGREDIENTS

» 2 tablespoons avocado oil, divided
» 2 pounds butternut squash
» 1 (13.5-oz) can coconut milk
» 4 cups chicken bone broth

## DIRECTION

1. Set oven at 400 degrees F and grease a baking sheet.
2. Arrange the butternut squash halves with open side up on the baking sheet.
3. Drizzle with half of the avocado oil and season with sea salt and black pepper.
4. Flip over and transfer into the oven.
5. Roast the butternut squash.
6. Cook remaining avocado oil over medium heat in a large pot and add the broth and coconut milk.
7. Let it simmer for about 20 minutes and scoop the squash out of the shells to transfer into the soup.
8. Puree this mixture in an immersion blender until smooth and serve immediately.

**NUTRITIONS:**
185 Calories, 12.6g Fats, 4.7g Protein

# 344. BAKED SHRIMP STEW

**COOKING: 25'**  **PREPARATION TIME:13'**  **SERVES: 6**

## INGREDIENTS

» Greek extra virgin olive oil
» 2 1/2 lb. prawns, peeled
» 1 large red onion
» 5 garlic cloves
» 1 red bell pepper
» 2 15-oz cans diced tomatoes
» 1/2 cup water
» 1 1/2 tsp ground coriander
» 1 tsp sumac
» 1 tsp cumin
» 1 tsp red pepper flakes
» 1/2 tsp ground green cardamom
» Salt and pepper, to taste
» 1 cup parsley leaves, stems removed
» 1/3 cup toasted pine nuts
» 1/4 cup toasted sesame seeds
» Lemon or lime wedges to serve

## DIRECTION

1. Preheat the oven to 375 degrees F
2. Using frying pan, add 1 tbsp olive oil
3. Sauté the prawns for 2 minutes, until they are barely pink, then remove and set aside
4. In the same pan over medium-high heat, drizzle a little more olive oil and sauté the chopped onions, garlic and red bell peppers for 5 minutes, stirring regularly
5. Add in the canned diced tomatoes and water, allow to simmer for 10 minutes, until the liquid reduces, stir occasionally
6. Reduce the heat to medium, add the shrimp back to the pan, stir in the spices the ground coriander, sumac, cumin, red pepper flakes, green cardamom, salt and pepper, then the toasted pine nuts, sesame seeds and parsley leaves, stir to combined
7. Transfer the shrimp and sauce to an oven-safe earthenware or stoneware dish, cover tightly with foil Place in the oven to bake for minutes, uncover and broil briefly.
8. allow the dish to cool completely
9. Distribute among the containers, store for 2-3 days
10. To Serve: Reheat on the stove for 1-2 minutes or until heated through. Serve with your favorite bread or whole grain. Garnish with a side of lime or lemon wedges.

**NUTRITIONS:**
977 Calories, 20g Fat, 41g Protein

# 345. CINNAMON SQUASH SOUP

## INGREDIENTS

- » 1 small butternut squash
- » 4 tablespoons extra-virgin olive oil
- » 1 small yellow onion
- » 2 large garlic cloves
- » 1 teaspoon salt, divided
- » 1 pinch black pepper
- » 1 teaspoon dried oregano
- » 2 tablespoons fresh oregano
- » 2 cups low sodium chicken stock
- » 1 cinnamon stick
- » ½ cup canned white kidney beans
- » 1 small pear
- » 2 tablespoons walnut pieces
- » ¼ cup Greek yogurt
- » 2 tablespoons parsley

## NUTRITIONS:

197 Calories, 11.6g Fat, 6.1g Protein

## DIRECTION

1. Preheat oven to 425 degrees F.
2. Place squash in bowl and season with a ½ teaspoon of salt and tablespoons of olive oil.
3. Arrange squash onto a roasting pan and roast for about 25 minutes until tender.
4. Keep aside squash to let cool.
5. Cook remaining 2 tablespoons of olive oil in a medium-sized pot at medium-high heat.
6. Sauté onions
7. Add dried oregano and garlic and sauté for 1 minute.
8. Mix squash, broth, pear, cinnamon stick, pepper, and remaining salt.
9. Bring mixture to a boil.
10. Once the boiling point is reached, add walnuts and beans.
11. Lower heat and cook for 20 minutes.
12. Remove the cinnamon stick.
13. Use an immersion blender and blend the entire mixture until smooth.
14. Add yogurt gradually while whisking
15. Season with some additional salt and pepper if needed.
16. Garnish with parsley and fresh oregano.

# CHAPTER 25
# SOUP AND STEW RECIPES PART 3

# 346. BULGARIAN LENTIL SOUP

**COOKING: 15'**　　　**PREPARATION:8'**　　　**SERVES: 10**

## INGREDIENTS

- » 2 cups brown lentils
- » 2 onions, chopped
- » 5-6 cloves garlic, peeled
- » 2-3 medium carrots, chopped
- » 1-2 small tomatoes, ripe
- » 4 tbsp olive oil
- » 1 ½ tsp paprika
- » 1 tsp summer savory

## DIRECTION

1. Cook oil in a cooking pot, add the onions and carrots. Add the paprika and washed lentils with 4 cups of warm water; continue to simmer.
2. Chop the tomatoes and add them to the soup about 15 minutes after the lentils have started to simmer. Add savory and peeled garlic cloves. Simmer soup. Salt to taste.

**NUTRITIONS:**
201 Calories, 12g Fat, 5g Protein

# 347. WHITE BEAN SOUP

**COOKING: 17'**　　　**PREPARATION:13'**　　　**SERVES: 6**

## INGREDIENTS

- » 1 cup white beans
- » 2-3 carrots
- » 2 onions, finely chopped
- » 1-2 tomatoes, grated
- » 1 red bell pepper, chopped
- » 4-5 springs of fresh mint and parsley
- » 1 tsp paprika
- » 3 tbsp sunflower oil

## DIRECTION

1. Submerge beans in cold water for 3-4 hours, drain and discard the water.
2. Cover the beans with cold water. Add the oil, finely chopped carrots, onions and bell pepper. Bring to the boil and simmer until the beans are tender.
3. Add the grated tomatoes, mint, paprika and salt. Simmer for another 15 minutes. Serve sprinkled with finely chopped parsley.

**NUTRITIONS:**
210 Calories, 11g Fat, 5g Protein

# 348. CAULIFLOWER SOUP

**COOKING: 40'**  **PREPARATION: 9'**  **SERVES: 8**

## INGREDIENTS

» 1 large onion finely cut
» 1 medium head cauliflower
» 2-3 garlic cloves, crushed
» 3 cups water
» ½ cup whole cream
» 4 tbsp olive oil

## DIRECTION

1. Cook olive oil in a large pot over medium heat and sauté the onion, cauliflower and garlic. Stir in the water and bring the soup to a boil.

2. Reduce heat, cover, and simmer for 40 minutes. Remove the soup from heat add the cream and blend in a blender. Season with salt and pepper.

**NUTRITIONS:**
221 Calories, 19g Fat, 8g Protein

# 349. MOROCCAN PUMPKIN SOUP

**COOKING: 54'**  **PREPARATION: 7'**  **SERVES: 6**

## INGREDIENTS

» 1 leek, white part only
» 3 cloves garlic
» ½ tsp ground ginger
» ½ tsp ground cinnamon
» ½ tsp ground cumin
» 2 carrots
» 2 lb. pumpkin
» 1/3 cup chickpeas
» 5 tbsp olive oil
» juice of ½ lemon

## DIRECTION

1. Heat oil in a large saucepan and sauté leek, garlic and 2 teaspoons of salt, stirring occasionally, until soft. Add cinnamon, ginger and cumin and stir. Add in carrots, pumpkin and chickpeas. Stir to combine.

2. Add 5 cups of water and bring the soup to the boil, then reduce heat and simmer for 50 minutes.

3. Pullout from heat, add lemon juice and blend the soup. Heat again over low heat for 4-5 minutes. Serve topped with parsley sprigs.

**NUTRITIONS:**
241Calories, 21g Fat, 4g Protein

# 350. POTATO SOUP

**COOKING: 7'**   **PREPARATION:16'**   **SERVES: 5**

## INGREDIENTS

- » 4-5 medium potatoes
- » 2 carrots
- » 1 zucchini
- » 1 celery rib
- » 3 cups water
- » 3 tbsp olive oil
- » 1 cup whole milk
- » ½ tsp dried rosemary

## DIRECTION

1. Cook olive oil over medium heat and sauté the vegetables for 2-3 minutes. Pour 3 cups of water, add the rosemary and bring the soup to a boil, then lower heat and simmer until all the vegetables are tender.

2. Blend the soup in a blender until smooth. Add a cup of warm milk and blend some more. Serve warm, seasoned with black pepper and parsley sprinkled over each serving.

**NUTRITIONS:**
211 Calories, 18g Fat, 6g Protein

# 351. LEEK, RICE AND POTATO SOUP

**COOKING: 17'**   **PREPARATION:9'**   **SERVES: 6**

## INGREDIENTS

- » 1/3 cup rice
- » 4 cups of water
- » 2-3 potatoes, diced
- » 1 small onion, cut
- » 1 leek, halved lengthwise and sliced
- » 3 tbsp olive oil
- » lemon juice, to serve

## DIRECTION

1. Heat a soup pot over medium heat. Add olive oil and onion and sauté for 2 minutes. Add leeks and potatoes and stir for a few minutes more. Add three cups of water, bring to a boil, reduce heat and simmer for 5 minutes.

2. Add the very well washed rice and simmer for 10 minutes. Serve with lemon juice to taste.

**NUTRITIONS:**
180 Calories, 11g Fat, 5g Protein

# 352. CARROT AND CHICKPEA SOUP

**COOKING: 18'**　　　**PREPARATION:9'**　　　**SERVES: 5**

## INGREDIENTS

- » 3-4 big carrots
- » 1 leek, chopped
- » 4 cups vegetable broth
- » 1 cup canned chickpeas
- » ½ cup orange juice
- » 2 tbsp olive oil
- » ½ tsp cumin
- » ½ tsp ginger
- » 4-5 tbsp yogurt, to serve

## DIRECTION

1. Cook oil in a huge saucepan over medium heat. Add leek and carrots and sauté until soft. Add orange juice, broth, chickpeas and spices. Bring to the boil.

2. Reduce heat to medium-low and simmer, covered, for 15 minutes.

3. Blend the soup until smooth; return to pan. Season with salt and pepper. Stir over low heat until heated through. Pour in 4-5 bowls, top with yogurt, and serve.

**NUTRITIONS:**

207 Calories, 13g Fat, 4g Protein

# 353. BROCCOLI, ZUCCHINI AND BLUE CHEESE SOUP

**COOKING: 22'**　　　**PREPARATION:11'**　　　**SERVES: 6**

## INGREDIENTS

- » 2 leeks, white part only
- » 1 head broccoli
- » 2 zucchinis, chopped
- » 1 potato, chopped
- » 2 cups vegetable broth
- » 2 cups water
- » 3 tbsp olive oil
- » oz blue cheese, crumbled
- » 1/3 cup light cream

## DIRECTION

1. Cook oil in a saucepan over medium heat. Sauté the leeks, stirring, for 5 minutes or until soft. Add bite sized pieces of broccoli, zucchinis, potato, water and broth and bring to a boil.

2. Reduce heat to low and simmer, stirring occasionally, for 10 minutes, or until vegetables are just tender. Remove from heat and set aside for 5 minutes to cool slightly.

3. Transfer the soup to a blender. Add the cheese and blend in batches until smooth. Return to saucepan and place over low heat. Add cream and stir to combine. Season with salt and pepper to taste.

**NUTRITIONS:**

301 Calories, 16g Fat, 4g Protein

# 354. BEETROOT AND CARROT SOUP

**COOKING: 32'**          **PREPARATION:12'**          **SERVES: 6**

## INGREDIENTS

- » 4 beets
- » 2 carrots
- » 2 potatoes
- » 1 medium onion
- » 4 cups vegetable broth
- » 2 cups water
- » 2 tbsp yogurt
- » 2 tbsp olive oil

## DIRECTION

1. Peel and chop the beets. Heat olive oil in a saucepan over medium high heat and sauté the onion and carrot until onion is tender. Add beets, potatoes, broth and water. Bring to the boil. Reduce heat to medium and simmer, partially covered, for 30-40 minutes, or until beets are tender. Cool slightly.

2. Blend the soup in batches until smooth. Return it to pan over low heat and cook, stirring, for 4 to 5 minutes or until heated through. Season with salt and pepper. Serve soup topped with yogurt and sprinkled with spring onions.

**NUTRITIONS:**
301 Calories, 21g Fat, 11g Protein

# 355. ROASTED RED PEPPER SOUP

**COOKING: 23'**          **PREPARATION:16'**          **SERVES: 7**

## INGREDIENTS

- » 5-6 red peppers
- » 1 large brown onion
- » 2 garlic cloves
- » 4 medium tomatoes
- » 3 cups chicken broth
- » 3 tbsp olive oil
- » 2 bay leaves

## DIRECTION

1. Grill the peppers or roast them in the oven at 450 F until the skins are a little burnt. Place the roasted peppers in a brown paper bag or a lidded container and leave covered for about 10 minutes. This makes it easier to peel them. Peel the skins and remove the seeds. Cut the peppers in small pieces.

2. Heat oil in a large saucepan over medium-high heat. Add onion and garlic and sauté, stirring, for 3 minutes or until onion has softened. Add the red peppers, bay leaves, tomato and simmer for 5 minutes.

3. Add in the broth. Season with pepper. Bring to the boil then reduce heat and simmer for 20 more minutes. Set aside to cool slightly. Blend, in batches, until smooth and serve.

**NUTRITIONS:**
311 Calories, 13g Fat, 5g Protein

# 356. LENTIL, BARLEY AND MUSHROOM SOUP

**COOKING: 38'**　　　　**PREPARATION:4'**　　　　**SERVES: 6**

## INGREDIENTS

- » 2 medium leeks
- » 10 white mushrooms
- » 3 garlic cloves
- » 2 bay leaves
- » 2 cans tomatoes
- » 3/4 cup red lentils
- » 1/3 cup barley
- » 3 tbsp olive oil
- » 1 tsp paprika
- » 1 tsp summer savory
- » ½ tsp cumin

## DIRECTION

1. Heat oil in a large saucepan over medium-high heat. Sauté leeks and mushrooms for 3 to 4 minutes or until softened. Add cumin, paprika, savory and tomatoes, lentils, barley, and 5 cups cold water. Season with salt and pepper.

2. Cover and bring to the boil. Reduce heat to low. Simmer for 35-40 minutes or until the barley is tender.

**NUTRITIONS:**
314 Calories, 19g Fat, 5g Protein

# 357. SPINACH SOUP

**COOKING: 21'**　　　　**PREPARATION:10'**　　　　**SERVES: 6**

## INGREDIENTS

- » 14 oz frozen spinach
- » 1 large onion
- » 1 carrot
- » 4 cups water
- » 3-4 tbsp olive oil
- » 1/4 cup white rice
- » 1-2 cloves garlic, crushed

## DIRECTION

1. Heat the oil in a cooking pot, add the onion and carrot and sauté together for a few minutes, until just softened. Add chopped garlic and rice and stir for a minute. Remove from heat.

2. Add in the chopped spinach along with about 2 cups of hot water and season with salt and pepper. Bring back to a boil, then reduce the heat and simmer for around 30 minutes.

**NUTRITIONS:**
291 Calories, 16g Fat, 7g Protein

# 358. SPINACH AND FETA CHEESE SOUP

**COOKING: 24'**          **PREPARATION:8'**          **SERVES: 4**

## INGREDIENTS

- » 14 oz frozen spinach
- » oz feta cheese
- » 1 large onion or 4-5 scallions
- » 2 -3 tbsp light cream
- » 3-4 tbsp olive oil
- » 1-2 cloves garlic
- » 4 cups water

## DIRECTION

1. Heat the oil in a cooking pot, add the onion and spinach and sauté together for a few minutes, until just softened. Add garlic and stir for a minute. Remove from heat. Add about 2 cups of hot water and season with salt and pepper.

2. Bring back to the boil, then reduce the heat and simmer for around 30 minutes. Blend soup in a blender. Crumble the cheese with a fork. Stir in the crumbled feta cheese and the cream. Serve hot.

**NUTRITIONS:**
251 Calories, 13g Fat, 5g Protein

# 359. NETTLE SOUP

**COOKING: 26'**          **PREPARATION:4'**          **SERVES: 6**

## INGREDIENTS

- » lb. young top shoots of nettles
- » 3-4 tbsp sunflower oil
- » 2 potatoes, diced small
- » 1 bunch spring onions
- » 1 ½ cup freshly boiled water
- » 1 tsp salt

## DIRECTION

1. Clean the young nettles, wash and cook them in slightly salted water. Drain, rinse, drain again and then chop or pass through a sieve. Sauté the chopped spring onions and potatoes.

2. Turn off the heat, add the nettles, then gradually stir in the water. Simmer until the potatoes are cooked through.

**NUTRITIONS:**
251 Calories, 13g Fat, 4g Protein

# 360. THICK HERB SOUP

**COOKING: 23'**     **PREPARATION:11'**     **SERVES: 4**

## INGREDIENTS

- » 2 oz mint leaves
- » 2 oz celery leaves
- » 4 tbsp butter or olive oil
- » 2 tbsp flour
- » 3 cups water
- » ½ cup thick yogurt
- » juice of a lemon
- » 2 egg yolks
- » 1 tsp salt

## DIRECTION

1. Wash the herbs, remove stalks and snip or chop finely. Heat butter or oil in a cooking pot, add prepared herbs, cover and simmer gently.

2. When the herbs are tender, add in the flour and stir to combine. Cook for a few moments before slowly adding the water, stirring all the time. Simmer for about 10-15 min.

3. Mix separately egg yolks, thick yogurt (or sour cream) and lemon juice. Add to the soup slowly, then stir well. The soup should not be allowed to boil any more.

## NUTRITIONS:

247 Calories, 13g Fat, 7g Protein

# CHAPTER 26
# VEGETARIAN RECIPES

# 361. RICE WITH VERMICELLI

**COOKING: 45'**   **PREPARATION: 5'**   **SERVES: 6**

## INGREDIENTS

- » 2 cups short-grain rice
- » 3½ cups water
- » ¼ cup olive oil
- » 1 cup broken vermicelli pasta
- » Salt

## DIRECTION

1. Rinse the rice under cold water until the water runs clean. Place the rice in a bowl, cover with water, and let soak for 10 minutes. Drain and set aside.
2. In a medium pot over medium heat, heat the olive oil.
3. Stir in the vermicelli and cook for 2 to 3 minutes, stirring continuously, until golden.
4. Add the rice and cook for 1 minute, stirring, so the rice is well coated in the oil.
5. Add the water and a pinch of salt and bring the liquid to a boil. Reduce the heat to low, cover the pot, and simmer for 20 minutes.
6. Remove from the heat and let rest, covered, for 10 minutes. Fluff with a fork and serve.

**NUTRITIONS:**

346 calories, 9g fat, 7g Protein

# 362. FAVA BEANS AND RICE

**COOKING: 35'**   **PREPARATION: 10'**   **SERVES: 4**

## INGREDIENTS

- » ¼ cup olive oil
- » 4 cups fresh fava beans
- » 4½ cups water
- » 2 cups basmati rice
- » 1/8 teaspoon salt
- » 1/8 teaspoon black pepper
- » 2 tablespoons pine nuts, toasted
- » ½ cup chopped fresh garlic chives

## DIRECTION

1. In a large saucepan over medium heat, heat the olive oil.
2. Add the fava beans and drizzle them with a bit of water. Cook for 10 minutes.
3. Gently stir in the rice. Add the water, salt, and pepper. Increase the heat and bring the mixture to a boil. Cover, reduce the heat to low, and simmer for 15 minutes.
4. Turn off the heat and let the mixture rest for 10 minutes before serving. Sprinkle with toasted pine nuts and chives.

**NUTRITIONS:**

587 calories, 17g fat, 17g Protein

# 363. BUTTERED FAVA BEANS

**COOKING: 15'**          **PREPARATION:30'**          **SERVES: 4**

## INGREDIENTS

- » ½ cup vegetable broth
- » 4 pounds fava beans
- » ¼ cup fresh tarragon
- » 1 teaspoon chopped fresh thyme
- » ¼ teaspoon black pepper
- » 1/8 teaspoon salt
- » 2 tablespoons butter
- » 1 garlic clove, minced
- » 2 tablespoons chopped fresh parsley

## DIRECTION

1. In a shallow pan over medium heat, bring the vegetable broth to a boil.
2. Add the fava beans, 2 tablespoons of tarragon, the thyme, pepper, and salt. Cook for 10 minutes.
3. Stir in the butter, garlic, and remaining 2 tablespoons of tarragon. Cook for 2 to 3 minutes.
4. Sprinkle with the parsley.

## NUTRITIONS:
458 calories, 9g fat, 37g Protein

# 364. FREEKEH

**COOKING: 40'**          **PREPARATION:10'**          **SERVES: 4**

## INGREDIENTS

- » 4 tablespoons Ghee
- » 1 onion, chopped
- » 3½ cups vegetable broth
- » 1 teaspoon ground allspice
- » 2 cups freekeh
- » 2 tablespoons pine nuts

## DIRECTION

1. In a heavy-bottomed saucepan over medium heat, melt the ghee.
2. Stir in the onion and cook for about 5 minutes, stirring constantly, until the onion is golden.
3. Pour in the vegetable broth, add the allspice, and bring to a boil.
4. Stir in the freekeh and return the mixture to a boil. Reduce the heat to low, cover the pan, and simmer for 30 minutes, stirring occasionally.
5. Spoon the freekeh into a serving dish and top with the toasted pine nuts.

## NUTRITIONS:
459 calories, 18g fat, 19g Protein

# 365. FRIED RICE BALLS WITH TOMATO SAUCE

**COOKING: 20'**  **PREPARATION:15'**  **SERVES: 4**

## INGREDIENTS

- » 1 cup bread crumbs
- » 2 cups cooked risotto
- » 2 large eggs, divided
- » ¼ cup freshly grated Parmesan cheese
- » 8 fresh baby mozzarella balls
- » 2 tablespoons water
- » 1 cup corn oil
- » 1 cup Basic Tomato Basil Sauce

## DIRECTION

1. Pour the bread crumbs into a small bowl and set aside.
2. In a medium bowl, stir together the risotto, 1 egg, and the Parmesan cheese until well combined.
3. Moisten your hands with a little water to prevent sticking and divide the risotto mixture into 8 pieces. Place them on a clean work surface and flatten each piece.
4. Place 1 mozzarella ball on each flattened rice disk. Close the rice around the mozzarella to form a ball. Repeat until you finish all the balls.
5. In the same medium, now-empty bowl, whisk the remaining egg and the water.
6. Dip each prepared risotto ball into the egg wash and roll it in the bread crumbs. Set aside.
7. In a large sauté pan or skillet over high heat, heat the corn oil for about 3 minutes.
8. Gently lower the risotto balls into the hot oil and fry for 5 to 8 minutes until golden brown. Stir them, as needed, to ensure the entire surface is fried. Using a slotted spoon, transfer the fried balls to paper towels to drain.
9. In a medium saucepan over medium heat, heat the tomato sauce for 5 minutes, stirring occasionally, and serve the warm sauce alongside the rice balls.

**NUTRITIONS:**
255 calories, 15g fat, 11g Protein

# 366. SPANISH-STYLE RICE

**COOKING: 35'**  **PREPARATION:10'**  **SERVES: 4**

## INGREDIENTS

- » ¼ cup olive oil
- » 1 small onion
- » 1 red bell pepper
- » 1½ cups white rice
- » 1 teaspoon sweet paprika
- » ½ teaspoon ground cumin
- » ½ teaspoon ground coriander
- » 1 garlic clove, minced
- » 3 tablespoons tomato paste
- » 3 cups vegetable broth
- » 1/8 teaspoon salt

## DIRECTION

1. In a large heavy-bottomed skillet over medium heat, heat the olive oil.
2. Stir in the onion and red bell pepper. Cook for 5 minutes or until softened.
3. Add the rice, paprika, cumin, and coriander and cook for 2 minutes, stirring often.
4. Add the garlic, tomato paste, vegetable broth, and salt. Stir to combine, taste, and season with more salt, as needed.
5. Increase the heat to bring the mixture to a boil. Reduce the heat to low, cover the skillet, and simmer for 20 minutes.
6. Let the rice rest, covered, for 5 minutes before serving.

**NUTRITIONS:**
414 calories, 14g fat, 6g Protein

# 367. ZUCCHINI WITH RICE AND TZATZIKI

**COOKING: 35'**  **PREPARATION:20'**  **SERVES: 4**

## INGREDIENTS

- » ¼ cup olive oil
- » 1 onion
- » 3 zucchinis
- » 1 cup vegetable broth
- » ½ cup chopped fresh dill
- » 1 cup short-grain rice
- » 2 tablespoons pine nuts
- » 1 cup Tzatziki Sauce, Plain Yogurt

## DIRECTION

1. In a heavy-bottomed pot over medium heat, heat the olive oil.
2. Add the onion, turn the heat to medium-low, and sauté for 5 minutes.
3. Add the zucchini and cook for 2 minutes more.
4. Stir in the vegetable broth and dill and season with salt and pepper. Increase the heat to medium and bring the mixture to a boil.
5. Stir in the rice and let it boil. Set to very low heat, cover the pot, and cook for 15 minutes. Remove from the heat and let the rice rest, covered, for 10 minutes.
6. Spoon the rice onto a serving platter, sprinkle with the pine nuts, and serve with tzatziki sauce.

**NUTRITIONS:**
414 calories, 17g fat, 11g Protein

# 368. CANNELLINI BEANS WITH ROSEMARY AND GARLIC AIOLI

**COOKING: 10'**  **PREPARATION:10'**  **SERVES: 4**

## INGREDIENTS

- » 4 cups cooked cannellini beans
- » 4 cups water
- » ½ teaspoon salt
- » 3 tablespoons olive oil
- » 2 tablespoons chopped fresh rosemary
- » ½ cup Garlic Aioli
- » ¼ teaspoon freshly ground black pepper

## DIRECTION

1. In a medium saucepan over medium heat, combine the cannellini beans, water, and salt. Bring to a boil. Cook for 5 minutes. Drain.
2. In a skillet over medium heat, heat the olive oil.
3. Add the beans. Stir in the rosemary and aioli. Reduce the heat to medium-low and cook, stirring, just to heat through. Season with pepper and serve.

**NUTRITIONS:**
545 calories, 36g fat, 15g Protein

# 369. JEWELED RICE

**COOKING: 30'**     **PREPARATION:15'**     **SERVES: 6**

## INGREDIENTS

- » ½ cup olive oil, divided
- » 1 onion, finely chopped
- » 1 garlic clove, minced
- » ½ teaspoon fresh ginger
- » 4½ cups water
- » 1 teaspoon salt
- » 1 teaspoon ground turmeric
- » 2 cups basmati rice
- » 1 cup fresh sweet peas
- » 2 carrots
- » ½ cup dried cranberries
- » Grated zest of 1 orange
- » 1/8 teaspoon cayenne pepper
- » ¼ cup slivered almonds

## DIRECTION

1. In a large heavy-bottomed pot over medium heat, heat ¼ cup of olive oil.
2. Add the onion and cook for 4 minutes. Add the garlic and ginger and cook for 1 minute more.
3. Stir in the water, ¾ teaspoon of salt, and the turmeric. Bring the mixture to a boil. Mix in the rice and boil. Select heat to low, cover the pot, and cook for 15 minutes. Turn off the heat. Let the rice rest on the burner, covered, for 10 minutes.
4. Meanwhile, in a medium sauté pan or skillet over medium-low heat, heat the remaining ¼ cup of olive oil. Stir in the peas and carrots. Cook for 5 minutes.
5. Stir in the cranberries and orange zest. Season with the remaining ¼ teaspoon of salt and the cayenne. Cook for 1 to 2 minutes.
6. Spoon the rice onto a serving platter. Top with the peas and carrots and sprinkle with the toasted almonds.

## NUTRITIONS:
460 calories, 19g fat, 7g Protein

# 370. ASPARAGUS RISOTTO

**COOKING: 30'**     **PREPARATION:15'**     **SERVES: 4**

## INGREDIENTS

- » 5 cups vegetable broth
- » 3 tablespoons unsalted butter
- » 1 tablespoon olive oil
- » 1 small onion, chopped
- » 1½ cups Arborio rice
- » 1-pound fresh asparagus
- » ¼ cup freshly grated Parmesan cheese, plus more for serving

## DIRECTION

1. In a saucepan over medium heat, bring the vegetable broth to a boil. Turn the heat to low and keep the broth at a steady simmer.
2. In a 4-quart heavy-bottomed saucepan over medium heat, melt 2 tablespoons of butter with the olive oil. Add the onion and cook for 2 to 3 minutes.
3. Add the rice and stir with a wooden spoon while cooking for 1 minute until the grains are well coated in the butter and oil.
4. Stir in ½ cup of warm broth. Cook, stirring often, for about 5 minutes until the broth is completely absorbed.
5. Add the asparagus stalks and another ½ cup of broth. Cook, stirring often, until the liquid is absorbed. Continue adding the broth, ½ cup at a time, and cooking until it is completely absorbed before adding the next ½ cup. Stir frequently to prevent sticking. After about 20 minutes, the rice should be cooked but still firm.
6. Add the asparagus tips, the remaining 1 tablespoon of butter, and the Parmesan cheese. Stir vigorously to combine.
7. Remove from the heat, top with additional Parmesan cheese, if desired, and serve immediately.

## NUTRITIONS:
434 calories, 14g fat, 10g Protein

# 371. VEGETABLE PAELLA

**COOKING: 45'**     **PREPARATION: 25'**     **SERVES: 6**

## INGREDIENTS

- » ¼ cup olive oil
- » 1 large sweet onion
- » 1 large red bell pepper
- » 1 large green bell pepper
- » 3 garlic cloves
- » 1 teaspoon smoked paprika
- » 5 saffron threads
- » 1 zucchini, cut into ½-inch cubes
- » 4 large ripe tomatoes
- » 1½ cups short-grain Spanish rice
- » 3 cups vegetable broth, warmed

## DIRECTION

1. Preheat the oven to 350°F.
2. In a paella pan or large oven-safe skillet over medium heat, heat the olive oil.
3. Add the onion and red and green bell peppers and cook for 10 minutes.
4. Stir in the garlic, paprika, saffron threads, zucchini, and tomatoes. Turn the heat to medium-low and cook for 10 minutes.
5. Stir in the rice and vegetable broth. Increase the heat to bring the paella to a boil. Reduce the heat to medium-low and cook for 15 minutes. Cover the pan with aluminum foil and put it in the oven.
6. Bake for 10 minutes or until the broth is absorbed.

## NUTRITIONS:
288 calories, 10g fat, 5g Protein

# 372. EGGPLANT AND RICE CASSEROLE

**COOKING: 35'**     **PREPARATION: 30'**     **SERVES: 4**

## INGREDIENTS

- » For sauce
- » ½ cup olive oil
- » 1 small onion
- » 4 garlic cloves
- » 6 ripe tomatoes
- » 2 tablespoons tomato paste
- » 1 teaspoon dried oregano
- » ¼ teaspoon ground nutmeg
- » ¼ teaspoon ground cumin
- » For casserole
- » 4 (6-inch) Japanese eggplants
- » 2 tablespoons olive oil
- » 1 cup cooked rice
- » 2 tablespoons pine nuts
- » 1 cup water

## DIRECTION

1. For sauce
2. In a heavy-bottomed saucepan over medium heat, heat the olive oil. Add the onion and cook for 5 minutes.
3. Stir in the garlic, tomatoes, tomato paste, oregano, nutmeg, and cumin. Bring to a boil. Cover, reduce heat to low, and simmer for 10 minutes. Remove and set aside.
4. For casserole
5. Preheat the broiler.
6. While the sauce simmers, drizzle the eggplant with the olive oil and place them on a baking sheet. Broil for about 5 minutes until golden. Remove and let cool.
7. Turn the oven to 375°F. Arrange the cooled eggplant, cut-side up, in a 9-by-13-inch baking dish. Gently scoop out some flesh to make room for the stuffing.
8. In a bowl, combine half the tomato sauce, the cooked rice, and pine nuts. Fill each eggplant half with the rice mixture.
9. In the same bowl, combine the remaining tomato sauce and water. Pour over the eggplant.
10. Bake, covered, for 20 minutes.

## NUTRITIONS:
453 calories, 39g fat, 6g Protein

# 373. MANY VEGETABLE COUSCOUS

**COOKING: 45'**     **PREPARATION:15'**     **SERVES: 8**

## INGREDIENTS

- » ¼ cup olive oil
- » 1 onion, chopped
- » 4 garlic cloves, minced
- » 2 jalapeño peppers
- » ½ teaspoon ground cumin
- » ½ teaspoon ground coriander
- » 1 (28-ounce) can crushed tomatoes
- » 2 tablespoons tomato paste
- » 1/8 teaspoon salt
- » 2 bay leaves
- » 11 cups water, divided
- » 4 carrots, peeled and cut into 2-inch pieces
- » 2 zucchinis
- » 1 acorn squash
- » 1 (15-ounce) can chickpeas
- » ¼ cup chopped Preserved Lemons (optional)
- » 3 cups couscous

## DIRECTION

1. In a large heavy-bottomed pot over medium heat, heat the olive oil. Stir in the onion and cook for 4 minutes. Stir in the garlic, jalapeños, cumin, and coriander. Cook for 1 minute.

2. Add the tomatoes, tomato paste, salt, bay leaves, and 8 cups of water. Bring the mixture to a boil.

3. Add the carrots, zucchini, and acorn squash and return to a boil. Reduce the heat slightly, cover, and cook for about 20 minutes until the vegetables are tender but not mushy. Remove 2 cups of the cooking liquid and set aside. Season as needed.

4. Add the chickpeas and preserved lemons (if using). Cook for 2 to 3 minutes, and turn off the heat.

5. In a medium pan, bring the remaining 3 cups of water to a boil over high heat. Stir in the couscous, cover, and turn off the heat. Let the couscous rest for 10 minutes. Drizzle with 1 cup of reserved cooking liquid. Using a fork, fluff the couscous.

6. Mound it on a large platter. Drizzle it with the remaining cooking liquid. Remove the vegetables from the pot and arrange on top. Serve the remaining stew in a separate bowl.

## NUTRITIONS:

415 calories, 7g fat, 14g Protein

# 375. BULGUR WITH TOMATOES AND CHICKPEAS

**COOKING: 35'**     **PREPARATION:10'**     **SERVES: 6**

## INGREDIENTS

- » ½ cup olive oil
- » 1 onion, chopped
- » 6 tomatoes
- » 2 tablespoons tomato paste
- » 2 cups water
- » 1 tablespoon Harissa
- » 1/8 teaspoon salt
- » 2 cups coarse bulgur #3
- » 1 (15-ounce) can chickpeas

## DIRECTION

1. In a heavy-bottomed pot over medium heat, heat the olive oil.

2. Add the onion and sauté for 5 minutes.

3. Add the tomatoes with their juice and cook for 5 minutes.

4. Stir in the tomato paste, water, harissa, and salt. Bring to a boil.

5. Stir in the bulgur and chickpeas. Return the mixture to a boil. Reduce the heat to low, cover the pot, and cook for 15 minutes. Let rest for 15 minutes before serving.

## NUTRITIONS:

413 calories, 19g fat, 11g Protein

# 374. KUSHARI

## INGREDIENTS

- » For sauce
- » 2 tablespoons olive oil
- » 2 garlic cloves, minced
- » 1 (16-ounce) can tomato sauce
- » ¼ cup white vinegar
- » ¼ cup Harissa, or store-bought
- » 1/8 teaspoon salt
- » For rice
- » 1 cup olive oil
- » 2 onions, thinly sliced
- » 2 cups dried brown lentils
- » 4 quarts plus ½ cup water
- » 2 cups short-grain rice
- » 1 teaspoon salt
- » 1-pound short elbow pasta
- » 1 (15-ounce) can chickpeas

## DIRECTION

1. For sauce
2. In a saucepan over medium heat, heat the olive oil.
3. Add the garlic and cook for 1 minute.
4. Stir in the tomato sauce, vinegar, harissa, and salt. Increase the heat to bring the sauce to a boil. Reduce the heat to low and cook for 20 minutes or until the sauce has thickened. Remove and set aside.
5. For rice
6. Line a plate with paper towels and set aside.
7. In a large pan over medium heat, heat the olive oil.
8. Add the onions and cook for 7 to 10 minutes, stirring often, until crisp and golden. Transfer the onions to the prepared plate and set aside. Reserve 2 tablespoons of the cooking oil. Reserve the pan.
9. In a large pot over high heat, combine the lentils and 4 cups of water. Bring to a boil and cook for 20 minutes. Drain, transfer to a bowl, and toss with the reserved 2 tablespoons of cooking oil. Set aside. Reserve the pot.
10. Place the pan you used to fry the onions over medium-high heat and add the rice, 4½ cups of water, and the salt to it. Bring to a boil. Reduce the heat to low, cover the pot, and cook for 20 minutes. Turn off the heat and let the rice rest for 10 minutes.6.
11. In the pot used to cook the lentils, bring the remaining 8 cups of water, salted, to a boil over high heat. Drop in the pasta and cook for 6 minutes or according to the package instructions. Drain and set aside.
12. To assemble: Spoon the rice onto a serving platter. Top it with the lentils, chickpeas, and pasta. Drizzle with the hot tomato sauce and sprinkle with the crispy fried onions.

## NUTRITIONS:
668 calories, 13g fat, 25g Protein

# CHAPTER 27
# VEGETARIAN RECIPES PART 2

# 376. CAULIFLOWER STEAKS WITH OLIVE CITRUS SAUCE

**COOKING: 30'**     **PREPARATION:15'**     **SERVES: 4**

## INGREDIENTS

- » 2 large heads cauliflowers
- » 1/3 cup extra-virgin olive oil
- » ¼ teaspoon kosher salt
- » 1/8 teaspoon black pepper
- » Juice of 1 orange
- » Zest of 1 orange
- » ¼ cup black olives
- » 1 tablespoon Dijon mustard
- » 1 tablespoon red wine vinegar
- » ½ teaspoon ground coriander

## DIRECTION

1. Preheat the oven to 400°F. Line a baking sheet with parchment paper or foil.

2. Cut off the stem of the cauliflower so it will sit upright. Slice it vertically into four thick slabs. Place the cauliflower on the prepared baking sheet. Drizzle with the olive oil, salt, and black pepper. Bake for about 30 minutes, turning over once, until tender and golden brown.

3. In a medium bowl, combine the orange juice, orange zest, olives, mustard, vinegar, and coriander; mix well.

4. Serve the cauliflower warm or at room temperature with the sauce.

**NUTRITIONS:**
265 Calories, 21g fat, 5g Protein

# 377. PISTACHIO MINT PESTO PASTA

**COOKING: 10'**     **PREPARATION:10'**     **SERVES: 4**

## INGREDIENTS

- » 8 ounces whole-wheat pasta
- » 1 cup fresh mint
- » ½ cup fresh basil
- » 1/3 cup unsalted pistachios, shelled
- » 1 garlic clove, peeled
- » ½ teaspoon kosher salt
- » Juice of ½ lime
- » 1/3 cup extra-virgin olive oil

## DIRECTION

1. Cook the pasta according to the package directions. Drain, reserving ½ cup of the pasta water, and set aside.

2. In a food processor, add the mint, basil, pistachios, garlic, salt, and lime juice. Process until the pistachios are coarsely ground. Add the olive oil in a slow, steady stream and process until incorporated.

3. In a large bowl, mix the pasta with the pistachio pesto; toss well to incorporate. If a thinner, more saucy consistency is desired, add some of the reserved pasta water and toss well.

**NUTRITIONS:**
420 Calories, 3g fat, 11g Protein

# 378. BURST CHERRY TOMATO SAUCE WITH ANGEL HAIR PASTA

**COOKING: 20'**      **PREPARATION:10'**      **SERVES: 4**

## INGREDIENTS

» Ingredients:
» 8 ounces angel hair pasta
» 2 tablespoons extra-virgin olive oil
» 3 garlic cloves, minced
» 3 pints cherry tomatoes
» ½ teaspoon kosher salt
» ¼ teaspoon red pepper flakes
» ¾ cup fresh basil, chopped
» 1 tablespoon white balsamic vinegar (optional)
» ¼ cup grated Parmesan cheese (optional)

## DIRECTION

1. Cook the pasta according to the package directions. Drain and set aside.

2. Heat the olive oil in a skillet or large sauté pan over medium-high heat. Add the garlic and sauté for 30 seconds. Add the tomatoes, salt, and red pepper flakes and cook, stirring occasionally, until the tomatoes burst, about 15 minutes.

3. Remove from the heat and add the pasta and basil. Toss together well. (For out-of-season tomatoes, add the vinegar, if desired, and mix well.)

4. Serve with the grated Parmesan cheese, if desired.

**NUTRITIONS:**
305 Calories, 8g fat, 11g Protein

# 379. BAKED TOFU WITH SUN-DRIED TOMATOES AND ARTICHOKES

**COOKING: 30'**      **PREPARATION:30'**      **SERVES: 4**

## INGREDIENTS

» 1 (16-ounce) package extra-firm tofu
» 2 tablespoons extra-virgin olive oil, divided
» 2 tablespoons lemon juice, divided
» 1 tablespoon low-sodium soy sauce
» 1 onion, diced
» ½ teaspoon kosher salt
» 2 garlic cloves, minced
» 1 (14-ounce) can artichoke hearts, drained
» 8 sun-dried tomato halves packed in oil
» ¼ teaspoon freshly ground black pepper
» 1 tablespoon white wine vinegar
» Zest of 1 lemon
» ¼ cup fresh parsley, chopped

## DIRECTION

1. Preheat the oven to 400°F. Line a baking sheet with foil or parchment paper.

2. In a bowl, combine the tofu, 1 tablespoon of the olive oil, 1 tablespoon of the lemon juice, and the soy sauce. Allow to sit and marinate for 15 to 30 minutes. Arrange the tofu in a single layer on the prepared baking sheet and bake for 20 minutes, turning once, until light golden brown.

3. Heat the remaining 1 tablespoon olive oil in a sauté pan over medium heat. Cook onion and salt for 6 minutes. Add the garlic and sauté for 30 seconds. Add the artichoke hearts, sun-dried tomatoes, and black pepper and sauté for 5 minutes. Add the white wine vinegar and the remaining 1 tablespoon lemon juice and deglaze the pan, scraping up any brown bits. Remove the pan from the heat and stir in the lemon zest and parsley. Gently mix in the baked tofu.

**NUTRITIONS:**
230 Calories, 14g fat, 14g Protein

# 380. BAKED MEDITERRANEAN TEMPEH WITH TOMATOES AND GARLIC

**COOKING: 35'**　　　**PREPARATION:25'**　　　**SERVES: 4**

## INGREDIENTS

- » For tempeh
- » 12 ounces tempeh
- » ¼ cup white wine
- » 2 tablespoons extra-virgin olive oil
- » 2 tablespoons lemon juice
- » Zest of 1 lemon
- » ¼ teaspoon kosher salt
- » ¼ teaspoon freshly ground black pepper
- » For tomatoes and garlic sauce
- » 1 tablespoon extra-virgin olive oil
- » 1 onion, diced
- » 3 garlic cloves, minced
- » 1 (14.5-ounce) can no-salt-added crushed tomatoes
- » 1 beefsteak tomato, diced
- » 1 dried bay leaf
- » 1 teaspoon white wine vinegar
- » 1 teaspoon lemon juice
- » 1 teaspoon dried oregano
- » 1 teaspoon dried thyme
- » ¾ teaspoon kosher salt
- » ¼ cup basil, cut into ribbons

## DIRECTION

1. For tempeh
2. Place the tempeh in a medium saucepan. Add enough water to cover it by 1 to 2 inches. Bring to a boil over medium-high heat, cover, and lower heat to a simmer. Cook for 10 to 15 minutes. Remove the tempeh, pat dry, cool, and cut into 1-inch cubes.
3. In a large bowl, combine the white wine, olive oil, lemon juice, lemon zest, salt, and black pepper. Add the tempeh, cover the bowl, and put in the refrigerator for 4 hours, or up to overnight.
4. Preheat the oven to 375°F. Place the marinated tempeh and the marinade in a baking dish and cook for 15 minutes.
5. For tomatoes and garlic sauce
6. Heat the olive oil in a large skillet over medium heat. Add the onion and sauté until transparent, 3 to 5 minutes. Add the garlic and sauté for 30 seconds. Add the crushed tomatoes, beefsteak tomato, bay leaf, vinegar, lemon juice, oregano, thyme, and salt. Mix well. Simmer for 15 minutes.
7. Add the baked tempeh to the tomato mixture and gently mix together. Garnish with the basil.

### NUTRITIONS:
330 Calories, 20g fat, 18g Protein

# 381. ROASTED PORTOBELLO MUSHROOMS WITH KALE AND RED ONION

**COOKING: 30'**　　　**PREPARATION:30'**　　　**SERVES: 4**

## INGREDIENTS

- » ¼ cup white wine vinegar
- » 3 tablespoons extra-virgin olive oil, divided
- » ½ teaspoon honey
- » ¾ teaspoon kosher salt, divided
- » ¼ teaspoon freshly ground black pepper
- » 4 (4 to 5 ounces) portobello mushrooms, stems removed
- » 1 red onion, julienned
- » 2 garlic cloves, minced
- » 1 (8-ounce) bunch kale, stemmed and chopped small
- » ¼ teaspoon red pepper flakes
- » ¼ cup grated Parmesan or Romano cheese

## DIRECTION

1. Line a baking sheet with parchment paper or foil. In a medium bowl, whisk together the vinegar, 1½ tablespoons of the olive oil, honey, ¼ teaspoon of the salt, and the black pepper. Arrange the mushrooms on the baking sheet and pour the marinade over them. Marinate for 15 to 30 minutes.
2. Meanwhile, preheat the oven to 400°F.
3. Bake the mushrooms for 20 minutes, turning over halfway through.
4. Heat the remaining 1½ tablespoons olive oil in a large skillet or ovenproof sauté pan over medium-high heat. Add the onion and the remaining ½ teaspoon salt and sauté until golden brown, 5 to 6 minutes. Add the garlic and sauté for 30 seconds. Add the kale and red pepper flakes and sauté until the kale cooks down, about 5 minutes.
5. Remove the mushrooms from the oven and increase the temperature to broil.
6. Carefully pour the liquid from the baking sheet into the pan with the kale mixture; mix well.
7. Turn the mushrooms over so that the stem side is facing up. Spoon some of the kale mixture on top of each mushroom. Sprinkle 1 tablespoon Parmesan cheese on top of each.
8. Broil until golden brown, 3 to 4 minutes.

### NUTRITIONS:
200 Calories, 13g fat, 8g Protein

# 382. BALSAMIC MARINATED TOFU WITH BASIL AND OREGANO

**COOKING: 30'**  **PREPARATION:40'**  **SERVES: 4**

## INGREDIENTS

- » ¼ cup extra-virgin olive oil
- » ¼ cup balsamic vinegar
- » 2 tablespoons gluten-free tamari
- » 3 garlic cloves, grated
- » 2 teaspoons pure maple syrup
- » Zest of 1 lemon
- » 1 teaspoon dried basil
- » 1 teaspoon dried oregano
- » ½ teaspoon dried thyme
- » ½ teaspoon dried sage
- » ¼ teaspoon kosher salt
- » ¼ teaspoon freshly ground black pepper
- » ¼ teaspoon red pepper flakes (optional)
- » 1 (16-ounce) block extra firm tofu

## DIRECTION

1. In a bowl or gallon zip-top bag, mix together the olive oil, vinegar, soy sauce, garlic, maple syrup, lemon zest, basil, oregano, thyme, sage, salt, black pepper, and red pepper flakes, if desired. Add the tofu and mix gently. Put in the refrigerator and marinate for 30 minutes, or up to overnight if you desire.

2. Preheat the oven to 425°F. Line a baking sheet with parchment paper or foil. Arrange the marinated tofu in a single layer on the prepared baking sheet. Bake for 20 to 30 minutes, turning over halfway through, until slightly crispy on the outside and tender on the inside.

**NUTRITIONS:**
225 Calories, 16g fat, 13g Protein

# 383. RICOTTA, BASIL, AND PISTACHIO-STUFFED ZUCCHINI

**COOKING: 25'**  **PREPARATION:15'**  **SERVES: 4**

## INGREDIENTS

- » 2 medium zucchinis
- » 1 tablespoon extra-virgin olive oil
- » 1 onion, diced
- » 1 teaspoon kosher salt
- » 2 garlic cloves, minced
- » ¾ cup ricotta cheese
- » ¼ cup unsalted pistachios
- » ¼ cup fresh basil
- » 1 large egg, beaten
- » ¼ teaspoon freshly ground black pepper

## DIRECTION

1. Preheat the oven to 425°F. Line a baking sheet with parchment paper or foil.

2. Scoop out the seeds/pulp from the zucchini, leaving ¼-inch flesh around the edges. Transfer the pulp to a cutting board and chop the pulp.

3. Heat the olive oil in a huge skillet over medium heat, sauté onion, pulp, and salt for 5 minutes. Add the garlic and sauté 30 seconds.

4. In a medium bowl, combine the ricotta cheese, pistachios, basil, egg, and black pepper. Add the onion mixture and mix together well.

5. Place the 4 zucchini halves on the prepared baking sheet. Fill the zucchini halves with the ricotta mixture. Bake for 20 minutes.

**NUTRITIONS:**
200 Calories, 12g fat, 11g Protein

# 384. FARRO WITH ROASTED TOMATOES AND MUSHROOMS

## COOKING: 1 HOUR     PREPARATION:20'     SERVES: 4

## INGREDIENTS

- » For tomatoes
- » 2 pints cherry tomatoes
- » 1 teaspoon extra-virgin olive oil
- » ¼ teaspoon kosher salt
- » For farro
- » 3 to 4 cups water
- » ½ cup farro
- » ¼ teaspoon kosher salt
- » For mushrooms
- » 2 tablespoons extra-virgin olive oil
- » 1 onion, julienned
- » ½ teaspoon kosher salt
- » ¼ teaspoon freshly ground black pepper
- » 10 ounces baby Bella mushrooms
- » ½ cup no-salt-added vegetable stock
- » 1 (15-ounce) can low-sodium cannellini beans
- » 1 cup baby spinach
- » 2 tablespoons fresh basil
- » ¼ cup pine nuts, toasted
- » Aged balsamic vinegar (optional)

## NUTRITIONS:
375 Calories, 15g fat, 14g Protein

## DIRECTION

1. For tomatoes
2. Preheat the oven to 400°F. Line a baking sheet with parchment paper or foil. Toss the tomatoes, olive oil, and salt together on the baking sheet and roast for 30 minutes.
3. For farro
4. Bring the water, farro, and salt to a boil in a medium saucepan or pot over high heat. Cover, reduce the heat to low, and simmer, and cook for 30 minutes, or until the farro is al dente. Drain and set aside.
5. For mushrooms
6. Heat the olive oil in a large skillet or sauté pan over medium-low heat. Add the onions, salt, and black pepper and sauté until golden brown and starting to caramelize, about 15 minutes. Add the mushrooms, increase the heat to medium, and sauté until the liquid has evaporated and the mushrooms brown, about 10 minutes. Add the vegetable stock and deglaze the pan, scraping up any brown bits, and reduce the liquid for about 5 minutes. Add the beans and warm through, about 3 minutes.
7. Remove from the heat and mix in the spinach, basil, pine nuts, roasted tomatoes, and farro. Garnish with a drizzle of balsamic vinegar, if desired.

# 385. BAKED ORZO

## COOKING: 1 HOUR     PREPARATION:20'     SERVES: 4

## INGREDIENTS

- » 2 tablespoons extra-virgin olive oil
- » 1 large (1-pound) eggplant, diced small
- » 2 carrots, peeled and diced small
- » 2 celery stalks, diced small
- » 1 onion, diced small
- » ½ teaspoon kosher salt
- » 3 garlic cloves, minced
- » ¼ teaspoon freshly ground black pepper
- » 1 cup whole-wheat orzo
- » 1 teaspoon no-salt-added tomato paste
- » 1½ cups no-salt-added vegetable stock
- » 1 cup Swiss chard, stemmed and chopped small
- » 2 tablespoons fresh oregano, chopped
- » Zest of 1 lemon
- » 4 ounces mozzarella cheese, diced small
- » ¼ cup grated Parmesan cheese
- » 2 tomatoes, sliced ½-inch-thick

## NUTRITIONS:
470 Calories, 17g fat, 19g Protein

## DIRECTION

1. Preheat the oven to 400°F.
2. Heat the olive oil in a large oven-safe sauté pan over medium heat. Add the eggplant, carrots, celery, onion, and salt and sauté about 10 minutes. Add the garlic and black pepper and sauté about 30 seconds. Add the orzo and tomato paste and sauté 1 minute. Add the vegetable stock and deglaze the pan, scraping up the brown bits. Add the Swiss chard, oregano, and lemon zest and stir until the chard wilts.
3. Remove from the heat and mix in the mozzarella cheese. Smooth the top of the orzo mixture flat. Sprinkle the Parmesan cheese over the top. Arrange the tomatoes in a single layer on top of the Parmesan cheese. Bake for 45 minutes.

# 386. BARLEY RISOTTO WITH TOMATOES

**COOKING: 45'** | **PREPARATION: 20'** | **SERVES: 4**

## INGREDIENTS

- » 2 tablespoons extra-virgin olive oil
- » 2 celery stalks, diced
- » ½ cup shallots, diced
- » 4 garlic cloves, minced
- » 3 cups no-salt-added vegetable stock
- » 2 (14.5-ounce) can no-salt-added diced tomatoes
- » 1 cup pearl barley
- » Zest of 1 lemon
- » 1 teaspoon kosher salt
- » ½ teaspoon smoked paprika
- » ¼ teaspoon red pepper flakes
- » ¼ teaspoon freshly ground black pepper
- » 4 thyme sprigs
- » 1 dried bay leaf
- » 2 cups baby spinach
- » ½ cup crumbled feta cheese
- » 1 tablespoon fresh oregano, chopped
- » 1 tablespoon fennel seeds, toasted (optional)

## DIRECTION

1. Heat the olive oil in a large saucepan over medium heat. Add the celery and shallots and sauté, about 4 to 5 minutes. Add the garlic and sauté 30 seconds. Add the vegetable stock, diced tomatoes, crushed tomatoes, barley, lemon zest, salt, paprika, red pepper flakes, black pepper, thyme, and the bay leaf, and mix well. Bring to a boil, then lower to low, and simmer. Cook, stirring occasionally, for 40 minutes.

2. Remove the bay leaf and thyme sprigs. Stir in the spinach.

3. In a small bowl, combine the feta, oregano, and fennel seeds. Serve the barley risotto in bowls topped with the feta mixture.

**NUTRITIONS:**

375 Calories, 12g fat, 11g Protein

# 387. CHICKPEAS AND KALE WITH SPICY POMODORO SAUCE

**COOKING: 35'** | **PREPARATION: 10'** | **SERVES: 4**

## INGREDIENTS

- » 2 tablespoons extra-virgin olive oil
- » 4 garlic cloves, sliced
- » 1 teaspoon red pepper flakes
- » 1 (28-ounce) can no-salt-added crushed tomatoes
- » 1 teaspoon kosher salt
- » ½ teaspoon honey
- » 1 bunch kale, stemmed and chopped
- » 2 (15-ounce) cans no-salt-added or low-sodium chickpeas
- » ¼ cup fresh basil, chopped
- » ¼ cup grated pecorino Romano cheese

## DIRECTION

1. Heat the olive oil in sauté pan over medium heat. Cook garlic and red pepper flakes for 2 minutes. Add the tomatoes, salt, and honey and mix well. Reduce the heat to low and simmer for 20 minutes.

2. Add the kale and mix in well. Cook about 5 minutes. Add the chickpeas and simmer about 5 minutes.

3. Remove from heat and stir in the basil. Serve topped with pecorino cheese.

**NUTRITIONS:**

420 Calories, 13g fat, 20g Protein

# 388. ROASTED FETA WITH KALE AND LEMON YOGURT

**COOKING: 20'**     **PREPARATION:15'**     **SERVES: 4**

## INGREDIENTS

» 1 tablespoon extra-virgin olive oil
» 1 onion, julienned
» ¼ teaspoon kosher salt
» 1 teaspoon ground turmeric
» ½ teaspoon ground cumin
» ½ teaspoon ground coriander
» ¼ teaspoon freshly ground black pepper
» 1 bunch kale, stemmed and chopped
» 7-ounce block feta cheese
» ½ cup plain Greek yogurt
» 1 tablespoon lemon juice

## DIRECTION

1. Preheat the oven to 400°F.
2. Cook olive oil in a huge ovenproof skillet or sauté pan over medium heat. Add the onion and salt; sauté until lightly golden brown, about 5 minutes. Add the turmeric, cumin, coriander, and black pepper; sauté for 30 seconds. Add the kale and sauté about 2 minutes. Add ½ cup water and continue to cook down the kale, about 3 minutes.
3. Remove from the heat and place the feta cheese slices on top of the kale mixture. Place in the oven and bake until the feta softens, 10 to 12 minutes.
4. In a small bowl, combine the yogurt and lemon juice.
5. Serve the kale and feta cheese topped with the lemon yogurt.

**NUTRITIONS:**
210 Calories, 14g fat, 11g Protein

# 389. ROASTED EGGPLANT AND CHICKPEAS WITH TOMATO SAUCE

**COOKING: 1 HOUR**     **PREPARATION:15'**     **SERVES: 4**

## INGREDIENTS

» Olive oil cooking spray
» 1 large (about 1 pound) eggplant
» 1 teaspoon kosher salt, divided
» 1 tablespoon extra-virgin olive oil
» 3 garlic cloves, minced
» 1 (28-ounce) can no-salt-added crushed tomatoes
» ½ teaspoon honey
» ¼ teaspoon freshly ground black pepper
» 2 tablespoons fresh basil, chopped
» 1 (15-ounce) can no-salt-added or low-sodium chickpeas, drained and rinsed
» ¾ cup crumbled feta cheese
» 1 tablespoon fresh oregano, chopped

## DIRECTION

1. Preheat the oven to 425°F. Prep two baking sheets with foil and lightly spray with olive oil cooking spray. Arrange the eggplant in a single layer and sprinkle with ½ teaspoon of the salt. Bake for 20 minutes, turning once halfway, until lightly golden brown.
2. Meanwhile, heat the olive oil in a large saucepan over medium heat. Cook garlic and sauté for 30 seconds. Add the crushed tomatoes, honey, the remaining ½ teaspoon salt, and black pepper. Simmer about 20 minutes, until the sauce reduces a bit and thickens. Stir in the basil.
3. After removing the eggplant from the oven, reduce the oven temperature to 375°F. In a large rectangular or oval baking dish, ladle in the chickpeas and 1 cup sauce. Layer the eggplant slices on top, overlapping as necessary to cover the chickpeas. Drizzle remaining sauce on top of the eggplant. Sprinkle the feta cheese and oregano on top.
4. Cover the baking dish with foil and bake for 15 minutes. Take out foil and bake an additional 15 minutes.

**NUTRITIONS:**
320 Calories, 11g fat, 14g Protein

# 390. BAKED FALAFEL SLIDERS

**COOKING: 30'**      **PREPARATION:10'**      **SERVES: 6**

## INGREDIENTS

» Olive oil cooking spray
» 1 (15-ounce) can low-sodium chickpeas
» 1 onion, roughly chopped
» 2 garlic cloves, peeled
» 2 tablespoons fresh parsley, chopped
» 2 tablespoons whole-wheat flour
» ½ teaspoon ground coriander
» ½ teaspoon ground cumin
» ½ teaspoon baking powder
» ½ teaspoon kosher salt
» ¼ teaspoon freshly ground black pepper

## DIRECTION

1. Preheat the oven to 350°F. Prep baking sheet with parchment paper or foil and lightly spray with olive oil cooking spray.

2. In a food processor, add the chickpeas, onion, garlic, parsley, flour, coriander, cumin, baking powder, salt, and black pepper. Process until smooth, stopping to scrape down the sides of the bowl.

3. Make 6 slider patties, each with a heaping ¼ cup of mixture, and arrange on the prepared baking sheet. Bake it for 30 minutes

## NUTRITIONS:
90 Calories, 1g fat, 4g Protein

# CHAPTER 28
# VEGETARIAN RECIPES PART 3

# 391. PORTOBELLO CAPRESE

**COOKING: 30'**     **PREPARATION:15'**     **SERVES: 2**

## INGREDIENTS

- » 1 tablespoon olive oil
- » 1 cup cherry tomatoes
- » 4 large fresh basil leaves, thinly sliced, divided
- » 3 medium garlic cloves, minced
- » 2 large portobello mushrooms, stems removed
- » 4 pieces mini Mozzarella balls
- » 1 tablespoon Parmesan cheese, grated

## DIRECTION

1. Prep oven to 350°F (180°C). Grease a baking pan with olive oil.
2. Drizzle 1 tablespoon olive oil in a nonstick skillet, and heat over medium-high heat.
3. Add the tomatoes to the skillet, and sprinkle salt and black pepper to season. Prick some holes on the tomatoes for juice during the cooking. Put the lid on and cook the tomatoes for 10 minutes or until tender.
4. Reserve 2 teaspoons of basil and add the remaining basil and garlic to the skillet. Crush the tomatoes with a spatula, then cook for half a minute. Stir constantly during the cooking. Set aside.
5. Arrange the mushrooms in the baking pan, cap side down, and sprinkle with salt and black pepper to taste.
6. Spoon the tomato mixture and Mozzarella balls on the gill of the mushrooms, then scatter with Parmesan cheese to coat well.
7. Bake for 20 minutes
8. Remove the stuffed mushrooms from the oven and serve with basil on top.

**NUTRITIONS:**
285 calories, 21.8g fat, 14.3g Protein

# 392. MUSHROOM AND CHEESE STUFFED TOMATOES

**COOKING: 20'**     **PREPARATION:15'**     **SERVES: 4**

## INGREDIENTS

- » 4 large ripe tomatoes
- » 1 tablespoon olive oil
- » ½ pound (454 g) white or cremini mushrooms
- » 1 tablespoon fresh basil, chopped
- » ½ cup yellow onion, diced
- » 1 tablespoon fresh oregano, chopped
- » 2 garlic cloves, minced
- » ½ teaspoon salt
- » ¼ teaspoon freshly ground black pepper
- » 1 cup part-skim Mozzarella cheese, shredded
- » 1 tablespoon Parmesan cheese, grated

## DIRECTION

1. Set oven to 375°F (190°C).
2. Chop a ½-inch slice off the top of each tomato. Scoop the pulp into a bowl and leave ½-inch tomato shells. Arrange the tomatoes on a baking sheet lined with aluminum foil.
3. Heat the olive oil in a nonstick skillet over medium heat.
4. Add the mushrooms, basil, onion, oregano, garlic, salt, and black pepper to the skillet and sauté for 5 minutes
5. Pour the mixture to the bowl of tomato pulp, then add the Mozzarella cheese and stir to combine well.
6. Spoon the mixture into each tomato shell, then top with a layer of Parmesan.
7. Bake for 15 minutes
8. Remove the stuffed tomatoes from the oven and serve warm.

**NUTRITIONS:**
254 calories, 14.7g fat, 17.5g Protein

# 393. TABBOULEH

| COOKING: 5' | PREPARATION:15' | SERVES: 6 |
|---|---|---|

## INGREDIENTS

» 4 tablespoons olive oil
» 4 cups riced cauliflower
» 3 garlic cloves
» ½ large cucumber
» ½ cup Italian parsley
» Juice of 1 lemon
» 2 tablespoons red onion
» ½ cup mint leaves, chopped
» ½ cup pitted Kalamata olives
» 1 cup cherry tomatoes
» 2 cups baby arugula
» 2 medium avocados

## DIRECTION

1. Warm 2 tablespoons olive oil in a nonstick skillet over medium-high heat.
2. Add the rice cauliflower, garlic, salt, and black pepper to the skillet and sauté for 3 minutes or until fragrant. Transfer them to a large bowl.
3. Add the cucumber, parsley, lemon juice, red onion, mint, olives, and remaining olive oil to the bowl. Toss to combine well. Reserve the bowl in the refrigerator for at least 30 minutes.
4. Remove the bowl from the refrigerator. Add the cherry tomatoes, arugula, avocado to the bowl. Sprinkle with salt and black pepper, and toss to combine well. Serve chilled.

## NUTRITIONS:
198 calories, 17.5g fat, 4.2g Protein

# 394. SPICY BROCCOLI RABE AND ARTICHOKE HEARTS

| COOKING: 15' | PREPARATION:5' | SERVES: 4 |
|---|---|---|

## INGREDIENTS

» 3 tablespoons olive oil, divided
» 2 pounds fresh broccoli rabe
» 3 garlic cloves, finely minced
» 1 teaspoon red pepper flakes
» 1 teaspoon salt, plus more to taste
» 13.5 ounces artichoke hearts
» 1 tablespoon water
» 2 tablespoons red wine vinegar

## DIRECTION

1. Warm 2 tablespoons olive oil in a nonstick skillet over medium-high skillet.
2. Add the broccoli, garlic, red pepper flakes, and salt to the skillet and sauté for 5 minutes or until the broccoli is soft.
3. Add the artichoke hearts to the skillet and sauté for 2 more minutes or until tender.
4. Add water to the skillet and turn down the heat to low. Put the lid on and simmer for 5 minutes.
5. Meanwhile, combine the vinegar and 1 tablespoon of olive oil in a bowl.
6. Drizzle the simmered broccoli and artichokes with oiled vinegar, and sprinkle with salt and black pepper. Toss to combine well before serving.

## NUTRITIONS:
272 calories, 21.5g fat, 11.2g Protein

# 395. SHAKSHUKA

**COOKING: 25'**          **PREPARATION:10'**          **SERVES: 4**

## INGREDIENTS

- » 5 tablespoons olive oil, divided
- » 1 red bell pepper, finely diced
- » ½ small yellow onion, finely diced
- » 14 ounces crushed tomatoes, with juices
- » 6 ounces frozen spinach
- » 1 teaspoon smoked paprika
- » 2 garlic cloves
- » 2 teaspoons red pepper flakes
- » 1 tablespoon capers
- » 1 tablespoon water
- » 6 large eggs
- » ¼ teaspoon freshly ground black pepper
- » ¾ cup feta or goat cheese
- » ¼ cup fresh flat-leaf parsley

## DIRECTION

1. Prep oven to 300°F (150°C).
2. Cook 2 tablespoons olive oil in an oven-safe skillet over medium-high heat.
3. Cook bell pepper and onion to the skillet for 6 minutes.
4. Add the tomatoes and juices, spinach, paprika, garlic, red pepper flakes, capers, water, and 2 tablespoons olive oil to the skillet. Stir and boil.
5. Turn down the heat to low, then put the lid on and simmer for 5 minutes.
6. Crack the eggs over the sauce, and keep a little space between each egg, leave the egg intact and sprinkle with freshly ground black pepper.
7. Cook for another 8 minutes
8. Scatter the cheese over the eggs and sauce, and bake in the preheated oven for 5 minutes
9. Drizzle 1 tablespoon olive oil and spread the parsley on top before serving warm.

**NUTRITIONS:**
335 calories, 26.5g fat, 16.8g Protein

# 396. SPANAKOPITA

**COOKING: 50'**          **PREPARATION:15'**          **SERVES: 6**

## INGREDIENTS

- » 6 tablespoons olive oil
- » 1 small yellow onion
- » 4 cups frozen chopped spinach
- » 4 garlic cloves, minced
- » ½ teaspoon salt
- » ½ teaspoon freshly ground black pepper
- » 4 large eggs, beaten
- » 1 cup ricotta cheese
- » ¾ cup feta cheese, crumbled
- » ¼ cup pine nuts

## DIRECTION

1. Set oven to 375°F (190°C). Coat a baking dish with 2 tablespoons olive oil.
2. Heat 2 tablespoons olive oil in a nonstick skillet over medium-high heat.
3. Add the onion to the skillet and sauté for 6 minutes or until translucent and tender.
4. Add the spinach, garlic, salt, and black pepper to the skillet and sauté for 5 minutes more. Keep aside
5. Combine the beaten eggs and ricotta cheese in a separate bowl, then pour them in to the bowl of spinach mixture. Stir to mix well.
6. Pour the mixture into the baking dish, and tilt the dish so the mixture coats the bottom evenly.
7. Bake for 20 minutes. Remove the baking dish from the oven, and spread the feta cheese and pine nuts on top, then drizzle with remaining 2 tablespoons olive oil.
8. Return the baking dish to the oven and bake for another 15 minutes
9. Remove the dish from the oven. Allow the spanakopita to cool for a few minutes and slice to serve.

**NUTRITIONS:**
340 calories, 27.3g fat, 18.2g Protein

# 397. TAGINE

**COOKING: 1 HOUR**  **PREPARATION: 20'**  **SERVES: 6**

## INGREDIENTS

- » ½ cup olive oil
- » 6 celery stalks
- » 2 medium yellow onions
- » 1 teaspoon ground cumin
- » ½ teaspoon ground cinnamon
- » 1 teaspoon ginger powder
- » 6 garlic cloves, minced
- » ½ teaspoon paprika
- » 1 teaspoon salt
- » ¼ teaspoon freshly ground black pepper
- » 2 cups low-sodium vegetable stock
- » 2 medium zucchinis
- » 2 cups cauliflower, cut into florets
- » 1 medium eggplant
- » 1 cup green olives
- » 13.5 ounces artichoke hearts
- » ½ cup chopped fresh cilantro leaves, for garnish
- » ½ cup plain Greek yogurt, for garnish
- » ½ cup chopped fresh flat-leaf parsley, for garnish

## DIRECTION

1. Cook olive oil in a stockpot over medium-high heat.
2. Add the celery and onion to the pot and sauté for 6 minutes or until the celery is tender and the onion is translucent.
3. Add the cumin, cinnamon, ginger, garlic, paprika, salt, and black pepper to the pot and sauté for 2 minutes more until aromatic.
4. Pour the vegetable stock to the pot and bring to a boil.
5. Turn down the heat to low, and add the zucchini, cauliflower, and eggplant to the pot. Put the lid on and simmer for 30 minutes or until the vegetables are soft.
6. Then add the olives and artichoke hearts to the pot and simmer for 15 minutes more.
7. Pour them into a large serving bowl or a Tagine, then serve with cilantro, Greek yogurt, and parsley on top.

## NUTRITIONS:
312 calories, 21.2g fat, 6.1g Protein

# 398. CITRUS PISTACHIOS AND ASPARAGUS

**COOKING: 10'**  **PREPARATION: 10'**  **SERVES: 4**

## INGREDIENTS

- » Zest and juice of 2 clementine
- » Zest and juice of 1 lemon
- » 1 tablespoon red wine vinegar
- » 3 tablespoons extra-virgin olive oil
- » 1 teaspoon salt
- » ¼ teaspoon black pepper
- » ½ cup pistachios, shelled
- » 1-pound fresh asparagus
- » 1 tablespoon water

## DIRECTION

1. Combine the zest and juice of clementine and lemon, vinegar, 2 tablespoons of olive oil, ½ teaspoon of salt, and black pepper in a bowl. Stir to mix well. Set aside.
2. Toast the pistachios in a nonstick skillet over medium-high heat for 2 minutes or until golden brown. Transfer the roasted pistachios to a clean work surface, then chop roughly. Mix the pistachios with the citrus mixture. Set aside.
3. Heat the remaining olive oil in the nonstick skillet over medium-high heat.
4. Add the asparagus to the skillet and sauté for 2 minutes, then season with remaining salt.
5. Add the water to the skillet. Turn down the heat to low, and put the lid on. Simmer for 4 minutes until the asparagus is tender.
6. Remove the asparagus from the skillet to a large dish. Pour the citrus and pistachios mixture over the asparagus. Toss to coat well before serving.

## NUTRITIONS:
211 calories, 17.5g fat, 5.9g Protein

# 399. TOMATO AND PARSLEY STUFFED EGGPLANT

**COOKING: 2 HOURS**    **PREPARATION:25'**    **SERVES: 6**

## INGREDIENTS

- » ¼ cup extra-virgin olive oil
- » 3 small eggplants, cut in half lengthwise
- » 1 teaspoon sea salt
- » ½ teaspoon freshly ground black pepper
- » 1 large yellow onion, finely chopped
- » 4 garlic cloves, minced
- » 15 ounces diced tomatoes
- » ¼ cup fresh flat-leaf parsley

## DIRECTION

1. Brush insert of the slow cooker with 2 tablespoons of olive oil.
2. Cut some slits on the cut side of each eggplant half, keep a ¼-inch space between each slit.
3. Place the eggplant halves in the slow cooker, skin side down. Sprinkle with salt and black pepper.
4. Cook remaining olive oil in a nonstick skillet over medium-high heat.
5. Add the onion and garlic to the skillet and sauté for 3 minutes or until the onion is translucent.
6. Add the parsley and tomatoes with the juice to the skillet, and sprinkle with salt and black pepper. Sauté for 5 more minutes or until they are tender.
7. Divide and spoon the mixture in the skillet on the eggplant halves.
8. Close and cook on HIGH for 2 hours.
9. Transfer the eggplant to a plate, and allow to cool for a few minutes before serving.

**NUTRITIONS:**
455 calories, 13g fat, 14g Protein

# 400. RATATOUILLE

**COOKING: 7 HOURS**    **PREPARATION:15'**    **SERVES: 6**

## INGREDIENTS

- » 3 tablespoons extra-virgin olive oil
- » 1 large eggplant
- » 2 large onions
- » 4 small zucchinis
- » 2 green bell peppers
- » 6 large tomatoes
- » 2 tablespoons fresh flat-leaf parsley
- » 1 teaspoon dried basil
- » 2 garlic cloves, minced
- » 2 teaspoons sea salt
- » ¼ teaspoon black pepper

## DIRECTION

1. Grease insert of the slow cooker with 2 tablespoons olive oil.
2. Arrange the vegetables slices, strips, and wedges alternately in the insert of the slow cooker.
3. Spread the parsley on top of the vegetables, and season with basil, garlic, salt, and black pepper. Drizzle with the remaining olive oil.
4. Cover on and cook on LOW for 7 hours until the vegetables are tender.
5. Transfer the vegetables on a plate and serve warm.

**NUTRITIONS:**
265 calories, 1.7g fat, 8.3g Protein

# 401. GEMISTA

**COOKING: 4 HOURS**   **PREPARATION:15'**   **SERVES: 4**

## INGREDIENTS

- » 2 tablespoons extra-virgin olive oil
- » 4 large bell peppers, any color
- » ½ cup uncooked couscous
- » 1 teaspoon oregano
- » 1 garlic clove, minced
- » 1 cup crumbled feta cheese
- » 1 (15-ounce) can cannellini beans
- » 4 green onions

## DIRECTION

1. Brush insert of the slow cooker with 2 tablespoons olive oil.
2. Cut a ½-inch slice below the stem from the top of the bell pepper. Discard the stem only and chop the sliced top portion under the stem, and reserve in a bowl. Hollow the bell pepper with a spoon.
3. Mix remaining ingredients, except for the green parts of the green onion and lemon wedges, to the bowl of chopped bell pepper top. Stir to mix well.
4. Spoon the mixture in the hollowed bell pepper, and arrange the stuffed bell peppers in the slow cooker, then drizzle with more olive oil.
5. Close and cook at HIGH for 4 hours or until the bell peppers are soft.
6. Remove the bell peppers from the slow cooker and serve on a plate. Sprinkle with green parts of the green onions, and squeeze the lemon wedges on top before serving.

**NUTRITIONS:**
246 calories, 9g fat, 11.1g Protein

# 402. STUFFED CABBAGE ROLLS

**COOKING: 2 HOURS**   **PREPARATION:15'**   **SERVES: 4**

## INGREDIENTS

- » 4 tablespoons olive oil
- » 1 large head green cabbage
- » 1 large yellow onion
- » 3 ounces (85 g) feta cheese
- » ½ cup dried currants
- » 3 cups cooked pearl barley
- » 2 tablespoons fresh flat-leaf parsley
- » 2 tablespoons pine nuts, toasted
- » ½ teaspoon sea salt
- » ½ teaspoon black pepper
- » 15 ounces (425 g) crushed tomatoes, with the juice
- » ½ cup apple juice
- » 1 tablespoon apple cider vinegar

## DIRECTION

1. Rub insert of the slow cooker with 2 tablespoons olive oil.
2. Blanch the cabbage in a pot of water for 8 minutes. Remove it from the water, and allow to cool, then separate 16 leaves from the cabbage. Set aside.
3. Drizzle the remaining olive oil in a nonstick skillet, and heat over medium heat.
4. sauté onion for 6 minutes. Transfer the onion to a bowl.
5. Add the feta cheese, currants, barley, parsley, and pine nuts to the bowl of cooked onion, then sprinkle with ¼ teaspoon of salt and ¼ teaspoon of black pepper.
6. Arrange the cabbage leaves on a clean work surface. Spoon 1/3 cup of the mixture on the center of each leaf, then fold the edge of the leaf over the mixture and roll it up. Place the cabbage rolls in the slow cooker, seam side down.
7. Combine the remaining ingredients in a separate bowl, then pour the mixture over the cabbage rolls.
8. Close and cook in HIGH for 2 hours.
9. Remove the cabbage rolls from the slow cooker and serve warm.

**NUTRITIONS:**
383 calories, 17g fat, 11g Protein

# 403. BRUSSELS SPROUTS WITH BALSAMIC GLAZE

**COOKING: 2 HOURS**     **PREPARATION:15'**     **SERVES: 6**

## INGREDIENTS

- » Balsamic glaze:
- » 1 cup balsamic vinegar
- » ¼ cup honey
- » Other:
- » 2 tablespoons extra-virgin olive oil
- » 2 pounds (907 g) Brussels sprouts
- » 2 cups low-sodium vegetable soup
- » 1 teaspoon sea salt
- » Freshly ground black pepper, to taste
- » ¼ cup Parmesan cheese, grated
- » ¼ cup pine nuts, toasted

## DIRECTION

1. Brush insert of the slow cooker with olive oil.
2. Make the balsamic glaze: Combine the balsamic vinegar and honey in a saucepan. Stir to mix well. Over medium-high heat, bring to a boil. Turn down the heat to low, then simmer for 20 minutes or until the glaze reduces in half and has a thick consistency.
3. Put the Brussels sprouts, vegetable soup, and ½ teaspoon of salt in the slow cooker, stir to combine.
4. Cover and cook at HIGH for 2 hours.
5. Transfer the Brussels sprouts to a plate, and sprinkle the remaining salt and black pepper to season. Drizzle the balsamic glaze over the Brussels sprouts, then serve with Parmesan and pine nuts.

**NUTRITIONS:**
270 calories, 11g fat, 8.7g Protein

# 404. SPINACH SALAD WITH CITRUS VINAIGRETTE

**COOKING: 0'**     **PREPARATION:10'**     **SERVINGS: 4**

## INGREDIENTS

- » Citrus Vinaigrette:
- » ¼ cup extra-virgin olive oil
- » 3 tablespoons balsamic vinegar
- » ½ teaspoon fresh lemon zest
- » ½ teaspoon salt
- » SALAD:
- » 1-pound (454 g) baby spinach
- » 1 large ripe tomato
- » 1 medium red onion

## DIRECTION

1. Make the citrus vinaigrette: Stir together the olive oil, balsamic vinegar, lemon zest, and salt in a bowl until mixed well.
2. Make the salad: Place the baby spinach, tomato and onions in a separate salad bowl. Drizzle the citrus vinaigrette over the salad and gently toss until the vegetables are coated thoroughly.

**NUTRITIONS:**
173 Calories, 14g fat, 4.1g Protein

# 405. KALE SALAD WITH PISTACHIO AND PARMESAN

**COOKING: 0'**          **PREPARATION:20'**          **SERVES: 6**

## INGREDIENTS

- » 6 cups raw kale
- » ¼ cup extra-virgin olive oil
- » 2 tablespoons lemon juice
- » ½ teaspoon smoked paprika
- » 2 cups chopped arugula
- » 1/3 cup unsalted pistachios
- » 6 tablespoons Parmesan cheese

## NUTRITIONS:

106 Calories, 9.2g fat, 4.2g Protein

## DIRECTION

1. Put the kale, olive oil, lemon juice, and paprika in a large bowl. Using your hands to massage the sauce into the kale until coated completely. Allow the kale to marinate for about 10 minutes.

2. When ready to serve, add the arugula and pistachios into the bowl of kale. Toss well and divide the salad into six salad bowls. Serve sprinkled with 1 tablespoon shredded Parmesan cheese.

# CHAPTER 29
# SALAD RECIPES

# 406. PEPPERS AND LENTILS SALAD

**COOKING: 0'**          **PREPARATION:10'**          **SERVINGS: 4**

## INGREDIENTS

- » 14 ounces canned lentils
- » 2 spring onions
- » 1 red bell pepper
- » 1 green bell pepper
- » 1 tablespoon fresh lime juice
- » 1/3 cup coriander
- » 2 teaspoon balsamic vinegar

## DIRECTION

1. In a salad bowl, combine the lentils with the onions, bell peppers, and the rest of the ingredients, toss and serve.

**NUTRITIONS:**
200 Calories, 2.45g Fat, 5.6g Protein

# 407. CASHEWS AND RED CABBAGE SALAD

**COOKING: 0'**          **PREPARATION:10'**          **SERVINGS: 4**

## INGREDIENTS

- » 1-pound red cabbage, shredded
- » 2 tablespoons coriander, chopped
- » ½ cup cashews halved
- » 2 tablespoons olive oil
- » 1 tomato, cubed
- » A pinch of salt and black pepper
- » 1 tablespoon white vinegar

## DIRECTION

1. Mix the cabbage with the coriander and the rest of the ingredients in a salad bowl, toss and serve cold.

**NUTRITIONS:**
210 Calories, 6.3g Fat, 8g Protein

# 408. APPLES AND POMEGRANATE SALAD

**COOKING: 0'**　　　　**PREPARATION:10'**　　　　**SERVINGS: 4**

## INGREDIENTS

- » 3 big apples, cored and cubed
- » 1 cup pomegranate seeds
- » 3 cups baby arugula
- » 1 cup walnuts, chopped
- » 1 tablespoon olive oil
- » 1 teaspoon white sesame seeds
- » 2 tablespoons apple cider vinegar

## DIRECTION

1. Mix the apples with the arugula and the rest of the ingredients in a bowl, toss and serve cold.

**NUTRITIONS:**
160 Calories, 4.3g Fat, 10g Protein

# 409. CRANBERRY BULGUR MIX

**COOKING: 0'**　　　　**PREPARATION:10'**　　　　**SERVINGS: 4**

## INGREDIENTS

- » 1 and ½ cups hot water
- » 1 cup bulgur
- » Juice of ½ lemon
- » 4 tablespoons cilantro, chopped
- » ½ cup cranberries
- » 1 and ½ teaspoons curry powder
- » ¼ cup green onions
- » ½ cup red bell peppers
- » ½ cup carrots, grated
- » 1 tablespoon olive oil

## DIRECTION

1. Put bulgur into a bowl, add the water, stir, cover, leave aside for 10 minutes, fluff with a fork, and transfer to a bowl. Add the rest of the ingredients, toss, and serve cold.

**NUTRITIONS:**
300 Calories, 6.4g Fat, 13g Protein

# 410. CHICKPEAS, CORN AND BLACK BEANS SALAD

**COOKING: 0'**      **PREPARATION:10'**      **SERVINGS: 4**

## INGREDIENTS

- » 1 and ½ cups canned black beans
- » ½ teaspoon garlic powder
- » 2 teaspoons chili powder
- » 1 and ½ cups canned chickpeas
- » 1 cup baby spinach
- » 1 avocado, pitted, peeled, and chopped
- » 1 cup corn kernels, chopped
- » 2 tablespoons lemon juice
- » 1 tablespoon olive oil
- » 1 tablespoon apple cider vinegar
- » 1 teaspoon chives, chopped

## DIRECTION

1. Mix the black beans with the garlic powder, chili powder, and the rest of the ingredients in a bowl, toss and serve cold.

**NUTRITIONS:**
300 Calories, 13.4g Fat, 13g Protein

# 411. OLIVES AND LENTILS SALAD

**COOKING: 0'**      **PREPARATION:10'**      **SERVINGS: 2**

## INGREDIENTS

- » 1/3 cup canned green lentils
- » 1 tablespoon olive oil
- » 2 cups baby spinach
- » 1 cup black olives
- » 2 tablespoons sunflower seeds
- » 1 tablespoon Dijon mustard
- » 2 tablespoons balsamic vinegar
- » 2 tablespoons olive oil

## DIRECTION

1. Mix the lentils with the spinach, olives, and the rest of the ingredients in a salad bowl, toss and serve cold.

**NUTRITIONS:**
279 Calories, 6.5g Fat, 12g Protein

# 412. LIME SPINACH AND CHICKPEAS SALAD

**COOKING: 0'**     **PREPARATION:10'**     **SERVINGS: 4**

## INGREDIENTS

- » 16 ounces canned chickpeas
- » 2 cups baby spinach leaves
- » ½ tablespoon lime juice
- » 2 tablespoons olive oil
- » 1 teaspoon cumin, ground
- » ½ teaspoon chili flakes

## DIRECTION

1. Mix the chickpeas with the spinach and the rest of the ingredients in a large bowl, toss and serve cold.

**NUTRITIONS:**
240 calories, 8.2g fat, 12g Protein

# 413. MINTY OLIVES AND TOMATOES SALAD

**COOKING: 0'**     **PREPARATION:10'**     **SERVINGS: 4**

## INGREDIENTS

- » 1 cup kalamata olives
- » 1 cup black olives
- » 1 cup cherry tomatoes
- » 4 tomatoes
- » 1 red onion, chopped
- » 2 tablespoons oregano, chopped
- » 1 tablespoon mint, chopped
- » 2 tablespoons balsamic vinegar
- » ¼ cup olive oil
- » 2 teaspoons Italian herbs, dried

## DIRECTION

1. In a salad bowl, mix the olives with the tomatoes and the rest of the ingredients, toss, and serve cold.

**NUTRITIONS:**
190 Calories, 8.1g Fat, 4.6g Protein

# 414. BEANS AND CUCUMBER SALAD

**COOKING: 0'**  **PREPARATION:10'**  **SERVINGS: 4**

## INGREDIENTS

- » 15 oz canned great northern beans
- » 2 tablespoons olive oil
- » ½ cup baby arugula
- » 1 cup cucumber
- » 1 tablespoon parsley
- » 2 tomatoes, cubed
- » 2 tablespoon balsamic vinegar

## DIRECTION

1. Mix the beans with the cucumber and the rest of the ingredients in a large bowl, toss and serve cold.

**NUTRITIONS:**

233 calories, 9g fat, 8g Protein

# 415. TOMATO AND AVOCADO SALAD

**COOKING: 0'**  **PREPARATION:10'**  **SERVINGS: 4**

## INGREDIENTS

- » 1-pound cherry tomatoes
- » 2 avocados
- » 1 sweet onion, chopped
- » 2 tablespoons lemon juice
- » 1 and ½ tablespoons olive oil
- » Handful basil, chopped

## DIRECTION

1. Mix the tomatoes with the avocados and the rest of the ingredients in a serving bowl, toss and serve right away.

**NUTRITIONS:**

148 Calories, 7.8g Fat, 5.5g Protein

# 416. ARUGULA SALAD

**COOKING: 0'**　　　**PREPARATION: 5'**　　　**SERVINGS: 4**

## INGREDIENTS

- » Arugula leaves (4 cups)
- » Cherry tomatoes (1 cup)
- » Pine nuts (.25 cup)
- » Rice vinegar (1 tbsp.)
- » Olive/grapeseed oil (2 tbsp.)
- » Grated parmesan cheese (.25 cup)
- » Black pepper & salt (as desired)
- » Large sliced avocado (1)

## DIRECTION

1. Peel and slice the avocado. Rinse and dry the arugula leaves, grate the cheese, and slice the cherry tomatoes into halves.
2. Combine the arugula, pine nuts, tomatoes, oil, vinegar, salt, pepper, and cheese.
3. Toss the salad to mix and portion it onto plates with the avocado slices to serve.

**NUTRITIONS:**
257 Calories, 23g Fats, 6.1g Protein

# 417. CHICKPEA SALAD

**COOKING: 0'**　　　**PREPARATION: 15'**　　　**SERVINGS: 4**

## INGREDIENTS

- » Cooked chickpeas (15 oz.)
- » Diced Roma tomato (1)
- » Diced green medium bell pepper (half of 1)
- » Fresh parsley (1 tbsp.)
- » Small white onion (1)
- » Minced garlic (.5 tsp.)
- » Lemon (1 juiced)

## DIRECTION

1. Chop the tomato, green pepper, and onion. Mince the garlic. Combine each of the fixings into a salad bowl and toss well.
2. Cover the salad to chill for at least 15 minutes in the fridge. Serve when ready.

**NUTRITIONS:**
163 Calories, 7g Fats, 4g Protein

# 418. CHOPPED ISRAELI MEDITERRANEAN PASTA SALAD

**COOKING: 2'**  **PREPARATION:15'**  **SERVINGS: 8**

## INGREDIENTS

» Small bow tie or other small pasta (.5 lb.)
» 1/3 cup Cucumber
» 1/3 cup Radish
» 1/3 cup Tomato
» 1/3 cup Yellow bell pepper
» 1/3 cup Orange bell pepper
» 1/3 cup Black olives
» 1/3 cup Green olives
» 1/3 cup Red onions
» 1/3 cup Pepperoncini
» 1/3 cup Feta cheese
» 1/3 cup Fresh thyme leaves
» Dried oregano (1 tsp.)
» Dressing:
» 0.25 cup + more, olive oil
» juice of 1 lemon

## NUTRITIONS:

65 Calories, 5.6g Fats, 0.8g Protein

## DIRECTION

1. Slice the green olives into halves. Dice the feta and pepperoncini. Finely dice the remainder of the veggies.

2. Prepare a pot of water with the salt, and simmer the pasta until it's al dente (checking at two minutes under the listed time). Rinse and drain in cold water.

3. Combine a small amount of oil with the pasta. Add the salt, pepper, oregano, thyme, and veggies. Pour in the rest of the oil, lemon juice, mix and fold in the grated feta.

4. Pop it into the fridge within two hours, best if overnight. Taste test and adjust the seasonings to your liking; add fresh thyme.

# 419. FETA TOMATO SALAD

**COOKING: 0'**  **PREPARATION:5'**  **SERVINGS: 4**

## INGREDIENTS

» Balsamic vinegar (2 tbsp.)
» Freshly minced basil (1.5 tsp.) or Dried (.5 tsp.)
» Salt (.5 tsp.)
» Coarsely chopped sweet onion (.5 cup)
» Olive oil (2 tbsp.)
» Cherry or grape tomatoes (1 lb.)
» Crumbled feta cheese (.25 cup.)

## DIRECTION

1. Whisk the salt, basil, and vinegar. Toss the onion into the vinegar mixture for 5 minutes

2. Slice the tomatoes into halves and stir in the tomatoes, feta cheese, and oil to serve.

## NUTRITIONS:

121 Calories, 9g Fats, 3g Protein

# 420. GREEK PASTA SALAD

**COOKING: 11'**         **PREPARATION:5'**         **SERVINGS: 4**

## INGREDIENTS

- » Penne pasta (1 cup)
- » Lemon juice (1.5 tsp.)
- » Red wine vinegar (2 tbsp.)
- » Garlic (1 clove)
- » Dried oregano (1 tsp.)
- » Black pepper and sea salt (as desired)
- » Olive oil (.33 cup)
- » Halved cherry tomatoes (5)
- » Red onion (half of 1 small)
- » Green & red bell pepper (half of 1 - each)
- » Cucumber (¼ of 1)
- » Black olives (.25 cup)
- » Crumbled feta cheese (.25 cup)

## DIRECTION

1. Slice the cucumber and olives. Chop/dice the onion, peppers, and garlic. Slice the tomatoes into halves.

2. Arrange a large pot with water and salt using the high-temperature setting. Once it's boiling, add the pasta and cook for 11 minutes Rinse it using cold water and drain in a colander.

3. Whisk the oil, juice, salt, pepper, vinegar, oregano, and garlic. Combine the cucumber, cheese, olives, peppers, pasta, onions, and tomatoes in a large salad dish.

4. Add the vinaigrette over the pasta and toss. Chill in the fridge (covered) for about three hours and serve as desired.

## NUTRITIONS:

307 Calories, 23.6g Fat, 5.4g Protein

# CHAPTER 30
# SALAD RECIPES PART 2

# 421. PORK AND GREENS SALAD

**COOKING: 15'**     **PREPARATION:10'**     **SERVINGS: 4**

## INGREDIENTS

» 1-pound pork chops
» 8 ounces white mushrooms, sliced
» ½ cup Italian dressing
» 6 cups mixed salad greens
» 6 ounces jarred artichoke hearts, drained
» Salt and black pepper to the taste
» ½ cup basil, chopped
» 1 tablespoon olive oil

## DIRECTION

1. Heat a pan with the oil over medium-high heat, add the pork and brown for 5 minutes.

2. Add the mushrooms, stir and sauté for 5 minutes more.

3. Add the dressing, artichokes, salad greens, salt, pepper and the basil, cook for 4-5 minutes, divide everything into bowls and serve.

**NUTRITIONS:**
235 Calories, 6g Fat, 11g Protein

# 422. MEDITERRANEAN DUCK BREAST SALAD

**COOKING: 20'**     **PREPARATION:10'**     **SERVINGS: 4**

## INGREDIENTS

» 3 tablespoons white wine vinegar
» 2 tablespoons sugar
» 2 oranges, peeled and cut into segments
» 1 teaspoon orange zest, grated
» 1 tablespoons lemon juice
» 1 teaspoon lemon zest, grated
» 3 tablespoons shallot, minced
» 2 duck breasts
» 1 head of frisée, torn
» 2 small lettuce heads
» 2 tablespoons chives

## DIRECTION

1. Heat a small saucepan over medium high heat, add vinegar and sugar, stir and boil for 5 minutes and take off heat.

2. Add orange zest, lemon zest and lemon juice, stir and leave aside for a few minutes. Add shallot, salt and pepper to taste and the oil, whisk well and leave aside for now.

3. Pat dry duck pieces, score skin, trim and season with salt and pepper. Heat a pan over medium high heat for 1 minute, arrange duck breast pieces skin side down, brown for 8 minutes, reduce heat to medium and cook for 4 more minutes.

4. Flip pieces, cook for 3 minutes, transfer to a cutting board and cover them with foil. Put frisée and lettuce in a bowl, stir and divide between plates.

5. Slice duck, arrange on top, add orange segments, sprinkle chives and drizzle the vinaigrette.

**NUTRITIONS:**
320 Calories, 4g Fat, 14g Protein

# 423. MEDITERRANEAN CHICKEN BITES

**COOKING: 10'**      **PREPARATION:10'**      **SERVINGS: 4**

## INGREDIENTS

» 20 ounces canned pineapple slices
» A drizzle of olive oil
» 3 cups chicken thighs
» A tablespoon of smoked paprika

## DIRECTION

1. Situate pan over medium high heat, add pineapple slices, cook them for a few minutes on each side, transfer to a cutting board, cool them down and cut into medium cubes.

2. Heat another pan with a drizzle of oil over medium high heat, rub chicken pieces with paprika, add them to the pan and cook for 5 minutes on each side.

3. Arrange chicken cubes on a platter, add a pineapple piece on top of each and stick a toothpick in each, and serve.

**NUTRITIONS:**
120 Calories, 3g Fat, 2g Protein

# 424. MEDITERRANEAN CHICKEN AND TOMATO DISH

**COOKING: 20'**      **PREPARATION:10'**      **SERVINGS: 4**

## INGREDIENTS

» Chicken thighs
» 1 Tablespoon thyme, chopped
» Garlic cloves, minced
» 1 Teaspoon red pepper flakes, crushed
» ½ cup heavy cream
» ¾ cup chicken stock
» ½ cup sun dried tomatoes in olive oil
» ¼ cup parmesan cheese, grated
» Basil leaves, chopped for serving

## DIRECTION

1. Preheat pan with the oil over medium high heat, add chicken, salt and pepper to taste, cook for 3 minutes on each side, transfer to a plate and leave aside for now.

2. Return pan to heat, add thyme, garlic and pepper flakes, stir and cook for 1 minute.

3. Add stock, tomatoes, salt and pepper, heavy cream and parmesan, stir and bring to a simmer.

4. Add chicken pieces, stir, place in the oven at 350 degrees F and bake for 15 minutes.

5. Take pan out of the oven, leave chicken aside for 2-3 minutes, divide between plates and serve with basil sprinkled on top.

**NUTRITIONS:**
212 Calories, 4g Fat, 3g Protein

# 425. CREAMY CHICKEN SALAD

**COOKING: 0'**     **PREPARATION:10'**     **SERVINGS: 6**

## INGREDIENTS

» 20 ounces chicken meat
» ½ cup pecans, chopped
» 1 cup green grapes
» ½ cup celery, chopped
» 2 ounces canned mandarin oranges, drained
» For the creamy cucumber salad dressing:
» 1 cup Greek yogurt cucumber, chopped garlic clove
» 1 teaspoon lemon juice

## DIRECTION

1. In a bowl, mix cucumber with salt, pepper to taste, lemon juice, garlic and yogurt and stir very well.
2. In a salad bowl, mix chicken meat with grapes, pecans, oranges and celery.
3. Add cucumber salad dressing, toss to coat and keep in the fridge until you serve it.

**NUTRITIONS:**
200 Calories, 3g Fat, 8g Protein

# 426. CHICKEN AND CABBAGE MIX

**COOKING: 6'**     **PREPARATION:10'**     **SERVINGS: 4**

## INGREDIENTS

» 3 medium chicken breasts
» 4 ounces green cabbage
» 5 tablespoon extra-virgin olive oil
» Salt and black pepper to taste
» 2 tablespoons sherry vinegar tablespoon chives
» ¼ cup feta cheese, crumbled
» ¼ cup barbeque sauce
» Bacon slices, cooked and crumbled

## DIRECTION

1. In a bowl, mix 4 tablespoon oil with vinegar, salt and pepper to taste and stir well.
2. Add the shredded cabbage, toss to coat and leave aside for now.
3. Season chicken with salt and pepper, heat a pan with remaining oil over medium high heat, add chicken, cook for 6 minutes, take off heat, transfer to a bowl and mix well with barbeque sauce.
4. Arrange salad on serving plates, add chicken strips, sprinkle cheese, chives and crumbled bacon and serve right away.

**NUTRITIONS:**
200 Calories, 15g Fat, 33g Protein

# 427. CHICKEN AND QUINOA SALAD

**COOKING: 20'**          **PREPARATION:10'**          **SERVINGS: 2**

## INGREDIENTS

- » 2 tablespoons olive oil
- » 2 ounces quinoa
- » 2 ounces cherry tomatoes, cut in quarters
- » 3 ounces sweet corn
- » Lime juice from 1 lime
- » Lime zest from 1 lime, grated
- » 2 spring onions, chopped
- » Small red chili pepper, chopped
- » Avocado
- » 2 ounces chicken meat

## DIRECTION

1. Fill water in a pan, bring to a boil over medium high heat, add quinoa, stir and cook for 12 minutes.
2. Meanwhile, put corn in a pan, heat over medium high heat, cook for 5 minutes and leave aside for now.
3. Drain quinoa, transfer to a bowl, add tomatoes, corn, coriander, onions, chili, lime zest, olive oil, salt and black pepper to taste and toss.
4. In another bowl, mix avocado with lime juice and stir well.
5. Add this to quinoa salad, and chicken, toss to coat and serve.

## NUTRITIONS:
320 Calories, 4g Fat, 7g Protein

# 428. SIMPLE PORK STIR FRY

**COOKING: 15'**          **PREPARATION:10'**          **SERVINGS: 4**

## INGREDIENTS

- » 4 ounces bacon, chopped
- » 4 ounces snow peas
- » 2 tablespoons butter
- » 1-pound pork loin, cut into thin strips
- » 2 cups mushrooms, sliced
- » ¾ cup white wine
- » ½ cup yellow onion, chopped
- » 3 tablespoons sour cream

## DIRECTION

1. Put snow peas in a saucepan, add water to cover, add a pinch of salt, bring to a boil over medium heat, cook until they are soft, drain and leave aside.
2. Preheat pan over medium high heat, add bacon, cook for a few minutes, drain grease, transfer to a bowl and also leave aside.
3. Heat a pan with 1 tablespoon butter over medium heat, add pork strips, salt and pepper to taste, brown for a few minutes and transfer to a plate as well.
4. Return pan to medium heat, add remaining butter and melt it. Add onions and mushrooms, stir and cook for 4 minutes.
5. Add wine, and simmer until it's reduced. Add cream, peas, pork, salt and pepper to taste, stir, heat up, divide between plates, top with bacon and serve.

## NUTRITIONS:
310 Calories, 4g Fat, 10g Protein

# 429. BEEF TARTAR

**COOKING: 0'**　　**PREPARATION:10'**　　**SERVINGS: 1**

## INGREDIENTS

- » 1 shallot, chopped
- » 4 ounces beef fillet
- » 5 small cucumbers
- » 1 egg yolk
- » 2 teaspoons mustard
- » 1 tablespoon parsley
- » 1 parsley spring

## DIRECTION

1. Incorporate meat with shallot, egg yolk, salt, pepper, mustard, cucumbers and parsley.
2. Stir well and arrange on a platter.
3. Garnish with the chopped parsley spring and serve.

**NUTRITIONS:**

210 Calories, 3g Fat, 8g Protein

# 430. MELON SALAD

**COOKING: 0'**　　**PREPARATION:20'**　　**SERVINGS: 6**

## INGREDIENTS

- » ¼ teaspoon sea salt
- » ¼ teaspoon black pepper
- » 1 tablespoon balsamic vinegar
- » 1 cantaloupe
- » 12 watermelons
- » 2 cups mozzarella balls, fresh
- » 1/3 cup basil, fresh & torn
- » 2 tablespoons olive oil

## DIRECTION

1. Spoon out balls of cantaloupe, then situate them in a colander over bowl.
2. Using melon baller to cut the watermelon as well
3. Drain fruits for ten minutes, then chill the juice.
4. Wipe the bowl dry, and then place your fruit in it.
5. Mix in basil, oil, vinegar, mozzarella and tomatoes before seasoning.
6. Gently mix and serve.

**NUTRITIONS:**

218 Calories, 10g Protein, 13g Fat

# 431. CELERY CITRUS SALAD

**COOKING: 0'**  **PREPARATION: 15'**  **SERVINGS: 6**

## INGREDIENTS

- » 1 tablespoon lemon juice, fresh
- » ¼ teaspoon sea salt, fine
- » ¼ teaspoon black pepper
- » 1 tablespoon olive brine
- » 1 tablespoon olive oil
- » ¼ cup red onion, sliced
- » ½ cup green olives
- » 2 oranges, peeled & sliced
- » 3 celery stalks

## DIRECTION

1. Put your oranges, olives, onion and celery in a shallow bowl.
2. Blend oil, olive brine and lemon juice, pour this over your salad.
3. Season with salt and pepper before serving.

**NUTRITIONS:**
65 Calories, 2g Protein, 0.1g Fat

# 432. BROCCOLI CRUNCH SALAD

**COOKING: 20'**  **PREPARATION: 10'**  **SERVINGS: 4**

## INGREDIENTS

- » 1 lb. Broccoli
- » 3 tablespoons olive oil, divided
- » 1-pint cherry tomatoes
- » 1 ½ teaspoons honey, raw & divided
- » 3 cups cubed bread, whole grain
- » 1 tablespoon balsamic vinegar
- » ½ teaspoon black pepper
- » ¼ teaspoon sea salt, fine

## DIRECTION

1. Set oven to 450, and preheat rimmed baking sheet.
2. Drizzle your broccoli with a tablespoon of oil, and toss to coat.
3. Pull out baking sheet from the oven, and scoop the broccoli on it. Leave oil in it, add in your tomatoes, then toss tomatoes with a tablespoon of honey. Put on the same baking sheet.
4. Roast for fifteen minutes, and stir halfway through your cooking time.
5. Add in your bread, and then roast for three more minutes.
6. Whisk two tablespoons of oil, vinegar, and remaining honey. Season. Drizzle over broccoli mix to serve.

**NUTRITIONS:**
226 Calories, 7g Protein, 12g Fat

# 433. SUMMER TOMATO SALAD

**COOKING: 0'**       **PREPARATION:20'**       **SERVINGS: 4**

## INGREDIENTS

- » 1 cucumber, sliced
- » ¼ cup sun dried tomatoes
- » 1 lb. Tomatoes, cubed
- » ½ cup black olives
- » 1 red onion, sliced
- » 1 tablespoon balsamic vinegar
- » ¼ cup parsley, fresh & chopped
- » 2 tablespoons olive oil

## DIRECTION

1. Mix all of your vegetables together. For dressing, mix all your seasoning, olive oil and vinegar. Toss with your salad and serve fresh.

**NUTRITIONS:**
126 Calories, 2.1g Protein, 9.2g Fat

# 434. CHEESE BEET SALAD

**COOKING: 0'**       **PREPARATION:15'**       **SERVINGS: 4**

## INGREDIENTS

- » 6 red beets
- » 3 ounces feta cheese
- » 2 tablespoons olive oil
- » 2 tablespoons balsamic vinegar

## DIRECTION

1. Combine everything together, and then serve.

**NUTRITIONS:**
230 Calories, 7.3g Protein, 12g Fat

# 435. CAULIFLOWER AND CHERRY TOMATO SALAD

**COOKING: 0'**     **PREPARATION:15'**     **SERVINGS: 4**

## INGREDIENTS

- » 1 head cauliflower
- » 2 tablespoons parsley
- » 2 cups cherry tomatoes, halved
- » 2 tablespoons lemon juice, fresh
- » 2 tablespoons pine nuts

**NUTRITIONS:**

64 Calories, 2.8g Protein, 3.3g Fat

## DIRECTION

1. Blend lemon juice, cherry tomatoes, cauliflower and parsley then season. Garnish with pine nuts, and mix well before serving.

# CHAPTER 31
## SALAD RECIPES PART 3

# 436. WATERMELON SALAD

**COOKING: 0'**    **PREPARATION:18'**    **SERVES: 6**

## INGREDIENTS

- » ¼ teaspoon sea salt
- » ¼ teaspoon black pepper
- » 1 tablespoon balsamic vinegar
- » 1 cantaloupe, quartered & seeded
- » 12 watermelon, small & seedless
- » 2 cups mozzarella balls, fresh
- » 1/3 cup basil, fresh & torn
- » 2 tablespoons olive oil

## DIRECTION

1. Scoop out balls of cantaloupe, and the put them in a colander over bowl.
2. With a melon baller slice the watermelon.
3. Allow your fruit to drain for ten minutes, and then refrigerate the juice.
4. Wipe the bowl dry, and then place your fruit in it.
5. Stir in basil, oil, vinegar, mozzarella and tomatoes before seasoning.
6. Mix well and serve.

**NUTRITIONS:**
218 Calories, 10g Protein, 13g Fat

# 437. ORANGE CELERY SALAD

**COOKING: 0'**    **PREPARATION:16'**    **SERVES: 6**

## INGREDIENTS

- » 1 tablespoon lemon juice, fresh
- » ¼ teaspoon sea salt, fine
- » ¼ teaspoon black pepper
- » 1 tablespoon olive brine
- » 1 tablespoon olive oil
- » ¼ cup red onion, sliced
- » ½ cup green olives
- » 2 oranges, peeled & sliced
- » 3 celery stalks, sliced diagonally in ½ inch slices

## DIRECTION

1. Put your oranges, olives, onion and celery in a shallow bowl.
2. Stir oil, olive brine and lemon juice, pour this over your salad.
3. Season with salt and pepper before serving.

**NUTRITIONS:**
65 Calories, 2g Protein, 0.2g Fat

# 438. ROASTED BROCCOLI SALAD

**COOKING: 17'**  **PREPARATION:9'**  **SERVES: 4**

## INGREDIENTS

- » 1 lb. broccoli
- » 3 tablespoons olive oil, divided
- » 1-pint cherry tomatoes
- » 1 ½ teaspoons honey
- » 3 cups cubed bread, whole grain
- » 1 tablespoon balsamic vinegar
- » ½ teaspoon black pepper
- » ¼ teaspoon sea salt, fine
- » grated parmesan for serving

## DIRECTION

1. Set oven to 450, and then place rimmed baking sheet.
2. Drizzle your broccoli with a tablespoon of oil, and toss to coat.
3. Take out from oven, and spoon the broccoli. Leave oil at bottom of the bowl and add in your tomatoes, toss to coat, then mix tomatoes with a tablespoon of honey. place on the same baking sheet.
4. Roast for fifteen minutes, and stir halfway through your cooking time.
5. Add in your bread, and then roast for three more minutes.
6. Whisk two tablespoons of oil, vinegar, and remaining honey. Season. Pour this over your broccoli mix to serve.

**NUTRITIONS:**
226 Calories, 7g Protein, 12g Fat

# 439. TOMATO SALAD

**COOKING: 0'**  **PREPARATION:22'**  **SERVES: 4**

## INGREDIENTS

- » 1 cucumber, sliced
- » ¼ cup sun dried tomatoes, chopped
- » 1 lb. tomatoes, cubed
- » ½ cup black olives
- » 1 red onion, sliced
- » 1 tablespoon balsamic vinegar
- » ¼ cup parsley, fresh & chopped
- » 2 tablespoons olive oil

## DIRECTION

1. Get out a bowl and combine all of your vegetables together. To make your dressing mix all your seasoning, olive oil and vinegar.
2. Toss with your salad and serve fresh.

**NUTRITIONS:**
126 Calories, 2.1g Protein, 9.2g Fat

# 440. FETA BEET SALAD

**COOKING: 0'**  **PREPARATION:16'**  **SERVES: 4**

## INGREDIENTS

- » 6 Red Beets, Cooked & Peeled
- » 3 Ounces Feta Cheese, Cubed
- » 2 Tablespoons Olive Oil
- » 2 Tablespoons Balsamic Vinegar

## DIRECTION

1. Combine everything together, and then serve.

**NUTRITIONS:**

230 Calories, 7.3g Protein, 12g Fat

# 441. CAULIFLOWER & TOMATO SALAD

**COOKING: 0'**  **PREPARATION:17'**  **SERVES: 4**

## INGREDIENTS

- » 1 Head Cauliflower, Chopped
- » 2 Tablespoons Parsley, Fresh & chopped
- » 2 Cups Cherry Tomatoes, Halved
- » 2 Tablespoons Lemon Juice, Fresh
- » 2 Tablespoons Pine Nuts

## DIRECTION

1. Incorporate lemon juice, cherry tomatoes, cauliflower and parsley and season well. Sprinkle the pine nuts, and mix.

**NUTRITIONS:**

64 Calories, 2.8g Protein, 3.3g Fat

# 442. TAHINI SPINACH

**COOKING: 6'**     **PREPARATION:11'**     **SERVES: 3**

## INGREDIENTS

- » 10 spinach, chopped
- » ½ cup water
- » 1 tablespoon tahini
- » 2 cloves garlic, minced
- » ¼ teaspoon cumin
- » ¼ teaspoon paprika
- » ¼ teaspoon cayenne pepper
- » 1/3 cup red wine vinegar

## DIRECTION

1. Add your spinach and water to the saucepan, and then boil it on high heat. Once boiling reduce to low, and cover. Allow it to cook on simmer for five minutes.

2. Add in your garlic, cumin, cayenne, red wine vinegar, paprika and tahini. Whisk well, and season with salt and pepper.

3. Drain your spinach and top with tahini sauce to serve.

**NUTRITIONS:**

69 Calories, 5g Protein, 3g Fat

# 443. PILAF WITH CREAM CHEESE

**COOKING: 34'**     **PREPARATION:11'**     **SERVES: 6**

## INGREDIENTS

- » 2 cups yellow long grain rice, parboiled
- » 1 cup onion
- » 4 green onions
- » 3 tablespoons butter
- » 3 tablespoons vegetable broth
- » 2 teaspoons cayenne pepper
- » 1 teaspoon paprika
- » ½ teaspoon cloves, minced
- » 2 tablespoons mint leaves
- » 1 bunch fresh mint leaves to garnish
- » 1 tablespoons olive oil
- » Cheese Cream:
- » 3 tablespoons olive oil
- » sea salt & black pepper to taste
- » 9 ounces cream cheese

## DIRECTION

1. Start by heating your oven to 360, and then get out a pan. Heat your butter and olive oil together, and cook your onions and spring onions for two minutes.

2. Add in your salt, pepper, paprika, cloves, vegetable broth, rice and remaining seasoning. S

3. Sauté for three minutes.

4. Wrap with foil, and bake for another half hour. Allow it to cool.

5. Mix in the cream cheese, cheese, olive oil, salt and pepper. Serve your pilaf garnished with fresh mint leaves.

**NUTRITIONS:**

364 Calories, 5g Protein, 30g Fat

# 444. EASY SPAGHETTI SQUASH

**COOKING: 45'**  **PREPARATION:13'**  **SERVES: 6**

## INGREDIENTS

» 2 spring onions, chopped fine
» 3 cloves garlic, minced
» 1 zucchini, diced
» 1 red bell pepper, diced
» 1 tablespoon Italian seasoning
» 1 tomato, small & chopped fine
» 1 tablespoons parsley, fresh & chopped
» pinch lemon pepper
» dash sea salt, fine
» 4 ounces feta cheese, crumbled
» 3 Italian sausage links, casing removed
» 2 tablespoons olive oil
» 1 spaghetti sauce, halved lengthwise

## DIRECTION

1. Prep oven to 350, and get out a large baking sheet. Coat it with cooking spray, and then put your squash on it with the cut side down.
2. Bake at 350 for forty-five minutes. It should be tender.
3. Turn the squash over, and bake for five more minutes. Scrape the strands into a larger bowl.
4. Cook tablespoon of olive oil in a skillet, and then add in your Italian sausage. Cook at eight minutes before removing it and placing it in a bowl.
5. Add another tablespoon of olive oil to the skillet and cook your garlic and onions until softened. This will take five minutes. Throw in your Italian seasoning, red peppers and zucchini. Cook for another five minutes. Your vegetables should be softened.
6. Mix in your feta cheese and squash, cooking until the cheese has melted.
7. Stir in your sausage, and then season with lemon pepper and salt. Serve with parsley and tomato.

**NUTRITIONS:**
423 Calories, 18g Protein, 30g Fat

# 445. ROASTED EGGPLANT SALAD

**COOKING: 36'**  **PREPARATION:14'**  **SERVES: 6**

## INGREDIENTS

» 1 red onion, sliced
» 2 tablespoons parsley
» 1 teaspoon thyme
» 2 cups cherry tomatoes
» 1 teaspoon oregano
» 3 tablespoons olive oil
» 1 teaspoon basil
» 3 eggplants, peeled & cubed

## DIRECTION

1. Start by heating your oven to 350.
2. Season your eggplant with basil, salt, pepper, oregano, thyme and olive oil.
3. Arrange it on a baking tray, and bake for a half hour.
4. Toss with your remaining ingredients before serving.

**NUTRITIONS:**
148 Calories, 3.5g Protein, 7.7g Fat

# 446. PENNE WITH TAHINI SAUCE

**COOKING: 22'**  **PREPARATION:16'**  **SERVES: 8**

## INGREDIENTS

- » 1/3 cup water
- » 1 cup yogurt, plain
- » 1/8 cup lemon juice
- » 3 tablespoons tahini
- » 3 cloves garlic
- » 1 onion, chopped
- » ¼ cup olive oil
- » 2 portobello mushrooms, large & sliced
- » ½ red bell pepper, diced
- » 16 ounces penne pasta
- » ½ cup parsley, fresh & chopped

## DIRECTION

1. Start by getting out a pot and bring a pot of salted water to a boil. Cook your pasta al dente per package instructions.
2. Mix your lemon juice and tahini together, and then place it in a food processor. Process with garlic, water and yogurt.
3. Situate pan over medium heat. Heat up your oil, and cook your onions until soft.
4. Add in your mushroom and continue to cook until softened.
5. Add in your bell pepper, and cook until crispy.
6. Drain your pasta, and then toss with your tahini sauce, top with parsley and pepper and serve with vegetables.

**NUTRITIONS:**
332 Calories, 11g Protein, 12g Fat

# 447. ROASTED VEGGIES

**COOKING: 26'**  **PREPARATION:14'**  **SERVES: 12**

## INGREDIENTS

- » 6 cloves garlic
- » 6 tablespoons olive oil
- » 1 fennel bulb, diced
- » 1 zucchini, diced
- » 2 red bell peppers, diced
- » 6 potatoes, large & diced
- » 2 teaspoons sea salt
- » ½ cup balsamic vinegar
- » ¼ cup rosemary, chopped & fresh
- » 2 teaspoons vegetable bouillon powder

## DIRECTION

1. Start by heating your oven to 400.
2. Get out a baking dish and place your potatoes, fennel, zucchini, garlic and fennel on a baking dish, drizzling with olive oil. Sprinkle with salt, bouillon powder, and rosemary. Mix well, and then bake at 450 for thirty to forty minutes. Mix your vinegar into the vegetables before serving.

**NUTRITIONS:**
675 Calories, 13g Protein, 21g Fat

# 448. ZUCCHINI PASTA

**COOKING: 32'**　　　**PREPARATION: 9'**　　　**SERVES: 4**

## INGREDIENTS

- » 3 tablespoons olive oil
- » 2 cloves garlic, minced
- » 3 zucchinis, large & diced
- » sea salt & black pepper to taste
- » ½ cup milk, 2%
- » ¼ teaspoon nutmeg
- » 1 tablespoon lemon juice, fresh
- » ½ cup parmesan, grated
- » 8 ounces uncooked farfalle pasta

## DIRECTION

1. Get out a skillet and place it over medium heat, and then heat up the oil. Add in your garlic and cook for a minute. Stir often so that it doesn't burn. Add in your salt, pepper and zucchini. Stir well, and cook covered for fifteen minutes. During this time, you'll want to stir the mixture twice.

2. Get out a microwave safe bowl, and heat the milk for thirty seconds. Stir in your nutmeg, and then pour it into the skillet. Cook uncovered for five minutes. Stir occasionally to keep from burning.

3. Get out a stockpot and cook your pasta per package instructions. Drain the pasta, and then save two tablespoons of pasta water.

4. Stir everything together, and add in the cheese and lemon juice and pasta water.

**NUTRITIONS:**
410 Calories, 15g Protein, 17g Fat

# 449. ASPARAGUS PASTA

**COOKING: 33'**　　　**PREPARATION: 8'**　　　**SERVES: 6**

## INGREDIENTS

- » 8 ounces farfalle pasta, uncooked
- » 1 ½ cups asparagus
- » 1-pint grape tomatoes, halved
- » 2 tablespoons olive oil
- » 2 cups mozzarella, fresh & drained
- » 1/3 cup basil leaves, fresh & torn
- » 2 tablespoons balsamic vinegar

## DIRECTION

1. Start by heating the oven to 400, and then get out a stockpot. Cook your pasta per package instructions, and reserve ¼ cup of pasta water.

2. Get out a bowl and toss the tomatoes, oil, asparagus, and season with salt and pepper. Spread this mixture on a baking sheet, and bake for fifteen minutes. Stir twice in this time.

3. Remove your vegetables from the oven, and then add the cooked pasta to your baking sheet. Mix with a few tablespoons of pasta water so that your sauce becomes smoother.

4. Mix in your basil and mozzarella, drizzling with balsamic vinegar. Serve warm.

**NUTRITIONS:**
307 Calories, 18g Protein, 14g Fat

# 450. FETA & SPINACH PITA BAKE

**COOKING: 36'**          **PREPARATION:11'**          **SERVES: 6**

## INGREDIENTS

- » 2 roma tomatoes
- » 6 whole wheat pita bread
- » 1 jar sun dried tomato pesto
- » 4 mushrooms, fresh & sliced
- » 1 bunch spinach
- » 2 tablespoons parmesan cheese
- » 3 tablespoons olive oil
- » ½ cup feta cheese

## DIRECTION

1. Start by heating the oven to 350, and get to your pita bread. Spread the tomato pesto on the side of each one. Put them in a baking pan with the tomato side up.

2. Top with tomatoes, spinach, mushrooms, parmesan and feta. Drizzle with olive oil and season with pepper.

3. Bake for twelve minutes, and then serve cut into quarters.

## NUTRITIONS:

350 Calories, 12g Protein, 17g Fat

# CHAPTER 32
# DESSERT RECIPES

# 451. VANILLA CREAM

**COOKING: 10'**  **PREPARATION: 2 HOURS**  **SERVINGS: 4**

## INGREDIENTS

- » 1 cup almond milk
- » 1 cup coconut cream
- » 2 cups coconut sugar
- » 2 tablespoons cinnamon powder
- » 1 teaspoon vanilla extract

## DIRECTION

1. Heat up a pan with the almond milk over medium heat, add the rest of the ingredients, whisk, and cook for 10 minutes more.
2. Divide the mix into bowls, cool down and keep in the fridge for 2 hours before serving.

**NUTRITIONS:**

254 calories, 7.5g fat, 9.5g Protein

# 452. BLUEBERRIES BOWLS

**COOKING: 0'**  **PREPARATION: 10'**  **SERVINGS: 4**

## INGREDIENTS

- » 1 teaspoon vanilla extract
- » 2 cups blueberries
- » 1 teaspoon coconut sugar
- » 8 ounces Greek yogurt

## DIRECTION

1. Mix strawberries with the vanilla and the other ingredients, toss and serve cold.

**NUTRITIONS:**

343 calories, 13.4g fat, 5.5g Protein

# 453. BROWNIES

**COOKING: 25'**     **PREPARATION: 10'**     **SERVINGS: 8**

## INGREDIENTS

- » 1 cup pecans, chopped
- » 3 tablespoons coconut sugar
- » 2 tablespoons cocoa powder
- » 3 eggs, whisked
- » ¼ cup avocado oil
- » ½ teaspoon baking powder
- » 2 teaspoons vanilla extract
- » Cooking spray

## DIRECTION

1. In your food processor, combine the pecans with the coconut sugar and the other ingredients except the cooking spray and pulse well.
2. Grease a square pan with cooking spray, add the brownies mix, spread, introduce in the oven, bake at 350 degrees F for 25 minutes, leave aside to cool down, slice and serve.

**NUTRITIONS:**
370 calories, 14.3g fat, 5.6g Protein

# 454. STRAWBERRIES COCONUT CAKE

**COOKING: 25'**     **PREPARATION: 10'**     **SERVINGS: 6**

## INGREDIENTS

- » 2 cups almond flour
- » 1 cup strawberries, chopped
- » ½ teaspoon baking soda
- » ½ cup coconut sugar
- » ¾ cup coconut milk
- » ¼ cup avocado oil
- » 2 eggs, whisked
- » 1 teaspoon vanilla extract
- » Cooking spray

## DIRECTION

1. In a bowl, combine the flour with the strawberries and the other ingredients except the cooking spray and whisk well.
2. Grease a cake pan with cooking spray, pour the cake mix, spread, bake in the oven at 350 degrees F for 25 minutes, cool down, slice and serve.

**NUTRITIONS:**
465 calories, 22g fat, 13.4g Protein

# 455. COCOA ALMOND PUDDING

**COOKING: 10'**      **PREPARATION:10'**      **SERVINGS: 4**

## INGREDIENTS

- » 2 tablespoons coconut sugar
- » 3 tablespoons coconut flour
- » 2 tablespoons cocoa powder
- » 2 cups almond milk
- » 2 eggs, whisked
- » ½ teaspoon vanilla extract

## DIRECTION

1. Fill milk in a pan, add the cocoa and the other ingredients, whisk, simmer over medium heat for 10 minutes, pour into small cups and serve cold.

**NUTRITIONS:**
385 calories, 31.7g fat, 7.3g Protein

# 456. NUTMEG CREAM

**COOKING: 0'**      **PREPARATION:10'**      **SERVINGS: 6**

## INGREDIENTS

- » 3 cups almond milk
- » 1 teaspoon nutmeg, ground
- » 2 teaspoons vanilla extract
- » 4 teaspoons coconut sugar
- » 1 cup walnuts, chopped

## DIRECTION

1. In a bowl, combine milk with the nutmeg and the other ingredients, whisk well, divide into small cups and serve cold.

**NUTRITIONS:**
243 calories, 12.4g fat, 9.7g Protein

# 457. VANILLA AVOCADO CREAM

**COOKING: 0'**          **PREPARATION:70'**          **SERVINGS: 4**

## INGREDIENTS

- » 2 cups coconut cream
- » 2 avocados, peeled, pitted and mashed
- » 2 tablespoons coconut sugar
- » 1 teaspoon vanilla extract

## DIRECTION

1. Blend cream with the avocados and the other ingredients, pulse well, divide into cups and keep in the fridge for 1 hour before serving.

**NUTRITIONS:**
532 calories, 48.2g fat, 5.2g Protein

# 458. RASPBERRIES CREAM CHEESE BOWLS

**COOKING: 25'**          **PREPARATION:10'**          **SERVINGS: 4**

## INGREDIENTS

- » 2 tablespoons almond flour
- » 1 cup coconut cream
- » 3 cups raspberries
- » 1 cup coconut sugar
- » 8 ounces cream cheese

## DIRECTION

1. In a bowl, the flour with the cream and the other ingredients, whisk, transfer to a round pan, cook at 360 degrees F for 25 minutes, divide into bowls and serve.

**NUTRITIONS:**
429 calories, 36.3g fat, 7.8g Protein

# 459. MEDITERRANEAN WATERMELON SALAD

**COOKING: 0'**     **PREPARATION: 4'**     **SERVINGS: 4**

## INGREDIENTS

- » 1 cup watermelon, peeled and cubed
- » 2 apples, cored and cubed
- » 1 tablespoon coconut cream
- » 2 bananas, cut into chunks

## DIRECTION

1. Incorporate watermelon with the apples and the other ingredients, toss and serve.

**NUTRITIONS:**
131 calories, 1.3g fat, 1.3g Protein

# 460. COCONUT APPLES

**COOKING: 10'**     **PREPARATION: 10'**     **SERVINGS: 4**

## INGREDIENTS

- » 2 teaspoons lime juice
- » ½ cup coconut cream
- » ½ cup coconut, shredded
- » 4 apples, cored and cubed
- » 4 tablespoons coconut sugar

## DIRECTION

1. Incorporate apples with the lime juice and the other ingredients, stir, bring to a simmer over medium heat and cook for 10 minutes.
2. Divide into bowls and serve cold.

**NUTRITIONS:**
320 calories, 7.8g fat, 4.7g Protein

# 461. ORANGE COMPOTE

**COOKING: 15'**    **PREPARATION:10'**    **SERVINGS: 4**

## INGREDIENTS

- » 5 tablespoons coconut sugar
- » 2 cups orange juice
- » 4 oranges, peeled and cut into segments

## DIRECTION

1. In a pot, combine oranges with the sugar and the orange juice, toss, bring to a boil over medium heat, cook for 15 minutes, divide into bowls and serve cold.

**NUTRITIONS:**

220 calories, 5.2g fat, 5.6g Protein

# 462. PEARS STEW

**COOKING: 15'**    **PREPARATION:10'**    **SERVINGS: 4**

## INGREDIENTS

- » 2 cups pears, cored and cut into wedges
- » 2 cups water
- » 2 tablespoons coconut sugar
- » 2 tablespoons lemon juice

## DIRECTION

1. In a pot, combine the pears with the water and the other ingredients, toss, cook over medium heat for 15 minutes, divide into bowls and serve.

**NUTRITIONS:**

260 calories, 6.2g fat, 6g Protein

# 463. LEMON WATERMELON MIX

**COOKING: 10'**  **PREPARATION:10'**  **SERVINGS: 4**

## INGREDIENTS

- » 2 cups watermelon
- » 4 tablespoons coconut sugar
- » 2 teaspoons vanilla extract
- » 2 teaspoons lemon juice

## DIRECTION

1. In a small pan, combine the watermelon with the sugar and the other ingredients, toss, heat up over medium heat, cook for about 10 minutes, divide into bowls and serve cold.

**NUTRITIONS:**
140 calories, 4g fat, 5g Protein

# 464. RHUBARB CREAM

**COOKING: 14'**  **PREPARATION:10'**  **SERVINGS: 4**

## INGREDIENTS

- » 1/3 cup cream cheese
- » ½ cup coconut cream
- » 2-pound rhubarb, roughly chopped
- » 3 tablespoons coconut sugar

## DIRECTION

1. Blend cream cheese with the cream and the other ingredients well.
2. Divide into small cups, introduce in the oven and bake at 350 degrees F for 14 minutes.

**NUTRITIONS:**
360 calories, 14.3g fat, 5.2g Protein

# 465. MANGO BOWLS

**COOKING: 0'**   **PREPARATION:10'**   **SERVINGS: 4**

## INGREDIENTS

- » 3 cups mango, peeled and cubed
- » 1 teaspoon chia seeds
- » 1 cup coconut cream
- » 1 teaspoon vanilla extract
- » 1 tablespoon mint, chopped

## NUTRITIONS:

238 calories, 16.6g fat, 3.3g Protein

## DIRECTION

1. Mix mango with the cream and the other ingredients, toss, divide into smaller bowls and keep in the fridge for 10 minutes before serving.

# CHAPTER 33
## DESSERT RECIPES PART 2

# 466. CHOCOLATE GANACHE

**COOKING: 16'**　　　**PREPARATION:10'**　　　**SERVINGS: 16**

## INGREDIENTS

» 9 ounces bittersweet chocolate, chopped
» 1 cup heavy cream
» 1 tablespoon dark rum (optional)

## DIRECTION

1. Situate chocolate in a medium bowl. Cook cream in a small saucepan over medium heat.
2. Bring to a boil. When the cream has reached a boiling point, pour the chopped chocolate over it and beat until smooth. Stir the rum if desired.
3. Allow the ganache to cool slightly before you pour it on a cake. Begin in the middle of the cake and work outside. For a fluffy icing or chocolate filling, let it cool until thick and beat with a whisk until light and fluffy.

**NUTRITIONS:**
142 calories, 10.8g fat, 1.4g Protein

# 467. CHOCOLATE COVERED STRAWBERRIES

**COOKING: 0'**　　　**PREPARATION:15'**　　　**SERVINGS: 24**

## INGREDIENTS

» 16 ounces milk chocolate chips
» 2 tablespoons shortening
» 1-pound fresh strawberries with leaves

## DIRECTION

1. In a bain-marie, melt chocolate and shortening, occasionally stirring until smooth. Pierce the tops of the strawberries with toothpicks and immerse them in the chocolate mixture.
2. Turn the strawberries and put the toothpick in Styrofoam so that the chocolate cools.

**NUTRITIONS:**
115 calories, 7.3g fat, 1.4g Protein

# 468. STRAWBERRY ANGEL FOOD DESSERT

**COOKING: 0'**      **PREPARATION:15'**      **SERVINGS: 18**

## INGREDIENTS

- » 1 angel cake (10 inches)
- » 2 packages of softened cream cheese
- » 1 cup of white sugar
- » 1 container (8 oz) of frozen fluff, thawed
- » 1 liter of fresh strawberries, sliced
- » 1 jar of strawberry icing

## DIRECTION

1. Crumble the cake in a 9 x 13-inch dish.
2. Beat the cream cheese and sugar in a medium bowl until the mixture is light and fluffy. Stir in the whipped topping. Crush the cake with your hands, and spread the cream cheese mixture over the cake.
3. Combine the strawberries and the frosting in a bowl until the strawberries are well covered. Spread over the layer of cream cheese. Cool until ready to serve.

## NUTRITIONS:
261 calories, 11g fat, 3.2g Protein

# 469. FRUIT PIZZA

**COOKING: 0'**      **PREPARATION:30'**      **SERVINGS: 8**

## INGREDIENTS

- » 1 (18-oz) package sugar cookie dough
- » 1 (8-oz) package cream cheese, softened
- » 1 (8-oz) frozen filling, defrosted
- » 2 cups of freshly cut strawberries
- » 1/2 cup of white sugar
- » 1 pinch of salt
- » 1 tablespoon corn flour
- » 2 tablespoons lemon juice
- » 1/2 cup orange juice
- » 1/4 cup water
- » 1/2 teaspoon orange zest

## DIRECTION

1. Ready oven to 175 ° C Slice the cookie dough then place it on a greased pizza pan. Press the dough flat into the mold. Bake for 10 to 12 minutes. Let cool.
2. Soften the cream cheese in a large bowl and then stir in the whipped topping. Spread over the cooled crust.
3. Start with strawberries cut in half. Situate in a circle around the outer edge. Continue with the fruit of your choice by going to the center. If you use bananas, immerse them in lemon juice. Then make a sauce with a spoon on the fruit.
4. Combine sugar, salt, corn flour, orange juice, lemon juice, and water in a pan. Boil and stir over medium heat. Boil for 1 or 2 minutes until thick. Remove from heat and add the grated orange zest. Place on the fruit.
5. Allow to cool for two hours, cut into quarters, and serve.

## NUTRITIONS:
535 calories, 30g fat, 5.5g Protein

# 470. BANANAS FOSTER

**COOKING: 6'**       **PREPARATION:5'**       **SERVINGS: 4**

## INGREDIENTS

- » 2/3 cup dark brown sugar
- » 1/4 cup butter
- » 3 1/2 tablespoons rum
- » 1 1/2 teaspoons vanilla extract
- » 1/2 teaspoon of ground cinnamon
- » 3 bananas, peeled and cut lengthwise and broad
- » 1/4 cup coarsely chopped nuts
- » vanilla ice cream

## DIRECTION

1. Melt the butter in a deep-frying pan over medium heat. Stir in sugar, rum, vanilla, and cinnamon.
2. When the mixture starts to bubble, place the bananas and nuts in the pan. Bake until the bananas are hot, 1 to 2 minutes. Serve immediately with vanilla ice cream.

**NUTRITIONS:**

534 calories, 23.8g fat, 4.6g Protein

# 471. CRANBERRY ORANGE COOKIES

**COOKING: 16'**       **PREPARATION:20'**       **SERVINGS: 24**

## INGREDIENTS

- » 1 cup of soft butter
- » 1 cup of white sugar
- » 1/2 cup brown sugar
- » 1 egg
- » 1 teaspoon grated orange peel
- » 2 tablespoons orange juice
- » 2 1/2 cups flour
- » 1/2 teaspoon baking powder
- » 1/2 teaspoon salt
- » 2 cups chopped cranberries
- » 1/2 cup chopped walnuts (optional)
- » Icing:
- » 1/2 teaspoon grated orange peel
- » 3 tablespoons orange juice
- » 1 ½ cup confectioner's sugar

## DIRECTION

1. Preheat the oven to 190 ° C.
2. Blend butter, white sugar, and brown sugar. Beat the egg until everything is well mixed. Mix 1 teaspoon of orange zest and 2 tablespoons of orange juice. Mix the flour, baking powder, and salt; stir in the orange mixture.
3. Mix the cranberries and, if used, the nuts until well distributed. Place the dough with a spoon on ungreased baking trays.
4. Bake in the preheated oven for 12 to 14 minutes. Cool on racks.
5. In a small bowl, mix icing ingredients. Spread over cooled cookies.

**NUTRITIONS:**

110 calories, 4.8g fat, g Protein

# 472. KEY LIME PIE

**COOKING: 8'**  **PREPARATION:15'**  **SERVINGS: 8**

## INGREDIENTS

» 1 (9-inch) prepared graham cracker crust
» 3 cups of sweetened condensed milk
» 1/2 cup sour cream
» 3/4 cup lime juice
» 1 tablespoon grated lime zest

## DIRECTION

1. Prepare oven to 175 ° C
2. Combine the condensed milk, sour cream, lime juice, and lime zest in a medium bowl. Mix well and pour into the graham cracker crust.
3. Bake in the preheated oven for 5 to 8 minutes
4. Cool the cake well before serving. Decorate with lime slices and whipped cream if desired.

**NUTRITIONS:**
553 calories, 20.5g fat, 10.9g Protein

# 473. RHUBARB STRAWBERRY CRUNCH

**COOKING: 45'**  **PREPARATION:15'**  **SERVINGS: 18**

## INGREDIENTS

» 1 cup of white sugar
» 3 tablespoons all-purpose flour
» 3 cups of fresh strawberries, sliced
» 3 cups of rhubarb, cut into cubes
» 1 1/2 cup flour
» 1 cup packed brown sugar
» 1 cup butter
» 1 cup oatmeal

## DIRECTION

1. Preheat the oven to 190 ° C.
2. Combine white sugar, 3 tablespoons flour, strawberries and rhubarb in a large bowl. Place the mixture in a 9 x 13-inch baking dish.
3. Mix 1 1/2 cups of flour, brown sugar, butter, and oats until a crumbly texture is obtained. You may want to use a blender for this. Crumble the mixture of rhubarb and strawberry.
4. Bake for 45 minutes.

**NUTRITIONS:**
253 calories, 10.8g fat, 2.3g Protein

# 474. CHOCOLATE CHIP BANANA DESSERT

**COOKING: 20'**     **PREPARATION:20'**     **SERVINGS: 24**

## INGREDIENTS

» 2/3 cup white sugar
» 3/4 cup butter
» 2/3 cup brown sugar
» 1 egg, beaten slightly
» 1 teaspoon vanilla extract
» 1 cup of banana puree
» 1 3/4 cup flour
» 2 teaspoons baking powder
» 1/2 teaspoon of salt
» 1 cup of semi-sweet chocolate chips

## DIRECTION

1. Ready the oven to 175 ° C Grease and bake a 10 x 15-inch baking pan.

2. Beat the butter, white sugar, and brown sugar in a large bowl until light. Beat the egg and vanilla. Fold in the banana puree: mix baking powder, flour, and salt in another bowl. Mix flour mixture into the butter mixture. Stir in the chocolate chips. Spread in pan.

3. Bake for 20 minutes. Cool before cutting into squares.

**NUTRITIONS:**
174 calories, 8.2g fat, 1.7g Protein

# 475. APPLE PIE FILLING

**COOKING: 12'**     **PREPARATION:20'**     **SERVINGS: 40**

## INGREDIENTS

» 18 cups chopped apples
» 3 tablespoons lemon juice
» 10 cups of water
» 4 1/2 cups of white sugar
» 1 cup corn flour
» 2 teaspoons of ground cinnamon
» 1 teaspoon of salt
» 1/4 teaspoon ground nutmeg

## DIRECTION

1. Mix apples with lemon juice in a large bowl and set aside. Pour the water in a Dutch oven over medium heat. Combine sugar, corn flour, cinnamon, salt, and nutmeg in a bowl. Add to water, mix well, and bring to a boil. Cook for 2 minutes with continuous stirring.

2. Boil apples again. Reduce the heat, cover, and simmer for 8 minutes. Allow cooling for 30 minutes.

3. Pour into five freezer containers and leave 1/2 inch of free space. Cool to room temperature.

4. Seal and freeze

**NUTRITIONS:**
129 calories, 0.1g fat, 0.2g Protein

# 476. ICE CREAM SANDWICH DESSERT

**COOKING: 0'**     **PREPARATION:20'**     **SERVINGS: 12**

## INGREDIENTS

- » 22 ice cream sandwiches
- » Frozen whipped topping in 16 oz container, thawed
- » 1 jar (12 oz) Caramel ice cream
- » 1 1/2 cups of salted peanuts

## DIRECTION

1. Cut a sandwich with ice in two. Place a whole sandwich and a half sandwich on a short side of a 9 x 13-inch baking dish. Repeat this until the bottom is covered, alternate the full sandwich, and the half sandwich.

2. Spread half of the whipped topping. Pour the caramel over it. Sprinkle with half the peanuts. Do layers with the rest of the ice cream sandwiches, whipped cream, and peanuts.

3. Cover and freeze for up to 2 months. Remove from the freezer 20 minutes before serving. Cut into squares.

## NUTRITIONS:
559 calories, 28.8g fat, 10g Protein

# 477. CRANBERRY AND PISTACHIO BISCOTTI

**COOKING: 35'**     **PREPARATION:15'**     **SERVINGS: 36**

## INGREDIENTS

- » 1/4 cup light olive oil
- » 3/4 cup white sugar
- » 2 teaspoons vanilla extract
- » 1/2 teaspoon almond extract
- » 2 eggs
- » 1 3/4 cup all-purpose flour
- » 1/4 teaspoon salt
- » 1 teaspoon baking powder
- » 1/2 cup dried cranberries
- » 1 1/2 cup pistachio nuts

## DIRECTION

1. Prep oven to 150 ° C

2. Combine the oil and sugar in a large bowl until a homogeneous mixture is obtained. Stir in the vanilla and almond extract and add the eggs. Combine flour, salt, and baking powder; gradually add to the egg mixture — mix cranberries and nuts by hand.

3. Divide the dough in half — form two 12 x 2-inch logs on a parchment baking sheet. The dough can be sticky, wet hands with cold water to make it easier to handle the dough.

4. Bake in the preheated oven for 35 minutes or until the blocks are golden brown. Pullout from the oven and let cool for 10 minutes. Reduce oven heat to 275 degrees F (135 degrees C).

5. Cut diagonally into 3/4-inch-thick slices. Place on the sides on the baking sheet covered with parchment — Bake for about 8 to 10 minutes

## NUTRITIONS:
92 calories, 4.3g fat, 2.1g Protein

# 478. CREAM PUFF DESSERT

**COOKING: 36'**　　　　**PREPARATION:20'**　　　　**SERVINGS: 12**

## INGREDIENTS

- » Puff
- » 1 cup water
- » 1/2 cup butter
- » 1 cup all-purpose flour
- » 4 eggs
- » Filling
- » 1 (8-oz) package cream cheese, softened
- » 3 1/2 cups cold milk
- » 2 (4-oz) packages instant chocolate pudding mix
- » Topping
- » 1 (8-oz) package frozen whipped cream topping, thawed
- » 1/4 cup topping with milk chocolate flavor
- » 1/4 cup caramel filling
- » 1/3 cup almond flakes

## DIRECTION

1. Set oven to 200 degrees C (400 degrees F). Grease a 9 x 13-inch baking dish.
2. Melt the butter in the water in a medium-sized pan over medium heat. Pour the flour in one go and mix vigorously until the mixture forms a ball. Remove from heat and let stand for 5 minutes. Beat the eggs one by one until they are smooth and shiny. Spread in the prepared pan.
3. Bake in the preheated oven for 30 to 35 minutes, until puffed and browned. Cool completely on a rack.
4. While the puff pastry cools, mix the cream cheese mixture, the milk, and the pudding. Spread over the cooled puff pastry. Cool for 20 minutes.
5. Spread whipped cream on cooled topping and sprinkle with chocolate and caramel sauce. Sprinkle with almonds. Freeze 1 hour before serving.

## NUTRITIONS:

355 calories, 22.3g fat, 8.7g Protein

# 479. FRESH PEACH DESSERT

**COOKING: 27'**　　　　**PREPARATION:30'**　　　　**SERVINGS: 15**

## INGREDIENTS

- » 16 whole graham crackers, crushed
- » 3/4 cup melted butter
- » 1/2 cup white sugar
- » 4 1/2 cups of miniature marshmallows
- » 1/4 cup of milk
- » 1 pint of heavy cream
- » 1/3 cup of white sugar
- » 6 large fresh peaches - peeled, seeded and sliced

## DIRECTION

1. In a bowl, mix the crumbs from the graham cracker, melted butter, and 1/2 cup of sugar. Mix until a homogeneous mixture is obtained, save 1/4 cup of the mixture for filling. Squeeze the rest of the mixture into the bottom of a 9 x 13-inch baking dish.
2. Heat marshmallows and milk in a large pan over low heat and stir until marshmallows are completely melted. Remove from heat and let cool.
3. Beat the cream in a large bowl until soft peaks occur. Beat 1/3 cup of sugar until the cream forms firm spikes. Add the whipped cream to the cooled marshmallow mixture.
4. Divide half of the cream mixture over the crust, place the peaches over the cream and divide the rest of the cream mixture over the peaches. Sprinkle the crumb mixture on the cream. Cool until ready to serve.

## NUTRITIONS:

366 calories, 22.5g fat, 1.9g Protein

# 480. BLUEBERRY DESSERT

**COOKING: 20'**         **PREPARATION:30'**         **SERVINGS: 28**

## INGREDIENTS

- » 1/2 cup butter
- » 2 cups white sugar
- » 36 graham crackers, crushed
- » 4 eggs
- » 2 packets of cream cheese, softened
- » 1 teaspoon vanilla extract
- » 2 cans of blueberry pie filling
- » 1 package (16-oz) frozen whipped cream, thawed

## DIRECTION

1. Cook butter and sprinkle 1 cup of sugar and graham crackers. Squeeze this mixture into a 9x13 dish.

2. Beat the eggs. Gradually beat the cream cheese, sugar, and vanilla in the eggs.

3. Pour the mixture of eggs and cream cheese over the graham cracker crust. Bake for 15 to 20 minutes at 165 ° C (325 ° F). Cool.

4. Pour the blueberry pie filling on top of the baked dessert. Spread non-dairy whipped topping on fruit. Cool until ready to serve.

## NUTRITIONS:

354 calories, 15.4g fat, 3.8g Protein

# CHAPTER 34
# DESSERT RECIPES PART 3

# 481. GOOD SWEET

**COOKING: 10'**  **PREPARATION:10'**  **SERVINGS: 2**

## INGREDIENTS

» Tomatoes, ¼ teaspoon, chopped
» Cucumber, ¼ teaspoon, chopped
» Honey, 2 tablespoons
» Other veggies/beans optional

## DIRECTION

1. Whisk the ingredients well.
2. In a bowl, toss to coat with honey as smoothly as possible.

**NUTRITIONS:**
187 Calories, 15.6g Fat, 2g Protein

# 482. A TASTE OF DESSERT

**COOKING: 0'**  **PREPARATION:15'**  **SERVINGS: 2**

## INGREDIENTS

» Cilantro, 1 tablespoon
» Green onion, 1 tablespoon
» Mango, 1 peeled, seeded and chopped
» Bell pepper, ¼ cup, chopped
» Honey, 2 tablespoons

## DIRECTION

1. Incorporate all the ingredients.
2. Serve when combined well.

**NUTRITIONS:**
21 Calories, 0.1g Fat, 0.3g Protein

# 483. HONEY CARROTS

**COOKING: 15'**  **PREPARATION:5'**  **SERVINGS: 2**

## INGREDIENTS

» Baby carrots, 16 ounces
» Brown sugar, ¼ cup

## DIRECTION

1. Boil carrots with water in a huge pot
2. Drain after 15 minutes, and steam for 2 minutes.
3. Stir in the sugar, and serve when mixed well.

**NUTRITIONS:**
402 Calories, 23.3g Fat, 1.4g Protein

# 484. FRESH CHERRY TREAT

**COOKING: 10'**  **PREPARATION:10'**  **SERVINGS: 2**

## INGREDIENTS

» Honey, 1 tablespoon
» Almonds, 1 tablespoon, crushed
» Cherries, 12 ounces

## DIRECTION

1. Preheat the oven to 350F, and for 5 minutes, bake the cherries.
2. Coat them with honey, and serve with almonds on top.

**NUTRITIONS:**
448 Calories, 36.4g Fat, 3.5g Protein

# 485. MILKY PEACHY DESSERT

**COOKING: 10'**  **PREPARATION:15'**  **SERVINGS: 2**

## INGREDIENTS

- » Peach, 1 fresh, peeled and sliced
- » Brown sugar, 1 teaspoon
- » Milk, 1 tablespoon

## DIRECTION

1. Prepare a baking dish with a layer of peaches and toss in the milk.
2. Top the peaches with sugar, and bake at 350F for 5 minutes.

**NUTRITIONS:**

366 Calories, 22.5g Fat, 1.9g Protein

# 486. CITRUS SECTIONS

**COOKING: 5'**  **PREPARATION:20'**  **SERVINGS: 2**

## INGREDIENTS

- » Grapefruit, 1, peeled and sectioned
- » Pineapple, ½ cup, chunks
- » Oranges, 1 small, sectioned into chunks
- » Brown sugar, ½ tablespoon
- » Butter, low fat and unsalted, ½ teaspoon, melted

## DIRECTION

1. Preheat an oven tray at 350F.
2. Set the fruits on the tray, and top with the brown sugar, mixed with the butter, and bake for 5 minutes.
3. Transfer to a platter.

**NUTRITIONS:**

279 Calories, 5.9g Fat, 2.2g Protein

# 487. AFTER MEAL APPLES

**COOKING: 25'**          **PREPARATION:15'**          **SERVINGS: 2**

## INGREDIENTS

- » Apple, 1 whole, cut into chunks
- » Pineapple chunks, ½ cups
- » Grapes, seedless, ½ cup
- » Orange juice, ¼ cup
- » Cinnamon, ¼ teaspoon

## DIRECTION

1. Preheat the oven to 350F.
2. Add all the fruits to a baking dish.
3. Drizzle with the orange juice and sprinkle with cinnamon.
4. Bake for 25 minutes, and serve hot.

**NUTRITIONS:**
124 Calories, 3.2g Fat, 0.8g Protein

# 488. WARM NUT BITES

**COOKING: 20'**          **PREPARATION:10'**          **SERVINGS: 2**

## INGREDIENTS

- » Honey, 4 tablespoons
- » Almonds, 2 cups
- » Almond oil, 1 tablespoon

## DIRECTION

1. Layer the almonds, whole, on a baking sheet.
2. Bake for 15 minutes at 350F.
3. Turn half way, and roll the almonds in honey.
4. Serve.

**NUTRITIONS:**
268 Calories, 19.7g Fat, 7.6g Protein

# 489. DIPPED SPROUTS

**COOKING: 10'**          **PREPARATION:12'**          **SERVINGS: 2**

## INGREDIENTS

- » Brussels sprouts, 16 ounces
- » Honey, 4 tablespoons
- » Raisins and nuts, crushed, 6 tablespoons

## DIRECTION

1. Boil water in a pot.
2. Add sprouts, and cook for 10 minutes until soft.
3. Glaze the sprouts in honey, and coat well. Add nuts and raisins.

**NUTRITIONS:**
221 Calories, 15.1g Fat, 5.3g Protein

# 490. PECANS AND CHEESE

**COOKING: 0'**          **PREPARATION:20'**          **SERVINGS: 2**

## INGREDIENTS

- » Cinnamon, ground, 1 teaspoon
- » Feta cheese, 4 ounces
- » Pecans, finely chopped, 2 ounces
- » Honey, 2 tablespoons
- » Rosemary, fresh, 2 sprigs, minced

## DIRECTION

1. Make small balls of the cheese.
2. Crush the pecans and place them in a shallow bowl with the cinnamon.
3. Roll the cheese in the pecans and cinnamon.
4. Drizzle honey over the balls.
5. Serve with rosemary on top.

**NUTRITIONS:**
234 Calories, 18.6g Fat, 7.5g Protein

# CHAPTER 35
# DESSERT RECIPES PART 4

# 491. HAZELNUT COOKIES

**COOKING: 21'**       **PREPARATION:8'**       **SERVINGS: 5**

## INGREDIENTS

- » 1 1/4 cups hazelnut meal
- » 6 tbsp. flour
- » 1 tbsp. brown sugar
- » 2 tbsp. powdered sugar
- » 1/2 tsp. kosher salt
- » 1/2 lemon zest
- » 1/2 lemon juice
- » 1/2 tsp. vanilla
- » 1/4 cup extra virgin olive oil

## DIRECTION

1. Heat the oven at 375 degrees F.
2. Take a bowl, add the hazelnut meal, brown sugar, flour, half of the powdered sugar, lemon zest, and salt. Next, whisk it well.
3. Whisk olive oil and vanilla.
4. Once the dough is crumbly, shape them into cookies and line them on the baking sheet.
5. Bake it until the edges are lightly brown, around 20 minutes.
6. Take out on a cooling rack Let it sit to cool.
7. Meanwhile, take a small bowl and add lemon juice, and the remaining powdered sugar.
8. Drizzle the syrup over the cookies before serving.

**NUTRITIONS:**
276 Calories, 3.6g Protein, 21.2g Fat

# 492. FRUIT DESSERT NACHOS

**COOKING: 13'**       **PREPARATION:9'**       **SERVINGS: 3**

## INGREDIENTS

- » 1 tbsp. sugar
- » a pinch of ground cinnamon
- » 1 1/2 whole wheat tortillas
- » 1/4 cup softened light cream cheese
- » 1 cup chopped assorted melon
- » 2 1/2 tbsp. light dairy sour cream
- » 1/2 tsp. finely shredded orange peel
- » 1 tbsp. orange juice

## DIRECTION

1. Preheat oven at 425 degrees F.
2. Grease huge baking sheet with cooking spray.
3. Take a small bowl, combine the cinnamon and half of the sugar.
4. Take the tortillas and lightly coat with cooking spray. Sprinkle each side with the sugar mix.
5. Cut the tortillas to make 8 wedges and place them on the baking sheet.
6. Bake the tortillas until they turn light browned, for about 7 to 8 minutes. Turn once halfway.
7. Meanwhile, take a small sized bowl and mix together the sour cream, cream cheese, 30 grams of orange juice, orange peel and the remaining sugar. Once smooth, set it aside.
8. Take a medium bowl and combine together melon and remaining orange juice.
9. Serve by adding a spoon of melon mix on each tortilla wedge, and a spoon of cream cheese mixture.

**NUTRITIONS:**
121 Calories, 5.3g Protein, 5.2g Fat

# 493. HONEY YOGURT WITH BERRIES

**COOKING: 0'**  **PREPARATION:12'**  **SERVINGS: 2**

## INGREDIENTS

- » 4 oz. hulled, halved strawberries
- » 1/6 cup Greek yogurt
- » 1/2 cup blueberries
- » 1/2 cup raspberries
- » 1 tsp. honey
- » 1/2 tbsp. balsamic vinegar

## DIRECTION

1. Take a large bowl and toss the berries with the balsamic vinegar.
2. Set it aside for 8 to 10 minutes.
3. Meanwhile, mix together the honey and yogurt in a bowl.
4. Serve it by topping the berries with honey yogurt.

**NUTRITIONS:**
111 Calories, 4.6g Protein, 3g Fat

# 494. CARAMELIZED APPLES WITH YOGURT

**COOKING: 9'**  **PREPARATION:14'**  **SERVINGS: 4**

## INGREDIENTS

- » 1/2 cup Greek yogurt
- » 2 tbsp. toasted, chopped walnuts
- » 1/4 cup heavy cream
- » 1 tbsp. sugar
- » 1/2 tbsp. honey
- » 1 tbsp. unsalted butter
- » 1 apple
- » a pinch of ground cinnamon

## DIRECTION

1. Take a bowl and add the yogurt, honey, and cream. Next, beat it with a hand blender or a whisk. Beat it until the mixture forms peaks and has thickened.
2. Place a large skillet on medium heat and warm the butter.
3. Add 21 grams of sugar and the apples in to the pan and mix it well.
4. Cook the apples for five to seven minutes while occasionally stirring, so it doesn't stick.
5. Once the apples soften, sprinkle the cinnamon and the remaining sugar on them.
6. Cook for 2 more minutes before removing from the heat.
7. Wait for the apples to appear warm.
8. Serve the whipped yogurt topped with apples and almonds.

**NUTRITIONS:**
315 Calories, 6.4g Protein, 22g Fat

# 495. RICOTTA BRULEE

**COOKING: 14'**          **PREPARATION:7'**          **SERVINGS:4**

## INGREDIENTS

- » fresh raspberries
- » 1 cup whole milk ricotta cheese
- » 1 tbsp. granulated sugar
- » 1/2 tsp. finely grated lemon zest
- » 1 tbsp. honey

## DIRECTION

1. Take a large bowl, stir in the lemon zest, ricotta, and honey.
2. Combine the ingredients well.
3. Place four ramekins and divide the batter among them.
4. Add sugar on top if you don't have a kitchen torch.
5. Add all of the ramekins on a baking sheet and place it on the oven rack.
6. Keep the rack on the highest level and turn the broiler on.
7. Once the ricotta is golden-brown and starts to bubble, turn the oven off.
8. Top with raspberries once it has cooled down. Serve it cold.

**NUTRITIONS:**
254 Calories, 12.8g Protein, 14.7g Fat

# 496. CHOCOLATE QUINOA BARS

**COOKING: 6'**          **PREPARATION:19'**          **SERVINGS: 10**

## INGREDIENTS

- » 1/4 tsp. vanilla
- » 2 oz. semi-sweet chocolate
- » 1/2 cup dry quinoa
- » 1/2 tbsp. powdered peanut butter
- » Peanut Butter Drizzle:
- » 1 tbsp. water
- » 9 tsp. powdered peanut butter

## DIRECTION

1. Place a large pot on medium heat.
2. Once the pot is hot, add the quinoa, 45 grams at a time.
3. Stir the quinoa occasionally, until you start hearing it pop.
4. Once the popping starts, stir continuously for a minute.
5. Once you see that the quinoa has popped, place it in a small bowl.
6. Set up a double boiler and melt your chocolate.
7. Take a large bowl and add the chocolate, peanut butter powder, vanilla, and quinoa.
8. Mix it well to combine.
9. Place a parchment paper on the baking sheet.
10. Spread the chocolate batter across, making it around half an inch thick.
11. Mix together water and peanut butter to make the drizzle, and then drizzle it over the chocolate.
12. Swirl it around with a fork.
13. Refrigerate for it to set, and then slice them into small bars.

**NUTRITIONS:**
170 Calories, 4g Protein, 8g Fat

# 497. ALMOND HONEY RICOTTA SPREAD

**COOKING: 15'**     **PREPARATION: 7'**     **SERVINGS: 3**

## INGREDIENTS

- » 1/2 cup whole milk ricotta
- » orange zest
- » 1/4 cup sliced almonds
- » 1/8 tsp. almond extract
- » 1/2 tsp. honey
- » sliced peaches
- » honey to drizzle

## DIRECTION

1. Take a medium bowl, and combine almonds, almond extract and ricotta.
2. Once you have stirred it well, place it in a bowl to serve.
3. Sprinkle with sliced almonds and drizzle some honey on the ricotta.
4. Spread a tablespoon of the spread to your choice of bread, top it with some honey and sliced peaches.

**NUTRITIONS:**
199 Calories, 8.5g Protein, 12g Fat

# 498. APRICOT ENERGY BITES

**COOKING: 0'**     **PREPARATION: 16'**     **SERVINGS: 10**

## INGREDIENTS

- » 1 cup unsalted raw cashew nuts
- » 1/4 tsp. ground ginger
- » 1/2 cup dried apricots
- » 2 3/4 tbsp. shredded, unsweetened coconut
- » 2 tbsp. chopped dates
- » 1 tsp. orange zest
- » 1 tsp. lemon zest
- » 1/4 tsp. cinnamon
- » salt to taste

## DIRECTION

1. Grind apricots, coconut, dates and cashew nuts in a processor.
2. Pulse until all a crumbly mixture has formed.
3. Add the spices, salt and citrus zest in the mixture.
4. Pulse it again to mix well.
5. Process the batter on high till it sticks together.
6. Take a dish or a tray and line it with parchment paper.
7. Shape the balls in your palm, make around 20 balls.
8. Keep in the refrigerator. Serve as needed.

**NUTRITIONS:**
102 Calories, 2g Protein, 6g Fat

# 499. PISTACHIO SNACK BARS

**COOKING: 0'**     **PREPARATION:17'**     **SERVINGS:4**

## INGREDIENTS

- » 10 pitted dates
- » 1/2 tsp. vanilla extract
- » 1 tbsp. pistachio butter
- » 10 tbsp. roasted, salted pistachios
- » 1/2 cup rolled oats, old fashioned
- » 2 tbsp. unsweetened, applesauce

## DIRECTION

1. Grind dates until pureed, in a processor.
2. Add the oats and 123 grams of pistachios and pulse a few times for 15 seconds each time.
3. Once there's a coarse and crumbly consistency, add the pistachio butter, vanilla extract, and applesauce until the dough becomes sticky.
4. Line a standard pan with parchment paper.
5. Place the dough on the pan, place another parchment paper on top, and press it down to evenly flatten the dough.
6. Sprinkle the remaining pistachios after removing the parchment paper.
7. Place the paper on top of the dough again and freeze for a while before cutting it into 8 equal bars.

**NUTRITIONS:**
220 Calories, 6g Protein, 12g Fat

# 500. OAT BERRY SMOOTHIE

**COOKING: 0'**     **PREPARATION:4'**     **SERVINGS:2**

## INGREDIENTS

- » 1/2 cup frozen berries
- » 1/2 cup Greek yogurt
- » milk
- » 4 1/2 tbsp. oats
- » 1 tsp. honey

## DIRECTION

1. Blend the berries, milk, and yogurt together until it's smooth.
2. Mix in the porridge oats, pour in a glass once it's mixed well, and drizzle some honey on top.

**NUTRITIONS:**
295 Calories, 18g Protein, 5g Fat

# CHAPTER 36
# 7-DAY MEAL PLAN

| DAY | BREAKFAST | MAIN DISH | SIDE DISH | DESSERT |
|:---:|:---:|:---:|:---:|:---:|
| 1 | Avocado Egg Scramble | Chicken Shawarma | Springtime Quinoa Salad | Vanilla Cream |
| 2 | Breakfast Tostadas | Honey Balsamic Chicken | Seafood Souvlaki Bowl | Blueberries Bowls |
| 3 | Parmesan Omelet | Garlic and Lemon Chicken Dish | Spaghetti Niçoise | Brownies |
| 4 | Watermelon Pizza | Crispy Mediterranean Chicken Thighs | Mediterranean Tostadas | Strawberries Coconut Cake |
| 5 | Ham Muffins | Greek Penne and Chicken | Vegetable Ratatouille | Cocoa Almond Pudding |
| 6 | Banana Quinoa | Yogurt-Marinated Chicken Kebabs | Citrus Cups | Vanilla Avocado Cream |
| 7 | Cauliflower Fritters | Zaatar Chicken Tenders | Mediterranean Frittata | Watermelon Salad |

# CONCLUSION

With the Mediterranean diet pattern, you will come closer to nature as the entire food concept depends on fresh produce. Mealtime, in these lands, is nothing short of a celebration. People, living in these parts have a tradition of eating together. It is time to nurture interpersonal relations as well.

It is the right time to get into the stride and do something that will not only improve your current state but will also gift you a healthy future. After all, there is no more significant wealth than the health of an individual.

The primary aim of the Mediterranean diet is to make a person fit from within. Eating these foods will not only help in enhancing the outer physical appearance but will bring out the healthy inner glow. People with cardiovascular issues, blood pressure, blood sugar, stress and anxiety, and stomach related ailments will be benefited from this dietary program. Additionally, it will also improve the development of brain cells and activities.

Keeping all these things in mind, it is safe to conclude that the Mediterranean diet will improve a person's immune system. Someone with a robust immune system will be able to resist diseases easily. Thus, your desire of leading a healthy, fulfilling and constructive life will be achieved successfully.

The goal was to provide a thorough look at this diet and all the advantages and disadvantages it can bring to your life. As always, when making dietary changes you should consult your physician first to ensure this is a healthy change for you to achieve your goals in regard to your individual health. With the Mediterranean diet, much research has proven it is the most efficient method to lose weight and improve your overall health.

With this book, wanted to provide a detailed look at the Mediterranean lifestyle and exactly what it entails. The more informed you are about this diet and exactly what you should and should not be eating, the greater your chances of success will be!

People love incorporating a Mediterranean diet lifestyle because of how user-friendly it is! There are no counting calories, decreasing your portion sizes, or counting your intake of macronutrients diligently all day. It's about learning what the diet entails and making those choices to fill your pantry and fridge with fresh, healthy ingredients that will promote better health. You will be cutting out the unhealthy things like processed foods, artificial sugars, refined grains, and soda from your diet which are known to cause blood sugar spikes and excess weight gains. Instead, you'll be shopping for ingredients rich in vitamins, minerals, good fats, and antioxidants that will improve your health! With a menu allowing whole grains, fish, seafood, fruit, vegetables, and even a glass of wine a day, the Mediterranean diet allows for such variety that you can't get sick of it!

As long as you do this and stick to the simple rules of a Mediterranean diet, you can attain all the benefits it offers. One of the major benefits of this diet is that it is perfectly sustainable in the long run, not to mention, it is mouth-watering and delicious.

Once you start implementing the various protocols of this diet, you will see a positive change in your overall health. Ensure that you are being patient with yourself and stick to your diet without making any excuses.

CPSIA information can be obtained
at www.ICGtesting.com
Printed in the USA
LVHW062047190121
676877LV00006B/295